CONSEQUENCES: THE IMPACT OF LAW
AND ITS COMPLEXITY

In North American society, there is increasing reliance on law in the attempt to grapple with complex political and social issues. What is the effect of this growing dependence on law and legal systems? In *Consequences* W.A. Bogart explores the impact of law on societies, and demonstrates how excessive reliance on law, particularly litigation, has generated difficulties regarding issues of social consensus and domestic policy.

Focusing mainly on the United States as the centre for post–Second World War legal culture, the book also takes into consideration other Western countries and their respective legal systems. Bogart begins by documenting the growth of law and the reasons for its enhanced influence, and then discusses the complex meanings of impact and the substantial difficulties in gauging outcomes produced by law. He illustrates his discussion with studies of five areas where the complexity of law's impact is evident: capital punishment, smoking, the environment, pornography, and discrimination against blacks. Detailing law's intricate ties to economic, social, and political issues, Bogart asserts that positive outcomes have occurred despite litigation's disappointing record. Timely and broad in scope, *Consequences* will make a substantial contribution to the study of law and society.

W.A. BOGART is Professor of Law at the University of Windsor. He is the author of *Courts and Country* (1994) and co-author of *The Civil Litigation Process* (5th edition, 1999).

CONSEQUENCES

The Impact of Law and Its Complexity

W.A. BOGART

UNIVERSITY OF TORONTO PRESS
Toronto London Buffalo

© University of Toronto Press Incorporated 2002
Toronto Buffalo London
Printed in Canada

ISBN 0-8020-3599-X (cloth)
ISBN 0-8020-8456-7 (paper)

Printed on acid-free paper

National Library of Canada Cataloguing in Publication Data

Bogart, W.A.
Consequences : the impact of law and its complexity

ISBN 0-8020-3599-X (bound)   ISBN 0-8020-8456-7 (pbk.)

1. Sociological jurisprudence.   2. Law – United States.   I. Title.

K237.B64 2001   340'.115   C2001-901965-3

This book has been published with the help of a grant from the Humanities
and Social Sciences Federation of Canada, using funds provided by the
Social Sciences and Humanities Research Council of Canada.

The University of Toronto Press acknowledges the financial assistance to its
publishing program of the Canada Council for the Arts and the Ontario
Arts Council.

University of Toronto Press acknowledges the financial support for its
publishing activities of the Government of Canada through the Book
Publishing Industry Development Program (BPIDP).

In Memory of
My Parents
Bernice and Arthur Bogart
and of
My Parents-in-Law
Emily and Joseph Bertoldi

'The work of righteousness shall be peace.'
Isaiah 32:17

Contents

Acknowledgments

A good many people helped this book along its way, though, of course, I alone am responsible for its shortcomings.

Virgil Duff and Chris Bucci of University of Toronto Press were enthusiastic about the manuscript from the start and masterfully guided it through the assessment process. I received very helpful comments from two anonymous reviewers now known to me – Austin Sarat and Wesley Pue – and from the Manuscript Review Committee of the Press. John St James provided careful editorial guidance.

I would like to thank my research assistants: Ted Betts, Laura Bliss, Carrie Fleming, Jack Huber, Gordon Jepson, Jeff Johnson, Brian Nicholson, Kurt Pereira, Vishva Ramlall, Virginia Shea, Gavin Smyth, and Tom Sutton. I wish to acknowledge particularly the help of Gabriel Fahel. Gabriel worked on the project at an advanced stage. He was first rate regarding research, organizing materials, editing, and in keeping me going on a book that seemed endless.

Many colleagues supported *Consequences*. Maureen Irish gave me the idea for the book in commenting on another of my manuscripts. Others greatly aided the enterprise by reading or discussing parts of the book or by supporting grant applications: Annalise Acorn, Jeff Berryman, Susan Bertoldi, Bob Brym, Sandra Burt, Paul Emond, Charles Epp, Scott Fairley, Neil Gold, Leslie Howsam, Bert Kritzer, Diane Labrèche, Rhonda Lenton, Mary Jane Mossman, Dick Moon, Jacqueline Murray, Betsy Ross, Peter Russell, Elisabeth Scarff, Bob Sharpe, Lynn Smith, Marcia Valiante, Neil Vidmar, and Juanita Westmoreland-Traoré. My secretary of many years, Annette Pratt, lent terrific administrative support to the project.

I received financial assistance to support research from the Ontario

Law Foundation, the University of Windsor, and the Social Sciences and Humanities Research Council of Canada. Progress on the book was greatly aided by a Research Professorship from the University of Windsor that permitted me to write full time for a term. Assistance in completing the book came as a result of being the Humanities Fellow, 1999–2000, awarded by the Humanities Research Group, University of Windsor. The HRG is a beacon for the humanities at the University and beyond with its director, Dr Jacqueline Murray, a tireless champion.

Finally, thanks to my household. Nanette Flores for keeping us all going. My daughter, Ab, for all her support that buoyed me during this long project. My wife – and editor – Linda Bertoldi, who ever demonstrates that corporate law, love of literature, and fine Italian cooking make an exceedingly good combination.

As I finish *Consequences* I am alone in the country. Ice is on the lake; snow has blanketed the cottage; it is cold and silent. The eternal relentlessness of nature is comforting as I complete a book on the unpredictable foibles of human institutions.

'Raspberries,' Lake Kawagama
February 2001

CONSEQUENCES

Introduction

The spirit of liberty is ... not too sure that it is right.

Learned Hand[1]

That law asserts an influence on society is scarcely an issue. But how it does so, the effects that are produced, and the gauging of those impacts raise complex questions to which there are frequently few easy answers. The interaction of law and other social forces is a complicated process. Difficult issues are involved including the determination of causation and the assessment of outcomes. What we know regarding many of these questions is sometimes little more than guesswork bolstered by enticing theories. The complexities of how to establish what are the consequences produced by law are evident. The extent to which such outcomes are linked to law – and to other social forces – looms large.

At the same time, persistent questions about the effects of law are a critical aspect of policy agendas, involving an array of issues. The following are examples of such quandaries. Responses to them will figure prominently in this book. What are the effects of America having the highest rate of imprisonment in the Western industrialized world and retaining capital punishment when all societies of a similar tradition have abandoned executions? Rates of smoking have dramatically decreased in many countries. To what extent has legal regulation been responsible for the decrease? To the extent that law has contributed to the decline in smoking, have some forms of law been more effective than others (requiring health warnings, banning smoking in public places, rates of taxation, tort litigation against tobacco companies, and so forth)? Efforts to improve the environment have been successful, at least in some significant areas. To what extent has law (and what kinds of law) contributed to this result? What are the outcomes when law attempts to suppress pornography? Will law be capable of banning smut in the face of technological developments, most prominently the Internet? Are laws combating discrimination effective in protecting those harmed by acts of prejudice? What are the consequences of affirmative-action programs in America, the society most associated with such initiatives?

One of the most obvious questions about outcomes concerns the extent to which there is compliance with law. Most people obey the law most of the time. But what of those who do not? Are there alternatives to deterrence and sanctions that will improve compliance? When laws are enacted or judicial decisions rendered, how do we determine what are the outcomes that they produce? How are we confident that it is these laws and decisions (and not other social forces) that have been responsible for such consequences? More generally, how do the effects of law relate to other influences and institutions in society in terms of various social phenomena?

In responding to these questions *Consequences* reviews studies of the impact of law and analyses debates about how it influences and interacts with society. *Consequences* urges more caution in turning to law as a solution to complex social, political, and economic issues when we know so little about what effects law actually produces. Such a caution is not 'anti-law' but, rather, a plea to devise ways to use a basic building block of society as effectively as we can. We need to ascertain as clearly as we are able the effects of law even as we acknowledge the challenges of establishing law's impacts. We need to be careful about turning to law in the face of much uncertainty about its outcomes. We need to be, to paraphrase the great judge quoted at the beginning of this introduction, 'not too sure that we are right' when we contemplate invoking law, when we make claims about its consequences.

This need to know more about the effects produced by law underscores the importance of empirical studies. Much of the analysis of law, especially in law schools and among judges and lawyers, proceeds at a theoretical level. Such theorizing is often eloquent and instructive regarding normative aspects of legalization. Nonetheless, often too little account is taken of the actual effects that are produced. Empirical studies of law have their own difficulties; for example, concerning perspectives brought to bear on any evaluations of impact, regarding methodologies that are employed, and in terms of hard issues such as those concerning causation. Most responsible statements regarding the effects of law are complicated ones. Yet such difficulties do not justify evading careful debate regarding law's consequences. Rather, such complexities should incite greater curiosity about impacts even as they engender modesty about making sweeping pronouncements in the name of one or other theory regarding the effects of legalization.

Law's role has expanded enormously since the Second World War. A survey of the last five decades of Western industrialized society would highlight, as a defining element, the insinuation of law into all manner of human endeavour. This growth of legalization has occurred especially in the United States. That great society's experiments with law have yielded a particularly rich and complicated terrain for assessment.

In many ways *Consequences* is intended for those in other countries looking to the Republic as a source for initiatives regarding legal policy who need to be mindful of the significant differences there can be between the United States and other societies. This book is written by someone also outside that country; one who has great admiration for America, but who is not uncritical of the way it forges domestic policy. This perspective, from an outsider looking in, may also be of help to policy-makers and students of the law within the United States who are immersed in the many experiments in legalization.

There are two main reasons why the USA looms large in the discussion of the impact of law. First, America, more than any other industrialized nation, is the land of law. Other societies also use law to achieve a variety of goals. Indeed, in some instances, other nations regulate certain areas much more extensively than the United States; for example, education, health care, and social assistance. Yet the United States is the society of detailed legal rules, deterrence-oriented enforcement practices, intensely adversarial procedures, and frequent judicial review of administrative orders and legislative enactments. It is the country of rights, most obviously in the courts, but also in the legislatures, in the media, and on the streets. It is the society that most invokes the heaviest machinery of the law, the criminal process culminating in litigation (prosecutions), as a primary response to crime. America leads Western industrialized nations, by a wide margin, in rates of imprisonment; the United States, alone among nations of a similar tradition, retains and imposes the most severe of sanctions: capital punishment.

Second, studies of the effects of law (at any rate those available in English) have mostly focused on the United States, either exclusively or on a comparative basis. Comparative studies explore crucial issues regarding impact, but interpreting their results is frequently complicated by the special way that America employs law. For better or for worse, the United States' invoking of law has become a standard against which the role of law in other societies is often compared.

Because of the particular way the USA uses law and because so many evaluative studies focus on that country, caution must be exercised about easily transferring discussions about the effects of law in America to other societies. *Consequences* does review, at a number of places, studies and statistics from countries other than America. It examines the forces that make the United States an outlier in its employment of law and it makes comparisons between the USA and other nations in several of the chapters. The lessons to be drawn from these pages can be useful for other countries – so long as a critical eye is brought to bear regarding the applicability of the American experience.

There is one point that is made throughout the book. Within the particular way that America employs law, litigation and the courts play a critical role. A lightning rod for this crucial function has been the 'rights revolution.' The expansion of rights over the last several decades has created a base for an array of claims, particularly in courts, but also in the larger society. Other forms of litigation, such as tort lawsuits, have also contributed to the growth of reliance on courts to provide redress and to forge policy. Yet another focus for the courts is as a response to crime. America, more than any other Western industrialized nation, uses the courts, and the punishments they mete out, as a primary response in controlling wrongdoing.

Law has achieved many successes in the United States in terms of policy goals. A number of these positive outcomes are discussed in *Consequences*. Yet, subject to some exceptions, such successes were not the product of litigation. Lawsuits are a particularly cumbersome means of making and putting into effect legal policy. Assessments of the impact of litigation suffer from all the vagaries associated with law that are examined in *Consequences*. In addition, court decisions may encounter particular problems in terms of implementation. What is more, such orders are prone to backlash that is not easily countered. These decisions are imposed by judges (and lawyers); they are not products of popular politics.

Reliance on courts to forge and implement policy contributes to the enervation of politics as elected and administrative officials back away from addressing contentious issues. The very exercise of making domestic policy, particularly of a progressive cast, becomes more difficult. Gun control, health care, educational reform, and social programs to assist the disadvantaged and to prevent crime, to name but a few, are shunted to the sidelines, lost in a swell of fractiousness as contests in courts come to occupy the policy-making terrain. The contention is not that courts should have no part in tackling complex social, political, and economic issues. Litigation has an important role in a society – but lawsuits should not be the engine driving policy formation and implementation.

There is a particular aspect of the quandary of transferring the United States' experience with law to other societies that has inspired *Consequences*. In 1982 Canada incorporated into its constitution the Charter of Rights and Freedoms. This document roughly corresponds to the United States Bill of Rights. The Charter has substantially expanded the scope of judicial review and the capacity of courts to negate the decisions of elected officials. It provides an interesting case study of a society that has significantly augmented the role of courts in forging and implementing policy. Other societies contemplating an increased role for their judiciary would do well to closely monitor developments in Canada.

Proponents of the Charter are optimistic that it can be used to protect fundamental freedoms without disturbing the temperate nature of Canadian society. The politics of Canada has been mostly centre-left and has created many social programs (including universal health coverage) that have been prominent on the world stage. Sceptics of the Charter are not so sure that Canada can have it both ways: a rights culture and compassionate politics. They fear that the adoption of an entrenched rights document will change the very tone of society. Canadian society will mimic America's approach to law and to rights discourse. Such convergence will bring with it the difficulties in forging domestic social policy associated with politics in the Republic. *Consequences* focuses primarily on the USA but it does, at various points, refer to Canada and its developing experience with 'rights talk.' I share much of the scepticism regarding the entrenchment of rights in Canada, a position that I have developed in detail elsewhere.[2] Nonetheless, I have tried to be balanced in presenting the issues and evidence; especially regarding the effects of using litigation to address fundamental values.

The complications posed by turning to litigation to tackle hard policy questions will be discussed in many places. Apart from litigation, law can be effective in achieving the goals set for it. Such outcomes are often much less precise than those claimed by advocates in any particular area. Unintended consequences can complicate matters substantially; such effects can even swamp the desired outcomes. However, the suppression of smoking, the backing of civil rights, and the protection of the environment – areas where the United States has played a prominent role – provide three important instances of the utility of law. Results in these three areas are a retort, on the one hand, to those who advocate only market solutions to social problems and, on the other, to those who insist that turning to law only deflects attention from such underlying issues. In contrast, attempts to control pornography and to implement affirmative-action programs have produced complex effects, which differ in some critical ways from the goals set by advocates of such policies. These outcomes cast doubt upon those policies and their implementation.

Law interacting with developing norms has been important to success in the three areas just mentioned (smoking, the environment, and civil rights). Public support can be critical in law achieving the goals set for it. Yet such support is not always sufficient to realize underlying objectives. Capital punishment enjoys high levels of public support in America. Nonetheless, to the extent that the death penalty's purpose is to curb murder, it cannot be counted a success. The burden of opinion is that executions do not deter. The death penalties (and sky-high rates of imprisonment) respond to America's enthusiasm for deterrence and punitiveness. However, the levels of lethal violence that persist suggest there is a misplaced confidence in such attitudes. Alternatives need to be explored. Yet America's enthusiasm for executions and incarceration push to the sidelines other ways to control crime. Punishing, imprisoning, and executing, all results accomplished through the courts, have become a misshapen attempt to impose responsibility as a reaction to the clamour for rights.

The invoking of law requires flexibility and pragmatism. Its use needs careful assessment of outcomes produced and requires a commitment to alter policies when results suggest another course of action. Its employment should be accompanied by more modesty and fewer sweeping statements about what it is sure to accomplish. Yet the deterrent, adversarial, litigious, and rights-regarding approach in America too often leads to law being viewed as a prize: something to be captured by the victor in a battle of wills, to be invoked in unquestioning pursuit of the winner's goal.

Consequences tackles the quandaries regarding the impact of law in four parts. Part 1, 'The Importance of Law,' documents the growth of law and the reasons for its expansion. Part 2, 'The Impact of Law,' addresses the fundamental concept of impact. Each chapter examines a different aspect of impact: one deals with compliance; a second discusses the complexities of assessing outcomes regarding any specific law or set of laws; and a third presents six basic ideas about the overall effects of law. Part 3, 'The Complexity of Law's Impact,' contains five case studies illustrating the ideas discussed in Parts 1 and 2. The case studies are on punishment and capital punishment; smoking; the environment; pornography; and discrimination, the law, and blacks in America. Part 4, 'Conclusions,' summarizes the general argument.

The following is a more extensive summary.

Part One: The Importance of Law

Consequences begins (chapter 1) by documenting the growth of law and the enlargement of its role. While the book does focus on the impact of law on society, still society is not some inert presence upon which law works its will. The influence of law and society goes both ways. Some insist that it is law *in* society that is crucial: how law emerges out of and is constituted within social relations. In any event, change results in people viewing their environment and relationships differently. Sooner or later these altered viewpoints can lead to demands for changes in law. Such demands, more often than not in the latter part of the twentieth century, have led to more – and more complex – law and, in turn, a range of societal reactions to it.

Quantitatively, there are many more statutes, regulations, and administrative agencies, more publications of and about law, more of the national income derived from legal services, more lawsuits (and variations such as alternative dispute resolution), and more lawyers. Qualitatively, law's influence has expanded to mediate an array of social, economic, and political quandaries. It has been extended to whole areas that were previously not regarded to be in need of such (re)structuring. A pattern of legal norms and institutions has become the common language for addressing problems. The United States is not the only society that has experienced this qualitative and quantitative expansion of law, but it is at the forefront.

America is especially prominent in the role that it has come to assign to litigation in courts. The list of issues in the USA remitted to courts is long and lengthening: housing, medical care, contraceptives and abortion, voting, privacy, bussing, affirmative action, pornography, defendant's rights (or lack thereof) are but a few. At the same time, the thrall of judges has cast a wide net, sweeping into it other kinds of lawsuits such as tort litigation with its claimed capacity to regulate all manner of social and economic issues. Other countries have also experimented with an enlarged role for courts. The experience of Canada in adopting, in 1982, the Charter of Rights and Freedoms and the ensuing focus on rights in that society will be referred to in several places. Yet the United States remains at the forefront in terms of using litigation to forge and implement policy.

Documenting the growth of law leads to the question of why. Why has its role expanded so appreciably? A number of factors can be looked to but two stand out. The first is the breakdown of other rules and norms, with an accompanying reliance on law as their substitute. Historically, a number of institutions stood between the state and the individual: schools, voluntary associations, local communities, religion, the family, and so forth. Such institutions, of course, still exist. Yet their size and numbers have decreased. At the same time, expectations regarding their roles have diminished even as those for law have increased.

The second factor is that politics has harnessed law across the ideological spectrum, most prominently in the United States. Of course, politics has always needed law. Politics is the cement holding a society together, providing a framework within which individuals, organizations, and businesses relate. When politics determines that action is to be taken it needs a vehicle to carry out those decisions. Law is not the only such vehicle, but it has long been a critical one. However, the last decades have seen, especially in the USA, a qualitative and quantitative change in how law – often litigation – is used to achieve political ends. There is faith that law will reconfigure society to bring it into conformity with the ends that are to be achieved. Consensus and agreement need not precede law. Rather law will bring about the desired change.

Part Two: The Impact of Law

Part 2 discusses the challenges of assessing the consequences of the growth of law. What effects have all this intense legal activity produced? To get at this assessment we will make constant reference to the idea of 'impact.'

At its most general level impact analysis addresses all policy-related effects of law. This wide net is meant to capture all significant outcomes relating to the presence of law in society. But that is a very wide net. Thus, within this broad framework, it is useful to think of impact as embracing three kinds of effects. These three are each dealt with in separate chapters (2 to 4).

Compliance with Law – Deterrence and Its Alternatives

Chapter 2 discusses an effect of law that is both obvious and critical: the extent to which it is obeyed. Most people comply with the law most of the time. While the task is not without difficulties, it is usually possible to determine, with reasonable accuracy, the extent to which there is compliance with a law or series of laws.

However, an important element of the wider impact of law is determining how to increase compliance among those not otherwise inclined to obey. Many strategies for the control of crime involve this element, but there are also implications for other areas such as tort litigation and enforcement by various regulatory officials. Discussion of compliance sparks a number of debates about the effectiveness of deterrence. The limits of deterrence lead to a search for alternatives that address underlying problems; for example, proactive measures, such as gun control, and initiatives to 'design out' the problem, such as employing air bags to lessen injury caused by hazardous driving. *Why* people obey the law is also an important issue. The extent of compliance and the degree to which a law is seen as legitimate are closely related. Yet what causes a law to be judged legitimate raises a number of issues that have not been fully resolved.

For all the criticisms levied against it, deterrence, as the cudgel enforcing obedience, still holds enormous appeal, especially in America and especially as a response to crime. Such enthusiasm in that society is a barrier to serious debate regarding other means to address crime and its underlying causes even as that nation is awash in lethal violence.

The Complexities of Assessing Impact

Chapter 3 focuses on the extent to which law has an effect on the underlying problem meant to be addressed. To a great extent it is this meaning of impact that people refer to when they urge or oppose implementation of any law: from arguments that minimum-wage laws raise the standard of compensation for people at the bottom of the economic ladder (or, conversely, that they are barriers to job creation) to assertions that pornography harms women and that laws prohibiting it will buttress gender equality (or, conversely, that such laws mangle free speech and/or result in the harassment of those with unconventional tastes in erotica).

Yet asserting that a law or set of laws has particular effects is one thing. Demonstrating that these consequences have occurred and that they have been caused by law is quite another. There may be heated debates about the underlying issue being addressed. A good example occurs in the case of pornography. There are protracted debates about whether pornography, in fact, causes harm and, if it does, whether the harm results from sexual explicitness, violence, or some combination of the two (questions taken up in detail in part 3). In other words, there may be deep controversy concerning whether the underlying issue is a problem that needs to be addressed by the law or, indeed, at all. Those doubting that an issue gives rise to problems that should be addressed by law are likely also to be sceptical regarding any outcomes produced by regulation. Conversely, those insisting that law should be invoked to respond to a perceived problem are likely to be inclined to judge outcomes as positive and to attribute such results to legal intervention.

In assessing the impact of a law or set of laws there is the significant question of perspective. Is there a neutral position from which to observe acts said to be the effect of law? Perhaps more importantly, is there an objective stance from which to assess and interpret these acts in order to draw conclusions in terms of impact? If such neutrality does not exist, can there be anything said about the impact of law that transcends a multiplicity of perspectives? If there is no objectivity can there be social 'science,' especially in gauging law's consequences?

In responding to these hard questions, the facts that appear to support contested values need to be examined. Conversely, judgments based on any set of values need to be open to being revisited by new perspectives and data. Social science, in its study of law, cannot be held out as a force to end debate. Yet it can be, amid divergent values, a critical tool of persuasion.

There can be a number of complications in terms of showing that a law actually caused any particular result. At the heart of causation issues is the need to control for 'plausible rival hypotheses.' In other words, in order to demonstrate that a law has had a particular effect, it is necessary to demonstrate that there were no other forces responsible for the specific result.

There are means available in specific instances to test rival hypotheses when assessing the impact of any particular law. To the extent that rival hypotheses can be eliminated, conclusions can be drawn with some confidence concerning a law having caused certain outcomes. However, it is also the case that, in circumstances when rival hypotheses cannot be controlled, claims about the capacity of law to achieve a determined set of outcomes are called into serious question.

Most of the time arguments over consequences focus on those that are foreseen, usually goals that proponents of the law wish to achieve in terms of the underlying social, economic, or other issues. Yet, laws can also be linked to effects that are not contemplated or, in any event, not intended by those involved with their implementation. Such unintended consequences demonstrate that law can be a more complicated instrument of policy implementation than many proponents care to acknowledge. These unwanted outcomes should promote more considered judgments about the efficacy of turning to law as a solution to any particular problem. Finally, they underscore the importance of a broad examination of assessments when gauging the impact of any law.

Six Ideas about the Impact of Law – America the Outlier

Chapter 4 suggests that the most important consequences of law reflect some larger pattern of influence in society. The impact of law is most clearly discerned in terms of broad contours of regulation. In discussing overall patterns of law's influence six basic ideas come to the fore. None of them, on its own, offers a comprehensive description of the effects of law. Yet, in total, these six ideas (and their intersections and collisions) articulate the range of views about the overall consequences of law in contemporary Western societies.

The first idea is instrumentalism: law is an independent tool that can be used to shape social, political, and economic forces. In this conception law can be used to achieve directly the goals of social engineering, as diverse as those ambitions may be. Second is the contention that law will only be effective in achieving intended goals when it acts in conjunction with social, political, and economic forces. The greater the alignment between any law and these forces, the more effective that law will be in achieving its ends. The third idea, strongly influenced by postmodernism, argues that law can reconstitute social and political relationships and thereby transform them, particularly in aid of progressive objectives. Yet such transformation is not direct, but takes place in diverse and contradictory ways. Such diversity and contradiction question the very assertion that law has impact separate from its relation to societal forces.

Fourth, it is alleged that law is essentially incapable of altering basic elements of society. There is both a left and right version of this assertion. Often linked to both these versions is a contention that, instead, law deflects attention away from forces that are responsible for establishing and for transforming basic societal arrangements. The fifth idea contends that there are different national styles of regulation. Accordingly, whatever is otherwise the explanatory power of the first four ideas, their effects, in turn, may vary appreciably depending on the different styles of regulation that various countries employ. This idea is subtitled 'American Exceptionalism' because so many of the analyses regarding national styles of regulation focus on the USA and that society's prominent adversarial disposition to lawmaking. Finally, the sixth idea claims that the effects of court decisions may be different than those of other kinds of law (from legislative and administrative processes) because of the institutional characteristics of courts. To be more specific, lawsuits cause significant social change only under a limited set of circumstances that are rarely met. This idea is also subtitled "American Exceptionalism" because of the critical role that courts and litigation play in the United States regarding the forging and implementing of policy.

The entire chapter is subtitled 'America the Outlier.' The role of law in the United States dominates writings about the effects of law. There are, of course, similarities between America and other countries in the way they employ law. Yet the USA stands out: the critical role of courts, the emphasis on individualism, the adversarialness, the enshrinement of rights, and the punitive response to criminal offences set that society apart. All six ideas examined here will be drawn upon to explain law's outcomes, particularly in the United States, with regard to the five case studies that are the subject of part 3.

Part Three: The Complexity of Law's Impact – Some Examples

To illustrate the growth of law, the reasons for its expansion, and the richness and complexity of all three kinds of impact in concrete settings, part 3 turns to five case studies: on capital punishment, smoking, the environment, pornography, and discrimination and blacks in America. They were selected to exemplify important social, political, and economic debates facing the United States and other societies in the last quarter of the twentieth century. Nevertheless, those criteria would also suggest several other candidates – as diverse as abortion, euthanasia, and securities regulation – that have not been covered. The availability of evaluative studies and the desirability of exploring a range of issues were prime criteria for selecting the topics. Each sheds light on the ideas discussed in parts 1 and 2.

Punishment and Capital Punishment

Capital punishment, discussed in chapter 5, is a startling instance of 'American Exceptionalism.' The infliction of the death penalty may be the best example of an exaggerated confidence in the capacity of deterrence and of punishment to regulate human behaviour. Generally, the United States is set apart by the extent of its reliance on punishment (through imprisonment) to combat crime, even as it has the highest rates of lethal violence among Western industrialized nations. More specifically, the United States stands isolated from other countries of a similar tradition in its continuing imposition of the death penalty. Many of the societies that have abolished the death penalty did so as a result of pressures exerted by elites. The termination of executions by those societies raises questions about law coming into force, being implemented, and persisting without popular support.

No such quandaries bother America. There the use of the death penalty is increasing, with public support for capital punishment at its highest level in decades. Meanwhile, litigation in the United States to have the death penalty declared unconstitutional demonstrates how ineffective litigation can be in terms of achieving reform. These lawsuits also provide a stunning example of unintended consequences. Far from bringing the death penalty to a halt they have resulted in the Supreme Court upholding the constitutionality of executions and have caused a backlash that has contributed to the quickening pace with which capital punishment is inflicted. At the same time, the patterns of executions are erratic, with substantial evidence that the death penalty is imposed discriminatorily.

Capital punishment is the foundation for the edifice of punishment, administered by courts. Punitiveness is a prime response to criminal behaviour in America. The society that is so absorbed by rights and freedoms searches frantically for some offsetting expression of responsibility. In some misdirected way that quest finds an outlet: in punishment, in incarceration – and in death.

Smoking

Smoking, discussed in chapter 6, furnishes a classic example of shifting attitudes regarding whether a problem exists that should be addressed by the law. Use of cigarettes has gone, in about a quarter of a century, from being a sophisticated and pleasurable pastime, to being considered a major health problem, to being seen now as a filthy habit that a sizable portion of the public believes should be heavily regulated. The regulation of smoking furnishes an example of how policy-making backed by law has worked in the United States. An important element of that success is that litigation, at any rate until recently, has had a subordinate role in the making and implementing of policies to suppress smoking.

Laws regulating tobacco and smoking illustrate the difficult questions of causation regarding the effects of regulation. There is little doubt that a general and steep decline in the consumption of cigarettes can be associated in time with the passage of laws dealing with such issues as regulating tobacco advertising, requiring warnings about health hazards on cigarette packages, imposing steep taxes on the sale of tobacco, and restricting smoking in public places. The difficult question is whether such laws 'caused' people to stop smoking or whether such regulations simply reflected an underlying change of attitudes toward tobacco consumption (because of health hazards, objections of non-smokers, and so forth). The burden of opinion suggests that both the effect of the law and changing social attitudes were essential and interacted in ways (not completely assessable) that have led to such a marked decline in consumption.

At the same time, certain efforts to constrain further the consumption of tobacco furnish an arresting example both of the limits of law and of unintended consequences that can result. Canadian officials, anxious to play a leading role in efforts to suppress smoking, have invoked a number of legal tools. Prominent among these were steep levels of sales tax on cigarettes. Yet such high rates of tax, rather than contributing further to declining rates of use, spawned a black market in cigarettes smuggled from the United States. This trafficking reached such proportions that the Canadian government was finally forced to cut taxes to undermine the price advantage of the contraband product.

Finally, the role of litigation in the suppression of smoking provides a complex tale of the effects of litigation on social phenomena. In the United States, tort litigation claiming damages on behalf of smokers has been almost completely unsuccessful. However, actions brought by state attorneys-general to recover monies expended on the care of smokers triggered a broad-based settlement with the tobacco industry in the late 1990s. The settlement has been severely criticized as not well designed to reduce consumption and as primarily rewarding tort lawyers with sky-high fees. Most significantly, the tobacco litigation and any settlements send out a signal that the hard work of popular politics can be bypassed and that the litigation route ought to be pursued in other contentious areas such as gun control. Popular politics is further eroded through desperate attempts in America to stitch together policy in the courts, however chancy the results.

The Environment

Protection of the environment, discussed in chapter 7, provides another example of the tremendous growth of law in the last quarter-century. It also furnishes an instance, from the perspective of both the left and the right, of the supposed futility of law. Extravagant positions on the left view legal efforts to protect the environment as little more than artifice that deflects any attempts at substantial political and social change necessary to safeguard the natural world. Meanwhile, the right views environmental regulation as a dramatic example of governmental tampering that ought to be ousted because of its futility in achieving any realistic objectives.

Yet a careful review of laws in the United States aimed at maintaining the environment suggests that such regulation and accompanying administrative enforcement have achieved positive effects in many areas. Furthermore, rather than diluting national efforts, international trade agreements may prod individual countries to further their efforts on behalf of the environment. At the same time, laws to protect the environment have received substantial public support that is critical to their effectiveness. What has not been successful, on the whole, is litigation around environmental issues. Lawsuits in America seeking compensation for damages caused by environmental degradation have particularly floundered for several reasons, including uncertainty regarding the source of pollutants and their effects.

Pornography

Pornography, discussed in chapter 8, illustrates the difficulty of defining a problem as an appropriate subject for redress by the law. The central issue with pornography again invites reconsideration of causation: this time not only in terms of the effects of law but also in terms of the phenomenon to be regulated. Those seeking to regulate pornography allege that it harms women by depicting them as objects of subordination. However, there is a raging debate over whether such harm, in fact, occurs. What is more, where harm can be established, there is heated controversy over whether the damage arises from the depiction of sex or whether the real villain is violence.

The discussion of pornography offers another opportunity to investigate the effects of litigation. Proponents of regulation were successful in having the Supreme Court of Canada rule that Criminal Code provisions prohibiting certain forms of pornography were constitutional. Limits on free speech were justified because of the perceived harm caused by such pornography. Many feminists cheered the holding as a great victory in the war against smut. Yet such evidence of the effect of the decision that has been gathered suggests that sexually explicit pornography involving women has not been suppressed to any greater extent. However, the erotica of other groups, most prominently gays and lesbians, has been subject to more harassment by the authorities, though probably not to the extent that some opponents of the decision (and of regulation of pornography generally) assert. The most marked outcome of the decision may be to splinter even further feminists and other progressive forces over questions of women's inequality and over gay and lesbian rights. Thus there may, indeed, be (re)constitutive effects of turning to law (one of the six ideas discussed in chapter 4); but in this instance the effect is to set back progressive issues.

Finally, the capacity for regulation of pornography on the Internet is uncertain. Whether and how the Internet can be regulated by individual countries, international agreements, the market, or some combination of these influences remains unanswered. Cyberspace tests the limits of the law, especially in achieving compliance with any regulatory scheme.

Discrimination, the Law – and Blacks in America

Discrimination and the condition of blacks in America are discussed in chapter 9. There is a strong consensus about basic protections from discrimination afforded by civil-rights laws. Developing norms and laws have interacted to promote a strong public ethos against racism. However, the impacts of civil-rights laws are less clear. Studies of the effects of a federal law banning discrimination in employment indicate that law did promote black economic progress for about a decade. Yet the effects of the law stalled in the 1980s and 1990s because of the stagnating economy for unskilled workers, a group in which blacks are disproportionately represented.

There is a war being waged over affirmative action. Studies of such programs in higher education establish that blacks admitted under affirmative action do not suffer from feelings of inferiority, do graduate at high rates, do take up lucrative careers, and are very active as community leaders. Yet affirmative action in higher education benefits only a handful of students at the most elite colleges and universities. Such programs do not respond to the problems of an inadequate public school system and the problems of poverty and social dysfunction that plague the lives of a disproportionate segment of blacks. Affirmative action deflects attention from these very issues and fans racial tensions.

As with affirmative action, at least some litigation can be demonstrated to have been "successful" in terms of its immediate goals. However, as with the effects of affirmative action, the results of litigation have done little to respond to underlying problems. Lawsuits to force desegregation of schools are illustrative. Many of these lawsuits have been successful; many more black children now attend integrated schools. The underlying problem is the quality of education that they receive. Litigation has had very little impact on that issue.

Part IV: Conclusions

Consequences concludes by underscoring the challenges raised by the impacts of law and with a specific warning regarding over-reliance on litigation to forge social policy. In particular, there is a strong reaction to Schudson's characterization of contemporary civic life in America as that of the 'rights regarding citizen.'[3]

Any such discussion about the place of rights and the role for litigation is probably too late for America. It is gripped by the thrall of lawsuits. The paradigmatic example of America being immersed in rights and in litigation is the spate of tort suits against gun manufacturers. A society that believes that such lawsuits, whether successful or not, are an appropriate response to lethal violence has probably gone too far down the litigation path. Other societies still have time. The formidable challenge is to achieve the promise of rights and to harness the advantages of litigation in addressing complex issues, while not debilitating popular democracy and other institutions of government.

Consequences ends with a plea for a cautious employment of law. The role of law should be pragmatic and flexible. Approaches need to be altered when the effects produced suggest another course of action. The spirit of the law, like the spirit of liberty, needs to be 'not too sure that it is right.'

PART ONE

The Importance of Law

CHAPTER ONE

So Decried, So Demanded

We might think of law and society as a two-way street with a boulevard down the middle. Law shapes society in complex and, often, unclear ways: a point woven through these chapters. At the same time, society is not passive, allowing law to work its will. Society also influences the quality and quantity of law. Of course social transformations do not translate into legal ones in a straightforward fashion. Society exerts its influence upon law in many complicated ways: '[S]ocial changes lead to changes in states of mind or opinion about law or legal institutions; and these states of mind in turn lead people to behave in certain ways, which do have an impact on law.'[1] It is not the coming of the automobile that produces legal change. It is the reaction to accidents, pollution that is caused, the need for faster and safer highways, and so forth that eventually results in the alteration – and growth – of law.[2]

The relationship between law and society is even more complex – thus the boulevard. Some of those who study that connection resist the pairing of law *and* society so as to suggest that the two are distinctive and independent of each other. The focus of research for the proponents of this view is on how law emerges out of and is constituted within social relations. This approach tends to be more interested in examining local, concrete, and specific situations than in attempting grand statements about the influence of law. Thus, the focus 'shifts away from tracking the causal and instrumental relationship between law and society toward tracing the presence of law *in* society.'[3]

This complex relationship of law and society and their influences upon each other will be discussed in later chapters.[4] What we pursue here is how society's need for law in the last several decades has led to an exponential increase in legalization. We also suggest answers to the question of why there has been such need for law over the last fifty-odd years.

Law's role has increased enormously, both quantitatively and qualitatively. The increase – in the number of lawyers, of statutes and regulations, of law reports, of administrative tribunals and agencies, in litigation (and variations such as 'ADR' – alternative dispute resolution), and in expectations about the issues courts can resolve – establishes the ways that law has entered into and shaped daily life, particularly since the Second World War. The United States is the exemplar, but there is evidence that the lure of law is strong in other societies as well.

There is widespread faith in the capacity of law to provide solutions to an enormous array of issues. Such optimism about the capabilities of law is especially prominent in America. This confidence occurs along the political spectrum, though sometimes for very different reasons. For many progressives law is the great counterweight to the market, constraining economic forces for an array of purposes, from recognition of collective bargaining by unions to provision of health care to requiring affirmative action. For many conservatives law is the great regulator of personal behaviour, from deterring violent crime to restraining pornography to protecting the unborn.

Yet even as law is demanded it is decried; nowhere more so than in the United States. It is seen to be responsible for all sorts of ills, however judged, from regulatory stranglehold to lack of choice in terminating pregnancies, from high insurance rates to oppressive criminal sanctions for those enmeshed by disadvantaged circumstances. It is robbing people of self-reliance and initiative even as it is destroying community and pulverizing the common good. There is altogether too much of it. Except when a particular perspective, group, or interest sees a need: then it is indispensable.

A fundamental question regarding this turning to law – such faith in it, such disparagement of it – is, Why? Why have societies come to have these expectations about law's ability to solve any number of problems even as so many are convinced that it is a major cause, or at least a reflection of, the malaise that besets us? Though a number of factors are part of the answer, two stand out and are particularly prominent in the United States: first, the breakdown of other rules and norms, with law being seen as a necessary substitute; second, politics harnessing law across the ideological spectrum, most prominently through the claiming of 'rights,' on the one hand, and an impulse to regulate behaviour by means of criminal sanctions, on the other.

The Growth of Law

So Demanded

It is doubtful that there was a time when law was unimportant in developed societies. People had conflict; they needed a means, short of violence, to settle those troubles. Governments, even those with modest roles, needed to regulate a wide range of human affairs, including branding an array of acts as criminal and sanctioning those who committed them.

In any event, the rise of the modern industrialized state has created a firm basis upon which an ambitious role for law rests. Law was called upon to regulate industrial enterprises, including providing a framework to keep markets competitive. As society became more urbanized land use needed to be regulated regarding such matters as drains and sewage, fire safety, density, placement and use of buildings, and expropriation for public purposes. Law came to structure other broad areas, such as employment relationships (for example, regarding occupational health and safety), recognition of the right to collective bargaining through unions, and, later, other conditions of work like the minimum wage.[5]

The role for law as the regulator of the industrialized state had emerged by the early decades of the twentieth century; for example, during the Progressive era in the United States. Yet it was given significant impetus by the Great Depression and the reaction to the excesses of unregulated markets. The Second World War only added to expectations that law could be harnessed to articulate and implement societal values.[6]

However, the fifty years since the war have seen a turning to law that dwarfed the otherwise significant experiences with regulation in the previous fifty-odd years. This period has witnessed extensive and complex intrusion of regulation into virtually every facet of daily life. A prime method by which such activity has been achieved has been through agencies and commissions performing a vast range of tasks and implementing an array of policies. A study done as long ago as the late 1970s in Canada, focusing upon only permanent agencies (thus excluding specifically appointed commissions, public inquiries, etc.), reported that in excess of 640 such agencies existed. A survey of similar bodies in the province of Ontario also done in the late 1970s identified 36 regulatory bodies, 44 licensing appeal tribunals, 8 compensation boards, 19 arbitral agencies, and 95 advisory boards.[7]

One reaction to this growth of law – and government – is the election of politicians committed to cutting back on such expansion. During the 1980s Thatcher and Reagan symbolized efforts to curtail regulation and to curb governmental agencies. Such developments came later in other countries, such as Canada, but were in place in some of the provinces of that country by the 1990s.

In many respects legal regulation became identified as both cause and effect of the huge debts and deficits weighing down governments in the last decade of the twentieth century. The impetus to use regulation as a response to an array of issues did abate and some programs were eliminated as 'privatization' and 'deregulation' became the new watchwords.[8] Nevertheless, it is by no means true that regulation uniformly shrank even in the United States and England under conservative, market-oriented governments.

In order to conform with Great Britain's obligations as a member of the European Union, the British parliament approved a welter of regulations in the early 1990s.[9] During that same period, the British government, with whatever misgivings, boosted environmental and other kinds of regulation: '... [T]he injection of an entrepreneurial spirit into the hierarchical institutions charged with promoting health, safety and environmental protection produced an unanticipated synergy.'[10] As a result, among other consequences, a large number of Self-Financing Regulatory Agencies (SEFRAs) grew up, including the National Rivers Authority, Her Majesty's Inspectorate of Pollution, the Waste Regulatory Authorities, the Planning Inspectorate, the Fishing Vessel Survey, the Data Protection Agency, and the Medicines Control Agency.[11]

There is a tendency to treat privatization and deregulation as the same phenomenon in terms of law when, in fact, the two can be negatively correlated: the more privatization there is, the more regulation there may be. When the Thatcher government privatized telecommunications, it established a regulatory agency to supervise the companies that could now engage in telecommunications.[12] When that same government implemented policies that caused a substantial shift from the public to the private sector in terms of nursing homes, there followed significant expansion of inspections by district health authorities. Indeed, these same inspectors increased scrutiny not only of the new private nursing homes but also of the public and charitable providers as well.[13] In the United States a form of privatization that has been advocated is a voucher system for education so that students could purchase education from any school they choose. Yet, it has been suggested that if vouchers were implemented they would be accompanied by all sorts of regulation and inspections in terms of ensuring minimum certification standards.[14]

In any event, many who support limited government in terms of any economic repercussions can be boosters of regulation of personal or moral behaviour.[15] Those who cry out for deregulation and privatization can also be the ones leading the charge for laws governing all sorts of other behaviour from criminal activity to the use of pornography to intimate personal relations like the domestic partnerships of gays and lesbians.

Along with the growth of law over this fifty-year period have come lawyers: the legal profession is flourishing. In many ways the increase of lawyers is a world-wide phenomenon for industrialized countries and even for some that are in the process of industrializing.[16] In England and Wales the two branches of the profession (barristers and solicitors) increased about 147 per cent from the early 1960s to the mid-1980s.[17] In the United States during about this same period the numbers of lawyers grew 129 per cent; they are still growing.[18] Canada led the way – in terms of percentage increase – with growth of the legal profession during the same period (mid-1960s to mid-1980s) expanding by 253 per cent.[19]

There are not only more lawyers but they are much more diverse in terms of age, education, race and ethnicity, and, most conspicuously of all, gender.[20] In the early 1960s women accounted for about 3 per cent of the profession in England, Canada, and the United States. In the late 1980s women made up about 15 per cent of lawyers in the United States and over 20 per cent in England and Canada, with the student body rising to close to half.[21] The rapid influx of women into such a staid calling leads to much wondering about possible transformations of the profession based on gender.[22]

With these more numerous and diverse lawyers has come societies' dependence on legal services. In the United States the portion of the national income and gross national product derived from legal services almost doubled from the early 1960s to the mid-1980s, and of these increasing expenditures a larger portion is spent by businesses than

individuals. It has been suggested that there have been parallel occurrences in Canada and the United Kingdom as evidenced by the growth
in the number and size of law firms that focus on business.[23] We do
know that total spending on civil legal services in Canada grew from
$1.9 billion in 1973 to $11 billion in 1993.[24] These expenditures easily
outpaced consumer spending generally. While per capita income rose
on average about 1.5 per cent during 1982–1992, the growth in legal
services spending, in most sectors, was nearly 5 per cent per year.[25]

With increased numbers of lawyers and increased expenditures has
come a significant increase in the amount of law.[26] There is no shortage
of claims that we are being engulfed in a legal morass.[27] Nevertheless,
because statistics on the legal system and empirical studies of its functioning are not what they should be, such expansion is difficult to
establish systematically and uniformly. At the same time, there are figures and other evidence available – from the United States, Canada,
and England – in a number of areas, that do document a qualitative
and quantitative shift in the way that at least those societies are invoking law.

Law has come to mediate a bewildering range of social, political,
and economic quandaries. This role for law during the last several
decades did not just suddenly arise. In America, it has been argued,
aspects of nineteenth-century society reflected 'powerful traditions of
governance, police, and regulation.'[28] The Progressive Era and the
New Deal were also periods in which there was concerted regulation
especially focused on business and its ramifications. However, one student of such regulation in the United States, writing from the vantage
point of the early 1980s, argued that the regulation of business that
occurred in the 1960s and 1970s, reflected the degree to which the role
of law had intensified in three ways: 'First, the degree of political conflict and debate over social regulatory policies in general and environmental and consumer protection regulations in particular was
significantly greater ... Secondly, there was a quantitative and qualitative increase in the scope and intrusiveness of federal controls over
corporate social performance. Finally, and most critically ... government regulatory policy became far more politicized.'[29]

Just a sampling of statistics substantiates the point that there was a
significant increase from the 1960s to the 1970s concerning regulation
of business activity. In the general area of consumer health and safety,
five new laws were enacted by the federal government during the Progressive Era, eleven during the New Deal, and a total of sixty-two

between 1964 and 1979. In respect of safety and other working conditions, there were five laws passed during both the Progressive Era and the New Deal, whereas twenty-one such laws were enacted from 1960 to 1978. In terms of the environment and energy, two statutes were passed by the federal government during the Progressive era, five during the New Deal, and thirty-two during the 1960s and 1970s.[30] In sum: 'In the course of a decade [1964–1975], the federal government put more regulatory laws on the books than it had in the country's entire prior history.' [31]

One indicator of just the volume of rules and other forms of subordinate legislation is the increase in the Federal Register (containing notices about regulation by the federal government): in 1960, 14,477 pages were added; in 1985, 53,480.[32] In 1955 the Canada Gazette (containing notices about regulations of the federal government) was a 3120-page/4-volume consolidation; by 1978 it was a 14,420-page/18-volume set.[33] Further annual volumes accumulated over 40,000 more pages by 1987. In the United Kingdom the average number of pages added annually to the statute book rose from 745 pages in the 1950s to 1525 pages in the early 1980s.[34]

The reporting of court decisions and legal scholarship has increased enormously. The judgments of state courts reported in one series (West Publishing) grew from 63 volumes with 61,057 pages in 1960 to 127 volumes with 151, 863 pages in 1985: a 149 per cent increase in the number of pages.[35] Cases reported in the federal court system expanded from 23 volumes (21,474 pages) in 1960 to 61 volumes (93,588 pages) in 1985: an increase of 336 per cent.[36] In 1960 the annual output of the Dominion Law Reports, a main service for publicizing judgments of Canadian courts, was 5 volumes with 3902 pages. By 1989 it was 11 volumes with 8448 pages.[37] Between 1960 and 1985, general law reviews grew from 65 to 186; specialized reviews increased from 6 to 140. During the period 1958 to 1980, in Canada, the number of law journals increased by 175 per cent.[38] Moreover, such statistics on printed sources scarcely does justice to an intense level of activity. On-line databases, which first appeared in the 1970s, have increased access to a vast range of legal material both published and unpublished.

Law has by no means a monopoly on innovations in information technology. Nevertheless, it is prominent in their use: '[A] rapid succession of new technologies – photo reproduction, computerisation, on-line data services, overnight delivery services, electronic mail and fax machines – have multiplied the amount of information that can be assembled and manipulated by legal actors and have greatly increased the velocity with which it circulates.'[39]

With more lawyers and more law come more roles for legalization in a complex diversity of human activity. Labels warn of dangers, instruct about use, and invite complaints if the consumer feels wronged. Notices in restaurants, on airline tickets, and at swimming pools inform about the limits of loss. Newspapers, plays, television, and the Internet are filled with legal images while asserting their claims to copyright. The lines between popular and legal culture have become blurred as the two collide and interact.[40]

Marc Galanter, examining 'law abounding'[41] in Canada, Great Britain, and the United States, observed that there has been an extension of law to whole areas of activity that were previously not regarded to be in need of such structuring.[42] In spite of some important differences, there is a pattern of legal norms and institutions as the common language of addressing problems. This pattern exists whether individuals experience difficulties with intimates or faceless entities. It occurs in such diverse areas as the environment, safety regulation, health care, employment, and sports:[43] 'From being ultimate but relatively unobtrusive, law has become pervasive.'[44]

For example, health care is provided in very different ways in Canada, Great Britain, and the United States. Yet it has undergone legalization in important aspects in each country: entitlement to treatment has undergone substantial regulation, with users increasingly turning to law for recourse for alleged deficiencies. Litigation has accompanied this expansion of law into health care. One study established that England, Canada, and the United States had experienced similar growth in medical malpractice litigation in the 1970s and 1980s.[45] It concluded that changes in underlying expectations – and not modifications in law – were primarily responsible for this increase: '[T]his growth must arise less from isolated doctrinal changes in one country than from changes in medical malpractice and social mores which occur roughly simultaneously in western countries.'[46]

Generally, there has been an increase in litigation and its off-shoots. There is more litigation, a quantitative expansion. Perhaps even more importantly, there are elevated expectations about the ability of litigation to forge solutions for complex issues, a qualitative expansion. In terms of more litigation, total filings in the US federal courts grew from 59,284 in 1960 to 273,670 in 1985. Comparable figures are not available for state courts but lawyers employed by those institutions grew in number from 7581 in 1960 to 18,674 in 1985. It is true that this increase has not been uniform. For instance, at times in the past, there is evidence of higher per capita filings of lawsuits in the United States. Nevertheless, per capita rates of filings have increased in recent decades in most areas of America.[47]

Data on courts are not highly developed in Canada. Yet we do know that the number of judges increased 177 per cent from 834 in 1961 to 2315 in 1986. In England and Wales, original proceedings in the High Courts increased from 140,003 in 1963 to 262,761 in 1988. In the county courts original proceedings expanded from 1,521,594 to 2,285,125 over the same period.[48]

We do know that money spent on legal-aid services in Canada increased enormously during the 1980s. In Ontario, the province where the growth of such expenditures was possibly the greatest, the total cost of legal aid rose almost 500 per cent between fiscal years 1980 and 1990.[49] Despite this galloping increase, the cost of legal aid in that province went on to almost double between fiscal 1990 and 1995[50] – before being reorganized.[51]

Meanwhile, even as litigation has grown, the role for other devices to resolve disputes has also been augmented. Three decades ago, alternatives to courts for resolving disputes (other than through administrative agencies) were limited to isolated areas, for instance, labour and (some) commercial arbitration. By the 1990s a whole area known as ADR (alternative dispute resolution) had put down substantial roots: 'The last decade has witnessed a great proliferation of ADR institutions and programmes; some free-standing, some attached to courts, and others embedded within organizations like corporations, hospitals, and schools.'[52] Many of the claims about the advantages of ADR are based on reactions to the forms and structures of established law, particularly as exemplified by courts and litigation. Nevertheless, there is little doubt that ADR is now dominated by lawyers and linked in significant ways to the fortunes of litigation and its increased role in society, including a counter-reaction to ADR itself.[53]

Qualitatively there has been an enormous enlargement of society's expectations concerning what litigation can – and should – do about complex social, political, and economic issues. These expectation are at their highest in America and, to a lesser extent, Canada. Nevertheless, there are indications of such elevated aspirations in several other countries,[54] including Great Britain.[55]

Nowhere are such claims made about the attributes of litigation and its ensuing effect with more flourish than in American constitutional law. Some US writers are unqualified in their extravagance. Consider, for example, Lawrence Tribe, author of perhaps the leading treatise on American constitutional law, and his assertions of what constitutional litigation in the Supreme Court has accomplished:

> [T]he most basic ingredients of our day-to-day lives are sifted and mea-sured out by the Supreme Court. When parents send their children to parochial schools, when men and women buy contraceptives, when workers organize a union, when friends share their intimate secrets in a telephone conversation without fear that others are listening, they enjoy rights and opportunities that would not exist if the Supreme Court had not secured them for us ...
>
> Justices are not just so many actors on the stage. To them has fallen a large share of a far more basic function – that of playwright and director. It is the Justices who decide which roles will be played by whom; which decisions about hours and wages will be made by government regulators and which will be left to the play of private bargains; which things of value – housing, medical care, legal services, voting opportunities – will only be sold on private markets and which will be available to all as a matter of right.[56]

Tribe is by no means alone in such hyperbole. He is joined by any number of others. Owen Fiss is perhaps the foremost proponent of using litigation to articulate and realize public values. America's genius for doing this is a matter to be countenanced:

> To conceive of the civil lawsuit in public terms as America does might be unique. I am willing to assume that no other country ... has a case like *Brown* v. *Board of Education* in which the judicial power is used to eradicate the caste structure. I am willing to assume that no other country conceives of law and case law in quite the way we do. But this should be a source of pride rather than shame. What is unique is not the problem, that we live short of our ideals, but that we alone among the nations of the world seem willing to do something about it.[57]

What is more, such dependency on litigation in America to navigate the rough waters of late-twentieth-century existence is not confined to constitutional issues. It has been suggested that tort litigation (encom-passing general wrongs for which there can be some redress) has come to play the central role in policing fundamentals: 'It is ... no exaggeration to see American tort law as the major means for setting norms and standards for social and economic behaviour.'[58] Indeed, some go so far as to fear that litigation is 'our basic form of government.'[59]

While Canadians may not have quite achieved the rhetorical flourishes that characterize Professors Tribe and Fiss, there seems little doubt that some are determined to head in that direction. This turning to litigation in Canada has been accelerated by the advent of the Charter of Rights and Freedoms (the approximate Canadian equivalent to the US Bill of Rights). Shortly after the Charter's entrenchment in 1982, one commentator felt sufficiently confident about the effects of litigation to characterize *Brown* v. *Board of Education* as 'such a moral supernova in civil liberties adjudication that it almost single-handedly justifies the exercise.'[60] A distinguished Canadian constitutional scholar, in the midst of decrying the 'notwithstanding' clause in the Charter (and its potential for legislatures to override judicial decisions) asserted:

> As a matter of principle we have adopted the notion that there are adjudicable public issues. Furthermore, we have come to terms with these issues being *ultimately* adjudicable – not subject to legislative review and revision. If Canada wants to say about human rights claims that not only are they adjudicable at the first stage of resolution, but they are adjudicable as a matter of ultimate resolution, this would be entirely consistent with our commitment to legalism in public ordering.[61]

What underlies such multifaceted expansion of law? Lawrence Friedman contends that the growth of law is inexorably linked to 'the concept of choice, the desire for choice and the experience of choice'[62] that pervade modern life.[63] This demand for choice is accompanied by veneration of individualism, whatever the reality of people's lives ('The culture of individualism does not depend on whether people are actually free to choose ... It is enough that they believe they are').[64] At the same time, most people see themselves as individualists but not as libertarians. Thus, the layers of rules and their structures for enforcement have come to be viewed as means to secure choice so that individualism can flourish, even as there may be radically different notions of how choice should be exercised and of what constitutes individualism. Three kinds of laws illustrate the widely accepted belief that rules and their structures protect freedom to choose.

First, law can provide 'traffic' rules so that there can be orderly use of scarce resources.[65] Such rules of the road, of course, embrace the many rules of the literal road: street and highway traffic safety. But a mere sample of the many others include regulation of access to television channels and radio frequencies; air-traffic-control laws; regulation of wilderness areas; laws about hunting and fishing; and enactments relating to energy conservation and consumption.

A second kind of law focuses on the uniqueness of the individual.[66] These civil-rights laws are meant to establish the right of individuals to be judged on their merits rather than on the basis of some alleged group characteristic. The civil-rights movement was crystallized with claims by American blacks. Nevertheless, once under way, that movement was fuelled by any number of minority groups who, at the same time, claimed recognition in the name of choice and of individualism: women, gays and lesbians, the handicapped, the elderly, prisoners, immigrants, and so forth. As these movements surged forth they were accompanied by endless controversy about the rights themselves (more about this later in the chapter).[67] Yet it was taken as truth that 'a framework of civil rights strongly supported by hard-edged legal institutions is a vital necessity.'[68]

Third, there are laws that regulate the economy. The welfare state, in its many different forms, assumed regulation of businesses, employers, landlords, and so on.[69] Whether the welfare state achieved its goals and whether particular forms of regulation made economic sense are important questions. Yet such issues may be beside the point in terms of the cultural meaning of such regulation. For example, antitrust laws garnered widespread acceptability by invoking choice and individualism as products of competition. Railroads, banks, and other huge entities required policing. The independence of farmers, small merchants, and shopkeepers had to be preserved; consumers needed choice. Similarly, income-maintenance programs, for instance for farmers, can be questioned as protectionist and anti-consumer. Yet they received widespread support by romanticizing the image of the sturdy rural family farm as a haven for individualism and choice in the ways of life.

Friedman, surveying this mass of laws, extols the obvious benefits that choice and individualism can bestow, particularly on the population at large. Yet he also issues a warning about their and law's excesses: 'Modern individualism, at its core, rejects passive acceptance of fate, a soft acquiescence in one's given life-station. It fosters pluralism, and at the same time, carried to extremes, it can destroy the ethical basis on which a plural society rests. Even at its best, it requires a delicate balance. That balance, alas, is not easily achieved or easily kept.'[70]

So Decried

This embrace of law has given rise to many concerns. Such angst is the stuff of colourful, sweeping – sometimes eloquent, sometimes hysterical – rhetoric. Given the United States' particular fascination with the law, the strongest reactions come from writers in the USA, whether regarding 'the litigation explosion,'[71] the 'suffocation of America' by the tentacles of detailed regulation,[72] or 'the crisis in the legal profession' concerning its dominance of national policy.[73]

This embrace of legalization is 'jurismania, the madness of American law,'[74] and is 'beyond all reason.'[75] Galanter sums up these anxieties:

Although the "rule of law" is praised as a good and noble thing, this excess of law is thought to produce – or at least accompany – a host of bads: palpable bads like high insurance rates, inefficiency and discouragement of product innovation. And beyond that, larger and more diffuse bads: atomisation, fragmentation, the decline of community, homogenisation and the decline of diversity, the loss of spontaneity, dignity, and self-reliance.[76]

In a widely publicized book, Howard equated the growth of law with the 'death of common sense.'[77] His target was the detail and intricacy of the law. The focus of this complaint is a society that has become obsessed with the search for precision in order to deal with every contingency. Yet with greater specificity there is an increased chance that something will be left unaccounted for. The solution? More specificity.[78]

Numerous examples illustrate the claim. A frequently repeated one involved Mother Teresa's prolonged attempt to open a desperately needed shelter for the homeless in New York.[79] The project was guided through a Byzantine approval process, but it ultimately foundered. There was an inflexible requirement stipulating that the building had to have an elevator; the nuns, because of their ascetic ways and their insistence that the maximum amount of funds go directly to the poor, refused to budge.

This specificity and its accompanying volume and complexity is of comparatively recent origin. As late as the 1960s forest rangers dealt with the many problems of running the national parks with a pamphlet of rules and their common sense. Now there are several volumes of fine print regulating their calling.[80] We have built 'a legal colossus unprecedented in the history of civilization, with legal dictates numbering in the millions of words and growing larger every day ... Is it a coincidence that almost every encounter with government is an exercise in frustration?'[81]

For others the growth of law reflects a paradox: as the widespread popular discontent with law increases, a heightened confidence in its ability to remedy social ills grows.[82] Glendon, in *A Nation under Lawyers*, comments: 'The same citizens who want to get annoying regulations out of their lives often believe that the way to deal with a broad range of social problems is to bring a lawsuit, to criminalize unwanted activity, or to augment the power of police and prosecutors.'[83]

Like Friedman, Glendon relates the growth of law to the increase in demand for individual choice. Such demand has loosened the bonds of marriage and family, and the commitment to children, jobs, and community. Thus, any number of standard-setting mechanisms have receded. Yet even as etiquette declines and orderly practices for business and economic life decrease, there is a need for some common source of authority. As a result, 'the heavy machinery of law is being wheeled out to deal with a growing array of personal, economic, and political matters to which it is poorly suited.'[84]

As society simultaneously reviles law while seeking more of it, enter the lawyers. Glendon acknowledges that lawyers have, in fact, always been central to American society. Yet, she also claims, that role has been radically transformed.[85]

At the dawning of America's republican experiment, Tocqueville saw law and the legal profession in the United States as a great bulwark for democracy. Lawyers were an antidote to the tendencies of popular government to focus on quick solutions even at the price of disorder and majoritarian oppression. Lawyers were the 'strongest barriers'[86] against the excesses of democracy. With their 'habits of order' and 'something of a taste for formalities'[87] they could be a force for moderation dampening a volatile society brash with its new-found freedom and its promise of popular participation.

Now lawyers appear in a very different light as they see themselves, and are seen, as central to solving an array of society's dilemmas. The result is a widespread inflation of expectations of law and deflation of the possibilities of popular democracy. Such habits of mind are sustained by an array of legal professionals anxious to join the vanguard:

'judges with grandiose visions of judicial authority, practitioners eager to blaze new trails to the nation's crowded courthouses, and legal scholars yearning to be philosopher-kings and -queens.'[88]

Such bombastic denunciations may have no counterpart, of least of such intensity, in other societies. Yet these descriptions, whatever there extravagance, hit a raw nerve. America is anxious about law's reach even as it seems compelled to invoke it. This hoopla surrounding law in the USA is scarcely conducive to sober discussion regarding its potential and its limits. Invoking law as a solution to societal problems often requires the scalpel. Yet such angst, in the Republic, frequently leads to the broadax – and, then, to yet more cries regarding the menace of law. Serious reflection on law's capabilities and its limits are shoved to the sidelines.

Why a Turning to Law?

Documenting the qualitative and quantitative growth of law is one thing. Explaining this phenomenon is quite another. Why has there been such a sizable growth of law? There are, doubtless, many contributing factors. Yet at the core of the explanation are two that have already been touched upon: first, the breakdown of other rules and norms, with law being seen as a necessary substitute, and second, law supplanting politics across the ideological spectrum.

The Breakdown of Other Rules and Norms

An important way of viewing law is as a set of rules governing behaviour, backed by the power of the state. Yet it is by no means the only means of influencing behaviour. Voluntary associations, the family, smaller urban communities, the school, and churches can all produce norms that can shape conduct, both formally and informally, promoting civic order and social mores. Just as there can be both good and bad laws, norms can be both constructive and detrimental. A consensus against littering and spontaneous disapproval of any such acts are widely endorsed as positive shaping of behaviour. An atmosphere (and accompanying acts) discouraging blacks from voting in the pre–civil rights South is now seen for the evil that it was.

These non-legal institutions and the structures they promote can be so central that some have seen in them the key that accounts for the fundamentals of any society. A startling example of this is Fukuyama's contention that the economic prosperity of a nation is directly related to the amount of social virtue that it fosters: first and foremost, 'trust.'[89] The claim is that a society's economic success is determined only partly by elements traditionally weighted by economists: competition, markets, skills, technology, and so forth. Vital as well is a culture that promotes citizens' willingness to cooperate with each other in economically productive ways; a culture that promotes 'trust.' Examples of 'high trust' nations are the United States, Germany, and Japan; of 'low trust,' China, France, and Italy.

Such sweeping claims about the connection of 'trust' to the economic lifeblood of nations, including the countries used as examples, have attracted sceptical reaction.[90] Commentators have been startled to have the United States coupled with Japan in terms of 'spontaneous sociability' when compared in terms of such measures as crime, lifetime employment, extremes of wealth and poverty, use of litigation, and social and geographical mobility.[91] Instead, it is the decline of a civic sense that many have seen as the hallmark of post–Second World War American society. This eclipse has important implications, to be pursued momentarily. (In fairness, Fukuyama, at points, recognizes both the decline of civil responsibility in America and the consequences of his argument.)[92]

Moreover, the examples of 'low trust' nations (if they do lack trust) seem to refute the central argument. China over the last decades has been the fastest-growing economy in the world. Since the end of the war France and Italy have been the third and fifth fastest-growing economies among developed nations; they were, in 1995, the fourth and fifth richest countries in the world.[93]

The point here, then, is not to assess precisely Fukuyama's claims. Rather, it is to use them to emphasize the vitality of roles that can be played by social institutions in the ordering of society, in the provision of basic human needs. Yet many of these other sources of influence for regulating conduct, for creating civil society, have been in eclipse during the last part of the twentieth century, perhaps particularly in the United States.

In 'Bowling Alone,' a much discussed article with a title as indicative as it is haunting, Putnam documented that decline.[94] In a subsequent book he answered his critics and reasserted his claims.[95] From 1980 to 1993 league bowling decreased by 40 per cent even as the number of individuals – those 'bowling alone' – increased by 10 per cent.[96] More-established markers also document the decline of civic institutions and the increase of social disengagement: voter turnout has decreased dramatically; church and union memberships are down; trust in government and attendance at community meetings has dropped; and membership in voluntary associations from the Boy Scouts to the Red Cross has been on the wane for some time.[97]

Putnam argues against received wisdom in much of the social sciences. That burden of opinion is that civic virtue is an adjunct of traditional societies. As societies modernize small organizations operating through custom are replaced with big ones operating by rules. Thus such virtue is bound to disappear. To the contrary, Putnam contends that even the largest and most modernized societies cannot operate satisfactorily, even perhaps economically, where civic commitment is weak. Conversely, there is a strong link between the vibrancy of associational life, good governance, and democracy. Involvement, in networks of relative equals, generates norms of reciprocity while sanctioning defectors and 'creates a culturally-defined template for future collaboration.'[98]

Putnam considered a number of explanations for the fall-off in civic activity. He dismissed the movement of women into the labour force, the decline in the size and stability of the family, and high rates of geographical mobility. He did focus on television as individualizing the use of leisure time. The amount of television watching has steadily increased so that such activity has 'dwarfed all of the changes in the way Americans spend their days and nights.'[99] At the same time, other technological developments – such as CD players, video recorders, and the Internet – markedly reduce interpersonal contact among individuals.[100]

Such trends in other countries may not be so marked. For example, some have argued that, despite battering from a number of forces, the French continue to maintain (and act upon) a vibrant 'sens civique.'[101] Nevertheless, less-systematic statistics do suggest some important similarities in comparable societies, for example, Canada.[102] At the same time, there are some countertrends in America, such as the growth of non-profit organizations and of 'support groups.'[103] Religion, despite declining numbers, may still occupy a position in the lives of ordinary people that elite opinion does not countenance.[104] What is more, some would claim – in contrast to Putnam – that the Internet is providing a very different, yet vital, way for people to form communities of interest – despite the fact that people, in using it, are geographically separated and isolated in their homes or offices. Both the Internet and the communities that are formed through its use are not dependent on law.

Indeed, they are mostly hostile to it. (We will pursue this wariness between the Internet and legal regulation in part 3 in the context of our discussion of pornography.)[105]

Critics of Putnam note the widespread popular response that greeted 'Bowling Alone.' They suggest that, whatever the goal of Putnam, his article serves a larger political agenda. At a time of anti-government fervour it is convenient to associate societal ills with widespread disengagement rather than inadequate, underfunded, and ill-supported public programs.[106] At the same time, they point out that Putnam does not account for the relationship between civic community, institutional performance, and democracy. He is not clear about what kind of society high social capital and democracy would – and should – produce: sceptics note that praising the PTA takes us back to a time when women were – and expected to be – in the home.[107]

Others question some of the statistics cited by Putnam. They suggest, among other things, that he has not accounted for all dimensions of associational life.[108] Still others insist that we should not think of civic participation as having so much declined as having changed. The source of the transformation has been the rise of rights, a matter turned to in detail below. The core of authority for civic action has moved from shared values rooted in the community to political action and elections to, now, individual rights guaranteed by the courts. Even if the epitome of former models, 'the informed citizen,' has not been totally displaced by the 'rights-bearing citizen,' it is the case that organized parties, elections, and voting are now less clearly the core acts of political participation. Instead, the '"political," carried on the wing of rights, has now diffused into everyday life.'[109]

Still, there is enough evidence of a decline, particularly in America, in civic participation to cause worry. The erosion of participation is associated with many social problems – broken families, poor schools, decaying urban cores, to name but a few. At the same time, there has been a strong correlation made between declining civic engagement and a demand for law to provide some framework for these societies of strangers: 'Law varies inversely with other social controls.'[110]

Put more elaborately, it can be said that law has risen in importance as the state has striven to fill the void created by the decline of family, clan, informal associations, and other forms of community. Such factors as increasing urbanization, the spread of liability insurance, and the advent of the welfare state have weakened the informal control system while expanding the domain of law. At the same time, technology has developed expectations of mobility and freedom in individuals (not always met, to be sure) that simultaneously loosen commitment to, and substitute for, any number of social structures, most prominently the family: 'Countless aspects of modern law are responses to mobility, and to its discontents. The very fact of law – the pervasiveness of law – is a reflex of a society made up of strangers; a society in which the most rapidly growing "family" unit is the single person living utterly alone.'[111]

This breakdown of forms of community has led to fears that law will come to be the only thing that will hold us together. If this is so, the worry is that the bond that law will create will be tenuous and fractious. There will be much talk of legalization and little achievement of justice: 'Law reflects but in no sense determines the moral wealth of a society. The norms of a reasonably just society will reflect themselves in a reasonably just law. The better the society, the less law there will be ... The worse the society, the more law there will be. In Hell there will be nothing but law, and due process will be meticulously observed.'[112]

Such apprehensions may be overdrawn, even as the sway of the law is undeniable. At any rate, the breakdown of other forms of community does not provide an entire account of the lure of legalization. A further explanation comes from a faith that law can be harnessed to achieve political ends, almost regardless of what those goals may be.

Politics Harnesses Law

Politics has always needed law. Politics is the cement holding a society together, providing a framework for individuals, organizations, and business entities to relate. When politics decides on action to be taken regarding a myriad of issues it needs a vehicle to carry it out. Law is by no means the only such vehicle, but it has long been an important one.

However, the last decades have seen a qualitative and quantitative change in how law is used to achieve political ends. Political activity and faith in government have been on the decline for some time. This was a point made in the last section in conjunction with the discussion of the decline in civic engagement. Just one statistic here will indicate how far faith in politics and government has eroded. In the United States there has been a drastic shift in the answer to the question 'How much of the time can you trust the government to do what's right?' In 1964, 76 per cent answered 'always' or 'most of the time'; in 1984, 44 per cent did so; in 1994, only 19 per cent did so.[113]

Law is now frequently seen to be the means to achieve the necessary agreement, or at least acquiescence, in society to effect particular goals. In other words, since government cannot be trusted to act for the common good, there is a race to get laws passed by legislatures or pronounced by courts. Such laws will reflect particular agendas without regard to the balance and compromise that politics, when well done, facilitates.[114] If law can be harnessed, it will reconfigure society to bring social and economic forces into conformity with the ends any group seeks to achieve. Consensus and agreement need not precede law. Rather law will bring about the desired change.

At first blush it might be thought that this fascination with law to achieve a particular agenda might be more prominent on the left wing of the political spectrum. In fact, some leftists want little to do with the law. It is said to be nothing more than a form of co-optation, preventing radical transformation. (Such warnings to stay clear of the law will be returned to in a subsequent chapter.)[115]

Nevertheless, those of a progressive cast who are willing to cede a role for law have long relied on it as a primary counterweight to the excesses of market capitalism. The expectations of the role for law, primarily because of the rise of rights, have now increased substantially. There are high hopes for law as a primary tool for reordering society through rights-claiming activism. This optimism, regarding the power of rights, is especially prominent in the United States.

Legalization is, however, also a siren call for conservatives. In matters economic, that end of the political spectrum turns to the market as the great engine of wealth production and distribution. In this depiction regulation is a constant source of harassment, burden, and annoyance. Nevertheless, for fighting crime and for matters moral, large segments of the right are prepared to harness law to achieve a multitude of ends from controlling pornography to restricting abortion to deciding who may adopt a child.

Of particular note is the right's willingness to rely on the heaviest machinery: the criminal law and its enforcement. Criminalization is the most drastic form of legalization because of its attendant threat of loss of personal freedom, its cost of enforcement, and the panoply of procedures should matters come before the judiciary. Nowhere is this fascination with the machinery of criminal law, enforced by the courts, more on display than in the United States. Nowhere is the weight of the law more evident than with the right's obsession with imprisonment and with capital punishment as a response to crime.

Rights and Transformation

Any number of progressives throughout the twentieth century saw law as a means of social, political, and economic reform. As the first section of this chapter documented, law was seen as the great counterweight to the excesses of market capitalism regarding protection of workers (in respect of occupational health and safety, collective bargaining, minimum wages, etc.), safeguarding the environment, guarding against anti-competitive practices and fraud, providing minimum security from poverty, and so forth. However, some time after the Second World War, in the United States, many progressives took another tack regarding the use of law to achieve particular agendas. The core of that strategy was the claiming of rights.[116]

When we speak of rights we may mean many things. But the sense of rights that most concerns us here is that involving an enforceable claim in law. Of course, the fact that some entitlement can be legally enforced is not, itself, the reason for the enchantment with law among progressives that the last several decades have witnessed. Rather, it was the claim of rights to transform the social and political order that seemed so attractive.

If laws are meant to recognize certain claims and to ensure that the holders of these claims obtain satisfaction, there is, for the most part, little problem in a role for rights in that enforcement. If someone is injured in a motor-vehicle accident (perhaps especially due to the negligence of another), we would want the person who is hurt to have a 'right' to recover. Or, if a society, for instance Canada, decides that there will be universal access to health care, we would want individuals to have a 'right' to receive treatment according to need on an equitable basis.

Instead, the 'rights revolution,' especially in America, focused on giving recognition to interests, individuals, and groups mainly through litigation. It was primarily courts, not politicians, that would confer entitlements, often constitutionalized. There were many ambitions for this revolution, but a primary one was to gain recognition legally that had not been obtained politically. At the core there was much to commend this approach. For example, protecting people either as individuals or as members of groups from discrimination can be a powerful, positive goal of law.

Such employment of law was particularly attractive, at least at the theoretical level, for those who have long been denied opportunities in society. A clear example of this are blacks in America. A prominent Afro-American woman, Patricia Williams, puts eloquently the case for rights: '"Rights" feels so new in the mouths of most black people. It is still so deliciously empowering to say. It is a sign for and a gift of self-hood ... The concept of rights, both positive and negative, is the marker of our citizenship, our participatoriness, our relation to others.'[117]

But from this laudable core the legalization of rights and the rightness of that which could be legalized proceeded apace.[118] An amalgam of progressives (activists, lawyers, academics, some media admirers – aided, for at least a period, by sympathetic courts) set about using rights to transform a politics that, at least in their view, was not responsive: 'Court majorities with an expansive view of the judicial role, and their academic admirers, propelled each other, like railway men on a handcar, along the line that led to the land of rights.'[119]

By the 1960s in the United States, one could talk about a public interest / rights movement. As exemplified by the work of Ralph Nader, law was to become an instrument of progressive change. By the 1970s, there were public-interest law firms representing a host of interests including environmentalists, consumers, women, the disabled, minorities, children, and prisoners as they pressed their agendas, largely through the claiming of rights in the political, legislative, and administrative processes, but most prominently through litigation, actual or threatened.[120]

'Rights talk,' it was insisted, revitalizes society's dulled sense of community. In this conversation the vulnerable and the powerful are brought together in a common forum: 'The language of the law enables lawyers to reform client problems in terms of broad standards of American law and culture and, thus, to convey the plight of the have-nots in terms that maximize the likelihood for a sympathetic response culturally as well as legally.'[121]

Thus it is contended that, when we entrench rights, we express values and, in turn, value each right holder. Here is one of the most optimistic accounts of what law can do for us if we but embrace it through 'rights': 'Legal rights, then, should be understood as the language of a continuing process rather than fixed rules ... [as] language we use to try and persuade others to let us win this round ... [We can take] the aspirational language of the society seriously and ... promote change by reliance on inherited traditions.'[122]

Yet many, perhaps particularly those aligning themselves with progressive causes, have argued that the meaning accorded 'rights' in law can be problematic and unpredictable.[123] This is so because there is no neutral standpoint from which to identify those who are to be the recipients of such rights. Because there is no uncontroversial means of determining the scope and nature of each particular right, there is no method that can be used to fairly adjudicate a clash of competing rights. The recognition of rights as fundamental, but not – ultimately – absolute means that balancing claims of individuals against the common interest is laden with difficulty. What is more, the costs of such rights and the drain they impose on resources that could be directed elsewhere is hardly ever seriously examined.[124] As a result, difficult trade-offs are ignored and the implications for benefits bestowed by the political process – public education and health care, welfare, public parks and urban cores – are not related back to the burdens that rights impose.[125] In sum: 'First, constitutional and legal symbols are not likely to be particularly useful for rallying those most in need. Second, with litigation at its core, mobilization tends to be divisive ... The net effect is to pit have not segments of the society against one another in a zero sum struggle over scarce resources.'[126]

Rights, in the sense we are employing the term, have become so controversial because of the kinds and number of interests in society demanding that their claims be recognized. Such claims are often aligned with 'extreme individualism,' which insists upon total vindication of specific interests. For example, some would argue that the high rate of marital breakdown is largely attributable to 'expressive divorce,' which suggests a right to leave a marriage 'if it becomes stultifying or simply boring,' without regard to the consequences, particularly for children.[127]

As a result, critics see us now living in a 'culture of complaint.'[128] Extremes of such critical reaction seek to pre-empt further discussion by levelling charges of 'political correctness' against many rights claimants (suggesting, among other things, that, in the case of the women's movement, a 'feminist agenda ... encourages women to ... kill their children').[129] It need not be said that such extremes are more objectionable than the phenomena they take to task.

Most recently, there are two kinds of responses being launched by defenders of rights. The first attacks the very idea of community, a concept that is often asserted to blunt the expansion of rights. 'Community' has too many, ill-defined meanings to be a foundation for a worthy politics. In its worst manifestations community can be a prescription for tyranny, stifling individualism, choice, and freedom. The American south once had a highly developed sense of community – that was oppressive and exclusionary towards blacks.[130]

The second asserts that there never was a time of a model politics. Instead, what constitutes good citizens and worthy political involvement has changed over the decades, with each stage having its attractions and its foibles. The 'rights bearing citizen' is the most recent manifestation of such transformations. Such change cannot be addressed by decrying it and wishing for the return of the 'long civic generation' that, in fact, probably never existed. Schudson is particularly eloquent in pleading for a coming to terms with this new way of conceiving of politics and of law: 'A rights-regarding citizenship does not "answer" democracy's discontents, but it is a necessary part of any answer. Moreover, it automatically implies respect for the rights of others and the willingness to engage in public dispute according to public norms and a public language. We have to recognize that the claiming of rights, though it should not be the end of a citizen's political consciousness, is an invaluable beginning to it.'[131]

Nevertheless, there are insistent questions as to how effective 'rights' are in terms of facilitating the goals of such claimants. Particularly interesting and complex issues arise regarding the effectiveness of litigation, especially in achieving the goals of progressive reform. America has most invoked litigation as the vehicle for the recognition and enforcement of rights, and the USA is the most studied society regarding the consequences produced by such an invocation of rights in courts. It is in America where debates are most intense concerning the impact of litigation over complex issues. Such studies and debates will occupy our attention at various points in subsequent chapters.

Holmes cautioned decades ago that 'all rights tend to declare themselves absolute to their logical extreme.'[132] That sentiment reflects worries about a cacophony of claims that will not be a route to empowerment. To the contrary, the fear is that such assertions will abet a swell of fractiousness, creating expectations for law that it cannot meet. At the same time, such societal dust-ups can blunt initiatives in tackling the very serious problems besetting common conditions. The hope that politics can be about 'measured care for our fellow humans'[133] will grow ever more distant.

Crime and Punishment

But fascination with the law is not confined to progressives. The right has also become enamoured with its use. To be sure, there is opposition whenever conservatives can be persuaded that a law will invade personal liberties. Since liberty is held to be closely aligned with the market, almost any form of economic regulation (from antitrust and consumer-protection measures to traditional forms of human-rights protection or more ambitious extensions such as pay-equity or affirmative-action measures) is likely to meet firm resistance. In such matters 'beware governmental regulation'[134] is ever the watchword.

Not so for crime. If the right can be persuaded that a matter is in a realm of conduct that ought to be prohibited by the state, then a very different set of attitudes and beliefs dominate. In combating crime, law and its enforcement is a sacred instrument for a holy mission. Atop this depiction capital punishment sits as a shining beacon, signalling to all that for the ultimate wrongdoing there will be the ultimate payment in terms of personal responsibility.

True, not all potential issues are characterized as fit subjects for criminalization. A classic example is gun control in America. Since the purpose of gun control is to lessen crime – violent crime at that – one might think that regulation of firearms would be a prime candidate for warm embrace by those whose rallying cry is law and order. But for the true conservative such a hug stands not a chance. The claim that laws regulating the sale and use of firearms will combat senseless killing is met by the cry that the right of peace-loving citizens to bear arms will be compromised.[135] Instead, there is unyielding faith that committing crime is all about individual choice and responsibility: 'Guns don't kill people. People kill people.' (Such unyielding faith, in the context of gun control, is a matter we look at in part 2.)[136]

Nevertheless, on many fronts, criminal law and its enforcement remain the prime means for the right to resist violence and mayhem.[137] There is accumulating evidence that rates of crime, including violent ones, are decreasing.[138] For some, such indicators verify that deterrence is the answer.[139]

Hardly a year has gone by in the recent decades without some scheme being hatched that has invoked some aspect of criminal law (or its enforcement, or the punishment it metes out) to fight crime. Among the many solutions on offer are capital punishment – more of it, more certain use of it; prison terms – increased, mandatory, and fixed curfews; the obligatory laying of charges; and shielding police from charges of discrimination and their use of violence.

All the while there is evidence indicating that

- capital punishment does not deter and may be applied discriminatorily;
- prisons are a breeding ground for crime; while in the United States

rates of imprisonment are the highest in the world (except for Russia), paradoxically America has some of the highest rates of violent crime in the world (though in decline);

– effective policing requires building the trust of the community to be policed and protected; and

– poverty, urban neglect, and unemployment can be dark hosts sponsoring the anti-social impulses that precede serious criminal conduct.

More temperate observers are likely to suggest that crime is most effectively combatted with a mix of policies: on the one hand, a variety of programs to fight the social conditions that spawn criminal conduct and, on the other, harsh measures for hard-core criminals, particularly when crimes of violence are involved. Such a view urges that we should be concerned about preventing the commission of crime in the first place by, among other things, being responsive to circumstances of deprivation that make crime so tempting. Yet, after the commission of serious crime – particularly of violence – our concern should shift to solicitude for the victims, with imprisonment often the appropriate punishment for the wrongdoer. At the same time, the death penalty is not, in Western industrialized nations – except for America – part of such policies.

What precisely the ingredients of this policy mix should be and how best to implement and assess responses are fit subjects for debate among reasonable people. Yet it is hard to have such discussions, particularly at a popular level, in the United States when tough sanctions meted out by the courts are presented as such a straightforward – and just – solution.[140]

The criminal law as an antidote for violence is not the only controversial area where the right has been attracted to legalization. There are any number of issues, which those more reluctant to use the law might term 'moral' (indicating conduct that may be questionable but not to be characterized as illegal). Indeed, for some such instances, an increasingly large percentage of the populace would consider the behaviour nothing but a matter of personal choice. Such issues include abortion, the production, sale, and consumption of pornography, use of a variety of drugs, and certain forms of sexual behaviour, most prominently homosexuality.

Many conservatives see these issues as evidence of personal corruption so great that the most drastic form of state intervention is justified.

Thus is the way paved for invoking the criminal law in such cases. This enthusiasm intensifies despite the fact that those who are otherwise their ideological allies issue warnings. These caveats particularly concern the harm that may come when criminalization of activity involving personal choice is too easily invoked. One danger is the failure to grapple with the inevitable complexities: '[T]he restoration of Puritan sex ethics is not realistic, and those who preach it are merely evading the difficult questions of policy.'[141]

An important aspect of these admonitions is that conservatives should be consistent. A wariness of government regulation of whatever nature should apply to areas of personal choice just as much as to market activity. There is also an openness, in such admonitions, to arguments that a certain amount of governmental presence could be sound policy. Such a role for government may be economically justified and may produce outcomes that improve individual lives, including making them less dependent on the state in the long run.[142]

Conclusions

Society asserts its influence and creates a demand for law. Legislation and lawyers proliferate, litigation and expectations of it grow. Law is meant to buttress choice and individualism, to transform society through rights, to provide what social capital no longer can, to deter violent crime and to halt erosion of traditional values and accompanying social disintegration. But there is too much of it and the ills of its excesses are everywhere apparent: it crowds out investment, it oppresses minorities, self-reliance is drained, the common purpose decays. Yet law invoked by the 'rights-regarding citizen' has become a central act – perhaps *the* central act – of civic participation. Nowhere are these multifaceted, contradictory aspects of law manifested as much as in America.

Can law do all these things – and simultaneously? How do we know what law does and how it does it? What are the consequences it produces? Are there ways of assessing law's outcomes? How precise are such assessments in terms of isolating the impact of law from the tangle of influences on individual, corporate, and governmental behaviour? Is there a set of fundamental ideas about the effects of law? If so, what are they based on? Are there areas of social, political, and economic activity that might be particularly illustrative of these questions – and their complicated answers?

Much of the focus regarding the impact of law will be on the United States. It is the land of the law in terms of detailed legal rules, deterrence-oriented enforcement practices, intensely adversarial procedures, and rights. It is the most studied society regarding the influence of law. It uses litigation more than any society to forge and implement policy. Such usage is fascinating, but the results produced suggest caution regarding the employment of lawsuits to forge and implement policy.

PART TWO

The Impact of Law

CHAPTER TWO

Compliance with Law – Deterrence and Its Alternatives

Most people obey most laws most of the time. Nevertheless, maximizing obedience is a crucial element in a law being successful. Thus, a straightforward measurement of whether a law is achieving its goals – of its impact – is the extent to which there is compliance with it.

Obedience to the law is clearly a central goal for the administration of criminal justice. Breaches of criminal law, especially violent ones, strike at the heart of civil society. Understandably, therefore, much of the literature on compliance focuses on upholding laws enjoining such behaviour. Yet compliance is an important focus of other areas of the law as well. The measure of success for regulatory provisions hinges, in good part, on the extent to which those who are regulated comply with such laws. Civil liability is directed at compensation for the victim whether the wrongdoing is a breach of contract, a violation of a trust, or a claim, in tort, for negligent or other behaviours. At the same time, such lawsuits are meant to discourage such wrongdoing so that compliance with appropriate levels of conduct (in terms of carrying out contracts, maintaining an appropriate standard of care, and so forth) is maximized.

At the heart of traditional notions of compliance was deterrence. It was thought that the best way to achieve obedience to a law was to threaten some form of sanction. Deterrence remains a large component in terms of achieving compliance. An important reason for this is that most laws are still couched in terms of 'command and control,' with the threat of some sanctions if they are not obeyed. Thus deterrence is meant to discourage disobedience and, therefore, to achieve compliance with such law. Hence, a critical question is how best to achieve maximum deterrence and, therefore, maximum compliance. There is little question that threats of punishment do have a deterrent impact. However, deterrence, especially by itself, often does not have the precise effects that proponents claim. Of course, imposing sanctions on wrongdoers punishes them as well. Thus retribution also looms large in criminal law.

Several alternatives to deterrence have been advanced and many have been tried in conjunction with particular laws. One of the crucial questions is, What is the best mix of deterrence and these other alternatives in order to obtain obedience in any particular circumstances? We will see that those who have studied this question provide some promising leads but offer no definitive solutions. For example, in terms of alternatives, many urge proactive measures that would regulate conduct so as to prevent objectionable behaviours from occurring; such measures are illustrated by the discussion of gun control. Similarly, there are intriguing possibilities in terms of 'designing out': attempting to eliminate the cause of the underlying problems that law might otherwise be called upon to address. However, as we shall see, such attempts can give rise to a number of technical and philosophical problems, as illustrated by the discussion of techniques as varied as airbags to blunt the effects of hazardous driving and social-intervention programs to curb crime.

Closely linked to compliance is legitimacy. If people believe that a law is legitimate, they are more likely to comply with it. Conversely, if they believe a law is illegitimate, a fundamental underpinning for obedience does not exist, though the law may be followed for other reasons. Theories abound about what constitutes legitimacy for individuals and for societies. Again, it will be seen that none of them is entirely satisfactory. Thus a central question is, How is a law seen to be legitimate? Included in this larger question is an important subsidiary one: Does legitimacy hinge only on the substance of a law or can the way a law is enforced and the procedures used to make decisions concerning that law also be important determinants of legitimacy?

A crucial theme that emerges in this chapter (and that is pursued in part 3) is the extent to which deterrence (linked to punitiveness) enjoys enormous currency in the United States. Rates of imprisonment in America have soared to unrivalled heights despite the fact that crime is actually falling. Courts are looked to as the agents and symbols of such deterrence and punitiveness. Incarceration as a response to wrongdoing enjoys such popular and political support that it is hard to have other responses to crime taken seriously. Such resistance is particularly strong against social programs that seek to foster law-abiding attitudes.

Atop all of this faith in punishment sits the death penalty as the ultimate statement regarding individual responsibility. Again, the role of courts is critical in imposing this ultimate sanction. Executions are the extreme testimony to a people's commitment to punitive measures whatever the costs and regardless of the evidence of lack of effectiveness.

Achieving Compliance?

The Bases of Compliance

Societies of liberal pluralism have three main ways of achieving compliance with policy goals: persuasion, exchange, and command.[1] All three rely on law to varying degrees. There are important distinctions among the three and their use of law. However, these differences do blur. For example, the last, often referred to as 'command and control,' can have important variations in the regulatory context. These variations may permit those regulated to use various means, including exchange, to achieve compliance with certain standards.[2] Nevertheless, it is useful to set out the basic distinctions among the three means for purposes of the discussion that will follow.

Persuasion relies on the power of argument and the invoking of norms and principles to achieve compliance. Historically, law's role was the most attenuated in terms of this form of obedience. Such institutions as those of education and religion were far more important. Yet, as we saw in chapter 1, the bonds of family, schools, and voluntary associations over the last several decades have been loosened in many critical ways. As a result, these institutions are not as effective as they once were in transmitting and developing norms. Then, too, societies of the late twentieth century are confronted by quandaries not otherwise associated with these secondary institutions: issues concerning environmental degradation, globalization, and so forth.

Thus, law has come to play a role even at this primary level of developing and garnering support for norms. Statutes creating programs and agencies may authorize them to expend funds for public education. An important example in this regard is the campaign against smoking (examined in detail in part 3). Governments have invoked a number of tools to curtail tobacco consumption. While the record is complicated, there is substantial evidence of success, particularly in Canada and the

United States. An important element of the campaign has been government education aimed at alerting the public to the hazards of smoking and at buttressing norms against consumption in both public spaces and private homes.

Exchange is the second means of achieving compliance with a goal. Compliance is voluntary but is achieved at a price: A induces B to comply by offering something of value in return. Exchange's major mechanism is the market, with negotiation an intricate element. Law's role here is to provide a structure in which the negotiations can take place and in which the market can operate. It does this through basic laws regarding the making and enforcement of contracts, including remedies for their breach.

Law also rules some ploys used in negotiating or contracting as out of bounds. There are basic common-law and statutory provisions against fraud, duress, or (sometimes) inequality of power. There are more elaborate statutory and regulatory regimes aimed at preventing widespread distortions such as those that may occur because of manipulation of securities markets or because of monopolies or other forms of anti-competitive behaviour.

In addition, exchange can operate by providing incentives. Laws can stipulate that certain benefits will flow if there is a stipulated course of conduct. Governments can use such incentives to achieve public-policy objectives in several contexts, for example, in some aspects of taxation. Moreover, parties can bargain regarding the extent to which there will be compliance with the standards otherwise stipulated by the law. Such bargaining can take place in many contexts: pleas in criminal charges, settlements in civil litigation, and following the regulatory standards of some administrative agency.[3]

The third form is command (with statutory law bearing this characteristic often referred to as 'command and control legislation'). Here compliance is achieved essentially by edict. Consent to the command may, indeed, be present, but it is not essential in order for the command to be effective. This is so because an essential aspect of a command is the threat of force in order to obtain obedience. The threat is meant to prevent disobedience, to ensure compliance.

Much of law works through commands. Obviously, the criminal-justice system does so. In addition, the vast array of the regulatory state is heavily dependent (some would say too dependent)[4] on command-and-control legislation. Further, much of the tax system relies heavily on command-and-control mechanisms. Finally, most laws dealing with domestic relations from grounds for divorce through to calculation of support payments and their enforcement can depend on command and control. The common law operates through command and control to the extent that standards are set by the judges in various areas (contract, tort, trust). If such standards are not met, then the wrongdoer can be subject to claims for compensation by the persons who have been harmed.

The role of law here is apparent. Law with its capacity to harness the force of the state is a crucial aspect of commands. Therefore, backing commands is the very apparatus of law: its making, application, and adjudication. Not surprisingly, then, legislatures, government departments and administrative agencies, and the courts have prominent roles when the law commands. To 'command' someone is to ensure that there is a sanction for disobedience. To stipulate a sanction is to have confidence that the threat of it will deter disobedience, that the command will be obeyed. Hence, the importance of deterrence in achieving compliance with command-and-control legislation looms large. Too large many would say. Thus we first examine deterrence in some detail, including its weaknesses. We then look at some suggested alternatives.

Deterrence and Its Alternatives

How Best to Deter

If much of law focuses on commands and most of those commands are negative ('Thou shalt not kill'), it is no surprise that enforcement would rely heavily on deterrence. If people are successfully deterred, then compliance with the command has been achieved. Yet, how best to achieve deterrence and whether deterrence is relied on too heavily, preventing other means of achieving compliance from being utilized, are insistent questions for those studying obedience to law.

In many ways the complexities arise not because deterrence does not work but because it does. Most people do not commit crimes, certainly not violent ones. They believe such acts are wrong; they fear any sort of punishment. Thus, for the vast majority deterrence works – or is just unnecessary because moral beliefs, informal social sanctions, or other controls blunt any impulse to break the law.[5] But a minority, even a small minority, can wreak havoc. How are their instincts to be curbed, especially at a time when other institutions have more than met their match on any number of fronts: 'The explosion in violent crime must mean that our society is unable to teach enough people to submerge themselves in a higher morality. The family loses its grip; the peer group, the gang, the crowd takes over.'[6]

Effecting change at the margins is where deterrence becomes complex.[7] A major problem is that punishment does not influence behaviour in a straight line. The relationship is a curve, one that flattens as greater numbers are deterred. Those who remain undeterred become increasingly difficult to change as punishment and behaviour interact – and fail to interact – and even apprehension of the offender becomes an issue. A study of crime in New York City in the 1970s illustrates the limits of deterrence. Of every 1000 felonies committed, only 540 were reported to the police; those reported yielded 65 arrests and convictions, with a mere 3 sentenced to jail for a year or more: 'If [the system] were four times as tough, the number might be *twelve*. Even a *tremendous* increase in conviction rates, without something more, would hardly make a dent in the problem of crime.'[8]

Those who boast of law's ability to control see deterrence as a main instrument in the armoury. Yet, upon close examination, the effectiveness of deterrence in problem areas – where it needs to deliver its wallop – is much more questionable. Part of the difficulty lies with the assumptions made by those who promote theories of deterrence. Such premises are weighted heavily towards the rationality of the potential criminal.

This would-be violator calculates gains from illegal activity against the probable sanctions, if caught, and then decides to do or to refrain. Yet much criminological research stresses the range of crimes committed on impulse, the absence of calculation by offenders of the consequences, and the multitude of motivations that may not be controllable by criminal law.[9] As a result: 'On the deterrent effects of legal sanctions in general it is impossible to offer confident conclusions from the results of numerous often inconsistent studies using a wide variety of methods and varying considerably in analytical sophistication.'[10] In other words, sanctions do have a deterrent effect. However, the extent of that effect and how it works in any specific area can be quite unclear.

We can glean further insights into questions regarding the effectiveness of deterrence by discussing three specific issues: problems regarding corporate crime; the controversy over severity versus certainty of sanctions; and the potential of civil liability in effecting deterrence.

Corporate Crime: As a matter of first impression, corporations, with their eye for the bottom line in terms of costs and benefits, should be highly responsive to deterrence. Such sensitivity should be present for two reasons. First, those in charge will worry about the loss of prestige that results from a criminal conviction. Second, organizations act rationally (unlike many individual offenders). Since sanctions imposed by the criminal law will greatly increase the cost of criminal behaviour, a rational calculation of the burdens imposed should lead to corporations avoiding conduct that will lead to such penalties.[11] Indeed, conventional views of the corporation see it as largely responsive only to threats of punishment. The amoral, profit-maximizing nature of corporations prevents them from responding to other inducements such as a sense of participation in the community, claims regarding larger public purposes, and so forth. In this depiction the corporation is an 'ingenious device for the maximisation of profit and the minimisation of responsibility.'[12]

However, it has been repeatedly demonstrated that deterrence is less effective in curbing wrongful corporate behaviour than theoretical analysis would suggest. There are several reasons for this disparity. First, managers can violate standards for reasons that can have little to do with rational choice. They can fail to comply because of incompetence, misunderstanding of the law, or improper attention to regulatory requirements. Second, calculation of the relevant costs and benefits may not be nearly as easy as the amoral-calculator model would suggest. Finally, the standards that are to be complied with and the consequent punishments are often not clear to the organization, to decision makers, or to the public.[13]

In terms of divergence between theories and the actual effect of deterrence regarding wrongful corporate behaviour, the record for prosecutions for death in the workplace is instructive. Despite some exceptions, the use of manslaughter provisions as a response to deaths in the workplace is very limited. In the cases in which they are successfully invoked the fines imposed are often inadequate. These provisions, therefore, have little influence on any rational cost-benefit calculation.

There are several explanations for this lack of success. Those prosecutions that do occur are seen to be politically motivated rather than prompted by the degree of wrongdoing involved. Mounting a prosecution for manslaughter requires a different enforcement strategy than that usually undertaken by health and safety agencies: training personnel to address relevant issues and gathering sufficient evidence remain major obstacles. There are substantial differences of opinion as to whether the organization or individuals in it should be held account- able. Those who argue for prosecution of individuals insist that it is only the people within the organization that can be deterred. Others argue, to the contrary, that the available defences make it unlikely that individuals can be convicted. At the same time, manslaughter provi- sions do not lend themselves to prosecution of organizations; major cases of this sort, costing the state considerable resources (and credibil- ity), have failed.[14]

As a result, contemporary discussions regarding corporate account- ability search for additional ways to foster compliance. The role of deterrence is recognized, but more as one of last resort. Increasingly there is interest in such factors as the dynamics of social organization, the role of persuasion, and the actual constituants of compliance in a given situation.[15] A prominent example of such a shift is the 'regula- tory pyramid.'[16] The base of this approach would consist of educa- tional/persuasive strategies that encourage trust and discourage defensiveness. Punitive sanctions would be reserved for situations where these other strategies have clearly failed. There is even talk of fostering 'corporate virtue.'[17] How successful this shift will be in terms of achieving compliance remains to be established. Here, again, the need for empirical studies to test the compatibility of theoretical approaches and actual results is obvious.[18] The point here is that, even at a theoretical level, the supremacy of deterrence has been dislodged in terms of its claimed power to shape the behaviour of corporate actors.

Severity versus Certainty: A second controversy regarding deterrence is the debate between the severity and the certainty of the penalty. The heart of deterrence theory is that the effectiveness of punishment is a function of severity, certainty, and swiftness. However, both theoreti- cally and empirically, there is less assuredness regarding the compara- tive efficacy of severity versus certainty.[19]

There is widespread support for certainty being more efficacious than severity. A prominent study of how best to prevent drunk driving surveyed studies focused on the severity/certainty debate. It con- cluded that 'a number of studies in widely different contexts seem to coalesce on support for the deterrent effect of measures aimed at increasing the certainty of punishment, though mainly in the short run, and on rejection of the deterrent effect of measures aimed at increasing the severity of punishment.'[20]

A body of economic theory also supports the superiority of certainty over severity in achieving compliance. That theory suggests that there is an expectation that increases in the probability of incarceration, in conjunction with reduction in the length of the term of imprisonment, will yield an increase in deterrence. Fines should also function in a similar manner. Laboratory experiments demonstrate that individuals are risk-adverse regarding financial losses.[21] Furthermore, it has been argued that there is a 'social influence' effect generated by high-certainty but low-severity strategies: '[I]ndividuals learn about the price of crime primarily from observing that a high percentage of those who choose to break the law are caught.'[22]

However, it is also the case that some economic analysis challenges the efficacy of certainty in isolation from severity.[23] Yet, while arguing that severity can deter, such analysis also acknowledges the complexities of relying only on increases in punishment. These issues are illustrated in Posner's discussion regarding the prevention of rape.[24] He endorses such measures as assigning more women to squads investigating such offences and rape-shield laws that protect women who testify as witnesses in the prosecution of their alleged assailant. Important for the issue at hand, he also endorses studies showing that rapists, like other criminals, respond to increases in the severity as well as the probability of punishment.[25] Problems would arise, however, because the impact on rapists would, probably, not be the only effect. Victims could be endangered. The narrower the difference in punishment for rape and for murder, the less the assailant has to lose in disposing of his victim. Moreover, he gains by killing the key witness against him.

Then, too, there is also the likelihood of more acquittals if rape were sanctioned more heavily. The heavier a punishment, the more likely a jury may be to resolve any doubts in favour of the accused. This tendency was observed, historically, in England when rape was a capital offence (as were all felonies under the common law).[26] That problem is said to be severe in modern Pakistan, where traditional Islamic law has been reinstated. That law decrees severe penalties, even death, for rape. Yet the imposition of the penalties is surrounded with so many procedural safeguards for the defendant as to make the law virtually unenforceable.[27]

Civil Liability: Finally, there is a persistent question whether civil liability – mostly through tort litigation – may offer an alternative to criminal sanctions in achieving deterrence. The first goal of such litigation is to compensate those who have been injured by wrongful conduct. In addition, the hope is that the civil system, with its reduced standard of proof ('balance of probabilities' versus 'proof beyond a reasonable doubt'), its private enforcement mechanisms (particularly tort litigation), and its respect for the parties' capacity to bargain in the shadow of litigation, can be an adjunct to the criminal system in terms of deterrence. The focus of civil liability is objectionable, often negligent conduct that nevertheless, does not call for the heavy machinery of criminal law. One seeks to impose such liability so that the sum of accident and avoidance costs will be minimized. The use of civil liability to curb wrongdoing is an idea that is debated generally. However, the actual employment of tort lawsuits for deterrent purposes is most closely associated with litigation in the United States.

A recent study looked at the effectiveness of deterrence in terms of tort litigation and of administrative regulation in America in five different areas: automobile accidents, medical malpractice, product-related accidents, environmental injuries, and workplace mishaps.[28] That study also evaluated the achievement of corrective and distributive justice in these areas. Here we will focus on the findings regarding deterrence.

The study analysed a large number of empirical investigations. It concluded, generally, that, regarding torts, '[t]he ... system performs unevenly in deterring the causes of personal injuries, so its scope should be restricted to situations where its effect seems likely to justify its high cost.'[29] In terms of regulatory alternatives, the study found that '[t]he regulatory system has achieved varying success in reducing personal injuries; its performance can be improved by reducing its use in areas in which it is ineffective, by expanding its use where it is more effective, and by improving its design.'[30]

For example, regarding torts and medical accidents, a major study of malpractice litigation in New York State had difficulty identifying a deterrent effect from such lawsuits. More complex analysis of the data supported the conclusion that this litigation results in a statistically significant, though still modest, reduction in injuries caused by negligence. At the same time, it is not clear that any marginal gains in injury reduction justify the costs. Such expenditures include legal services, the court system, and the parties' and witnesses' time, but also defensive medicine, engaged in primarily to limit exposure and not for therapeutic purposes.[31]

In terms of administrative regulation and product liability, the study concluded that a 'striking' result is that the cost per life saved or injury avoided by regulatory intervention varies dramatically across the regulatory system. The implication is that significant reallocation of resources based on rigorous cost-benefit analysis could 'vastly' improve results on the whole, without increased total costs.[32]

Generally, the study acknowledges the theoretical desirability of using civil liability to deter undesirable conduct. Yet it emphasizes that careful examination of the facts reveals the gap between idea and reality: 'The great disappointment that the deterrent effect of tort is limited and uneven or cannot be established by existing studies suggests that considerable intellectual effort has been expended on models that omit some crucial facts about the real world.'[33]

Alternatives to Deterrence

The foregoing indicates the dissatisfaction with deterrence and its capacity to effect and to explain compliance (and non-compliance) with the law. Empirically, a number of studies have demonstrated levels of compliance that cannot be explained by any deterrent effects of the law. Conversely, there are any number of instances where deterrence is not as effective as its proponents suggest it should be, most prominently in terms of controlling violent crime. Theoretically, there is reaction to the underlying premises of deterrence and their depiction of individuals as amoral, risk averse, and utility maximizing.

These critiques of deterrence have prompted searches for alternatives in achieving compliance. Here we will discuss three reactions to deterrence: rewards, proactive measures, and behavioural decision theory. This part closes by emphasizing the importance of context when examining the effectiveness of deterrence or any substitutes.

Rewards: One reaction to deterrence advances the potential of its opposite – that is, rewards – in effecting compliance. Proponents believe that rewards have greater possibilities in achieving compliance with law than has yet been tried. Enthusiasts point to the fact that many other institutions in society (for example, business and religion) rely on rewards to enforce their norms. Indeed, university faculties work almost entirely on the reward system (tenure, promotion, merit increases, grants, etc.). (Whether the public would judge academic institutions to be models for the regulation of behaviour may, however, be a question.) In any event, proponents seek to take lessons learned from other institutions regarding positive reinforcement and apply them to law.[34] In this regard, they emphasize the extent to which industry uses rewards in areas such as absenteeism, productivity, and occupational safety and the degree to which there is a major reward component in many management schemes.[35]

One instance in law where rewards are used to some extent is in the administration of criminal justice. For example, informers are sometimes paid – as distasteful as this might be – in order to secure necessary evidence. Then, in the running of prisons, persons who are of good conduct receive time off for good behaviour, a better chance for parole, and better accommodation and privileges. In addition, there has been some experimentation with rewards to support other aspects of criminal justice: to the police for decreases in the crime rate; to localities for the use of probation rather than jail; and to district attorneys who cut down on long-term detainees awaiting trial.[36]

Enthusiasts of rewards would extend their potential to other areas. For instance, to control mayhem on the highway they would look beyond deterrence to several other tools. They claim that rewards could be usefully employed by acknowledging the record of good drivers through decreased insurance rates, free licences, or lottery tickets with the chance of a substantial prize.[37] They point to field experiments regarding the use of seat belts and rewards and certain incentives-based safety programs, such as used by the Toronto Transit Commission with its employees, as evidence of the potential regarding traffic safety.[38]

The case for rewards should be explored through carefully designed and evaluated experiments. Nevertheless, the potential for incentives will, more often, be confined to a defined group. It will be more difficult to use incentives to prevent action (e.g., 'Do not steal') since the admonition applies to everyone.[39] In any event, one basis for the claim that rewards are the new way is questionable. Advocates writing in the eighties suggested that a main reason why rewards had not been used in the past was that the state could not afford them. However, 'today,' with the 'enormous wealth' of governments, that obstacle has been removed.[40] From the vantage point of the austere nineties and beyond this basis for rewards is wobbly.[41]

Nevertheless, there are prominent examples of governments using incentives to promote public policy. For instance, in federal systems the central government, through its spending power, sometimes uses transfer payments to achieve policy goals in areas where it does not have constitutional authority to act. A conspicuous instance of this phenomenon is the Canadian system of universal health insurance. This system is essentially uniform throughout a diverse country, including in terms of the various provinces' ability to pay, and despite the fact that the central government has no, or at any rate a sharply curtailed, constitutional competence over health care. It has been achieved through a federal statute that commits the central government to funding a large portion of the health-care system in each of the provinces so long as these governments maintain systems that adhere to a set of requirements designed to achieve universal access.[42]

Finally, governments are increasingly turning to incentives provided by market forces to encourage attainment of policy objectives. The reaction in the 1980s and 1990s to big government and its central authority has led several commentators to promote the use of such stimulants to achieve public-policy objectives.[43] Such 'performance'- or 'incentive'-based regulation should be focused on achieving the overall policy objectives while leaving the means to do so to a great extent to those who are regulated.[44] For instance, such regulation should

- stipulate only the goals leaving wide play to market incentives for those subject to the regulation to achieve those goals.

- be largely self-enforcing, regulators ensuring that the overall conduct of those regulated entities comply or that the appropriate tax or charge on harmful activity is paid.

- achieve any redistribution through taxes and transfers, not the setting of prices and rates.[45]

An example of this approach to regulation, in the context of environmental issues, are tradeable pollution permits. In this instance, the overall level of pollution permitted is legally stipulated. However, the allocation of resources to not exceed this level is left to market forces, including through the use of tradeable pollution permits. Thus, the total emissions permitted are legally regulated: those for whom it costs little to not pollute will do so the least and those for whom it costs most to pollute will negotiate for and use the permits.

Proactive Measures: Another alternative to deterrence would seek to achieve obedience largely through proactive measures such as persuasion, licensing, and inspection. This alternative is linked to the movement typified by the 'regulatory pyramid' and efforts to foster 'corporate virtue,' discussed in the previous section, in which deterrence is de-emphasized and efforts to achieve compliance through education and persuasion are encouraged. If infractions are to be sanctioned, administrative penalties would generally be invoked. The criminal law would be relied on only for clear and egregious violations.[46] This flexibility in sanctioning would be used to capture the respective strengths of the two systems.

The administrative process can be quicker and less costly. Offenders who deserve sanctioning are more likely to be identified in this process because previous offences are taken account of in assessing liability. Moreover, offenders can be punished for causing risk (and not only injury) in a system that applies the civil standard of proof. What is more, this process can impose more penalties and, as a result, create greater incentives to comply with regulatory standards: so long as enforcers are reasonably aggressive in setting about their tasks. In contrast, the criminal process is more expensive, slower, and constrained by the applicable rules of evidence. At the same time, however, there is a belief that criminal sanctions pack more punch because they are more stigmatizing, although there is little empirical substantiation of this point in the administrative context.

In any event, those who have looked at these issues tend to advocate a dual system of administrative and criminal penalties. The former would be utilized for the vast majority of regulatory offences, while the latter would be applied only to the most serious offences. The reduced cost of the administrative process would result in offenders being penalized sufficiently frequently to furnish a financial deterrent to infractions. In contrast, the rare high-profile prosecution would underscore the stigma incurred if the law is violated.[47] Again, the need for careful evaluative studies regarding the actual effectiveness of these efforts to find the right mix of persuasion and flexibility in sanctioning should be emphasized.[48]

As indicated, alternatives based on persuasion, licensing, and inspection de-emphasize the threat of prosecution and criminal sanctions. At the same time, they often advance measures designed to avoid infractions in the first place. Illustrative of such proactive techniques, using licensing in particular, is gun control.[49] A discussion of gun control also raises issues of the effectiveness of similar laws in different societies: particularly Canada and the United States.

In terms of the deterrence of crimes resulting from guns, the United States and Canada, as well as many other countries, take roughly similar approaches. Also similar are measures, in the two countries, designed to incapacitate those believed likely to misuse firearms because of a history of such offences or because of substance abuse, etc.; though in some instances Canadian legislation goes farther, allowing (and, in some situations, compelling) courts to make specific orders barring firearms.[50]

However, Canadian and American legislation have differed, for some time, with respect to more proactive measures. Such measures include various requirements for licensing, screening prior to acquisition or possession, controls on use, and restrictions or complete prohibitions on particular kinds of guns. These policies are well established in Canada – and are increasing. There are virtually no counterparts in the United States, particularly at the federal level. Any relevant proposals in America are enmeshed in deep controversy.[51]

Deaths from handguns in the United States substantially exceed those in Canada, despite the fact that Canada and the United States share a common border and common language, and most Canadians live in the south in close proximity to the United States. Accounting for this difference regarding deaths by handguns leads to interesting issues regarding cause and effect. Some believe that a greater respect for law and order on the part of Canadians plays a significant role – the rate for violent crime, generally, is substantially lower than in the United States.[52]

Others argue a very different conclusion. They point to statistics showing that, though their rates of deaths by guns are substantially different, the United States and Canada have comparable rates of violent crime when guns are not involved. They suggest, therefore, that the critical difference between the two countries is not some deeper structural element (e.g., the United States is a revolutionary, frontier society, Canada a counter-revolutionary, orderly society) but, rather, that one has an ambitious and reasonably effective gun-control policy, the other does not.[53] This lack of effective gun control in America may be a particularly important factor regarding violence committed by juveniles.[54]

Another complicating factor is the fact that there are other countries where citizens can be heavily armed (e.g., Israel and Switzerland) and yet the rates of violent crime are low.[55] A further complexity has been added recently. Some who are opposed to controls argue, based on a highly controversial analysis of statistics, that, in a society as awash in lethal violence as is America, law-abiding citizens need guns to defend themselves. What is more, possession of such arms deters crime. Restricting these citizens from having guns, it is asserted, results in even more crime, as predators act upon the knowledge that the law abiding are less likely to brandish a gun to repel attackers.[56] Not unexpectedly, the empirical bases for such claims have been challenged.[57]

The explanation of the significant differences between Canada and the United States probably lies somewhere in between the extremes of the accounts just outlined. The difference in regulation and licensing provisions is an important, but not determinative, variable.[58] Canadians need to ponder what their society would be like without an effective gun-control policy. American advocates of gun control need to acknowledge that guns are an important element, but only a part of a complex explanation, of the reason the United States is burdened by lethal violence.

Behavioural Decision Theory: Yet another approach to compliance would turn away not only from deterrence (and rewards for that matter) but also from the theory underlying deterrence, which rests on a conceptual base of the amoral, risk-averse, and utility-maximizing individual. In this depiction it is claimed that the 'expected utility model' (EUM) informs most decisions.

EUM holds that the decisions regarding compliance are made on the basis of the costs of complying versus the costs of not complying. So, for instance, in the context of occupational health and safety, this model claims that the amount of risk in a plant reflects the optimal level of safety expenditures. In turn, those expenditures are determined by assessing their marginal costs relative to the expected savings from accidents being prevented.[59]

Nonetheless, in several contexts there is evidence that there is compliance in excess of what EUM would predict. For example, most individuals do not engage in income-tax evasion and most insist that they would not even if afforded a safe opportunity to do so.[60] Likewise, studies of occupational health and safety indicate compliance with relevant laws in excess of that posited by EUM.[61]

To explain such results (inconsistent with EUM) some have turned to behavioural decision theory (BDT). BDT builds on psychological literature which holds that people use various simplifying strategies ('heuristics') in coming to conclusions about what action to take.[62] Whereas EUM emphasizes conscious and rational choice with full information in decision making, BDT suggests that behaviour is better explained by looking at the way individuals view decisions and the relatively simple guidelines used in deciding. In de-emphasizing decisions based on cost-benefit calculations and in emphasizing explanations (and results) based on the larger context and on a range of motivations, BDT is linked to such other initiatives as the 'regulatory pyramid' and efforts at promoting 'corporate virtue,' discussed earlier in the chapter.

In the context of occupational health and safety, one study suggests that managerial attention does respond to regulatory enforcement actions.[63] Specifically, inspections, sometimes imposing penalties, reduced injury rates in inspected firms to a greater extent than could be explained if firms simply abated violations. BDT claims these results demonstrate that regulatory law plays an important, but limited, role in guiding human behaviour.

Regulation is turned to when existing motivations lead to socially undesirable behaviour. To change such behaviour regulations must not only overcome a set of existing motivations but also call the attention of citizens to particular behaviour in need of changing. Citations by enforcement agents help the process of change by interpreting legal duties in concrete situations.

For a minority, avoiding future penalties may be the only motivation capable of inducing compliant behaviour. However, for the majority, such citations focus attention on a set of behaviours that citizens may not have fully integrated with their own beliefs about social responsibility. BDT claims that inspections function like other forms of persuasive communications.[64]

Thus, inspections (with sanctions for violations) are most likely to succeed in changing behaviour if they gain attention, point out behaviour and a relation to normative beliefs, and suggest that compliance is more consistent with the beliefs and obligations of those inspected. Most importantly, BDT claims that even imperfect regulatory strategies pursued by politically controlled agencies with limited capabilities can effectively advance goals embodied in the law one is seeking to enforce. Nevertheless, as with the related approaches of the 'regulatory pyramid' and 'corporate virtue,' discussed earlier, the need for careful empirical evaluation of the assertions of BDT is obviously warranted.

The Importance of Context: Finally, in discussing deterrence or any alternative, the importance of context must not be ignored. The subject matter of the law, the reasons for the law, and the relative ease with which the law may be complied with may be very important factors regardless of whether deterrence or any of its alternatives, or some combination of them, are invoked. This point regarding context emerges in a study of two different attempts to regulate environmental pollution in Ontario.[65]

One attempt involved mercury discharge from chlor-alkai plants; the other sought to control sulphur dioxide discharges. The former was a clear success. Mercury discharges were reduced by 95 per cent in one year, and within three years were less than 1 per cent of their previous amount. Results in the latter case were much less impressive: sulphur dioxide emissions were reduced by only 50 per cent over a fifteen-year period.[66]

What is of interest, for the purpose of this discussion, are the reasons for the difference in the results of the two attempts. Neither penalties nor any form of subsidy or other inducement accounted for the disparity. Instead, the findings appear to be explained, in large part, by the differing characteristics of the two pollutants: mercury is a serious health problem, whereas the effects of sulphur dioxide inhalation are thought to be much more subject to speculation; the sources of mercury pollution can be easily traced, but not those of sulphur dioxide; and mercury pollution, unlike the effects of sulphur dioxide, can be controlled by available technology at moderate cost.[67]

Designing Out the Problem

Yet a different approach to compliance would focus on the underlying problem that the law seeks to address. Such an approach would rely much less on using law to sanction inappropriate behaviour and much more on 'designing out' the problem itself. The issue, of course, is how to succeed in eliminating the problem and any other related difficulties.

Proponents of this approach focus on 'controlling opportunities.' For instance, the vast majority of us would like there to be less theft. One obvious response is to make robbery a criminal offence. Yet another is to control opportunities for such theft. Such control, for motor vehicles, might be accomplished by either encouraging or requiring (by law) cars to be equipped with steering-wheel locks.

Does the control of opportunities work? In some specific instances it appears to. The classic example of success is the elimination of carbon monoxide from gas for domestic use in England in the 1960s. Death by domestic-gas poisoning accounted for over 40 per cent of the suicides in England in 1963. Between 1963 and 1975 lethal agents were eliminated from gas for domestic use. For those same years suicides in the rest of Europe rose. Yet, in England during those years, suicides – from all causes – declined from 5714 to 3963.[68]

Nevertheless, there are difficulties that can arise from designing out. Prominent among these is displacement; that is, if one behaviour is controlled, yet another, perhaps more negative, may be substituted.[69] Requiring exact fare for buses may help eliminate robbery of public transportation vehicles, but maybe perpetrators will simply turn to more convenient sources. Likewise, more intensive policing in one area of the city may lead to more crime in another. Or, to return to an earlier example, putting steering locks on certain cars may shift theft to cars, say older ones, without such devices.

Traffic Safety

Many of the issues around designing out are illustrated by discussing the regulation of traffic safety.[70] Most efforts in the past to control vehicular accidents have been focused on changing driver behaviour, primarily through surveillance and prosecution. Recently in Ontario there have been over a million convictions a year for violations of traffic laws.[71] Proponents of designing out argue that resources have been concentrated too heavily on changing driver behaviour. Conversely, they maintain that switching some of those resources to improving car and road design and to curtailing activity levels (for instance, through licensing and pricing systems) would increase safety.[72]

This switch could be facilitated by adopting an epidemiological approach. The starting point for that perspective is the fundamental observation – one running throughout this book – that legislators, lawyers, police (and the rest of us) tend to think that law is the best way of controlling behaviour. Instead, advocates of epidemiology claim that attention should not be focused exclusively on driver behaviour but should also be heavily concentrated on the reduction of damage when crashes occur.[73]

The 'Haddon matrix' (named after the epidemiologist who did much to develop it) provides an analytic framework for much work in traffic safety.[74] It distinguishes human, vehicle, and environmental factors in accidents and breaks down mishaps into pre-crash, crash, and post-crash phases for analysing potential intervention. Some concrete developments of the Haddon approach are safety belts and airbags.

Yet there have been some strong challenges to the efficacy of such developments. Prominent among these are allegations of displace-ment;[75] in this context displacement carries its own term, 'risk homeo-stasis.'[76] The argument is that all safety improvements are used up by the population as a whole in riskier driving.[77] Careful evaluators acknowledge some such displacement, but insist that the develop-ments provide a net improvement in terms of safety.[78]

In addition, the efficacy of many of these developments depends on how their design actually works. A device may counteract certain neg-ative results, may compensate for the law's inability to mandate behav-iour, only to contribute to other problems. Air bags are an example of design difficulties calling into question the overall benefit of the device. They were heralded as a significant innovation for traffic safety in blunt-ing the effects of hazardous driving that the law's admonitions could not prevent. What is more, they (unlike most safety belts) were not to depend on any positive action by occupants and were said to be highly effective in insulating drivers and passengers from the effects of a crash.

However, there is increasing concern that air bags also cause their own problems, including opening at low speeds and causing damage, even death, particularly in the case of young children, who are too short and too fragile for the force of the air bags in an accident.[79] As a result, many safety advocates urge the development of 'smart' air bags that would electronically take into account the size and position of the occupant and respond with appropriate force in the event of a crash. Meanwhile it would appear that some affirmative conduct on the part of occupants is necessary: seat belts should also be worn and children under ten should not sit in the front seat.[80]

With all these developments, it is difficult to determine overall how best to effect traffic safety: '[W]e do not know ... where lies the greatest pay-off on the marginal dollar devoted to traffic safety. This is the cen-tral policy issue that traffic safety research has barely begun to con-front.'[81]

Crime – and Crime in America

A similar remark could be made for designing out generally. Tackling crime and preventing it through early social programs forcefully illus-trates the complexities of designing out – and the political vagaries of implementation, especially in the United States. Donohue and Siegel-man, after a careful attempt to identify the various costs and benefits, argue vigorously that spending less money on prisons (and incarceration) and applying more funds to programs to support disadvantaged children and their families would constitute a much better strategy in preventing – designing out – crime.[82]

This is not the place to examine in detail the models, calculations, projections, and estimates that Donohue and Siegelman use. The point is that they make an arguable case. They contend that doubling the current prison population in the United States – at an additional cost of about $36 billion – would reduce crime by only about 15 per cent, for benefits of about $30 billion[83] (and ignoring the human costs that incarceration imposes).

On the other hand, social programs can help prevent crime in the first place. Yet many social programs have been ineffective. However, there is a body of research indicating that properly designed programs for early-childhood intervention can reduce criminal behaviour. Successful programs have three characteristics: they intervene with very young children – in all cases before the age of four; they involve the children's families so that basic child-care skills, including techniques for effective discipline, could be communicated and the social environment improved; and they are small scale, of high quality – and costly. Such programs have produced lasting gains in socialization, school functioning, self-esteem, and family relationships (but not in measures of cognitive functioning). The programs that tracked the behaviour of the children involved found that juvenile delinquency was significantly reduced in terms of indicators such as the number of arrests and the severity of crimes when arrests did occur.[84]

The crucial question for these authors is whether these intervention programs could be replicated on a nation-wide basis. If they could, then by curtailing the present policy of continuing large increases in imprisonment and by directing the saved social resources to intervention programs, crime could be reduced at lower social costs. Moreover, other investment and consumption benefits that flow from such social programs would be generated, as well as the advantages of fostering compliance through a justice system that is less punitive.[85]

Yet Donohue and Siegelman know that their proposal will be a hard sell. The beneficiaries of these programs are a minority who are otherwise disadvantaged and who lack political clout. Further such programs would breed resentment in those only marginally better off but sufficiently so to disqualify them from the benefits of these initiatives. Meanwhile, the better off are likely to oppose any short-term cuts in crime control arising from curtailing the financing of prisons.[86]

Beyond these specific reasons for resisting intervention programs lies America's fascination with deterrence and punishment as a response to crime. Thus far in the chapter we have been talking about using criminal law and the threat of punishment to deter wrongful conduct. Of course, punishment can also stand on its own as retribution for the evil done by the particular perpetrator.

In the United States these two motivations for punishment – deterrence and retribution – have mixed together over the last two decades as fear of crime, especially involving physical harm, has escalated: 'It is the violent strain in American social life that leads to the special destruction and disorganization caused by crime, and spreads such corrosive anxiety and fear.'[87] As a result prison incarceration rates have soared. America now has by far the highest rates of imprisonment in the world save for Russia. To take but one statistic, Canada and England in 1995 had incarceration rates of 115 and 100 per 100,000 respectively. The rate in the United States was six times greater, at 600 per 100,000 (Russia's was 690).[88] In addition, the rate of imprisonment in America has continued to climb. By 1997 it had increased to 645 per 100,000.[89] Meanwhile, the building and running of prisons has become a boom industry with no sign of abating as the popular clamouring for imprisonment as the response to crime intensifies.[90] Crime, even violent crime is falling, but thus far the cries for punishment have not lessened. Punitiveness and an exaggerated confidence in deterrence may be permanently ingrained in the American popular consciousness.

Capital punishment crowns this bastion of retribution and deterrence. America, alone among countries of a similar tradition, continues to impose this ultimate sanction. Indeed, the pace of executions has intensified in the last decade and shows every indication of quickening even further. The right, in particular, has an abiding faith in the law's capacity to deter and, in any event, to exact retribution in a way that enshrines the individual as solely responsible for crime. Thoughtful doubts about the effectiveness of deterrence combined with careful suggestions about alternatives[91] are paved over in the rush to start construction on that next jail, to house more and more in prisons, and to exact the ultimate sanction from those convicted of murder.

It is this very particular turning to law – to deterrence, to retribution acted out through the courts – that sets apart the administration of criminal justice in the United States from that in so many other societies. The irony is that even as it is one of the most punitive countries it is also one of the most dangerous regarding lethal violence. We will return to this paradox at length in part 3, when we discuss punishment and the death penalty in America.

For the moment this section concludes with a question taken from a recent study of prisons in the United States: 'What explains the paradox of a country that prides itself as being the citadel of individual liberty, yet imprisons more persons per capita than any other nation in the world with the possible exception of Russia?'[92]

Compliance and Legitimacy

Why do people obey the law? Part of the answer to that question is found in the discussion we have just had about compliance. But compliance is mostly about *how* to get people to obey. Here we want to focus on *why* they obey, while recognizing these are related questions. Of course these issues presuppose the luxury of liberal democracy. In regimes where the boot and the barrel of a gun are the stock and trade of daily life people do obey, even as legitimacy is beside the point.

The burden of opinion suggests that legitimacy counts heavily in explaining why people obey the law in liberal democracies. If people perceive the law and its administration as legitimate they tend to obey it; if not, then not. If this is so, we are led to ask yet another question: What makes a law legitimate? This question does not yield a simple answer.

Legitimacy and Internalization

One important account of legitimacy focuses on internalization. People accept a law when they come to believe in a society's underlying values; that is, rules, values, and behaviour are internalized. This, of course, leads to yet another question: How is internalization achieved? As with other critical questions regarding compliance, there are many interesting answers, none of which is definitive.

Regarding this question theories abound.[93] For example, in terms of individual development, one idea suggests a sequence of levels orienting people to law; this sequence is, itself, linked to cognitive development generally.[94] The first level includes conformity merely to avoid punishment. The ultimate level reflects obedience only when law mirrors proper ethics, a development that few reach. At the same time, socialization into the legal order is seen as dependent on wider processes of cognitive development.

This theory has caused a stir. It has been criticized on the grounds of rigidity of the developmental sequence and as embodying judgments about moral progress reflecting only Western values.[95] This sequence approach has also attracted feminist criticism for denying the female 'voice,' which emphasizes relationships, caring, and connection.[96] In any event, empirical substantiation of the theory remains unclear.

However, there is a related aspect regarding socialization and legitimacy that has recently come to prominence. It is argued that there is a marked correlation between an individual's compliance with a law and her perception of how others react to that law: '[A] person's beliefs about whether other persons in her situation are paying their taxes plays a much more significant role in her decision to comply than does the burden of the tax or her perception of the expected punishment for evasion.'[97]

This view of the importance of social influence upon legitimacy and, in turn, upon obedience is advanced as part of a broader perspective about the critical interaction between law and norms (a point of view that we will return to in chapter 4).[98] It may, indeed, be true that individuals are influenced by others' reactions to law. Yet, to the extent this proposition is accurate, 'others' and their response also raise questions, similar to those already discussed, about the circumstances under which 'others' view a law as legitimate (or not) and obey it (or not).

One of the most comprehensive explanations of internalization was provided by Weber. In his depiction, law has a central importance for the economic foundations of capitalism: in facilitating forms of social action on which capitalism depends. As a result, law is accepted not because of such factors as the sanctioning power of the state or the charisma of political leaders. It is internalized because it provides a comprehensive framework of predictable rules making it possible for individuals to engage in social action not only for economic goals, but well beyond them too.[99]

As with most explanations pitched at the level of society in general, there are problems with this theory when it is applied to individuals.[100] It may, indeed, be true that law generally facilitates capitalism and that most people think that system is a good idea or, at any rate, a better one than any other economic arrangements put on offer in this century. However, even if law generally facilitates capitalism, this is not an explanation of why certain laws are seen to be more legitimate than others within various capitalist countries or why a minority of individuals are inclined to defy law generally.

Some debates about this question of what makes a law legitimate parallel more general discussion regarding compliance. The psychologist B.F. Skinner insisted that positive reinforcement (rewards) was the best way to achieve internalization. But many disagree, claiming that moderate levels of punishment administered by a caring agent, such that the connection between individual behaviour and adverse outcome is clear, can be just as effective.[101]

However, there appears to be general agreement that too much coercion will work against internalization. Individuals who judge that they have been coerced into conformity will be less likely to internalize moral – and legal – standards. Thus, there should be a heavy emphasis on techniques that minimize coercion. Prominent among such techniques are persuasion, education, and reasoning, which do not rely on law or at least on law emphasizing deterrence and sanctions.[102] Of course, such debates about the relationship between coercion and internalization lead us back to discussions regarding the comparative effectiveness of deterrence and alternatives, discussed at length earlier in this chapter.

A concrete example of internalization can be provided by discussing recommendations aimed at curbing domestic violence. There must be punitive consequences for those who perpetrate such acts. Yet there should also be efforts to educate regarding why such conduct is wrong and the effects it has on the family. Such efforts would include effective treatment programs for abusers. These programs would be directed at changing their behaviour, including by having them internalize a different set of values.[103] In addition, it has been urged that the structure of families must be more egalitarian. The premise is that greater equality yields less violence.[104]

Legitimacy and Process

Another important account of legitimacy and the law focuses on the processes used to enforce it. Do people care only about outcomes? Are they only concerned with winning or losing? Or, is how a decision is made important as well? If procedures are relevant, how are they connected to legitimacy and, more generally, to compliance? A study by Tyler (*Why People Obey the Law*) tackled these questions and maintains that procedures are highly relevant to judgments about the legitimacy of law.

Citizens in Chicago were interviewed about their views and behaviour concerning law. A subset were reinterviewed about the same topics one year later.[105] The main questions asked by the study were closely linked to issues around internalization discussed in the previous section. More specifically, the study examined the extent to which normative factors influence compliance with the law independently of deterrence. Such factors take account of the extent to which what people regard as just and moral (as opposed to what is in their self-interest) influences their perceptions and behaviour. An important premise is that people will voluntarily assume an obligation to follow legal rules if they view compliance as appropriate because of their attitudes about how they should behave. They will feel committed to obeying the law regardless of the risk of punishment for breaking it.

An important aspect of Tyler's inquiry regarding normative factors was the significance of procedures. An instrumental – or deterrent – perspective on procedure suggests that assessments of procedural fairness are based on favourability of outcomes. From this perspective, aspects of procedures not linked to outcomes will contribute little to an understanding of whether people feel fairly treated.

However, a normative perspective views people as concerned with aspects of their experience with law not linked to whether they win or lose. Such aspects would include neutrality, lack of bias, honesty, efforts to be fair, politeness, and a basic respect for rights. To the extent this normative perspective is correct, procedures can influence the degree to which people internalize an obligation to obey the law.[106]

Generally, the study found that normative issues do matter and that a perception of legitimacy does have an independent effect on law-abidingness. More specifically, not only are procedures relevant to legitimacy, but 'affect, evaluation of performance, and legitimacy are all more strongly influenced by procedural fairness than by favourability of outcome or fairness of outcome.'[107] Also of significance is the finding that these views regarding the relevance of procedures appear not to be influenced by such demographic characteristics as age, gender, or race.[108] In addition, the prominence of procedures is underscored by their ability to insulate: '[I]f people receive fair procedures, outcome is not relevant to their reactions,'[109] or if 'unfavourable outcomes are delivered through procedures viewed as fair, the unfavourable outcomes do not harm the legitimacy of legal authorities.'[110]

Perhaps not surprisingly, Tyler's study has attracted wide attention[111] – and some sharp criticism. One criticism involves the subject matter of the questions people were asked: speeding, parking illegally, disturbing the peace, littering, driving while intoxicated, and shoplifting. All were about criminal infractions. Thus the study could say little about law more generally. In addition, those who believe in deterrence would suggest that the narrow range of laws involved may not adequately trigger the interest of individuals so as to give play to the importance of self-interest.

Another reaction arises from one of the study's findings. It reported that 82 per cent of those asked thought that '[p]eople should obey the law even if it goes against what they think is right.'[112] Such a finding seems to fly in the face of a central contention of the study – that people are influenced to an important degree by social values about what is right and proper. A subsequent study suggests that such factors as race and gender may be important variables regarding individuals' reactions to outcomes described to them that they believe to be unjust.[113]

Yet another criticism involves the claim of neutrality of the study. At one point Tyler states: 'The study of procedural justice is neutral about the quality of the existing legal system?'[114] What can 'neutral' mean here?[115] This was, after all, an examination of such influential concepts as legitimacy and obedience in relation to the power of the state to deter and to punish. Analysed in one way, the study's findings can be reassuring. Despite all its problems, people appear to have faith in the system and its procedures. However, viewed from another angle, the study is disturbing. People are determined to support the system no matter how enfeebled and unjust it is. Regardless of how they are viewed, these issues should not be sidestepped through claims of neutrality.

Nevertheless, Tyler's study is an important basis for re-examining issues around compliance and the criminal law system generally. Individuals' perceptions of the processes in which they have been involved are an important factor in how they view the law – and whether they obey it. Fostering positive attitudes to fair procedures may be a way of improving compliance without imposing burdensome costs on the administration of justice.[116]

Conclusions

In terms of impact, compliance, in critical ways, is the most straightforward behaviour: most people obey the law most of the time. But the percentage who do not obey raise a host of questions to which there are few definitive answers.

Traditionally, deterrence has been the centrepiece in achieving compliance. On close scrutiny, though, it is unclear to what extent deterrence is effective when it counts: for the minority who are tempted to violate the law. Theories of deterrence emphasize the rationality of the potential offender who weighs the yields from illegal activity against the sanctions if apprehended. Yet much of the results of criminological research demonstrates how many crimes are committed on impulse without calculation of the consequences or are influenced by motivations not reachable by sanctions. For example, many observers point to the United States as evidence of the limits of deterrence. America has one of the highest rates of incarceration and is one of the few Western industrialized nations that retains the death penalty. Yet, even though crime has decreased recently, the USA nevertheless has one of the highest rates of violent crime in the world. Similarly, there are any number of elaborate theoretical statements of why civil litigation ought to effectively deter; in fact, the actual results are mostly otherwise.

At the same time, a host of questions surround alternatives to deterrence. For example, proactive measures that attempt to control the situations in which crime may occur have, in certain contexts, enjoyed success. An example of positive results would be laws in Canada regulating gun control. Opportunities for access to guns, particularly handguns, are circumscribed; therefore, fewer shooting deaths and injuries occur. America, by contrast, has a much looser system of gun control and death from handguns exceeds the Canadian rate by as much as twenty times. However, whether this lower death rate is a function of stricter gun control or is a product of a less violence-prone society or is somehow a combination of these two factors remains a question.

Yet another alternative to deterrence involves de-emphasizing law altogether and, instead, 'designing out' the underlying problem itself that would otherwise be regulated. 'Designing out' is a promising technique. Its use signals an acceptance of the limits of law, particularly of deterrence. Nevertheless, there are critical issues regarding this technique's feasibility and whether any positive effects it engenders are displaced by other untoward consequences. A case in point is air bags. Initially they were hailed as a measure to minimize death and injury on the highway (beyond the laws commanding drivers not to be negligent, not to drive at excessive speeds, and so forth). However, there is growing worry that they are also responsible for other problems; for example, by opening at low speeds and causing damage, even death, especially to young children.

Those advocating more social programs to curb crime provide an even more complex example of the difficulties surrounding designing out. American proponents contend that spending more on properly designed intervention programs will decrease crime more cost effectively than continuing to build prisons and incarcerating convicted criminals. Nevertheless, they also recognize how difficult it is to garner support for intervention programs as a crime-fighting technique. The beneficiaries of such interventions are disadvantaged minorities lacking political clout, and such programs tend to cause resentment among those not qualified to receive benefits. More generally, such initiatives collide with America's enthusiasm for deterrence and for retribution as a response to crime.

Legitimacy and its role as an underpinning for compliance also raises quandaries. Indeed, the fact that there are no confident and clear answers as to why people obey the law is a dramatic illustration of how little is known about compliance when knowledge counts: how to make the minority who flout the law cross the line to obedience.

In important ways this chapter is a prelude to fundamental points made in this book. Despite some claims to the contrary that we will discuss, law *is* important. It is much in demand; it works most of the time, certainly to the extent that compliance is an indicator. But how it works, and what effects it has on specific issues and the workings of society more generally, is much less clear. Regarding compliance it is possible to know more. Careful experiments and thoughtful debate regarding the effects of deterrence and alternatives to it can edge us along. All the while there needs to be critical evaluation of actual effects and attention to variations dependent on context.

Yet myth can rush in to fill the void. Such embrace of claims about the working of law, whatever the reality, is aptly illustrated by the administration of criminal justice in the United States. For all the criticisms levied against it, deterrence, as the cudgel enforcing obedience, still holds enormous appeal, first and foremost in America. Such enthusiasm is a barrier to serious debate regarding other responses to crime even as that nation is awash in lethal violence. We will return to the thrall of deterrence, commingled with retribution, in our discussion in part 3 of capital punishment in the United States.

CHAPTER THREE

The Complexities of Assessing Impact

A couple of years ago an article appeared in The *New York Times Sunday Magazine* reporting a debate between Floyd Abrams, a prominent First Amendment attorney, and the well-known feminist and advocate of legal measures to curb pornography, Catharine MacKinnon.[1] It will surprise no one to hear that there was little common ground between them. Positioning free speech and equality as irreconcilable opponents, as perhaps only these two antagonists could, is, itself, wrongheaded. Nevertheless, the important issue of how these two principles might be reconciled is one that we will leave to the side.

What was remarkable for the questions occupying us in this book, however, was the degree to which both Abrams and MacKinnon premised their philosophical and policy arguments on claims concerning the impact of pornography and, conversely, of laws to curb it. For example:

- Pornography results in antisocial, abusive activity (MacKinnon).
- In countries where there are no legal restraints on sexually explicit materials the incidence of sexual crimes is much lower than in the United States (Abrams).
- The data is inconclusive; the definition and categories of sexual offences were changed at the same time pornography was decriminalized; reporting may well have dropped – if governments support pornography, reporting sexual abuse seems totally pointless to women (MacKinnon)
- Those countries that are harshest on pornography are also harshest on women; in China promulgation of pornography leads to capital punishment, but China is not a good nation for women to live in (Abrams).

The Abrams/MacKinnon debate is a vivid example of how important claims about impact are to normative arguments concerning law. Assertions regarding the effects of pornography, on the one hand, and of laws curbing it, on the other, are important and complex to assess. For that reason we shall return to questions around evaluating the consequences of pornography and laws against it in part 3. For the moment, the Abrams/MacKinnon exchange underscores both the importance of determining the impact of a law or set of laws and the quandary involved in doing so.

Thus, in this chapter we concentrate on the second aspect of impact described in the Introduction. We focus on the extent to which law has an effect on the underlying issues being addressed and the difficulties of isolating and assessing such outcomes. In other words, in addition to issues of compliance with a law (or judgment), (addressed in chapter 2), what effect does the law (or judgment) have on the problem for which a remedy is being sought?

Needless to say, law is not the only discipline that wrestles with such problems. Issues of proof, of causation, and of consequence are woven through the social sciences and humanities.[2] A classic work in history once argued that it was the only discipline that could aspire to be a 'science' of human nature. This was because only history could (unlike science) claim an 'a priori imagination,' yet (unlike the artistic imagination) have a respect for evidence.[3] Even among historians such a statement is now likely to be regarded as an eloquent boast.[4] However, it does call our attention to the concerted efforts among various disciplines to build and assess theories of proof, impact, and related issues.[5]

The effect of a law on the underlying problem it was meant to address is the aspect of impact that people often refer to when they urge or oppose an enactment or ruling. Such assertions abound in a host of areas: from arguments that minimum-wage laws raise the standard of compensation for people at the bottom of the economic ladder (or, conversely, that they are barriers to job creation) to assertions that pornography harms women and that laws prohibiting it will buttress gender equality (or, conversely, that such laws mangle free speech and/or result in the harassment of those with unconventional tastes in erotica)[6] to contentions that 'no fault' regimes compensate personal injuries caused by accidents more comprehensively, more cheaply, and more quickly than do compensatory systems based on fault as determined by the courts (or, conversely, that such 'no fault' regimes encourage reckless behaviour by removing the threat of sanctions for negligent conduct).

Yet asserting that a law has particular effects is one thing. Demonstrating that it, in fact, has these consequences and explaining why they have occurred is quite another. There are any number of complexities involved in establishing that a particular law is responsible for any changes regarding the problem it was meant to address. There may be heated debates about the underlying issue being responded to and whether it is a problem or, in any event, a problem that ought to be remedied by law (see, for instance, the battle over pornography, depicted in the opening paragraphs of this chapter). In assessing the impact of a law or set of laws there is the significant question of perspective. Is there a neutral position from which to observe acts said to be the effect of law? Is there a generally agreed upon methodology that can assess and interpret these acts in order to draw conclusions in terms of impact? There can be complications in terms of showing that a law actually caused any particular result. More specifically, to demonstrate that a law has had a specific effect, it is necessary to demonstrate that there were no other social, political, economic, or other forces responsible for the specific result. Under what circumstances can there be such a demonstration? Finally, laws can produce effects that are not contemplated or, in any event, not intended by those involved with their enactment and implementation.

What, If Anything, Is the Problem?

The debates around outcomes can start before any law comes into play. If one does not believe the phenomenon in question is a problem at all or, at any rate, is one that the law should solve, then one is more likely to be sceptical about the effects produced by any law that is invoked as a solution. Such scepticism may include predictions that undesirable results will occur. Conversely, those urging a legal response to a claimed problem may be inclined to view outcomes produced by intervention as positive, ignore any warnings about undesirable consequences, and conclude that any good effects (as judged by the proponents of the law) are the result of the law or series of laws meant to respond to the ill that is to be remedied.

Whether a situation is viewed as a problem or not involves a world view that can have a right/left split. Of course, there are moderate positions in between on many issues. Still, any temperateness has to contend with more extreme positions ever ready to stake out their territory.

The right considers outcomes produced by the market as desirable just because they have come about in this way. Even if there are problems, the overall attitude is that what the market has caused it can solve – and woe unto the government who tampers, especially by invoking regulation. Thus, those earning low wages need to equip themselves, through education and training, for better jobs so as to compete in the job market. They – and a well-ordered economy – do not need laws mandating minimum wages.[7] Women experiencing a gender gap in earnings need to make rational choices regarding pursuing education, childrearing, flexibility in moving to accept promotions, and so forth. They – and a well-ordered economy – do not need laws mandating comparable-worth (pay-equity) adjustments. Those experiencing discrimination (when the events in question can be so characterized) should let market forces work to punish the perpetrators.[8] They – and a well-ordered economy – do not need civil-rights codes; they most certainly should not be the objects of affirmative action.[9]

In contrast, many on the right see a compelling need to use law to regulate morals. In this view the heaviest machinery of regulation – the criminal process – should often be hauled out to suppress all manner of objectionable behaviour from gay and lesbian sexual activity to consumption of drugs to abortion. This vantage point places great faith in the deterrent and punitive effects of law: if people feel the heavy threat of sanctions they will do as they are told.

Conversely, the left tends to be shy of regulating individuals' decisions about what is regarded as their personal lives, especially if the regulations restrict choice. Indeed, if law is to be invoked at all in such areas it is to be used to facilitate the exercise of that choice. Thus, laws constricting the range of options regarding, for example, birth control, abortion, marriage and divorce, and sexual partners (homo- or heterosexual), and consumption of at least certain kinds of drugs are viewed with hostility and said to cause all manner of undesirable outcomes: for instance, retaining 'fault' as the basis of divorce is an impediment to autonomy, generates adversarial posturing, promotes inequality, and so forth.[10]

More generally, the whole apparatus of the criminal law and its reliance on deterrence is viewed with suspicion by the left as a site for oppression of individuals, particularly the poor and minorities. Few would argue that there should be no criminal law at all, but progressives insist on the futility of prisons as a route to curb crime. Most prominently, they rail at the death penalty as the jewel of paste in the crown of deterrence.[11] Better to use law to get at the root causes of poverty and discrimination in the first place.[12]

In contrast, many of those toward the left of the spectrum are predisposed to use law to counter alleged negative effects of market forces. From that vantage point, there is need for minimum-wage laws, occupational health and safety regulation, civil rights codes, detailed environmental protections, and so on. All manner of law should be invoked to counter the market and to promote individual and group rights. What is more, what the legislatures and the administrative processes will not do the courts will have to do for them while pulling a dulled citizenry along.

Still, not all controversies about social phenomena as candidates for intervention by law fit easily into a right/left divide. Pornography, a topic that began the introduction to this chapter and that will be pursued in part 3, is an issue where those wishing to invoke law form an amalgam including some feminists and religious fundamentalists. Likewise, those who resist characterizing pornography as a problem requiring a legal solution range from many media interests to other feminists and minority groups such as some gays and lesbians who adamantly maintain that any legal intervention will do more harm than good – in terms not only of restricting pornography but of curtailing access to all kinds of literature and information, and erotica.[13]

Smoking is an example of a phenomenon that has moved from being viewed as a sophisticated and pleasurable pastime to being treated as a noxious addiction that poses health risks, and, finally, as a deadly blight that must be eradicated and whose suppression is opposed primarily by corporate interests that directly profit from the sale of cigarettes. This transformation is an interesting tale in itself that will be told later on (in part 3). Of course, achieving such consensus about the existence of a problem and invoking law to formulate and realize a solution are two different matters.[14]

The point here is that law's effect on an underlying problem raises many complexities that often start at the very beginning. Some see a fact of daily life and view it as a problem crying out for regulatory intervention – the costs, however measured, are sure to be dwarfed by the benefits. Others cast their gaze on the same happenings and shrug with indifference or, at any rate, are certain that any legal solution will impose far more harm than good. These very different world views lead to the question entertained in the next section: how, if at all, can the effects of law be assessed objectively?

The Quandary of 'Impartial' Perspective

Is there a neutral position from which to observe acts said to be the effect of law? Perhaps more importantly, is there an objective stance from which to assess and interpret these acts in order to draw conclusions in terms of impact? If such impartiality does not exist, can there be anything said about the impact of law that transcends a multiplicity of perspectives? If there is no objectivity, can there be social 'science,' especially in assessing law's consequences?

The Enlightenment promised that rationality would provide an evolutionist and progressive accumulation of knowledge. This knowledge would be objective and realized in a number of ways, including through neutral scientific procedures. Yet as the twentieth century ended such claims were challenged in numerous ways.[15] One such challenge relates to the very way we express ourselves: language. In this depiction, language is the 'paradigm case of cultural construction.' Because language is 'constructed,' there can be no assurance that 'our discourses stand in some relation of "correspondence" to a reality independent of consciousness.'[16] In other words, there can be no guarantee that any sets of debates and discussion at any time and place can produce verifiable and objective access to that reality.

It is all very well to contend that law and its influence can only be fully understood through systematic empirical assessment. Yet we live in a world confronted with substantially different understandings and perspectives concerning the driving forces in society and, of course, in law. Such differences can have many sources, including race, gender, and class. What is more, even as claims are made that language is culturally constructed, there are similar assertions that social science is embedded in a set of particular and changeable assumptions. The very notion of what constitutes a fact – 'nuggets of experience detached from theory' – becomes contentious.[17] In the face of such disarray can there be a single understanding concerning the impact of law?

The terrain is even more complicated by divisions about the very relationship of law and society. Such differences can be illustrated by two different accounts of that relationship (ignoring, to be sure, important subtleties in between).[18] One represents the preponderance of empirical and theoretical studies on legal impact. It maintains that there can be intelligible analyses of 'law' and 'society' and searches for how they influence each other even as this account acknowledges the complexity of such undertakings.[19]

Generally, this account relies heavily on a model of causation that seeks evidence regarding how discrete stimuli (independent variables) produce clear changes in the behaviour of targeted individuals or institutions (the dependent variable). At the risk of oversimplification this account will be referred to as 'positivism.' Positivism's model of causation is inspired by that of the physical sciences.[20] Thus, results that show covariance – that is, a showing that can be measured indicating that dependent variables are altered uniformly with variations in the independent variable – are particularly valued. A less than flattering account of the claims of this model suggests a comparison with bowling balls: '[T]he causal significance of ... law ... is lik[e] ... a bowling ball rolled down an alley; impact is measured by how many pins succumb to the force of the ball; if many fall, the impact is great, but if all or most remain standing, the toss was casually insignificant and the bowling agent ineffective.'[21]

In its most robust version, positivism contends that it does not seek to explain why law changes or behaves in any way but, rather, to observe and to measure correlations between the behaviour of law and other quantifiable social phenomena. Evaluation, interpretation, and analysis of law's ideals or its effects are to play no role in such observation and measurement.[22]

A second account asserts that law and society cannot be conceived as external to each other. Rather, the critical issue to be addressed is the way that society is produced within law and how law is insinuated into social practices. In this depiction, the main focus is on 'the context which is assumed and reproduced by law as a bearer of traditions or of ideological constructions or forms of discourse.'[23] In this account law is viewed not only as a system of commands or norms, but also as a framework of interpretation, as discourse.[24] To understand the workings of law, researchers must go beyond examining legal institutions and their linkages with other elements of social life. In addition, 'legality' must be studied: 'the meanings, sources of authority, and cultural practices that are commonly recognized as legal, regardless of who employs them or for what ends.'[25] Again, at the risk of oversimplification, this account will be referred to as 'interpretivism.'

Interpretivism emphasizes that 'causal explanations are partial, imperfect, problematic intellectual contrivances to help us to make sense of ourselves and the world in which we live but cannot fully "know."'[26] This view rests on three specific reservations about positivism and its enthusiasm for clear relationships between dependent and independent variables.

First, it is contended that positivist models do not adequately take account of the nuances of human interaction. Their conceptions of causality slight the 'dynamic, indeterminate, contingent, interactive processes of judgment, choice, and reasoned intentionality of people in action.'[27] As a result, positivism is inclined to be reductionist or evasive regarding the motives and goals of much complex human activity such as political action.

Second, it is contended that positivism has a myopic view of social context in which particular actions take place. That account emphasizes the isolation of various elements that make up context into 'discrete, insular, commensurable, variables, that can be measured for relative independent casual significance.' In contrast, interpretivism lays great emphasis on the contention by the dynamically interacting factors that make up any social context. As a result, '[h]uman relations are viewed as ongoing, dialectical processes rather than as aggregations of isolated causal collisions.'[28]

Third – and most important – is the understanding of the relationship between subjectivity and context that influences interpretivism. Thus, it is contended that institutional forces are manifested in the culturally defined intersubjective knowledges, conventions, and norms that people act on. As a result, conventions and knowledge, including legal norms, are 'constitutive' of meaning and activity. Hence, 'this focus on meaning construction further highlights the inherently indeterminate, variable, contingent aspects of human interaction about which positivist causal models offer quite limited analytical insight.'[29]

With the rise of these controversies about the study of law, society, and the role of empiricism, some have abandoned any attempt to achieve objectivity in their assessment of impact or, indeed, in their understanding of law itself. (This is largely the case for those who adhere to 'legal mobilization,' an idea about the impact of law that we will discuss in chapter 4).[30] Since 'human interaction is heterogeneously experienced and indeterminate in character,' it follows that there is 'no transcendent or impartial perspective for the analyst to assume' in collecting, documenting, and assessing behaviour that could offer evidence of impact. Indeed, 'there is no essential reality of law to discover independent of multiple partially constitutive legal practices.'[31]

A more temperate position – between some extreme positions taken by positivism and interpretivism – acknowledges the importance of perspective while yet claiming some role for the scientific method as traditionally understood. In this view, the goals that law seeks to reflect cannot be ignored. Positivism is valuable in reminding us of the tenets of the scientific method: reliance on observed data as the basis for considered judgments; a refusal to speculate beyond what observed experience will justify as plausible. But positivism can be severely limiting in preventing recognition of the elaborateness of the law and the complexity of its impact.[32]

At the same time, issues posed by a multiplicity of perspectives and by the relations of law and society must be addressed. The values of researchers that affect their studies of law and its influence need to be evaluated; the conceptual frameworks that researchers bring to their investigations need to be assessed. Thus, such values and conceptual frameworks should, to the greatest extent possible, be isolated and made explicit.

One formulation of a middle ground has been referred to as the 'empirically grounded social construction approach' (rather a mouthful). Proponents of this method maintain that it does not simply catalogue facts remaining at the level of individual experience to the detriment of more structural understandings of social forces. Instead, 'the blend of data, theory, and reflexive awareness yields informative analysis of the way law impacts people's lives, and of the way people respond to and shape the realization of law in practice.'[33]

Perhaps we need to talk in terms of possibilities. The facts that appear to make these values and frameworks plausible need to be continuously re-examined. Similarly, judgments based on these values and frameworks need to be reconsidered in the light of new arguments and new data. In this depiction, social science, in its study of law, is conceded not to be 'powerful or authoritative enough to end arguments.' At the same time, even in this world of diverse and divergent values and perspectives, empirical assessment 'continues to keep alive the hope that science can serve as a tool of persuasion, albeit a limited one.'[34]

The possibility of science is that of ultimately documenting and interpreting law and its social reality. This may remain only a possibility; yet it is still critical as a goal. Such assessments should bear in mind two guiding objectives: 'first, a clear and explicit recognition that all perspectives on experience are necessarily partial and incomplete and, secondly, the serious (but necessarily never completed) attempt to overcome the limitations of partial perspectives through systematic collection, analysis, and interpretation of the empirical data of experience.'[35]

The Difficulties of Assessing a Particular Law

How do we determine the effect of a law or set of laws? By what means can we conclude that the law has had an effect on the underlying problem sought to be addressed or any other impact for that matter? Or to put the issue another way, if there has been some redress of the ills that are meant to be remedied, how can we be confident that the law in question – and not some other factor – was responsible?

Social scientists who are focused on legal studies are well versed in the methodological difficulties of assessing the impact of law. However, many others are not. In particular, those who are legally trained may be much more accustomed to thinking in terms of individual situations and cases rather than in terms of overall outcomes produced by a law or set of laws. (Moreover, they may be very focused on litigation, the effects of which will be examined more specifically in chapter 4).[36] In any event, the following is a brief description, for non-specialists, of the methodological difficulties that need to be tackled by those who undertake assessments of the effects of a particular law or set of laws.

These questions concerning the difficulties of determining the outcomes produced by a law or set of laws return us to many of the issues that we discussed in the last section. Not surprisingly, those more inclined to positivism than to interpretivism are more likely to believe that there are methods that can respond to such questions. Nevertheless, even enthusiastic proponents of positivism admit that the social sciences can rarely control the environment in order to isolate all the factors that might have contributed to a certain outcome; indeed, sometimes there are difficulties even ascertaining with precision what the outcomes are. The dynamics of causation are insufficiently understood to state starkly that any specific casual claims are definitively right or wrong.[37] Yet such limitations should not bar assessments; rather, they sound strong notes of caution about arriving at conclusions.[38] Moreover, in terms of both method and the drawing of conclusions, the wise positivist will pay careful attention to the critiques of interpretivism, which raise several vital points regarding the effects of law, including the nuances of human interaction, the importance of social context, and the constitutive role that legal norms can play in terms of interpreting the actions of those affected.[39]

That said, causal influence, in terms of the consequences of law, is assessed, as best it can be, using three kinds of information. First, the types of influence and their relationships must be indicated clearly.

Second, the evidence that could substantiate these sources and connections must be ascertained. Third, all other possible explanations for the change, other than the law being examined, need to be explored and evaluated.[40] Further, the indicators used to measure the effects can be problematic (as they can be for social-science investigations in general). Such indicators must be specified and justified as appropriate gauges of the impact being examined.[41]

Thus, a legal-impact study attempts to establish how a particular law or set of laws affects conduct and attitudes of those individuals, groups, or other relevant units located in jurisdictions where that law is in force.[42] The study involves an essential comparison: between actual behaviour patterns in jurisdictions having the law in question and behaviour patterns that would have existed in those same jurisdictions had the law in question never been enacted.

One way, in theory, to test such impact is through an experiment. However, true experiments require randomized assignments of subjects to experimental and control groups. For obvious reasons, the application of most laws cannot be limited so as to establish the latter. As a result, experiments are usually not feasible as a means of testing impact.

Thus, the question remains how best to estimate what the behaviour patterns would have been in a certain jurisdiction had the law in question never existed. In essence there are three ways in which this comparison can be made:

- First, the jurisdictions subject to the laws being studied can be compared before and after the law in question. Any behavioural changes that seem to follow as a result of the passage of the law can be documented. This method is usually referred to as having an 'interrupted time-series' design.[43] The purpose of such a design is to study the impact of a particular treatment on a variable that is repeatedly measured over a period of time, both before and after the application of the treatment.
- Second, jurisdictions that have been subject to the laws being studied can be compared with those that have not. Any disparity in behaviour may be attributable to such laws so long as the jurisdictions are otherwise comparable.
- Third, the first and the second approaches can be combined. Behaviour in jurisdictions subject to the law can be examined both before and after passage. In addition, such behaviour (before passage, after

passage) can be compared, over the same period of time, with jurisdictions not having the law in question.

The acid test for these three ways of making such comparisons is how well they control for 'plausible rival hypotheses.'[44] Such hypotheses are non-experimental variables that could reasonably explain behaviour apart from the law or set of laws that are the subject of investigation. (Social scientists would, more generally, speak about 'threats to internal validity.')[45]

There are several factors that are sources of 'plausible rival hypotheses.' These include the following:

1 History: The observed change may be due to simultaneous events other than the experimental treatment.
2 Selection: Biases may occur because of differential selection of respondents for the comparison group.
3 Maturation: The change could be attributable to a long-term trend.
4 Instrumentation: The measured change may be based on a change in the means of measuring, rather than in the thing being measured.
5 Testing: The change may be caused by the initial measurement rather than by the treatment.
6 Instability: The apparent change may be no more than a chance or random variation.
7 Mortality: There is a differential loss of respondents from the comparison group.
8 Regression: If the group was selected because it was extreme on some measure, statistical reasoning indicates that it will appear less extreme on subsequent tests, even though the intervening treatment may be completely ineffectual.[46]

Most of these factors can be controlled for through a properly designed study. However, 'History' and 'Selection' are especially problematic as sources of rival hypotheses in legal-impact studies. History is particularly plausible in 'before and after' studies. Its nub as a rival explanation is that a coincidental happening can often explain a perceived change. To counter such a possibility, geographically well-distributed groups of jurisdictions subject to the law should be compared with a similar group of jurisdictions without the law. If such a comparison can be made, history may usually be ruled out as an explanatory cause for changes in behaviour in the jurisdictions with the law.

'Selection' cautions that a study of the impact of a law has to confirm that that law is more than an expression of the popular will of the people and that people would be acting differently without the law. For example, suppose it could be demonstrated that the French legal structure has long subjected the voluntary associations of that country to regulations that hinder their formation and influence. In contrast, America protects, constitutionally, the right of association. Suppose further that it could be demonstrated that the French have fewer ties with such associations than do comparable groups of Americans.

Without more evidence, it could not be concluded that such Franco-American differences in voluntary-association participation could be explained on the basis of differing laws. A rival hypothesis would be that for several reasons, including cultural ones, the French and Americans view the importance of voluntary associations differently and act in divergent ways based on those views. These differences and divergences have been reflected in laws. They have not been caused by them. Without more findings, the only reliable statement that might be made is that the French laws have not assisted directly the role of voluntary associations.[47]

Selection can usually be controlled by using a group of jurisdictions subject to the law and a similar group that are not. The question is, Do people in various jurisdictions having a particular law act in one way and people in the other jurisdictions without that law act in another way (with regard to the subject of the law)? If there are such differences in behaviour, then the regulative (rather than the expressive) aspect of law would appear to have been responsible for them.

There are a number of designs available for evaluation.[48] The best is 'multiple time series.' The serious practical difficulties there may be in utilizing this preferred model of assessment only emphasize the importance of careful analysis of the complexities. The essential features of this design are the presence of several jurisdictions in both the group subject to the law and the groups not subject to it and a testing of the behaviour in question both before and at several points after passage of the law. If behaviour patterns are similar until the law is introduced in the experimental states, then an investigator can attribute subsequent changes over time to the law with a high degree of certainty.

If only two jurisdictions are being compared, there is a chance that history/selection interaction has been the cause of any resultant change. Nevertheless, it is very unlikely that people of two states will be alike for an extended period of years and then undergo a sudden differentiation in their population's characteristics. If there is differentiated behaviour, then it is likely that the law has caused it. It is less likely that an underlying attitude difference suddenly developed between the people of the jurisdictions. Such a rival hypothesis becomes even less plausible with the inclusion of states that are heterogeneous.

There is still the possibility of another rival hypothesis: that extra-legal changes are causing the difference in behaviour. However, this becomes less likely the more jurisdictions are put into the two categories (subject to the law / not subject to the law). This is the case because even when laws are similar on the books, extra-legal patterns tend to be differentiated. If, on the one hand, extra-legal patterns differ relatively randomly among the jurisdictions and, on the other, behaviour patterns between the two categories are systematically differentiated, then it is probable that the law is causing those differences.

Lempert pointed out that, in the case of the United States, the fifty jurisdictions are 'natural laboratories.' Therefore, there ought to be many opportunities to subject law to the rigorous scrutiny of a 'multiple time series' so as to determine 'exactly how certain laws influence specific behavioural patterns.'[49] He concludes optimistically: 'Once there is more information as to how this occurs there will be a more reasoned basis for determining "why" the patterns occur as they do.'[50]

Such admonitions are valuable in both demonstrating the difficulties of assessing impact and, at the same time, providing a framework for such assessment. However, there can be severe practical limitations in using interrupted time series generally and multiple time series in particular. First, the discussion assumes the availability of multiple jurisdictions to provide a basis of comparisons. America, a federation, has such multiple jurisdictions; most countries do not. It is possible that different countries can be utilized, but real issues of comparability of social, political, and legal structure may arise.

Indeed, jurisdictions within the same country, even at the level of cities, may give rise to issues of comparability. The goal is to have control and intervention groups 'constitute naturally assembled collectives ... as similar as availability permits.'[51] The difficulty raised is the determination of whether two or more such jurisdictions are sufficiently similar to justify a comparison.

Take the issue of gun control, which, in the United States, can have a municipal dimension. Suppose the issue investigated is the effect of gun control on the rate of violent crime.[52] The goal might be to compare two cities: one subject to some form of gun control and one not. However, there are several ways in which the cities might not be comparable cross-sectionally: for example, regarding racial composition, socio-economic status, and existing rates of violence. In addition, the trends for violent crime in the two cities might be at odds, a cross-temporal issue. For example, the intervention city could be trending downward in crime before the legislation came into effect while the control city could be trending upward. Generally, it is considered that if the choice is between cross-sectional and cross-temporal similarity, the former is more important since there are ways to adjust statistically for different trends in the two sites[53] and for trends generally.[54]

Second, even when a country is a federation the law may be of national application. In that instance, differentiation among the jurisdictions for the purpose of studying impact will not be possible. In Canada, two such examples would involve the effect of laws implementing universalized medical care and those regulating gun control.

Third, there may be interactive effects among different kinds of laws. Such outcomes may be a puzzle to assess. For example, we know that the murder rate in Western Europe is much lower than in the United States. Yet western Europe has no capital punishment, while many states in America retain it. However, it is also the case that western Europe has a much fuller economic safety net and more developed social programs than the United States. How do we compare the social programs of the United States and Europe and how do we determine the relative impact of capital punishment and social programs in lessening the murder rate? (Further, how can we confidently compare the social and political structure of Western Europe and America regarding these issues?: see the first point, discussed just above.)

Fourth, the impact model being used for any investigation must be clearly specified. There are two issues that frequently arise regarding specification. The first concerns the timing of the intervention: When is the change in law or policy supposed to have an effect on the target variable? The second concerns how the law influences the target variable: What is the mechanism that results in a change? Or to put the second issue another way: Is the effect of the law immediate and permanent, immediate but temporary, or gradual but permanent?

Concerning the first issue, the most frequently chosen intervention point in policy-impact research is the officially effective date of the law. However, the problem is that there are many points where the law's impact could begin. For example, with regard to a penal statute, various points would include the time when the law is first publicly proposed or introduced, the law is passed by a legislative committee, the law is designated to be in effect, or a large enough number of violations are punished so that 'word gets out in the street.' The date of a law coming into effect may be quite arbitrary in terms of impact. Yet '[p]olicy impact assessments have rarely considered alternatives or tested for apparent effects when differing intervention points may be appropriate.'[55]

The second issue in terms of specification is how the law influences the target variable. In a number of situations it may not be possible to specify whether the change in law should have an abrupt and permanent, abrupt and temporary, or gradual and permanent effect on the target variable. In those instances where there is some expectation about how the law ought to affect the target variable based on some theory, prior research, and so forth that specification should be chosen and tested.[56] At the same time, if the specification does not fit, that is, the hypothesis of an intervention of a specified form is rejected, a reasonable implication is that the law may not have had an effect on the target variable.[57]

Finally, there may be problems regarding the specification of the time series. Frequently, the length of the time series is determined solely by data availability. It is rare for researchers to study whether there would be different results with the use of a time series with different start and end points or of a time series of a different length. A time series is a continuous set of observations at consecutive points. It is, therefore, not a random sample of all time points. In actuality, the time series evaluated in impact studies tend to be arbitrary in the sense that they are generally chosen in terms of data availability.

Thus, results can vary sharply depending on exactly which set of time points is used, particularly if, as is frequently the case, the sample size is small.[58] In evaluations using time-series data the issue could be addressed by re-estimating models premised on varying sets of time points; often this is not done. Yet, if outcomes differ substantially when varying subsets of time points are employed, such variations effect the robustness of the conclusions. Or, in other words, since the evaluations of the effectiveness of a law may differ with the specific time series employed, research outcomes may vary – indeed, may be manipulated – merely through the timing of the study.[59]

Even if robust conclusions can be drawn about the effects of a law in one jurisdiction (including when compared with others), very difficult questions can arise regarding the extent to which such outcomes are generalizable to any other jurisdictions. (Social scientists would, more generally, speak about 'threats to external validity.')[60] Different social, political, and economic structures and their effects can make it very difficult to compare the outcomes of even similar laws in Arkansas, New York, and Sweden, and so forth.

We can sum up this rather intricate section as follows. In determining the effect of a law or set of laws on an underlying problem we face substantial difficulties around the question of causation, including those posed by the diverse approaches of positivism and interpretivism (discussed in the previous section). Legal-impact studies respond to such complexities by establishing a comparison between actual behaviour patterns in jurisdictions subject to the law in question and behaviour patterns that would have existed in those same jurisdictions had the law in question never been enacted. The goal in assessing the outcomes of a law is to control for 'plausible rival hypotheses,' non-experimental variables that could reasonably explain behaviour rather than the law that is the subject of investigation.

The best design for a legal-impact study is one based on 'multiple time series.' The essential features of this design are the presence of several jurisdictions in both the group subject to the law and the groups not subject to it and a testing for the behaviour in question both before and at several points after passage of the law. If behaviour patterns are similar until the law is introduced in the experimental states, then an investigator can attribute subsequent changes over time to the law with a high degree of certainty. However, there can be severe limitations in using such a design. First, multiple jurisdictions may not be available. Second, even when a country is a federation (with many jurisdictions) the law in question may be of national application. Third, there may be interactive effects among laws that are very difficult to identify and isolate. Fourth, the particular details of the evaluative model must be clearly specified, for example, regarding the timing of the legal intervention and the nature of the effect being tested; that is, is it immediate and permanent, immediate but temporary, and so forth. Fifth, there may be problems regarding the specification of the time series. Finally, there can be very difficult issues regarding the extent to which any findings about the effects of a law in one jurisdiction are generalizable to other societies.

These complexities in evaluation underscore the importance of rigorous assessments of laws. They also heighten the fact that such evaluations are sometimes simply not possible or at any rate must be done in some compromised fashion. The need for high-quality evaluations of effects must be recognized and supported even as the limitations of evaluative studies must be squarely faced.

In terms of limitations, the critiques of interpretivism may be critical. Interpretivism suggests that even a 'successful' legal-impact study will be limited in the understanding it provides if the context in which the law is produced and acted upon is not carefully evaluated as well. Study of the context could include, where appropriate, interpretive in-depth interviews of those affected by the law – or absence of the law – in question.[61]

In all of this, fiery point/counterpoint exchanges – such as the one between Mackinnon and Abrams (quoted at the beginning of this chapter) – may be energetic and eloquent. But they are no substitute for sober study and careful debate about the outcomes of law or the situations that it ought to address.

Surprise – Unintended Consequences

The need to understand impact is compellingly illustrated by the phenomenon of unintended consequences. In some critical ways unintended consequences offer dramatic reproof to instrumentalism. We shall have much more to say about instrumentalism in the next chapter. Basically, however, this view contends that law is capable of directly reshaping social forces. Unintended consequences are a sharp retort to such contentions.

Unintended consequences speak to the disparity between the intended effects of a law or sets of laws and the actual impact. Such disparity becomes especially dramatic when the consequences that result are not only unintended but are essentially at odds with the ends one sought to achieve. When these adverse effects occur, the very underpinnings of an instrumental conception of law get turned on their head.

Law, of course, is not the only area of human endeavour that must contend with unintended consequences. In *Why Things Bite Back: Technology and the Revenge of Unintended Consequences* Tenner traces the many ways in which technological 'advances' have produced effects that were not intended and have been, in many instances, quite harmful. Here are but a few diverse examples on a very long list:

Intensive antibiotic therapy has removed the horror of some of the nineteenth century's most feared infections, yet it has also promoted the spread of even more virulent bacteria. Massive shielding of beaches from the energy of waves has deflected their intensity to other shores or robbed these beaches of replenishing sand. Smoke jumpers have suppressed small forest fires but have thereby helped build reservoirs of flammable materials in the underbrush for more intense ones ... Rigid molded ski boots have helped prevent ankle and tibia fractures at the cost of anterior cruciate ligament injuries.[62]

Tenner insists that technology requires more, not less, human intervention, because even as it may solve acute problems technology can also introduce more insidious ones.[63]

In the legal domain the phenomenon of unintended consequences has captured the attention of students of the impact of law across the political spectrum.[64] Nevertheless, those wary of activist government, at least in the economic realm, are especially inclined to invoke the danger of unintended consequences as a rallying cry in their efforts to roll back the public sector.[65] Again, Tenner is instructive as he links wayward technology to wayward law, at least so far as those inclined to the right of the political spectrum are concerned: 'If hidden risk is the concern of the liberal distrustful of corporate assurances of safety through technology, displaced risk is the objection of the conservative to regulation. And conservative scepticism is directed less often at technologies themselves than at attempts to limit, regulate, or impose them.'[66]

The general line of argument (not confined to the regulation of technology) is that any particular law will not achieve the desired results, will create economic distortions, is philosophically bad because of the burden that government imposes, and so forth. In addition, it is contended that the law may have any number of undesirable results, even from the perspective of the proponents of the law who would (of course) not intend them. The upshot of this line of argument, generally, is that attempting to regulate human behaviour is a hazardous, unpredictable enterprise, with law a particularly unwieldy tool. Hence, government regulation should mostly stay clear of such matters; indeed, it should shrink.

In some quarters the lessons of unintended consequences and neo-conservatism (at least in the United States) are especially closely linked. The tenets of neo-conservatism are difficult to pin down. Nevertheless, one of its architects has emphasized the insistence that the complexity of social reality means that effective change is likely to

prove difficult. Such difficulties pave the way for unintended consequences: '[G]overnment programs often do not achieve their objectives
or do achieve them but with high or unexpected costs. A true conservative may oppose change because it upsets the accumulated wisdom
of tradition ... [A] neoconservative questions change because, though
present circumstances are bad and something ought to be done, it is
necessary to do that something cautiously, experimentally, and with a
minimum of bureaucratic authority.'[67]

A favourite target for this and related lines of argument are laws
imposing minimum wages. Progressives began promoting such regulation over a half-century ago. In doing so they argued that those at the
bottom of the workforce were entitled to a wage that lets them live in
at least some dignity. In addition, it was contended that a fair minimum wage would prevent sweatshops and encourage people to
eschew welfare for work.

Those on the right target such laws as a clear illustration of unintended consequences. They contend that one of the main effects of such
regulation is that it actually hurts those it is intended to help.[68] Generally, the position taken is that the market will often react to economic
regulation in a way that harms the least well off. In the instance of minimum wage laws the reaction of employers is simply not to hire. Thus,
the effect of such regulation is to raise unemployment at the bottom of
the ladder; hardly a desirable – or intended – consequence for those
championing such provisions.

Yet this example of minimum-wage laws also suggests that conservative promotion of the phenomenon of unintended consequence may,
itself, be overblown. Sophisticated proponents of such regulation challenge the assertion that minimum-wage laws, or raising the levels of
those that exist, necessarily result in loss of jobs.[69] At least some
employers may actually invest in training programs.[70] In any event, it
is argued that, even if this regulation causes some loss of jobs for those
whose existing marketable skills do not 'justify' a minimum wage, the
law needs to be viewed in a larger regulatory context. A minimum
wage should be linked to unemployment-insurance provisions and job
retraining to create a system that encourages work and re-education to
do it and, at the same time, ensures that all employment complies with
minimal standards of safety, economic dignity, and so forth.[71]

The point here is not to attempt to settle debates about the effects of
minimum-wage laws or about the values used to assess such impacts.
Rather, it is to illustrate the economic right's fascination with unin-

tended consequences and to show that the claims about that phenomenon can, themselves, be applied in overdrawn ways. At the same time, it is clear that unintended consequences are an aspect of impact that is critical and needs much fuller investigation and assessment as part of the larger study of the effect of law.

There are many contemporary examples of unintended consequences. We will turn to some of these momentarily. However, a classic example from the earlier part of the twentieth century is America's experiment with prohibition. The illustration is made more dramatic because, in this instance, resort was had not only to ordinary law but also to the Constitution of the United States. The Eighteenth Amendment prohibited the manufacture, sale, and transportation of intoxicating liquors.[72] Some 750,000 individuals were arrested for violation of the prohibition laws from 1920 until their repeal in 1932. There were thousands of convictions, seizures of distilleries, and fines imposed running to millions of dollars.[73]

These laws did curb the consumption of alcohol (with a lowering of the incidence of related diseases) and contributed, in the long run, to changing attitudes to the dangers of excess.[74] What also occurred, however, was the proliferation of organized crime enjoying a highly profitable trade in illegal alcohol. Enforcement was inadequate in terms of both resources and the will to curtail drinking among otherwise law-abiding citizens. Neither Congress nor individual states sufficiently underwrote the costs necessary to achieve compliance. Meanwhile, trafficking in alcohol became lucrative. So forces in the underworld were quick to seize the opportunity, becoming more organized and successful than the forces of law and order.[75]

More broadly, prohibition reflected – and aggravated – rural and urban divisions in society despite the wide support the laws received when first enacted. Robust consumption of alcohol was substantially an urban phenomenon. Prohibition was an attempt by rural forces to assert their influence. Laws forbidding consumption were enacted. Still, drinking continued, albeit at a lower rate, especially among the working class.[76] Moreover, illicit trade in alcohol flourished and the influence of country folk waned.[77] All the while, efforts on behalf of repeal were helped along by concerted efforts on the part of the alcohol industry.[78]

At the level of symbolism the prohibitionists were clearly successful.[79] Yet the instrumental effects of such laws were largely at odds with that symbolism. Such consequences eventually overwhelmed and largely obliterated the values, at least expressed in law, that the Eighteenth Amendment was meant to enshrine. The 'American faith in the power of law to correct all evils'[80] had been badly misplaced.

While prohibition provides a dramatic, historical example, it by no means stands alone. A number of contemporary examples can be cited.[81] Here we will discuss two very different ones: sanctions in international law and the no-fault movement reflected in two divergent areas – marriage breakdown and compensation for automobile-accident injuries. There is controversy concerning the precise effects of law in both these examples. Yet, more to the point, there is compelling evidence of actual consequences very much at odds with the intent of advocates.

Sanctions in International Law

The international order of law has always been subject to debate. Seen through the eyes of domestic legal regimes, international ones come up short for several reasons, including their inability to enforce their norms. International-law advocates respond to this allegation in varied ways.[82] Those promoting such an order argue that there are ways that nations violating accepted norms can be brought to heel; one of the most important of these means is sanctions, most prominently economic ones.

Sanctions, when deployed, are typically used by Western states to protest against what they consider to be fundamental human-rights violations and other morally reprehensible acts. Recent examples of such objectionable events are the Iraqi invasion of Kuwait, the massacre in Tiananmen Square, and apartheid in South Africa. It is true that justifications for sanctions vary. Yet a consistent rationale is avowedly instrumental. The purpose is to have target countries act to eliminate or at least reduce the objectionable acts by complying with the demands of those countries imposing sanctions. There is also a more symbolic function, that is, reinforcing collective international standards that certain fundamental acts of individual countries should be judged and buttressing the principles regarding how such acts ought to be assessed.[83]

Nevertheless, for our purposes, the issue is the effectiveness of sanctions. Too often sanctions suffer from what has been called the 'termination trap.'[84] Effective application of sanctions requires clear and achievable objectives that, in turn, result in the lifting of those sanctions when their objectives are met. Yet most sanctions are imposed with unclear objectives, resulting in the sanctioner maintaining them indefinitely, for example, on such nations as North Korea, Cuba, and Vietnam. One survey of the employment of sanctions throughout the twentieth century is very guarded about their effectiveness as measured against their announced objectives: '[E]conomic sanctions have only rarely attained the declared goals ... Even in the few cases where economic sanctions appear to have attained their goals, it is often questionable whether it was the economic sanctions or other measures, or a combination of the economic sanctions and other measures which brought ultimate success.'[85]

That said, there are instances where sanctions have had at least some effects linked to avowed purposes. The measures taken against South Africa to bring to an end the apartheid regime may be one such example. Moreover, such measures carried with them additional moral force because they resulted, in good part, from calls for sanctions that came from within that country from leaders opposed to racial segregation.

However, the entire chronicle of sanctions is littered with instances of ineffectiveness. For example, embargoes on North Korea, Vietnam, and Cuba have been in place for nearly three decades with virtually no impact on the governments of those countries.[86] In another instance, sanctions in Serbia had a devastating effect on the economy, including rocketing inflation and massive unemployment. Yet, a gangster class thrived in a burgeoning black market and the ruling elite was largely immunized from the devastating effects.[87]

Indeed, the example of Serbia illustrates what are often the most salient effects of sanctions: the groups most responsible for the harms escape the ruinous consequences of sanctions while innocent ordinary people must bear them. What is more, there is evidence that the harshest effects of such measures fall upon women and children. Children are most likely to feel the effects of the collapse of health, education, and food-supply systems. Women are most likely to be the ones who have to cope with such effects on children and themselves.[88] One study that focused on a statistical analysis of sanctioning episodes[89] argues that financial sanctions (for example, freezing of assets) may be more effective than other strategies such as import/export restrictions. At least financial sanctions target the elite rather than ordinary citizens in a country being sanctioned.[90] The same study suggests that the chances of sanctions succeeding are also dependent on the amount of costs imposed, the length of the episode, and the degree of instability created in the country that is targeted.[91]

Thoughtful students of sanctions do not argue that they should never be used. They do insist, however, that the probabilities of their success and the likelihood that they will impose substantial suffering upon ordinary people be carefully weighed. They call for debate about 'other tools of statecraft that can produce political change more effectively without inflicting deprivations on the innocent.'[92]

The 'No Fault' Movement

The 'no fault' movement of the 1970s and 1980s sought to alleviate the acrimony and inaccessibility of court-adjudicated fault determinations with systems resolving problems on the basis of simply providing compensation, the harmonious resolution of conflict, and so forth. The consequences intended by those advocating such laws were understandable. Experiments in America were the more laudable considering all the criticisms (as noted here) that the United States relies too heavily on litigation for any number of purposes. The results regarding critical aspects of these ventures were a different story. Here we will discuss the two most prominent examples of 'no fault': compensation for harm done in auto accidents and as grounds for granting divorce.

Courts and their adherence to a fault-based system in addressing compensation for personal injuries, with their attendant loss of time and other costs, have long been the subject of criticism. The concerns have been voiced most anxiously in the context of redress for injuries in automobile accidents. In North America car crashes are responsible for the most numerous and costly incidents of personal injuries. For example, in 1989 in the USA there were about 34 million automobile accidents; of that number, 47,000 people were killed and another 5 million suffered personal injuries.[93]

Among the general shortcomings of the tort system, it is contended, there is an inability to deliver compensation to all who are injured (because fault will not always be established); the mandatory once-and-for-all payment can either under-compensate or over-compensate, depending on the circumstances; and, funds, otherwise available for compensation (usually provided because of the existence of insurance), are excessively consumed by administrative and legal costs.

As a result, many jurisdictions have turned to schemes based wholly or substantially on 'no fault.' In these schemes compensation for injury from automobile accidents is not assessed on the basis of who is at fault but, rather, only on the basis of whether the injury occurred as a result of the mishap. Moreover, such compensation, or at least a sub-stantial part of it, is usually determined through some administrative scheme, thus excluding resort to the courts.

There is strong evidence that no-fault does compensate more vic-tims, more quickly and at less cost than the tort system. However, there are disquieting results regarding the impact on the deterrence effects of such regimes. The empirical evidence respecting such schemes in the United States is mixed, due, partly, to the fact that they are frequently a combination of elements of fault and no-fault.[94] However, studies of the schemes in Australia, New Zealand, and Quebec, which are entirely no-fault, clearly have some troubling, unexpected implications regarding the loss of deterrence effects on dangerous driving when tort actions are abolished and no-fault schemes are substituted.[95] These problems can be illustrated by discussing assessments of the Quebec scheme.[96]

In that jurisdiction, all court actions for compensation for bodily injury from automobile accidents are banned. In exchange, an agency of the provincial government provides earnings – related benefits at a high level (though there is a cap). The regime is funded by flat-rate lev-ies.[97] Gaudry, using multivariate analysis, concluded that bodily inju-ries grew by 26.3 per cent a year and fatalities by 6.8 per cent after the initiation of the scheme.

It may be that the increase in bodily injuries can reflect a reporting bias, but this would not be the case with fatalities. Gaudry suggests that the increase in both these rates is due, at least partly, to two fac-tors: first, compulsory insurance requirements that cause previously uninsured motorists to drive less carefully and, second, flat premiums that significantly decrease insurance for high-risk drivers, resulting in more accidents, when before the differential rates would have priced them off the highway. Another study of no-fault in Quebec was even more insistent that such compensation produces, on average, less care-ful driving and increases the incidence of automobile accidents[98] – scarcely consequences intended by advocates of such alternative schemes.

The point here is not that no-fault must inevitably lower driver safety and increase injuries, even fatalities. The studies purporting to reach these conclusions have been criticized for failing to distinguish between the impact of any liability system and the particular insurance scheme linked to that system.[99] At the same time, it has been argued that no-fault schemes, properly designed and implemented, can achieve deterrence incentives: through experience-rated premiums or direct levies on driving activities (e.g., gasoline taxes) or both.[100] Still, the point remains: '[T]he empirical evidence does indicate that without added financial deterrence incentives, no-fault schemes are likely to lead to increased accident rates, injuries and fatalities.'[101] Such consequences are clearly at odds with the avowed purposes of such regimes.

Our second example of unexpected consequences involving 'no fault' focuses on divorce. The acrimony around the dissolution of marriage has long prompted calls for a more humane way to resolve issues surrounding divorce. As a result, many jurisdictions in Canada and the United States have passed legislation authorizing no-fault divorce.

Reformers' hopes were high. These laws were meant to minimize arguments about responsibility for the breakdown of the relationship. Instead, the focus was to be on a humane dissolution of the marriage so as to facilitate fair and equitable division of assets and to ease post-divorce parenting. Most prominently, for our purposes, these laws were meant to eliminate antiquarian assumptions about women's subordinate role, instead recognizing wives as equals in marriage.

Yet, to the reformers' dismay, the unexpected economic consequences for women and children were, frequently, devastating. The removal of the levers of fault, on the one hand, and, on the other, the contention that women were the economic equals of men (despite the manifest evidence to the contrary that the traditional marriage provided) spelled financial disaster for many women and children. The most prominent study on the effects of no-fault divorce concluded: 'The result is often hardship, impoverishment, and disillusionment for divorced women (and their children) ... [O]n the average, divorced women and the minor children in their households experience a 73 per cent decline in their standard of living in the first year of divorce. Their former husbands, in contrast, experience a 42 per cent rise in their standard of living.'[102]

Such conclusions have not, themselves, been free of controversy. It has been claimed that the magnitude of the statistical disparity presented in the excerpt just quoted is in error to a significant degree.[103] Still other studies contend that no-fault did not cause such disparities. Rather, it is divorce itself – whatever the basis of its being granted – that has enormously adverse economic impact for many women and children.[104] However, even if this contention is well founded, no-fault still had the consequence of providing a 'legal' solution that was no solution at all. At the same time, the no-fault 'solution' deflected attention away from the economic inequalities that traditional marriage (and divorce) imposes on most women.

This point about the disparity between the aspirations of reformers and the actual results, however precisely caused, has been captured eloquently, if a bit selectively, by Mary Ann Glendon. She complains generally that '[i]n peddling an idea of law that promised too much, legal opinion leaders for the past thirty years set the stage for disappointment, disillusion, and disrespect.'[105] More specifically, relevant to the issues at hand, she asserts: 'In a country where the majority of divorces occur between couples with minor children, how can one explain that reformers took childless couples as the norm and treated couples with children as exceptions? Or that, in utter disregard of the economic realities of single parenthood, they constructed the marital property and support law around an image of spousal "self-sufficiency" after divorce?'[106]

This discussion of unintended consequences and 'no fault' should not be taken as an indictment, root and branch, of the latter. Indeed, many of those who have led the initiatives in documenting its untoward effects often do not wish to discredit the underlying ideas and impulses for improvement. Rather, they seek to demonstrate the unanticipated (or, sometimes, the ignored) outcomes so that such weaknesses will not impede the larger aims of the reforms.[107]

For example, a major study of redress for automobile accidents concludes that there is compelling evidence that improperly designed no-fault regimes can fail to deter negligent driving to the maximum extent. At the same time, it insists that tort litigation (except in very clear and constrained circumstances) is not the answer, particularly for the purposes of achieving compensation. No-fault can compensate more victims, more quickly, and insurance will cost no more and could, possibly, cost less. As a result, in response to deterrence issues, the study suggests that extensive risk-rating be used and that there be better enforcement of regulatory policies that can reduce the accident rate.[108]

The phenomenon of unintended consequences requires us to sort through issues of impact as best we can: both in terms of evaluating the effects that any law has actually had and in terms of possible results – perhaps outcomes to be avoided – when law is being turned to as a solution. Tenner, in his book on the unintended consequences of technology discussed at the beginning of this section, documents many unforeseen effects – some of which are truly frightening. Yet he knows that technology will – and should – advance. Hence, he urges some reservation even as he accepts technology's modifications: 'I am arguing not against change, but for a modest, tentative, and sceptical acceptance of it.'[109] Could such watchwords be applied to alterations we seek to achieve by law?

Conclusions

A straightforward reaction regarding the effect of any law is to ask what impact it has had on the problems it has sought to address. It turns out, however, that such a direct question may not be so easy to answer.

In the first place, there may be substantial disagreement about whether there is a problem at all. Does pornography, in fact, harm? Indeed, what is pornography? If one does not believe the phenomenon in question is a problem at all or, in any event, is one that the law ought to redress, then one will probably be very sceptical regarding outcomes produced by any law that is supposed to provide a solution.

Then, too, there may be significant disagreement regarding the values brought to the task of assessing impact. Ours is a world with substantially divergent understandings (based on race, gender, class, and so forth) regarding the forces that shape society and law. Assertions that social science is embedded in a set of particular and changeable assumptions confront claims to objectivity and neutrality. Such assertions are highlighted by the divergence between positivism and interpretivism as methodologies for empirical studies. Do such contentions permit an insistence that there can be a single understanding regarding the impact of law? If there is no such understanding, what is the value of empirical studies?

In any event, there can be substantial questions about cause and effect concerning the impact of a law and any changes regarding the underlying problem that law is meant to address. What is more, positivists are more likely to be optimistic than interpretvists concerning the possibility of clear answers. In terms of such questions, the notion of 'plausible rival hypotheses' suggests that all other reasonable explanations for any measurable change must be eliminated before there can be confidant conclusions that law caused those modifications. Theoretically, the best way to control for such other causes is to compare the jurisdictions that have enacted the law being studied with ones that have not.

Yet, practically, there may be all sorts of problems establishing such comparisons of jurisdictions. It may be that there are simply none available. And if they are available, there may be difficult comparability issues; for example, around rates of violent crime in the case of gun-control legislation. In addition, there may be issues about whether related laws are interacting to produce effects that cannot be attributed to either. There can also be questions regarding the model that is used to gauge effects, particularly regarding the timing of the intervention and the nature of the effects of the law being measured.

Finally, when effects can be established, they may be sharply at odds with those meant to be produced. What is more, these unintended consequences may swamp those that were supposed to result. Prohibition may have lowered the amount of drinking, but did not end it. What did result was the proliferation of organized crime enjoying a highly profitable trade in illegal alcohol and strong reaction against prohibition, especially among urban dwellers. Economic sanctions authorized by international law often do not achieve their announced goals, while frequently producing negative consequences for the ordinary people who are subjected to them. More currently, the 'no fault' movement, whether in the context of compensation for personal injuries or relating to divorce, has yielded results at odds with those sought by its advocates.

The point of this chapter is a question. Law surely has significant effects – but what are they? The consequences of a law are often much less straightforward and assessable than either its proponents or opponents might claim. The need for rigorous evaluations of the effects of law is vital if we are to achieve an understanding of how law functions, of its limits – and of its potential. At the same time, qualifications about the feasibility of evaluative studies and controversies surrounding the methods that they employ and the results they produce must be squarely faced. The potential of such evaluations and their limits will be discussed in specific contexts in part 3 when we examine the effects produced by capital punishment, the regulation of smoking and of the environment, the impact of pornography and attempts to control it, and the results produced by laws to combat discrimination and programs to implement affirmative action to benefit blacks in America.

CHAPTER FOUR

Six Ideas about the Impact of Law – America the Outlier

This chapter examines the third aspect of the impact of law: the overall effects of law's interaction with social, political, and economic forces. A number of ideas contend that the outcomes produced by law are most clearly discerned in terms of broad contours of regulation. The third aspect of impact is not primarily concerned with gauging the consequences of any particular law (the focus of the previous chapter) but, rather, with exploring the relationship of law and society generally.

The ideas discussed in this chapter vary substantially. There are instrumental assertions about law that suggest that it can single-handedly cause changes in societal conditions. There are claims that talking about the impact of law is, itself, mistaken: law and society are so inextricably related that one cannot coherently talk about law affecting society; rather, the focus ought to be on the complexities of their interaction. None of these ideas provides a complete account of the effect of law. They are more a body of general directions of thought. Some of them are more assertions about law's influence – or lack of influence – than detailed accounts about how law interacts with social, economic, and political forces to assert its presence. Even so, these ideas, taken together, capture the range of views about the overall consequences of law in the contemporary societies of Western, developed nations.

The modifier 'contemporary,' just used, needs some further elaboration. This book examines the expansion of the role of law in the last part of the twentieth century, accounting for that enlarged role and assessing the effects that the increased presence of law has had.[1] Historical ideas are referred to in this chapter[2] and others[3] as is appropriate to the particular issues being discussed.[4]

Attempts to assign law overarching effects run the risk of trailing off into vague generalities. The contention that law asserts its influence more as 'a system of cultural and symbolic meanings than as a set of operative controls'[5] is an important statement emphasizing that law is not just commands ordering people about in some direct manner. Yet what precisely does the contention, just quoted, mean? 'Cultural and symbolic meanings' produce outcomes as well. But what are they? In any event, has all this time and energy spent on law over the last decades been expended largely for the sake of symbolism? (We will examine the symbolic uses of law and the outcomes produced in conjunction with the discussion of capital in punishment in part 3.)

Chances are that individuals and groups as diverse as, say, environmentalists, manufacturers' associations, gay and lesbian rights activists, and minimum-wage opponents think there are more tangible outcomes at stake. They may be wrong regarding such effects, but those efforts and the outcomes produced are not satisfactorily accounted for by labelling them and the entire enterprise 'symbolic.' A more complex and multi-faceted account of the consequences of law is required.

Stepping back from the wealth of writing that asserts theories and hypotheses about the relationship of law and society, we can discern six major ideas regarding the impact of law. The first four are general accounts of law. The last two focus on particular aspects of law and underscore the dominance of America in debates about the influence of legalization.

1 Instrumentalism:
   This idea asserts that law is an autonomous instrument that can be used to effect (or curb) various social, political, and economic consequences.
2 Law Acting in Concert with Social and Political Forces:
   This idea claims that the impact of law will most closely correspond to its intended goal when that law and related social and political forces are in harmony – the greater the alignment, the more likely that the law will have the effect its proponents predict.
3 Law (Re)Constituting Social and Political Relationships:
   This idea, like 2, acknowledges the link between law and social/ political forces and institutions. However, its advocates, usually interested in progressive reform, claim that law can be used in important ways to constitute and reconstitute such social and political arrangements.
4 The Ineffectiveness of Law:

This idea contends that law largely impedes the proper workings of society – whatever they may be. Some progressives (in contrast with those embracing idea 3) see law, not as a vehicle for change, but as a deflection of forces that could effect reform. At the same time, some conservatives have their own brand of scepticism regarding law's ability to respond to social issues (in addition to a general hostility regarding any interference with market forces).

5 National Styles of Regulation – 'American Exceptionalism' I:
   This idea claims that there may be different ways in which societies use law and implement it and, therefore, law may have different effects in different societies. It contends that, whatever the explanatory power of ideas 1–4, they, in turn, may be dependent, in significant ways, on national differences across societies. Of particular note is 'American Exceptionalism,' that is, the notion that the United States is an outlier in its expectations about law and its litigation/rights-dominated approach.

6 The Impact of Litigation Regarding Social Change – 'American Exceptionalism' II:
   This idea (like idea 5) is closely associated with law in the United States. No other society accords such importance to courts. America relies heavily on litigation to regulate an array of important social, economic, and political issues. In particular, the judiciary dominates many critical issues because of an entrenched bill of rights and the role the Republic assigns to courts in nullifying legislation and controlling public officials.

   Yet idea 6 asserts that litigation can rarely cause significant changes in society. Lawsuits can bring about change only under a very limited set of circumstances that are almost never met. This hypothesis suggests that discussions of the effects of law must be careful to distinguish the influence of courts from other agencies of government (particularly legislatures and administrative bodies) and from markets and other institutions.

   Debates about the impact of litigation focus on courts in America. At the same time, such controversies raise important issues for other countries contemplating an expanded role for courts, especially regarding an entrenched bill of rights. Does an enhanced role for courts lead to a diminished role for popular politics?

These six ideas do not exist in isolation from each other. Each may have adherents who claim that their idea and only that idea accounts for the influence of law. Yet there are critical overlaps. Such blurring among these ideas is an important element of their explanatory power. For example, we will see that within 'Law Acting in Concert with Social and Political Forces' (idea 2) is a variant that suggests greater use of self-regulation. That variant has many similar aspects in common with those of 'normativity,' discussed in conjunction with 'the Ineffectiveness of Law' (idea 4). 'The Impact of Litigation Regarding Social Change' (idea 6) in many ways focuses on diluting the claims of Instrumentalism (idea 1) regarding the impact of courts. In other words, each of these six ideas contains a core that urges a particular view of how law exerts its influence and that justifies separate treatment. At the same time, the ways that the totalities of these ideas interconnect (and collide) with each other is critical in accounting for law's consequences and the role it plays in contemporary societies.

Two of the ideas (5 and 6) are subtitled 'American Exceptionalism' because they reflect so directly the special role that law plays in that society. But the entire chapter is subtitled 'America the Outlier.' The role of law in the United States dominates writings about the effects of law. This is no surprise given that nation's use of law, expectations of law, and contests about how and when it will be invoked. There are, of course, similarities between America and other countries. Yet the United States employs law in a particular way. The predominance of courts, the emphasis on individualism, the adversarialness, the enshrinement of rights, and the punitiveness for criminal offences set that society apart. In quality and quantity the United States is an outlier regarding the role of law. Other societies contemplating invoking law in the hope that it will produce desired outcomes need to answer many questions. A critical one is, Is this a role for law or is this a task that would be (should be?) assigned to law, particularly to litigation, only in America?

Six Ideas about the Impact of Law

1. Instrumentalism

The belief that law can be used to directly engineer society is most closely associated with instrumentalism. This idea asserts that law is an autonomous instrument which can be used to produce various social, political, and economic consequences: '[S]ince it voices decisions from which there is no appeal, we regard it as able to decide and effect anything at all.'[6]

While instrumentalism itself can be depicted in many ways, the core of it is the view that 'legal rules do cause social phenomena because of what they prescribe, and that prescription in legal rules must therefore figure in the explanation of social phenomena.'[7] The manifestation of these beliefs is heard in numerous debates about law: '[I]t simply does not occur to lawyers (or, for that matter, to most sociologists of law) to discuss legal rules without involving, implicitly or explicitly, their supposedly intended consequences.'[8] In this depiction, law is a formidable instrument available to effect change. Simultaneously, it is a source of principles and standards for structuring society: 'Instrumentalist writings are filled with analogies and metaphors that identify law and government with "instruments", "tools", machines, and even "engines"; law is viewed as a technology, legal personnel as "social engineers", and law's uses as "social engineering." '[9]

A high-water mark for this attitude came with public-policy analysis of law, its foremost proponents being Lasswell and McDougal of Yale Law School.[10] The assertion of public-policy analysis was as straightforward as it was simplistic: good public analysis would produce good law; good law would produce good societies. The agents of such goodness would be lawyers.

Public-policy analysis of law has been characterized as 'probably the most exaggerated conception ever imagined of the importance of lawyers.'[11] Yet this analysis was confident that legal education should be properly oriented 'toward achieving the distinctive values and conditioning variables of a free society.'[12] If it were, lawyers would be 'more effective instruments for the achievement of the public good than they have been in the past.'[13]

Nevertheless, some have seen a form of 'pragmatic instrumentalism' playing a critical role in transforming the role of law in America. This instrumentalism repudiated the formalistic, static, and conservative conception of law that was so influential at the end of the nineteenth century.[14] Such instrumentalism asserted three distinguishing claims. First, the primary task of legal theory is the provision of coherent ideas so that law can be more valuable to policy-makers. Second, legal rules are essentially tools for practical ends rather than general norms laid down by officials in power, secular reflections of natural law, or social phenomena historically grounded. Third, the focus of law ought to be on the goals it may serve, the machinery that implements it, the sorts of means–goal relationships, and its efficacy and limits.[15]

Still, however worthy its intentions, any number of perspectives have demonstrated that the claims of instrumentalism have been excessively optimistic.[16] Much credit for the debunking of instrumentalism can be given to 'gap' studies in law. Such investigations, in many contexts, established disjunctions between legal pronouncement, whatever the source, and the actual effect of any particular law on social behaviour. These studies exposed naivety regarding the instrumental capacities of law to effect change.

A good example of such research is Nelken's examination of the effects of the 1965 Rent Act in Great Britain. One of the main goals of the act was to restrain harassment of tenants by landlords. It 'was hailed as "a tenants' *Magna Carta*" and "one of the most courageous and valuable Bills ever placed before Parliament."'[17] However, detailed investigation demonstrated that many commercial landlords were able to shape investigations and official decisions so that they escaped prosecution for what was objectionable behaviour. Instead, the landlords prosecuted and convicted of harassment of tenants tended to be small residential landlords in personal disputes with their tenants.[18] Taking issue with assertions that the law would effect change in a linear manner, Nelken suggests that, rather than talking about its 'impact' on society, the legislative process, generally, should be viewed as framed by internal and external constraints. Such constraints result in law being a means by which society is simultaneously maintained and changed. At the same time, Nelken acknowledges that the ways in which legislation asserts its influence within these constraints raises many unanswered questions.[19]

Commenting on the cumulative effect of various investigations on the outcomes produced by law, Trubek contends: 'As the result of over two decades of gap studies, impact studies, and implementation research, we have come to doubt the independent power of law to reshape social arrangements.'[20] The exaggerations of instrumentalism can be illustrated by discussing two examples drawn from two very different areas – 'law and development' and torts – where law has had effects. Yet such impact is much more complicated and difficult to assess than the effects asserted by an instrumentalist conception.

The 'Law and Development' movement sought to bring 'modern' law to societies in transition in Asia, Africa, and Latin America. As such societies transformed themselves politically and economically, law – and lawyers – would be there to provide the framework, to be the catalyst: 'Ideas of liberty and freedom travel fast and far and are contagious. Yet their adaptation to particular societies requires trained people, disciplined people, dedicated people. It requires lawyers.'[21] 'Backward' legal systems were seen to be a substantial impediment to development; conversely, the importing of Western legal concepts, institutions, and processes was taken to promote it. Examples of the importance attributed to law in affecting change were its role in the reform of land tenure to facilitate modern agriculture, in population control, in commercial investment, and in achieving lower crime rates.[22] It was contended that 'behaviour can be consciously modified by appropriate alterations of ... rules.'[23] Thus, there was need for 'instrumental research designed to ascertain the legal changes needed to achieve some specific developmental goals.'[24]

Soon, however, the bloom was off the rose. Those who had once been enthusiastic then declared the reverse: exporting law was responsible for any number of ills, even reaction and repression.[25] This migration of legal norms was a way of controlling developing nations for the benefit of industrialized countries, and a means of preventing structures other than liberal capitalism from taking hold.

Whether – as policy – 'Law and Development' was intended to facilitate progressive change or to be an instrument of control and suppression or, even, whether its agents understood clearly what they were trying to do is a fit subject for debate. The point here is that instrumental assumptions about the capacity of law were woefully inflated. What did become obvious was the discrepancy between actual social and political relations and the newly imported norms.[26] Rightly or wrongly, part of the discrepancy was underscored by the failing confidence in the legal system that was to be exported: '[M]uch of the early faith that America is a beacon of freedom and a model of realization of human welfare [has been abandoned]. From this perspective, the effort to export our legal institutions makes little sense.'[27]

Both the perky optimism of the instrumentalists' statements at the dawning of the law and development project and the (self)flagellation at its dusk are likely to leave moderates cold. They might go further and suggest that these extreme oscillations were, themselves, at least in part, responsible for the project's unravelling. Suffice it to say that, in the end, the record of the actual effects of this migration of Western law as agent of progress, as cudgel of repression, or as anything else is murky.[28] More recently, there have been renewed efforts, often under the banner of globalization, to aid in buttressing the legal systems of developing nations.[29] These efforts need to develop a much more nuanced approach than the original law and development movement,[30] an approach more aware of the complex outcomes that could be produced.[31]

A second example of instrumentalism and its deficiencies is provided by reference to torts, possibly the most pliant area of the law. At base, a tort is a wrong, other than breach of contract, that the law will redress by an award of damages or some other remedy. The influence of instrumentalism on torts, particularly the American version, is palpable. Tort litigation is meant to contour all sorts of economic and social behaviour. There is abundant confidence in its ability to shape human conduct. Indeed, one prominent commentator has contended: 'It is ... no exaggeration to see American tort law as the major means for setting norms and standards for social and economic behaviour.'[32] At the same time, there have been intense debates concerning how tort litigation should accomplish that purpose: through compensation? deterrence? some form of corrective justice?

Yet the empirical evidence concerning actual impact suggests that the effects of tort litigation are often at odds with the goals assigned to it.[33] A recent study surveyed outcomes regarding tort litigation, in the United States, in five accident areas: automobile, medical, product-related, environmental, and workplace.[34] That study confirmed the disparity between the actual impact of tort litigation and various claims about its effects, including when those claims are measured against comparable regulatory or compensatory schemes. Overall the study asserted: '[T]ort has expanded far beyond the areas in which it is cost effective; it must be substantially contracted.'[35]

Here, by way of illustration, we highlight only a few of the study's findings. Tort litigation produces the strongest deterrence in terms of auto accidents; weakest in terms of environmental lawsuits. In between, the role of tort and deterrence for medical- and product-related hazards is difficult to assess. Regarding workplace accidents, tort litigation has been largely replaced by administrative schemes ('workers' compensation boards') during this century. That said, workers' compensation levies seem to deter better than the tort system did (or would if it were to be revived). Regarding compensation, tort lawsuits 'fail badly in all five areas,' especially in terms of environmental, product, and medical accidents.[36] In terms of corrective justice, tort appears to do 'reasonably well' for automobile accidents, 'much less well' for medical and environmental injuries, and its effects regarding product-related accidents is unclear.[37]

A specific instance, in the context of injuries arising out of medical treatment, may be useful in illustrating the uncertain effects of instrumentalist assertions regarding tort litigation. The example is provided by the results of another study,[38] which examined the aftermath of a Supreme Court of Canada decision on informed consent to medical treatment.[39] When judgment was rendered there were various sweeping statements made concerning the effect it would have.[40] Yet the study of surgeons throughout Canada, conducted shortly after the decision of the Court, found that 70 per cent were not aware of the decision, and a majority of those who were aware expressed views inconsistent with it.

In a follow-up study ten years later, the author concluded that the decision had had small significance for the severity and frequency of malpractice claims.[41] Further, it had had little impact on developments in other areas of health law or in jurisdictions outside Canada. There is some evidence that doctors now do spend more time discussing the risks and benefits of treatment with patients, but such discussions have also increased in jurisdictions that have expressly declined to follow the rule propounded in that case.

The claim here is not that tort litigation has no effect on behaviour. In the specific example being discussed – informed consent to medical treatment – other studies demonstrate a complicated relationship between rules laid down in such cases and behaviour supposedly based on them.[42] Rather, the general point being made is more limited – but, nevertheless, critical: any substantial consequence of such rules is possible, but its likelihood is often in question. Instrumentalist claims concerning cause and effect regarding deterrence, compensation, and so forth may be realized in particular circumstances.[43] Yet the extent of the achievement of such goals is by no means certain, even as other effects may be produced by the law in question.[44] Such disparity is well accounted for by the study of torts discussed earlier: '[M]any assertions in the academic literature about the efficacy of the tort system have been supported principally by theory and assumption with little or no empirical analysis.'[45]

Still instrumentalism maintains a hold on both lawyers and the public. In this world of complexity and many-faceted troubles, a solution that seems to provide certainty and closure is often tempting. Many prominent legal scholars still hold law out as having a great capacity to provide solutions.[46] These boosts for law contain dark warnings about the 'value-discourse so primitive and vulgar' that will arise if even highly educated non-lawyers displace 'the American legal mind from the heights of power.'[47]

More broadly, the supposed capacity of law to directly affect social, political, and economic conditions is still touted when particular circumstances seem to warrant such an approach.[48] The bitter debate over laws mandating affirmative action is one such example. However, as we shall see later in the book,[49] the effects of such programs are not nearly as clear as either proponents or detractors frequently suggest. Yet another example of faith in the power of law is the right's abiding belief that law can deter criminal behaviour. As discussed in chapter 2, there are, on the one hand, high and uncomplicated hopes for deterrence (mixed with an appetite for vengeance) and, on the other, a much more complex record of results. We shall have another look at the disparity between the expectations regarding vengeance and deterrence and their actual outcomes when we examine capital punishment in Part 3.

In many ways, debunking instrumentalism is the easy part in a search for a statement about the effects of law. The much more difficult assignment is to provide a model or models that capture the complexity of law's influence. The next five ideas respond, in various ways, to that task.

2. Law Acting in Concert with Social and Political Forces

This idea claims that the impact of a law will most closely correspond to its intended goal when that law and related social and political forces are aligned – the greater the harmony, the more likely that the law will have the effect that its proponents predict.[50] The operation of law is heavily predicated on such prior factors as custom, morality, religion, and tradition. Thus, law's effectiveness is frequently dependent on other institutions such as family, church, and school and on professional, vocational, and other associations that foster those prior factors.[51]

Therefore, any substantial divergence between the intended effects of a law and the relevant social and political forces will result in the law being ineffective, at least in terms of its announced goals.[52] At the same time, it is contended that, to the extent that a law is supported by the institutions it affects, there is less need for intricate law. As a result, details and implementation can be left to those institutions through some form of self-regulation.[53]

It is said that there are three difficulties that law can confront when it seeks to initiate reform 'rather [than be] the echo ... of social change.'[54]

First, there may be popular resistance. If the changes decreed disturb the settled practices of people or seek to further goals that do not enjoy popular support, then resistance may be generated that will thwart such reform. Second, mobilization of organizational support critical to effect reforms may be a problem. When the changes are substantial, the necessary institutions are likely non-existent. If they can be created, it is even more of a struggle to impose such new organizations upon the established order without severe disruption. Third, there are complexities involved in allocation. If resources and human services are deployed as stipulated by reforms, then other social goals and undertakings that also need such resources and services may go wanting or may need to be abandoned altogether. These three difficulties frequently bode ill in terms of the outcomes hoped for through legal change: '[L]egal intervention often fails of its purpose and creates as many difficulties as it removes because it does not take into proper account the conditions that it must satisfy if it is to be effective.'[55] Indeed, some sharing similar views go farther, maintaining that 'the legal institution does not generally alter social behaviour and remedy social problems.'[56]

There are three very different variations on the contention that the effect of law is predicated on its alignment with social forces. The three agree on the importance of the convergence of law and society. However, they part company regarding the significance of such overlap. First, the left points to this hypothesis as affirmation of the conditions of dominance in this society. Second, there is the role of other institutions in determining the effectiveness of law – and the effect of law on these other institutions. Here we will look at the economic right's insistence that law must be in harmony with the market. Third, there is the claim that, if law converges with other institutions, then self-regulation can be used to augment the effectiveness of law and to bolster such agreement.

There is an important sense in which many on the left are willing to affirm that law is effective when it acts in concert with societal forces.[57] However, for this strand of the left, this symbiosis between law and social/political forces spells domination for working folk. From the top down such convergence may be a happy tale of consensus, but from the bottom up it is oppression writ large.

In this depiction – heavily influenced by Marxist analysis of society – it is law's affirmation of the social and economic relations existing within capitalist society that makes the legal order sinister.[58] So, for instance, property law is not just based on the inequality of ownership.

The law buttresses such disparity by permitting and helping owners to use that property as capital. Hence, rules relating to mortgages, leases, and so forth allow property to be so employed; contracts and commercial doctrines reflect the market and its mechanisms. Likewise, labour law bolsters free enterprise by giving effect to the dependence of the majority on the sale of their capital and by reflecting the control of working men and women, including their hiring and firing.

Beyond the effect of individual rules lies the more pervasive impact that law has on the depoliticization of issues through an appeal to universality. Criminal law defends the person and property of all members of society. Yet such protection disguises fundamental class differences, treating the capital of the employer and the personal belongings of the worker as if they were the same. Thus, the view is promoted that all classes have a common interest in the protection of private property. Social unity is asserted and encouraged even while there is manifest class differentiation in capitalist society.

While law is produced by conflict and instability, because of changes in society it is '*by its very nature* directed at the maintenance of order.'[59] However, law is not directly controlled by a unified ruling establishment. Rather, law develops as the state manages frequently conflicting pressures while maintaining its own legitimacy.

Thus a range of regulation, at least in the United States, is explained as a device responding to the needs of capitalism. The demands of such an economy for stable and predictable social relations led to a complex state that could manage the costs of disorder (poverty, unemployment, crime, etc.) associated with capitalism. The state took responsibility for 'externalities' of production processes to promote economic growth by private entities. Yet, such activity by government produced contradictory results both for the state and for capitalists. As the state acted to guard private interests from the full consequences of the costs such interests imposed on society, it also established itself as the forum where aggrieved interests could seek redress and argue for constraints on capitalism.[60]

Nevertheless, the essential power of law resides in the integration of the two effects just described: affirmation of the social and economic relations of capitalism and the fundamental depoliticization of issues through an appeal to universality.[61] Law thereby achieves control for the interests of dominant groups, whether with regard to socio-economic status, gender, race, or other characteristics. Simultaneously, law provides a justification for such oppression by appealing to higher, universal needs. The claim is that law is essentially the product of and vehicle for the interests of the rich and powerful. As a result, capitalism can relegate the vast majority of citizens to systematic inequality with very little resort to coercion.

The second variation of the contention that law is effective when it is in harmony with society essentially issues a warning: should law imperil other institutions, its effectiveness will be weakened. This issue of law's relationship with other forces in society has already been raised earlier in our discussion about the reasons for the growth of law.[62] It is said that if other institutions perform their functions effectively and if they are sufficiently strong to secure respect for their views, they can serve as mediators between law and society.

Institutions make two contributions to the effectiveness of law.[63] The first reflects the fact that associations are more closely geared to various segments of social order. Thus, they can ensure that the legal apparatus is conversant with prevailing social conditions. Such knowledge can go far to ensure that the measures law proposes will be acceptable. The second contribution of institutions is their critical role in forming human character and conduct. As a result, they can ensure that the legal apparatus will be responsive to these needs, as complex and varied as they may be. Hence the family, the school, churches, voluntary associations, and smaller urban communities can promote social mores and civic order.

However, as we saw earlier, according to this hypothesis, an important problem has developed because of the growth of law.[64] Law has asserted a presence that is now stultifying and crowding out other institutions, including the very workings of the institutions themselves: '[L]aws should complement and police rather than smash the internal rules of private institutions.'[65]

This is not to say that law does not have an important relationship with other institutions. Law is indispensable because it furnishes a force that is both sovereign and principled. Law, therefore, can and should intervene to contain the shortcomings of institutions and individuals in two ways: by correcting institutional abuses and by restraining individual defiance of institutions. Yet too much intervention by law establishes it as the sole principle of order, raising expectations that are bound to be disappointed.

More generally, the fear is that law and its blandishments are crowding out all manner of institutions. Social capital dwindles as membership falls in all sorts of organizations that foster and buttress individuals and society. Yet law abounds, such that 'the growth of an overly central-ized, regulatory and legalistic American state in the last 25 years has crowded out our once-flourishing civil society.'[66]

One institution is particularly singled out by economic conserva-tives as they resist tampering by law: the market. Regulation is bound to produce misguided consequences precisely because it is at variance with market principles. Economists, at least those of a neo-classical bent, place great faith in regimes of private exchange and ordering. Generally, they are sceptical of the capacity of lawmakers – legislators, regulators, or even courts – to enact provisions the effect of which is to increase net welfare.[67] In addition to economic justifications, there are closely related political arguments advanced by classical liberals. Autonomy is seen as a paramount value and a precondition to indi-vidual freedom; law is regarded as more likely to hamper autonomy than to establish conditions for its exercise.

Hence both economic conservatives and classical liberals are attracted to minimalist intervention by law, to a legal structure that privileges private ordering. Such preferences focus, therefore, on the law of contracts: 'The law of contracts, just because it is rooted in promise and so in right and wrong, is a ramifying system of moral judgments working out the entailments of ... principles that determine the terms on which free men and women may stand apart from or combine with each other. These are indeed the laws of freedom.'[68] In this depiction, contracts, refereed by the courts and enforced by them with minimum legislative and regulatory tampering, constitute the least intrusive and the best ordered regime of law. Mutual obligations of individuals coming from self-imposed commitments will reflect convergence of interest in their contracts. In this view, any public inter-est – resource allocation, economic growth, or income distribution – is realized as an incident of numerous, self-regarding decisions to con-tract for trade or exchange.

Yet even some of those attracted to an ambitious application of eco-nomic analysis to a wide range of issues seriously doubt that the law of contract (focused as it is on self-regarding individualism) should always be the model for law. Such reservations suggest that claims that autonomy will produce the greater good as a by-product are over-drawn by proponents of the private-ordering paradigm.[69] At the same time, communitarian values raise important issues about 'whether the individualistic orientation of both neo-classical economics and classi-cal liberalism can be reconciled with the essentially social nature of people.'[70]

As a result, it is argued that there is a role for regulation in a range of areas to give expression to such common aspirations. For instance, programs designed to enhance human development are investments with significant public-goods aspects. The benefits of such initiatives would be inadequately realized if left to private interests and would, in turn, be claimed at an insufficient level because of inequalities among the people such programs are meant to assist.[71] In short, the functioning of the regulatory state is to be rigorously evaluated, but its underlying purpose and the role for law is not to be abandoned. Rather, law and the regulatory state are to be used in a more discriminating way that engages market forces for constructive ends: 'Achievement of social justice is a higher value than the protection of free markets ... Whether free markets promote social justice is an impossible question to answer in the abstract. Far more progress can be made by examining the contexts in which markets, adjustments of markets, and alternatives to markets are proposed as solutions.'[72]

The third variation of 'law acting in concert with social and political forces' focuses on the essentials of how self-regulation can augment the effectiveness of law. The popular image is of governments in a process of deregulation, that is, a pruning or even the elimination of governmental presence in many areas of the economy. In fact, we are in a state of regulatory flux, 'an era when dramatic regulatory, deregulatory, and re-regulatory shifts are occurring simultaneously.'[73]

One answer to the regulatory quagmire is 'responsive regulation.'[74] We have already looked at this approach in chapter 2 in conjunction with the discussion of compliance. The underpinning of this solution is to have government regulation encourage and focus on the effectiveness of private regulation. Government would delegate more of its powers to associations to create and enforce standards. Nevertheless, there would be recognition that delegation may not always be appropriate. Further, the particular form of appropriate delegation must be shaped by the industry structure and how the market is failing. Effectiveness would depend on a combination of market forces, norms of the associations, involvement of and monitoring by citizen groups, such as consumers' associations, and the threat of and actual intervention by government. In this depiction, regulators will be most successful if they appear willing to escalate intervention up the pyramid or to deregulate down the pyramid in response to an industry's performance in achieving regulatory objectives. There is even hope that such an approach will encourage 'corporate virtue,' resulting in more effective and less intrusive and costly intervention by government.

Moreover, the state can and should have a vital role in constituting associational orders, including a policy empowering citizen groups in regulatory deliberations.[75] Public-interest groups can be powerful. They can invest significant resources to affect behaviour, for instance, stopping drunken driving, saving the dolphins from drift nets, and so forth. Because informed public-interest groups can magnify competitive forces by demanding higher standards of quality and behaviour unregulated firms will be forced to comply.

There has been little empirical investigation of self-regulation.[76] However, what exists suggests that there are, indeed, competing sets of advantages and disadvantages for both regulation by government and for self-regulation.[77] For example, generally, self-regulation tends to be too lax and governmental regulation too strict in standard setting. Nonetheless, this is not always the case. In some areas, such as aviation safety, self-regulation has set stricter standards. Further, the private sector usually intervenes earlier trying to anticipate problems and forging responses to them. The importance of context – the kind of regulation, the manner of enforcement, the size of the corporation, the amount of flexibility employed by the regulator, and so forth – appears to loom large.

The second idea about the impact of law has implications for activists. Not surprisingly, the contention that law is effective when it is aligned with societal forces is unattractive to those, across the spectrum, seeking to use law to achieve change. Whether with regard to curbing smoking, suppressing pornography, or fighting discrimination – to give three varied examples pursued in part 3 – this idea holds that creating social and political consensus must essentially precede any relevant laws – a tall order to be sure. In this depiction, law can cement and enforce social norms; it rarely can create them.

Instead, what is required is 'more effective action by other social forces and institutions, directed toward assuring a stable and coherent social order in which there is a sense of shared values and purposes, agreement on the priority to be assigned to various social goals and needs, accepted standards of behaviour, and an acknowledgment by all of the duties that go with the rights that are claimed.'[78] Not a welcome prescription for activists – of any political stripe.

3. Law (Re)Constituting Social and Political Relationships

This third idea, like the second one, acknowledges the close link between law and social/political forces and institutions. Its advocates, however, often interested in progressive reform, make quite a contrary claim to that of the second: law can be used in important ways to constitute and reconstitute such social and political arrangements.

This hypothesis has two important sources. The first was a reaction against Marxist conceptions of law (discussed in the previous subsection as the first variant on the idea that law is effective when it acts in concert with societal forces). In particular, there was a strong reaction to the claims of Marxists regarding determinism. Central to the assertion of determinism was that, while capitalism relegated the people to systematic inequality, it did so with very little direct coercion. Instead, it achieved its ends through a web of social relations, with law an important ingredient. Therefore, law could be accounted for as a direct product of and vehicle for the interests of the dominant class.

Such a simple account of law's working in society was bound to be revisited, even by those otherwise influenced by Marx. Law's effect on society, as difficult and controversial as it is to determine, could simply not be accounted for by characterizing it as always in the service of the powerful. The twentieth, and even the nineteenth, century provided too many contrary examples where law intervened specifically to alleviate the misery of those with little economic or political power.

A sympathetic critic, assessing critique of the law by the left, indicates a broad recognition of the inadequacies of determinism, which lie 'in positing both a necessary and direct connection between class interests on the one hand and either the content of legal rules or the outcome of the legal process.'[79] Thus, any number of those on the left have sought to – somehow – use law to effect the change they seek while at the same time not being – in their rendering – ensnared by it in a way that controls their larger project of change.

The second source of this reconstitutive idea about the influence of law is a reaction to the extravagant hopes of instrumentalism (discussed above) held by some progressives. That reaction was sparked by instrumentalism's confidence and univocalism in its capacity to effect change. Instrumental claims, for example, to solve problems of poverty and dependency by creating new substantive entitlements and extending due process have backfired, 'stifling professional service ideals and miring well-intended programs in bureaucratic formalism, rigidity and insensitivity.'[80]

While reactive to the claims of instrumentalism, this third, reconstitutive approach, nevertheless means to take law very seriously. This view of the reconstitutive possibilities of law has been strongly influenced by postmodernism and its emphasis on diversity and contradiction. Such contentions view law not as a set of determinate commands or even as structured but contradictory sets of rules. Rather, law becomes a series of fragments invoked through a wide range of processes and practices.

It is these 'fragments of law' that both constrain change and offer it as a possibility. Various interpretations regarding these fragments – along with the opportunities for 'transformation' they provide – become the focus of attention.[81] Such ideas about 'law as fragments' have a strong appeal for postmodernists. While postmodernism can mean many things, it is characterized, in matters of law and politics, as being highly suspicious of liberalism's appeal to universality, on the one hand, and of Marxist accounts of society in terms of class and economic differences, on the other. Instead, postmodernists insist on the critical importance of multiple perspectives and experiences in interpreting the world: from vantage points of gender, race, sexual identity, class, religion, age, and so forth.

Sometimes the constitutive approach to law focuses on how such diverse perspectives are shaped by law – how law matters for the 'legal consciousness' of individuals in their day-to-day lives. Engel suggests three lessons that can be derived from such research:

1 Different substantive areas of law are associated with different perceptions, understandings, and behaviours and must therefore be distinguished in research on legal consciousness.
2 Law in society is multi-centred and assumes many different shapes. It is not necessarily an instrument of state power, and its connection with the state is a problem to be studied rather than a fact to be assumed.
3 In some instances, official law directly touches and influences the lives of individuals, but more often law is mediated through social fields that filter its effects and merge official and unofficial systems of rules and meanings.[82]

These lessons cover a lot of territory. At the same time, this 'law as fragments' reaction is, in some ways, strikingly modest. Its watchwords are 'partial, tentative, and limited.'[83] Its own advocates also acknowledge that it runs the risk of being branded 'muddled-headed,'[84] 'hesitant and confused.'[85] Even what is to count as law is unspecified.[86] If law is something in addition to statutes, judgments of courts, and decisions of regulatory agencies, where is the line drawn between law and other societal forces?: '[O]nce we expand our understanding of law from determinant rules to indeterminate knowledges and conventions, and once we range beyond study of official legal institutions (courts and the like) and actors (judges) as sites of legal practice, how do we specify what counts as legal?'[87] The limited, qualified, and unspecified elements of the account provide only a tentative explanation of the effects of law. Still, as we shall see momentarily, its proponents view such lack of certitude less as a weakness and more as a strength.

One example of '[l]aw guarantees nothing ... [b]ut ... nothing is impossible,' just described, focuses on the need for more flexible service systems for the disempowered.[88] Altruistic professional norms must be revitalized and a role for practical discretion must be affirmed. At the heart of such transformation is dialogue: 'both solution and method; both symbol and substance.'[89] Dialogue will engender genuine community by taking human-service agencies beyond adversarial entrenchment, professional paternalism, and cynicism. Dialogue can move citizens and agencies to a place where values and policies are negotiated with trust and respect.

Another variant of 'law does not guarantee but it does create possibilities' has been advanced in the context of campaigns for pay equity based on gender. McCann proffers a model of legal mobilization in his study of these campaigns in the United States.[90] One of the complicating factors of legal mobilization as a theory is that it is focused very heavily on litigation as law, though nowhere does McCann expressly so limit it. That there might be important differences between litigation and other forms of law is an issue that we will turn to, below, in our discussion of the sixth idea about the impact of law. At the same time, legal mobilization provides a full and recent attempt to present law's (re)constitutive effects.

Legal mobilization does not refute the thrust of critics who emphasize the conservative character of institutionalized legal practices in most official state forums. The theory assumes that law is the primary medium of social control and domination. Authoritative legal forms and relational logics are, by definition, products of long-evolving historical struggles in which some interests, groups, norms, and arrangements have tended to prevail in relatively systematic fashion. Specifically, an analysis of pay equity emphasizes ways in which legally defined wage-setting practices have contributed to the maintenance of gender and class hierarchies.

Yet 'system-wide patterns of hegemonic order are always maintained by a complex, volatile process of multiple site-specific accommodations between domination and resistance.'[91] (Those adhering to the (re)constitutive-capacity-of-law approach have a tendency to talk in mouthfuls.) As a result, a decentred view of law is advanced. That depiction holds that law is pluralistic and relatively independent of the state while having a role in sustaining traditional hierarchies. Potential strategies of resistance vary significantly among different terrains of social struggle. Hence, legal mobilization focuses upon tactical options concerning particular sites, terms, and timing of struggle.

Some legal-mobilization theorists adopt a view that has considerable overlap with instrumentalism and its faith in the power of law to directly alter societal conditions. 'Direct' effects of formal legal action must determine a movement's strategy and impact. In this view, legal action is employed primarily to win short-term remedial relief for victims of injustice or to develop case-law precedents capable of producing long-term institutional change. However, other approaches examine the indirect effects and secondary tactical uses of official legal action. It is claimed that these indirect effects can build a movement, generate public support for new rights claims, and provide leverage to supplement other political tactics. Indeed, given the copious evidence that judicial victories produce uneven or negligible impacts on targeted social practices, such indirect effects and uses of litigation may be the most important of all for political struggles by social movements.

The foregoing is the basis for a further point. Legal mobilization is one among many constitutive dimensions of most social movements. The focus on indirect effects of formal legal action suggests a limited and often secondary role in a larger multidimensional political campaign.[92] Thus, legal-mobilization factors should identify those contextual variables most and least favourable to a movement's success.

This emphasis on the contingent nature of legal mobilization suggests a utility in disaggregating social movements into distinct stages, which are helpful in examining how legal mobilization may contribute in different ways and with varying impacts at different points in 'ongoing struggles.' McCann suggests that there are four such stages:

- *movement-building process* of raising citizen expectation for political change, activating potential constituents, building group alliances, and organizing resources for tactical action;
- *struggle to compel formal changes in official policy* addressing movement demands, at least in principle;

- *struggle for control over actual reform-policy development and implementation* that evolves among interested parties;
- *transformative legacy of legal action* for subsequent movement development, articulation of new rights claims, and alliance with other groups, policy-reform advocates, and social struggle generally.

As with theory, so with methodology. The tenets that guide McCann's study of his legal mobilization in the context of pay equity complement the essentials of the theory.[93] Thus, he is sceptical regarding the traditional scientific goals of defining clear causal relations and developing a strong predictive capacity. This is because every historical movement is subject to multiple contingencies that no theory can predict with any degree of accuracy. (In chapter 3 this 'interpretivist' approach, with its emphasis on multiple contingencies / heterogeneous experience, was contrasted to 'positivism,' with its emphasis on the traditional scientific method in determining the effect of law).[94]

The interpretivist rendering holds that social action is generated out of ever-changing processes of human conceptualization. Thus, even if the contextual complexity could be fully accounted for by social scientists (which it cannot), future subjects will act from their own understanding of their different situation; that is, human interaction is heterogeneously experienced and indeterminate in character. Finally, legal mobilization presumes no transcendent or impartial perspective for the analyst to assume while researching law in action. Thus, there is an edginess regarding even talking about the 'impact of law,' since so much of this approach emphasizes the inextricable relationship between law and social forces – a relationship that cannot be easily separated for the purposes of investigation and analysis.

Not surprisingly, this (re)constitutive/interpretive perspective on law's influence has been taken to task. A specific critique, by a 'positivist,' of McCann's study of pay equity is instructive in this regard.[95] Positivists lay great store in constructing and testing models that will permit statements about cause and effect to be made. In such an approach questions of case selection, representative samples, and controls for alternative explanations are crucial.[96] In the particular subject matter being examined – pay equity – positivists would think it crucial to ask and answer such questions as '[H]ow important was the law in the various phases of the pay equity movement? What factors made law more or less influential?'[97]

The thrust of this critique is that the strengths of this third, reconstitutive idea about the influence of law (and studies in aid of it) are also its weaknesses. In particular, the criticism insists that the emphasis on context has severe limitations regarding any ability to draw conclusions about cause and effect; in this case, the outcomes regarding attempts to achieve pay equity. For example, one of the main problems is that, in this instance, only cases where pay-equity campaigns were waged were examined. As a result, all that the study was able to describe was the role of law and courts where such campaigns occurred. What is more, no reliable statements can be made about what caused the movements: law, courts, and the assertion of rights may not have played any appreciable role.[98]

The critique acknowledges that McCann (and the interpretivist approach) might insist that the interest is not in explaining what caused pay-equity struggles but, rather, in understanding the many and contingent ways in which law shapes and interacts with other factors in such campaigns. However, 'positivist methodology maintains that McCann can't answer his question because he can't separate the effects of law from the effects of other variables.'[99] In any event, it is contended that McCann goes on to make several statements about cause and effect: for example, 'litigation is most successful when it works as an unfulfilled threat'[100] and 'equity activists derived substantial power from legal tactics despite only limited judicial support.'[101]

This positivist critique insists that such statements are unpersuasive because of particularism and lack of controls. 'Particularism' means that because of the non-representative nature of the sample, any claims are confined to the cases examined and there can be no generalization. Lack of controls gives rise to even more drastic limitations: because the study cannot separate out the effects of law from those of other factors, even in the particular cases, there can be no generalizations regarding the impact of law.[102]

Still, (re)constitutive possibilities have become a powerful way of looking at the effects of law. In diverse societies viewed from multiple perspectives this idea reflects the many paradoxes, contingencies – and the drift – that face societies as the new millennium dawns. The viewpoint of (re)constitutive possibilities is a compelling account of protest movements and their use (or non-use) of courts and litigation. Thus, its attraction to many American progressives, fixed on litigation as the vehicle of change, is no surprise.

We will see particular applications of this reconstitutive view of the influence of law when we look at the case studies in part 3, especially as relating to pornography. In other areas examined in part 3, where litigation has played a small role or an unsuccessful one, the reconstitutive possibilities of law are largely irrelevant – or have been stood on their heads.

4. The Ineffectiveness of Law

We said earlier that political progressives are by no means united in saluting the power of law to transform the plight of individuals and groups. The doubters see law not as a vehicle for change but as a deflection of forces that could effect reform. Conservatives (apart from a general wariness of regulating as a substitute for the market) also have their own brand of scepticism regarding law's ability to respond to social issues. There is, as well, scepticism concerning the effectiveness of law that focuses on the capacity of litigation and the courts regarding social change (discussed separately, below, as idea 6).

A large part of the doubting on the left regarding law is attributable to Marx and his claim of determinism; that is, that law is simply a vehicle for the dominant class and is dictated by their interests. In reaction to what increasingly came to be regarded as a simplistic account of the relationship of law to societal conditions, some scholars on the left turned to the concept of 'relative autonomy.' This idea asserts that law is relatively independent of the interests of the dominant classes but, at the same time, is shaped by social forces strongly influenced by the privileged. But what, precisely, does 'relative' mean in this context? A sympathetic critic suggest that this concept's label signals its deficiencies: 'unless [relative autonomy] is capable of being linked to some account that specifies the boundaries or limitation of autonomy it [rests on] the assertion of either autonomy or determinism coupled with an expression of faith that on the one hand autonomy has determined limitations or, on the other, that determination is tempered or postponed.'[103] Such fiddling with airy concepts has led to the suggestion that some on the left simply do not take law seriously.[104]

In some respects, one strand of the left would virtually do just that. It dismisses law, warning that, if anything, it deflects real change.[105] There are several examples of such judgments about the effects of law ('social problems are largely unresponsive to regulation by the legal system'),[106] including the workings of the administrative state.[107] We will pursue claims about the ineffectiveness of law and its capacity to blunt forces that could achieve progressive change when we examine the impact of law on the environment[108] and pornography[109] later in the book.

However, to illustrate these ideas more generally, here we will look at the work of a group of feminist scholars and their scepticism about law's capacity to better the lot of women, particularly disadvantaged women. In this regard the work of Carol Smart is of particular note.[110] She asserts that the feminist movement has been all too ready to invoke law to achieve its goals. This attempt to harness law often occurs when feminists are deeply critical of a law. The solution is then deemed to be a new, better law.

But for Smart, law's language, methods, and procedures are fundamentally anti-feminist. In engaging with law to produce law reforms the women's movement is tacitly accepting the significance of law in regulating the social order. As a result, the idea that law is a means – perhaps *the* means – to resolve social problems gains strength. At the same time, the idea that lawyers are the technocrats of unfolding betterment becomes taken for granted. While it is possible that some law reform may benefit women, 'it is certain that all law reforms empower law.'[111] Conversely, it is important to insist on 'feminism's ability to redefine the wrongs of women which law too often confines to insignificance.'[112]

Smart draws parallels between law reform and the iatrogenic potential of medicine.[113] Medicine sometimes creates illness and disease in the process of attempting to cure a particular malady. Similarly, in turning to law we may produce effects that make conditions worse and, in worsening conditions, we can make the mistake of assuming that we need to apply more doses of legislation.[114] Smart's position echoes many of the points made in our discussion of 'unintended consequences' in the previous chapter. Her conclusions, however, lead her to a general scepticism about any positive effects of law.

Smart illustrates iatrogenic aspects of law by discussing a number of issues, including sexual abuse. She maintains that it is well established that the legal process itself creates its own harms. For example, in her estimation, the criminal law does not provide a remedy for sexual abuse. Yet it is still assumed by many, including advocates on behalf of victims, that the solution is *to encourage* more women and children *into* the legal system.[115]

At the same time, efforts to apply criminal sanctions against the abuser hurt victims, particularly children. Often the criminal proceedings against the perpetrator are not successful. Even if they are, the process itself further traumatizes children. In Smart's account, the real problem is masculine sexuality and its aggressive nature; hence there is a need to treat the causes of sexual abuse, not the aftermath. Yet, whatever solutions are necessary to respond to the social regulation that produces aggressive male sexuality, the answers, likely lie beyond law: '[H]ow [have] we arrived in a situation where child sexual abuse is publicly deplored while the criminal law seems designed to make it almost impossible to prosecute, or at least seems to ensure that the child is damaged in the process.'[116]

Many of the assertions of Smart may seem utopian, especially the idea that serious human problems can be resolved without the leadership, or at least the backing, of law. Yet, when we discuss the environment and pornography, in part 3, we will see that some progressives are extremely suspicious of a turn to law. This retreat from law, has, itself a set of consequences – some of which are by no means intended by those wary of legal intervention.

The right is often suspicious of law to the extent it can be characterized as interfering with the market. Conversely, many on the right are supportive of legal intervention if the regulated act involves morality or issues of public safety so characterized: intimate personal relations, the rearing of children, substance abuse, pornography, and so forth. Yet another strand worries that law may corral attempts by groups and associations to develop their own norms of conduct. To some extent this view harkens back to one of the main causes of the rise of law: the ebbing of other forms of community, a matter discussed at length in chapter 1. Proponents of this strand contend that law is not only a result of this waning; it can also be a cause as it crowds out forms of community.

Such arguments take various forms,[117] but one of the most prominent is contained in the work of Ellickson.[118] His study of a group of cattle ranchers (in Shasta County, California) revealed that they more often resolve their disputes through a system of informal norms than through recourse to formal legal action. In one sense his conclusions are modest and predictable: law is not the only means of avoiding or containing conflict; rather, informal social controls are likely to supplant law in close-knit communities such as the one he studied. However, he also claims that social order itself often arises spontaneously ('it ... cannot be repeated too often').[119] When this occurs, people may supplement and even pre-empt the state's rules with rules of their own. Accordingly, 'social engineers' should take note: '[L]egal activists have been especially prone to exaggerate what the Leviathan can accomplish.'[120]

Ellickson asserts that for this spontaneity to occur people must have continuing relationships, reliable information about behaviour, and effective countervailing power to deal with the inevitable tensions that will arise. These conditions should be fostered so that norms can be constructed and implemented: '[L]awmakers who are unappreciative of the social conditions that foster informal cooperation are likely to create a world in which there is both more law and less order.'[121]

Ellickson's broader assertions were bound to draw fire for several reasons,[122] including the obvious one that he bases his conjectures on one atypical example.[123] In fairness, Ellickson has continued to apply his ideas about law and norms to other contexts (such as the impairment of the enjoyment of public spaces by the judicially created right to panhandle).[124] Another criticism is very much to the point for our purposes. While Ellickson is insightful in arguing for more coordination between law and norms, he never articulates the proper role for law in achieving such coordination. He neither explains how law, in fact, impedes development of informal norms nor does he stipulate how, when, and to what extent law ought to intervene in private ordering.[125]

Yet Ellickson's book has spawned interest in others, many of whom are linked to the University of Chicago, who believe that 'normativity' (the relationship between the workings of laws and norms) is the new frontier for the study of law's effectiveness. In turn, 'normativity' has attracted wider public notice, at least partly because it seems to respond to the widespread belief that there is too much law and too much indiscriminate use of it.[126] Many of the themes being explored by normativists echo concerns expressed under the second variant of 'Law Acting in Concert with Social and Political Forces' (idea 2): institutions can serve as mediators between law and society; thus law must take care not to imperil their effectiveness. However, normativists emphasize the direct examination of norms and their functioning. They suggest that such study has essentially been ignored by students of the law, with norms treated as an uninteresting given.[127]

Those working on 'normativity' vary in many respects; their views tend to span a broad range on the political spectrum. What is common among 'normativists' is a scepticism about the capacity of law to alter behaviour directly and, more importantly, an emphasis on the vital role of norms in controlling conduct. Thus, there is a belief that policy goals will more likely be achieved if norms, existing or altered, support those ambitions. In this depiction law becomes subsumed. It becomes merely a means, albeit an extremely important one, to assist in the creating or changing of norms. What is more, normativists caution that the consequences of law are not always benign: misapplied, it can obstruct or even destroy norms that are critical in achieving policy objectives.

One strand of normativity is attempting to articulate more generalized statements (than those of Ellickson's) concerning norms and their relation to law. An aspect of this attempt examines the relation of law and norms in a variety of contexts from smoking rates among black teenagers[128] to rates of crime in inner cities.[129] A second strand is trying to link norms to the social meaning of law and, in turn, law's effectiveness. One author insists that the critical reason the public is not interested in major experiments with alternatives to imprisonment is the social meaning of prison as an unambiguous denunciation of crime. He, therefore, claims that there should be a search for other alternatives that exhibit such denunciation. This leads him to make a persuasive case for 'shaming.' At the same time, he demonstrates the critical role of norms in the selection of effective – and publicly acceptable – punishments.[130]

A third strand is struggling to demonstrate how norms and their careful altering can improve compliance with the law while achieving underlying policy goals.[131] Here there is talk of 'norm cascades' in which society can shift very rapidly in terms of its beliefs in appropriate conduct and regarding the actual conduct itself: rates of smoking constitute a prominent example in this regard.[132] (Smoking is examined in detail in part 3.) Those taken with the idea of 'norm cascades' believe that government should, in some instances, seed pilot programs – 'norm perturbation' – so that the possibility of desirable conduct can be fostered while guarding against the costs of experiments gone wrong.[133] A fourth strand is more focused on law's influence on the norms of groups.[134] For example, there is concern that law may actually impede, in some instances, the capacity for self-regulation of organizations.[135]

Needless to say, such ideas have elicited strong reactions, including within the ranks of normativists themselves. Government using norms to alter behaviour looks like the wolf in sheep's clothing to some eyes: big government and its appetite for regulation will have just put on a different garb as it pursues its impulses to manipulate individuals' preferences.[136] Others worry that sanctions like shaming will have a perverse effect: unleashing the appetite of people to hound and, thus, reducing even further the possibility of those convicted turning their lives around.[137]

A further worry goes to the vitality of norms themselves and their being called upon to rescue the haplessness of law. It was asserted in chapter 1 that there has been a breakdown of norms and the institutions that foster them. To the extent that this is true, the ambitions of the 'normativists' may rest on a weak foundation. What is more, for law to attempt to rekindle norms may be yet another manifestation of its arrogance. Thus there may be bitter irony here. Society has been flooded with law that has crowded out other institutions and their ability to create and buttress norms. Yet, that harm done, some now have the effrontery to suggest that norms – victims of law's aggression – can be turned to for a solution for legal ineffectiveness.

Still, the role that norms may play in achieving policy goals does raise critical issues. There is surely an important link between norms and law. The problem is determining what it is and how that connection relates to law's (in)effectiveness. The interplay between law and norms is a subject to which we will return in part 3, particularly when we discuss smoking, the environment, and discrimination.

5. National Styles of Regulation – 'American Exceptionalism' I

This idea claims that there are different ways in which societies use law and implement it.[138] Thus, whatever the explanatory power of ideas 1 to 4, they, in turn, are, in significant ways, dependent on national differences. At the same time, the precise nature of the differences and the extent to which they are responsible for the varied impact of similar laws are issues requiring careful analysis.[139]

The importance of exploring differences in the way societies use law is often raised as an important general line of inquiry. Yet in various studies examining such differences one country looms large: the United States.[140] The following is a sampling of areas in which national styles of regulation have been advanced as a possible explanation of differing outcomes produced by law: occupational health and safety – the United States and Sweden;[141] environmental regulation – the United States and Great Britain;[142] gun control – the United States and Canada;[143] and regulation of industry through negotiation versus litigation – the United States and Great Britain[144] and various studies regarding the United States and Japan.[145]

There are many reasons why America should feature so prominently. Its size, its wealth, and its great universities and research institutions (sponsoring all manner of study) position it to be the subject of an array of projects in a host of areas. More particularly, the United States is the home of the Law and Society Association, a group of scholars from several disciplines that focuses on a wide variety of theoretical and empirical issues regarding the use and effects of law. It is not surprising then that the United States' employment of law would often be the starting place in comparative inquiries. But beyond these important factors is the very centrality that law plays in that society – 'American Exceptionalism.'[146]

Lipset comes to the point: 'This country is an outlier. It is the most religious, optimistic, patriotic, rights-oriented, and individualistic.'[147] He points to the following factors as some of those setting the country apart: it is the wealthiest in real income; the most productive in worker output; the first in proportion of people who graduate from or enrol in higher education; the leader in upward mobility into professional and other high-status occupations; the least egalitarian among developed nations with respect to income distribution; at the bottom regarding welfare benefits; the lowest in savings; and the least taxed.[148]

More specifically, in terms of our inquiry, the United States is 'a society profoundly rooted in law.'[149] To illustrate that proposition he lists the following: regarding crime, the highest rates; with respect to jails, the most persons incarcerated; in terms of litigiousness, the most lawyers per capita and very high rates of tort[150] and other lawsuits[151] and the stupendous damages that are sometimes awarded.

To further depict America as an outlier respecting both law and society ('Is this excessive litigiousness indicative of our inability to deliberate and form amicable agreements among ourselves?'[152]) Lipset compares the United States with Japan. Japan and the significance of law in that society and in the USA has been the subject of several other studies.[153] These investigations, including Lipset's, reach similar conclusions regarding the role of law in Japan – and the contrast with the United States: 'Japan represents the extreme version of a legal culture where law remains to a large degree peripheral; that is the consequence of many explicit public choices. In Japan relationships are tied more closely to ideas of community and various types of everyday interdependence than to formal, legally established relationships.'[154]

It has recently been argued that, in terms of substantive rules, there may be more similarities between Japanese and American law than has been contended.[155] Nevertheless, the way law is used and the influences it has in the two societies do seem to underscore important distinctions. For Lipset the starting point is the differences in the two societies. Arising out of revolution the USA lacked established mechanisms of social control and respect for authority that have been the hallmark of Japanese society. As a result, the serious crime rate in the former is over four times the total crime rate in the latter:[156] 'Japan and the United States occupy the opposite poles in the distribution of violent and property crimes among major capitalist countries.'[157] In terms of commercial dealings, agreements are spelled out in much less detail in Japan, guided by the assumption that if conditions change the agreement will be modified appropriately. If conflict does arise, mediation is the preferred outcome. In short: 'In no other industrial society is legal regulation as extensive or coercive as in the United States or as confined and as weak as in Japan.'[158]

More generally, in terms of America and its use of law, several studies in a wide range of areas all point in the same direction: the United States' form of regulation is highly legalistic, contentious, and costly compared with that of any other society which has been the subject of study. This proposition can be illustrated by focusing on an examination, by Vogel, of environmental regulation in Great Britain and the United States during the 1970s and 1980s.[159]

Comparing the effects of environmental-protection laws is not easy. In this case, for example, the priorities in the two countries were different. The United States concentrated more on curbing motor-vehicle emissions, while Great Britain focused more on preserving green belts. Nevertheless, 'both nations made measurable though uneven progress in reducing pollution levels, safeguarding public health, and preserving amenity values.'[160] Moreover, there is no clear evidence that 'either nation's environmental policies have been significantly more or less effective than the other's.'[161]

However, Vogel's examination of a large number of case studies revealed that the nations clearly differed in the way in which environmental regulation was implemented. The United States displayed a far more legalistic and adversarial 'regulatory style,' including the form of laws, the ways in which they were made and enforced, and the level of contentiousness that pervaded policy making and implementation. Vogel's study focused on environmental regulation. Yet he indicates that this American 'style' appears in cross-national studies in other spheres: occupational safety, worker exposure to vinyl chloride fumes, carcinogenic chemical products, pre-marketing testing of pharmaceuticals, and the regulation of sales and banking.[162]

At first blush the United States may have seemed more ambitious in terms of the environmental regulation studied by Vogel. Yet it faltered in enforcing detailed standards. In contrast, Great Britain may have done as well because demands that were made were moderate, consensually developed, and better tailored to particular conditions and, therefore, perceived as reasonable. In any event, the study concludes that '[t]he American system of regulation is distinctive in the degree of oversight exercised by the judiciary and the national legislature, in the formality of its rulemaking and enforcement process, in its reliance on prosecution, in the amount of information made available to the public, and in the extent of the opportunities provided for participation by nonindustry constituencies.'[163] Simultaneously, 'in no other nation have the relations between the regulated and the regulators been so consistently ... strained'[164] 'or resulted in so much open legal and political contestation.'[165]

Similarly, in a comparative study of the United States and Sweden regarding occupational safety, inspectors were asked questions about the trustworthiness of business. They were asked to place themselves along a scale, one end of which was characterized by the statement 'Without the penalty-imposing powers we have, many employers would simply ignore the standards.' Of the Swedish inspectors, only 15 per cent placed themselves at that end of the scale, whereas 56 per cent of the American inspectors did so.[166]

Why there is such a difference between the United States and other countries is a critical question. Vogel emphasizes the culture of the business community in the USA and Britain and the resulting pattern of public attitudes toward business and government–business relations. Britain has had a highly respected civil service, a business community prepared to cooperate with government officials, and public acceptance of large corporations. Indeed, more generally, it has been observed that relations between business and governments in western Europe and Japan are not as likely to be characterized by the mutual mistrust and public hostility that is the hallmark of such interactions in America.[167] Instead, the United States is a 'business civilization': a society where successful business people are seen as the most important elite, and where government intervention in the economy is widely regarded as suspect.[168]

Yet whether 'the culture of the business community' holds the key to explaining the differences is debatable. For instance, it has been pointed out that American legal methods are often uniquely legalistic and adversarial in policy areas far removed from the regulation of big business. At the same time, it is not true that all regulation in the United States is more adversarial and legalistic. Moreover, in some areas that country does not have as much law as other nations: the Dutch regulate land-use planning more intensively; the Swedes have stricter control regarding dismissal of employees; Canadians have appreciably tighter gun control; and many countries more intensely regulate prices, entry into business, and so forth, while the United States leaves such issues largely to contract.[169] In areas of social welfare such as social assistance for the unemployed, health care, and education, many other societies have elaborate schemes implemented by law; by comparison, the efforts of America regarding most of these issues are meagre.

An alternative explanation points to the fragmented, pluralistic, and permeable political structure of the United States. Such a structure creates possibilities and inducements for legalistically formulated and administered policies. At the same time, a particular legal culture encourages activists to view law as a manipulable political instrument, and to value strongly worded rights and protections. Yet because the political structure is permeable, it is also open to those who believe that the public interest would be served by less rigidly defined rights, by reduced adversarial contestation, and by more moderate penalties. Thus, any number of views can assert their interests regarding how, when, and where regulation will occur. What is more, the structure of litigation, with provisions such as those for class actions and for attractive cost arrangements (such as contingency fees), acts as an inducement for an array of issues to be litigated.[170]

Finally, it has been contended that those in charge of regulation in western Europe and Japan seem more sensitive to the economic outcomes compared to their counterparts in America. Such solicitude has been manifested not only on the part of conservative governments but also in countries that have had periods of social-democratic rule. For instance, such attitudes were apparent for many years regarding consumer-protection policies in Europe: many regulations were motivated more by a need to improve the internal competitiveness of that country's products than by a desire to protect consumers.[171]

Whatever the explanation, there does seem to be general agreement that the United States turns to law more often than not in a way that sets it apart: detailed legal rules, deterrence-oriented enforcement practices, intensely adversarial procedures, and frequent judicial review and reversal of administrative policies and legislative enactments. As a result, 'the United States ends up with a uniquely costly and politically contentious legal process.'[172]

There is yet a further area where America's use of law sets it apart: criminal sanctions. We discussed in chapter 2 how anxieties about lethal violence over the last two decades have contributed to the administration of criminal justice taking a very punitive turn. Prison rates have soared both absolutely and comparatively. The United States has by far the highest rates of imprisonment in the world, save for Russia. To cite but one comparison, the rate of imprisonment in America is six times greater than that in Canada and in England. Crime, including that involving violence, has fallen, but the clamour to put more people away continues as the building and running of jails has taken on a life of its own. Over this thirst for punishment looms the ultimate sanction: the death penalty. The United States, alone among Western industrialized nations, continues to impose capital punishment. The pace of executions has intensified and more states are imposing the death penalty.

The implications of this uniqueness are surely complex. In terms of crime, the thrall of punishment and deterrence means that there is very little interest in proactive measures, particularly social programs, to help individuals avoid wrongdoing in the first place. Such indifference to prevention through proactive programs also sets the United States apart from many other societies.

Yet, in other areas America's costly and contentious legal process may, in fact, bestow benefits on other societies – 'US Imperialism' with a benign aspect. Most products and processes that could carry risks are, nonetheless, traded freely across borders. The open, sharp battles (often waged with awesome resources) over such products and processes provide cost-free information to the rest of the world: other countries acquire the knowledge with no (or much less) conflict. For example, it may be that small nations such as the Nordic countries and Australia have better systems of drug regulation because they can take advantage of the American system: 'If what America is exporting is the clash of earnestly held alternative ideas about how modern industrial processes might be designed more safely, then maybe U.S. imperialism is not such a bad thing.'[173]

But in terms of implications, the aspect of America's legal system that surely sets it apart is the prominence of rights determined by courts. Litigation is an engine that drives the judiciary to a central place in that society in terms of policy formation and implementation.

In the United States, law delivers trophies in complex political and litigious disputes: '[I]n its simple American form, the language of rights is the language of no compromise. The winner takes all and the loser has to get out of town. The conversation is over.'[174] Meanwhile this emphasis on rights and the courts has been accompanied by disarray in the political process, especially in terms of formulating domestic policy. Other societies of a similar tradition are more inclined to recognize most legal rights – and impose most obligations – when there is agreement about them reached, with whatever difficulty, through the political process. Kagan, referring to America's 'adversarial legalism,' sums up the fears regarding policy making and its implementation: 'Legislatures and courts mandate new goals, new benefits, and new regulatory protections. Yet implementing agencies are constrained by formal legal requirements, buffeted by threats of litigation and judicial review. In this harried condition government seems doomed to fail.'[175]

We will look at 'American Exceptionalism' and its implications in a number of places in part 3. More immediately, we need to take a closer look at this prominence of courts and of rights. Specifically, we now turn to examine the dominance of litigation in the United States in terms of the consequences that ensue from it, especially in terms of social change.

6. The Impact of Litigation Regarding Social Change –
'American Exceptionalism' II

The United States as Outlier

A number of post–Second World War societies have sought to harness litigation and the courts to effect social and political change.[176] These attempts have been most conspicuous in American society. The power of courts is especially prominent regarding judges' capacity, because of an entrenched bill of rights, to strike down the laws of elected officials and to nullify regulatory decisions: '[T]he United States is the outlier in the extraordinary power that its ... courts exercise in reviewing the constitutionality of legislation.'[177] Using litigation to effect change has had its adherents across the political spectrum. However, progressive reformers (in America, 'liberals') have placed the highest faith in the courts' willingness and ability to do their bidding.[178]

The list of issues that have been placed before courts in the United States in the last decades seems endless. A mere sampling would include school desegregation, voting rights, the constitutionality of the death penalty, abortion, euthanasia, anti-trust regulation, innumerable aspects of product liability, the effects of smoking, protection of the environment, questions regarding civil rights and affirmative action, and the constitutionality of rape-shield legislation.

An initial reaction to this description of heightened judicial activity in the United States (and elsewhere) might be to ask why litigation is receiving separate treatment in a book on the impact of law. Discussing the impact of law is problematic on any number of fronts – a point woven through the book. What is so special about litigation and its outcomes as to justify separate consideration?

There is talk of dialogue between politics and courts. Yet a predictable result of an enhanced role for courts, especially for those who are sceptical about it, is that the more judicial power increases the more political power wanes. These trade-offs are most marked in societies, such as the United States and Canada, where entrenched bills of rights equip courts to nullify legislation that has been enacted by elected officials.

Politicians, no matter how wrong-headed, can point to the power of the ballot as the source of legitimacy of their actions: the force they wield rests on the base of the democratic process. Life, for courts, is more complicated. Since the power they exercise can, by definition, be anti-majoritarian, proponents of an ambitious judicial role have to offer a rationale that does not depend on popular will or authority. When all is said and done, advocates of courts usually assert some form of betterment for society – however judged – as the premium achieved against the loss to democracy that judicial powers brings.

Conservatives tend to hold fast to a core of essential freedoms that, it is claimed, courts will protect from marauding governments. However, political progressives are called upon to vigorously justify the judicial enterprise, since so many of them, over the last decades, have put such store by courts and the desirability of their intervention in a range of issues. As a result, progressives tend to justify the dilution of political power by asserting that litigation, and the acknowledgment of rights, will effect reform. The marginalized will be empowered in ways that the political process of an unresponsive majority has blocked. But how effective have the courts, in fact, been in bringing about social change and what evidence exists to answer this question? Gauging the impact of litigation becomes critical in debates about the desirability – the legitimacy – of an ambitious role for courts in developing social policy.

At the same time, a scepticism about the capacity of the courts to contour the social and political terrain and, in any event, about the wisdom of democracy permitting them to do so, has run parallel to the high hopes expressed for that institution.[179] While not exclusively so, some strong doubters have also allied themselves with progressive politics.[180] This scepticism has recently gained renewed strength in the United States.[181]

The argument is not that litigation has no effects. Individuals and organizations constantly use litigation (or threaten to) as they assert myriad claims (and defences). The outcomes produced by their doing so raise important issues, including the effects of differentials based on financial power, frequency of involvement with lawsuits, and so forth.[182] With regard to such outcomes it is not invariably the case that the American court system is more solicitous towards victims' claims.[183] However, the focus here is on the capacity of lawsuits to bring about major social change. The contention is that litigation can produce such change only under limited circumstances that are not often present, and as a result the ambitions of those turning to lawsuits are often frustrated.

Rosenberg, in his book *The Hollow Hope*, focused on the Supreme Court of the United States and its role in social change. He provides the best description of both the potential and limits of litigation to 'cause' change.[184] He makes two points. One focuses on judicial and extra-judicial paths regarding change.[185] A second describes the constrained and dynamic models of courts.

Causality moves along both judicial and extra-judicial paths. The judicial path emphasizes the direct outcome of court judgments and examines whether any change by the courts was made. For example, if a Supreme Court decision ordering an end to segregation caused such a result, lower courts should be observed requiring officials to comply, a community to respond accordingly, and segregation to actually disappear.

The extra-judicial path makes claims about change other than those brought about by the courts. These claims suggest that judgments may lead to substantial change because they cause individuals to act or to alter their views. Judgments may be powerful symbols for reform by transforming the intellectual climate. Manifestations of such impact might be seen in media coverage, public-opinion data, and public responses that support change.

There are two starkly different models presented in *The Hollow Hope* of the capacity of courts themselves to cause change: the constrained and the dynamic. The constrained model focuses on barriers that prevent courts from being effective agents of change.[186] First, it is argued, the limited nature of constitutional rights, the constraints of legal culture, and the general caution of the judiciary will make it very difficult for proponents of change to persuade courts that the (often novel) rights they are claiming are required by either the constitution or the language of a particular statute. Second, because of their deference to other government institutions and potential limitation by these institutions' actions, courts may be reluctant to move away from the mainstream of politics. Third, even if the first and second barriers are overcome, litigants still need to have judicial orders implemented. Because courts do not have tools of enforcement, their decisions can be stymied if there is strong opposition to them. In any event, the strong prescriptive claim for this model is that American society should be left to govern itself without interference from non-elected officials.

The dynamic-court model, in sharp contrast, takes as a point of pride that America's version of democracy includes 'the world's most powerful court system, protecting minorities and defending liberty, in the face of opposition from the democratically elected branches.'[187] A key claim on behalf of the dynamic court is that access and influence are not premised on political and economic leverage. Professional lobbying, with the persistence and compromise required for effective influence on bureaucracies or legislation, is not necessary for victory in litigation.[188]

From this vantage point, groups with few resources can harness litigation not only to achieve change directly but also to strengthen their presence with other branches of government, obtaining validity from the courts to assert their positions. Independent and tenured (at least in the case of federal appointments) judges are able to offer sanctuary 'from the pathologies of rigid bureaucracies, ossified institutions, and a reluctant or biased citizenry.'[189]

Combining the constrained and dynamic models, Rosenberg concludes that, theoretically, courts can be effective causes of significant change but only under certain conditions: when (1) there is ample legal precedent for change; (2) there is support for change from substantial numbers in Congress and from the executive; and (3) there is either support from some citizens or at least minimal opposition from all citizens and (a) positive incentives are offered to induce compliance, or (b) costs are imposed to induce compliance, or (c) court decisions allow for market implementation, or (d) key administrators and officials are willing to act and see court orders as a tool for leveraging additional resources (or, conversely, as a screen to hide behind).[190]

The Hollow Hope caused a firestorm for several reasons, not the least of which are the conclusions Rosenberg reached after applying his set of conditions:[191] 'U.S. courts can *almost never* be effective producers of significant social reform.'[192] Though major victories in the courts can be cited, Rosenberg concludes that almost invariably their long-range impact was minor, 'often more symbolic than real,' so that there was 'only an illusion of change.'

Rosenberg could find no evidence that court decisions mobilized supporters of significant social reform. Instead, he contends, there is evidence that litigation may actually galvanize opponents who are already very aware of the issues and related developments. Courts give rise to the 'fly-paper phenomenon.' Litigation is a 'lure' that entices groups and organizations to use it. They hope to provoke responses from bureaucracies, to counter the advantages of the better-endowed in the legislative processes, and to force recalcitrant majorities to desist from their unprincipled ways. Instead what occurs, overwhelmingly, is that these groups exhaust sparse resources that could have been better spent in the electoral, legislative, and administrative processes to make democracy live up to its ideals.[193]

The *Hollow Hope* has attracted much attention – and criticism. Some assert that Rosenberg is simply wrong in making such sweeping claims about the ineffectiveness of courts. These critics, examining areas as diverse as prison reform,[194] school financing,[195] and the availability of sexual material,[196] claim that courts have been responsible for substantial change. In addition, there is scepticism regarding Rosenberg's set of conditions used to judge the effectiveness of the courts.

Shuck in his review of the *Hollow Hope* has criticized the analysis as incomplete in fundamental ways.[197] Rosenberg nowhere tackles the meaning of the concept of causality; indeed, he expressly disclaims any such attempt.[198] He is also accused of neglecting the repetitive, dialogic nature of the interactions between courts, legislatures, agencies, and other social processes. Further, Rosenberg's measure of court effectiveness appears to give excessive weight to whether litigation advances the avowed agendas of public-interest litigators and too little weight to more modest reform goals and to the substantive merits of the policies actually involved in the litigation.

Finally, it is alleged that Rosenberg does not differentiate between constitutional litigation and lawsuits turning on statutory interpretation. Administrative agencies can have a fundamental role in implementing statutory schemes of regulation designed to deal with social and political problems. The agencies' relationship to legislatures, to the regulated, to the greater public, and to the courts may be central to how courts' decisions are reached and how they are reacted to.

The real problem, in Shuck's view, is that there is **no** account of the judicial enterprise that will adequately describe how courts exert their influence: 'The many threads of causality are simply too tightly knotted to disentangle.'[199] He urges that students of courts confess that 'we ... are guided more by our professionally honed, often intuitive grasp of an elusive social reality than by any robust scientific theory worthy of the name.'[200]

A variation of Shuck's critique has been made by McCann. The debate encapsulated by the difference between McCann and Rosenberg has been discussed already in this chapter[201] and the previous one.[202] These differences between Rosenberg and McCann reflect the wide divergence between 'positivism' and 'interpretivism' as to assessing the influence of law. McCann's essential point is that the methodology employed by Rosenberg is misdirected.

Rosenberg clings to 'positivism,' which insists, in this context, that the influence of litigation can be measured in direct and linear ways employing means that echo scientific models for assessing actions and reactions in the physical world.[203] In contrast, the 'interpretivist' approach to understanding law insists that 'causal explanations are partial, imperfect, problematic intellectual contrivances to help us to make sense of ourselves and the world in which we live but cannot fully "know."'[204] For McCann the effect of courts cannot be compared to the effect of bowling balls; cause and effect in terms of courts is much more complicated than counting the number of pins hit or missed. Instead, the influence of courts arises out of a context that must be carefully examined by taking account of such factors as the nuances of human interaction, the dynamic relationship of all relevant elements, and an understanding that legal norms are 'constitutive' of meaning and activity.

Rosenberg has countered that McCann's methodology confines him to the very context that the latter insists is so important. This is so because interpretivism suffers from particularism and lack of controls. The former contends that, to the extent that non-representative samples are employed, any conclusions are confined to the cases examined and there can be no generalization. The latter asserts that interpretivism cannot separate the effects of law from other factors even in particular cases; thus, there can be no generalizations regarding the impact of law.[205]

Nevertheless it is Shuck, in his eagerness to demonstrate the incompleteness of Rosenberg's framework and its conclusions, who may actually underscore the latter's most fundamental point: those who place faith in litigation to effect change have only that faith; they cannot, in fact, demonstrate that law has any such capacity. If the fundamental conclusion is that there is no theory – let alone reliable evidence – to account for the impact of courts, no sensible way to analyse cause and effect relating to their decisions, then, equally, any claims about their capacity to achieve any change must surely be thrown on the scrap heap as well. Most importantly, if the effects of litigation reflect, as Schuck insists, an 'elusive social reality,' what is the normative basis for an ambitious judicial role, one that confounds the basic democratic legitimacy that elected officials are apt to claim?

We will examine the impact of litigation on many issues in part 3: capital punishment, smoking, the environment, pornography, and affirmative action. McCann and Shuck are right: assessing such results is more complicated than Rosenberg maintains. Yet Rosenberg is also right: those advocating litigation to affect change are, mostly, too optimistic.

The Impact of Litigation on Popular Politics: Canada Experiments

The debate in the United States largely focuses on the effects of litigation on specific issues or sets of issues: women's rights, prison reform, bussing, and so forth. However, there is a broader question regarding the impact of litigation that is of special interest to those societies contemplating giving courts an enhanced role, particularly through an entrenched bill of rights. Does equipping courts with the power to nullify the enactments of elected officials change the political process, making the forging of policy through popular politics more difficult? Do rights anchored in courts mean less agreement regarding the common good?

This question has been of concern in America, particularly among those who believe the pursuit of individualism through the assertion of rights in and around courts has gone too far. Those of this view tend to search for ways to restore a sense of community in various contexts.

One expression of community are legislative enactments brought about by forging agreement in the political process.

Yet many now view politics as fractious, disputatious, and impotent, particularly regarding domestic policy, whether in terms of health care, education, support for families, welfare entitlement, or the prevention of crime. They believe that a major cause of this state of affairs is excessive reliance on courts and litigation to address complex social, political, and economic issues and the way judicial pronouncements stymie political processes. The fear is of 'atrophy in the democratic processes of bargaining, education, and persuasion that take place in and around legislatures ... [B]y too readily ... blocking the normal political avenues for change, courts leave the disappointed majority with no legitimate political outlet.'[206] Litigation is so entrenched in America that any hope for turning back from judicial oversight and the dominance of courts and rights in policy debates may be wishful thinking. Society may have been so transformed that the very bedrock of civic engagement is not popular politics, but the 'rights regarding citizen.'[207]

Yet the way in which entrenched rights, accompanied by an enhanced role for the judiciary, may change the political process remains a critical question for other societies contemplating an altered role for the courts. The evolving experience of Canada with an entrenched bill of rights is instructive. In 1982 Canada adopted the Canadian Charter of Rights and Freedoms.[208] The text of the Charter differs in important ways from the US Bill of Rights, including an express instruction that any rights are subject to 'reasonable limits prescribed by law as can be demonstrably justified in a free and democratic society.'[209] At the same time, it does empower judges to strike down legislation and nullify acts of public officials that contravene a set of enumerated rights.

After some hesitation, Canadian courts have now warmed to the task, involving themselves in questions relating to abortion, mercy killing, assisted suicide, language rights, and an array of issues relating to the administration of criminal justice, to name but a few. So significant has been this alteration in the role of the judiciary that a study comparing the role of the supreme courts in four countries, including the United States, has characterized the shift, resulting from several factors, as 'Canada: a Great Experiment' and the result as 'Canada's Dramatic Rights Revolution.'[210]

Canadian and American societies share a long, undefended border. They are alike in many ways: wealthy, well educated, ethnically and geographically diverse. However, many commentators point to important differences between the two countries.[211] Up to the adoption of the Charter at least, American society was viewed as individualistic and liberal; Canadian as communitarian and conservative. Canadian society was influenced by conservative English Protestants who fled the American revolution and conservative French Catholics who escaped the French one. In contrast, the United States was forged in revolution by those rebelling against religious and governmental authority. As a result, Canadian political and legal culture was more amenable to collective solutions to problems agreed to through legislative processes and implemented through governmental programs. This communitarian impulse in government was fed both, on the left, by a social-democratic party (during the latter twentieth century the New Democratic Party) – virtually unthinkable in the United States – and, on the right, by 'red' Toryism (a conservative party that was very influential until the 1990s, known as the Progressive Conservatives).[212] Thus Canada, at least up to the Charter, had a moderate politics and, with some dark exceptions, enjoyed an international reputation in its respect for human rights.

Those sceptical of the Charter worry that the entrenchment of rights with an enhanced role for the judiciary will make the society much more individualistic and much more hostile towards government. As courts become more important, popular politics will wane.[213] As a result, there will be much less commitment to the public good as manifested in policies relating to health care, education, urban renewal, basic income entitlement, and social programs to prevent crime. It is not that the rights of minorities and the disadvantaged should be excluded. It is that these protections – and other policy goals, just listed – could have been accomplished through an evolving popular politics. Yet such a possibility has now been foreclosed through the dominance of courts and the obsession with rights.[214]

What is the evidence thus far? There is certainly little indication of the excesses of America in terms of criminal sanctions. As in the United States, crime, including the violent variety, has fallen. However, unlike in the United States, there has been no substantial increase in the rates of incarceration. Moreover, except for the occasional outburst, there has been no sustained call for a return to the death penalty.[215]

On the other hand, politics in Canada have generally taken a right turn in terms of economic equality. Government budgets have been drastically cut and there have been few initiatives regarding social programs in the last decade or so. Ontario, the most populous province, has, in the 1990s, twice elected a very conservative regime, pledged to shrink government. It has implemented many stringent measures in terms of health care, education, and worker protection. At the same time, support for social-democratic parties, particularly the New Democratic Party, at the national level and in many provinces is on the wane.[216] Meanwhile, the disparity between rich and poor in terms of income and wealth, though not as great as in the United States, has increased in the last fifteen years.[217] Maybe there are other explanations for governments becoming more conservative. Huge public debts had been accumulated by governments of every stripe in the previous decades, making austerity regarding social programs virtually inevitable in the 1990s. However, many countries of Western Europe have faced debts and deficits without disavowing the programs themselves.[218] At the same time, disparities in income and wealth in most countries of Europe have not increased to the same extent as in Canada (to say nothing of the United States).[219]

The evidence of the impact on Canadian society is ambiguous. However, there are enough negative indications to put at issue proponents' claims that the Charter and the courts would bring about a new era in progressive politics. There are enough worrisome signs to suggest that the very notion of using popular politics to forge common agreement may be in jeopardy.[220]

In part 3 we will look at Canada's use of law in the era of the Charter regarding smoking and pornography. Sceptics' worries may be inflated. But the proponents of the Charter, particularly those of a progressive political bent, have little about which to be enthusiastic.

Conclusions

Law has become a pervasive and complex system of language, institutions, actions, and symbols. Once any sort of sophisticated notion of impact is brought to bear, few are prepared to any longer defend the idea, in the abstract, that law can directly contour economic, political and social forces. At the same time, instrumental *claims* are constantly heard from both proponents and opponents of a specific law or set of laws. Simplistic accounts of law in the media and sloganeering by politicians, lobbyists, and advocacy groups are to blame for such blustery contentions.

Yet legal academics have played their part too. The recent spate of work so sceptical of the capacity of litigation to achieve change (Rosenberg and others) has, itself, been subject to much criticism about its accuracy. Still that work, questioning the effects of lawsuits, has thrown into stark relief the bald – instrumentalist – claims regarding litigation's ability, particularly compared with the political and administrative processes, to reconfigure societal issues. A large part of the explanation for such unsubstantiated contentions is the fact that academics – perhaps especially legal academics – operate in a domain that lulls them into the belief that if an idea is theoretically elegant it must be accurate. If, for example, there are compelling arguments why the tort system should deter negligent behaviour, it must be the case that it does. Never mind the evidence. Never even contemplate the challenges that empirical investigations might entail.

Similarly, critics of the law – from both the left and right – who insist that it mostly deflects the pursuit of larger social goals may offer a largely erroneous account. Can it really be argued that the environment would be better off if there were no regulation of it? (This is a question that will, in fact, be addressed in part 3.) Nonetheless, these critics provide a vital corrective to the inflated claims of instrumentalism regarding law's capacity to contour social, economic, and political forces. They admonish us to consider, at the least, a more discriminating use of law concerning a wide range of goals.

What of the idea that law is effective only when it converges with societal norms? At one level this claim seems accurate in many situations. Certainly compliance with law, discussed at length in chapter 2, is heavily dependent on the fact that most people believe most of the time that it is critical to a well-ordered society that the law be obeyed. In a very different context, Canadians have a universal health-care system because a series of laws say that they will. At the same time, those laws and that system enjoy large levels of public support (despite ongoing debate about quality of care and levels of public financing).

Yet, if law is to be effective, what does society do if the bases for forming consensus have waned? Those espousing law as (re)constituting relationships may get carried away with their insistence that society is composed of multiple 'perspectives' where meaning is 'constructed' and where human interaction is 'inherently indeterminate,' 'variable,' and 'contingent.' Yet the fact remains that in large, decentralized, and heterogeneous countries such as the United States – and Canada – there is a growing angst regarding a lack of agreement about essentials, let alone details. In such a context, law presents the possibility of providing a common language concerning the basis of society while yet providing many opportunities for contests about the interpretation, the significance, the meaning of that common language.

It is not a coincidence that the most diverse society – the United States – also has the most costly, most complicated, most litigation-driven system of legal regulation. Thus, the effect of law in the United States may be different in many situations because its source and its framework of implementation are different. In quality and quantity, for better or for worse, America is exceptional. It is an outlier in the predominance of its courts, the emphasis on individualism, the adversarialness, the enshrinements of rights, and the punitive attitude to crimes.

There is no doubt that there is a relationship between law and society, that law has effects on broader social forces. No one idea discussed in this chapter captures that relationship and those effects. However, the six ideas examined here, taken together, come closer to succeeding. Much of their explanatory power depends on the issues being examined. In part 3 we look at five different areas – capital punishment, smoking, the environment, pornography, and civil rights / affirmative action – that are very much at the forefront of contemporary society, particularly in the United States. We will use these topics to reflect upon the ideas presented in this chapter. All six ideas are required to explain law's outcomes. Looming large is the special role that law plays in the United States. There much influence is ceded to litigation even as much disappointment ensues.

PART THREE

The Complexity of Law's Impact:
Some Examples

CHAPTER FIVE

Punishment – and Capital Punishment

Much of the growth of law in the last thirty years is attributable to the left side of the political spectrum. Progressives have long viewed law as a counterweight to market excesses and failures. Environmentalism, affirmative action, and the campaign against smoking – all topics addressed in this part – are illustrations of progressive forces seeking to harness law to achieve results at odds, in important ways, with the dictates of the marketplace. Regulation as diverse as minimum-wage laws to tax laws stipulating progressive rates to programs ensuring health care can all be accounted for, in many ways, as a reaction to the deficiencies of market forces.

But the right as well has long had a love affair with law, though the basis of attraction is different. That side of the political spectrum tends to see law as a means to control personal behaviour it believes ought to be proscribed. That viewpoint is an impetus for the control of pornography – a topic also examined in this part. But the right is keen to lead the charge regarding many other aspects of personal behaviour from restricting access to abortion to circumscribing the lives of gays and lesbians to controlling the recreational use of drugs.

More generally, it is in the control of crime that the right's faith in law is clearly illustrated. Nowhere is such evidence provided so obviously as in the United States. Most industrialized nations have adopted a mix of policies with regard to suppressing wrongdoing. On the one hand, violations are deterred through punishment, with imprisonment often reserved for the most serious crimes and the most hardened criminals. On the other hand, programs are implemented to redress the social causes of crime (such as poverty, discrimination, unemployment, poor education, and weak family and community structures) and to 'design out' situations associated with crime; for instance, by restricting access to guns, by promoting busy urban cores, and, in some instances – and more controversially – by decriminalizing the use of drugs.

However, the United States relies much more heavily on deterrence and punishment than do other industrialized countries. Conservatives in America have dominated policy agendas with the message that *the* response to crime is punishment by imprisonment and, in the case of murder, by the death penalty. Such robust faith in the power of punitive measures has crowded out rational debate of many other policies designed to redress the underlying causes of crime. Whatever other reservations conservatives have in invoking law, many of them demonstrate no such inhibitions regarding its heaviest machinery: the criminal process, incarceration, and capital punishment. Yet such measures have been conspicuously unsuccessful.

An examination of the policies of punishment in the United States presents this paradox regarding the criminal-justice system: among the highest expenditures per capita and highest per capita rates of imprisonment yet, at the same time, the highest per capita rate of violent crimes, especially murder. Underscoring this paradox is 'American Exceptionalism' writ large – capital punishment, which the United States, alone among countries of a similar tradition, continues to impose in determined isolation.

Many of the countries that have abolished executions did so despite widespread opposition to ending the death penalty. The halting of capital punishment in these societies raises questions concerning the enactment and enforcement of law that is not supported by public norms. Yet America is not troubled by such questions regarding capital punishment. The incidence of executions is increasing, with public support at its highest levels. At the same time, attempts to abolish the death penalty through the courts furnish a clear example of the failure of litigation-based reform[1] and provide a striking instance of unintended consequences.[2] Such lawsuits did not end the death penalty. Instead, the Supreme Court has upheld the constitutionality of capital punishment. What is more, there has been a backlash regarding such suits: the number of states providing for executions has increased and the pace with which the death penalty is imposed has intensified. Finally, examination of the cases in which it is inflicted illustrates how erratically that sanction is employed. Yet the death penalty plays a critical role in bolstering a system determined to use punishment – the heaviest machinery of the law – as a prime response to crime.

The policies of widespread incarceration and the retention of the death penalty – accomplished through the courts – separate America from all other nations of a similar heritage and, again, mark it as an outlier in its use of law.[3] It is the society of liberty and of rights that now imprisons far more people, on a relative basis, than any other country in the world except Russia. A recent work on the history of imprisonment in America asks: 'How is it that the United States, which epitomizes and sanctifies democracy, continues to build and maintain such a huge and growing complex of totalitarian institutions in its midst?'[4]

Why has this 'growing complex of totalitarian institutions' come to be? Is there a relationship between the fact that, among nations of a similar heritage, the United States is the society most absorbed by rights and, yet, is also the one that is the most punitive? Can it be that such widespread imposition of punishment buttresses the expansiveness of rights? There are myriad complaints that the spreading of rights, including through the courts, has not been accompanied by a corresponding observance of responsibilities.[5] Perhaps the criminal-justice system, administered by the courts, has become the misplaced repository for an unfocused but determined insistence on such responsibility. If individuals have so many rights, then they alone are responsible for their criminal acts – and deserve to be punished, to lose their freedom. Astride this machinery of accountability is the ultimate sanction for individual wrongdoing – capital punishment.

Thus is America locked in a rigid trade-off hugely dependent on law, and largely administered by the courts. Progressives get to clamour for rights. Conservatives get to push for punishment, incarceration, and electrocution.

Deterrence and Crime

If much of the law focuses on commands and most of those commands are negative ('Thou shalt not kill'), it is no surprise that enforcement would rely heavily on deterrence.[6] Thus, deterrence is invoked in many contexts to achieve obedience to the law. In civil suits, tort law, in the wide range of situations to which it applies, depends heavily on deterrence to prevent acts that will be characterized as wrongful. In a different area, regulatory regimes may depend on civil penalties and their potential for deterrence to achieve compliance with the particular scheme that is to be implemented. The results of such exercises in deterrence may be another matter. The deterrent effects of tort lawsuits, for which there is most enthusiasm in the USA, appear to be far less than proponents have claimed.[7] Civil penalties for regulatory infractions (as opposed to criminal prosecutions) may have more potential, in some contexts, than has been fully exploited.[8]

The most obvious area where deterrence is fundamental is criminal law. A critical determinant of the success of criminal law is the extent to which acts that society wishes to prohibit are, in fact, not committed. Most people do not judge the administration of criminal justice by the quality of policing, the efficiency and fairness of the courts, or the state of prisons – though all these raise important issues. People first rate the success of a society and its criminal laws according to the extent that they are not victims of crime, that is, the extent that unlawful acts are prevented.

The uncertainties surrounding deterrence bring us back to the core issue of this book: assessing its effectiveness in curtailing proscribed acts. When we talk of deterrence in criminal law we are confronted by ideological polarities. At one end is the contention that attaching unpleasant consequences to behaviour will reduce the tendency of people to engage in that behaviour. When instances are presented of failure to achieve a deterrent effect such examples are said to indicate simply the need for more severe and certain retribution.

At the other pole is the insistence that deterrence is essentially irrelevant to the incidence of violations of the law: 'At best the criminal law is merely epiphenomenal, a dependent variable shaped by current mores and prevailing norms. At worst the threat of punishment is likely to provoke more of the behaviour it is intended to control or suppress.'[9]

Nonetheless, this polarity is mostly misconceived: the end points are not mutually exclusive. Rather, they underscore the complexity around determining the impact of deterrence in different contexts. We generally seek to avoid unpleasant consequences; a threat of such unpleasantness tends to deter. Yet not all criminal prohibitions are, in all ways, effective. These antagonistic propositions have, more or less, force depending on the quandaries raised by the specifics addressed. Thus, while it is always possible to argue that some threat could have been more effective, it is also always possible to find examples of deterrence failing. The critical issue is whether any particular policy creates benefits worth its costs – fundamentally, whether crime declines.[10]

Such quandaries raise complicated issues about the effect of the criminal-law. Nowhere are such questions more difficult than in the United States, a land that relies so heavily on the machinery of criminal law enforcement. Consider American courts and their entanglements with due process on behalf of the accused. At a rhetorical level, due process marks a great divide between liberals who focus on 'rights' and conservatives who want 'law and order.' Yet the well-known criminal lawyer and academic Alan Dershowitz is prepared to say flatly that such judicial rulings have virtually no consequences:

> The courts have almost no impact on crime rates. Whether the 'Miranda' or other exclusionary rules are expanded, contracted, or abolished will have no discernible effect on the number of murders, rapes, muggings, or burglaries committed or prosecuted in any given jurisdiction ... If the entire right-wing law-and-order agenda were suddenly to be enacted ... there would be no real decrease in violent crime. Neither would there be a discernible increase if suddenly Earl Warren and his liberal court of the 1960s were resurrected and adopted the agenda of the American Civil Liberties Union.[11]

Such unqualified assertions are likely to be greeted sceptically. The courts' obsession with due process and the heated debate that surrounds their rulings must have some impact. If nothing else, such judicial activity and the reaction it provokes may sideline reasoned discussion and attempts to grapple with the underlying causes of crime.[12] Clearly the administration of criminal justice, in that country, has some effects, if in no other way than by occupying the hundreds of thousands who are swept into its net as victims, accused, police, judges, and lawyers. But beyond these obvious effects lie many unanswered questions.

In his history of crime in America, Lawrence Friedman is acutely aware of the importance of the question of impact. However, he is not prepared to venture more than a guess about the actual consequences of the system's capacity to deter: 'Clearly, there must be *some* impact, some deterrent effect, some influence on morality and behaviour. How much, is completely unknown. It is pretty certain that it is less than most people think; the constant clamour for more prisons, more executions, more police, assumes a potency that is almost surely a delusion.'[13] This 'potency that is ... a delusion' is the hallmark of the administration of criminal justice in the United States. The American response to crime yields especially punitive results while the underlying problem of violence remains largely unchanged, especially compared with other industrialized nations.

America and Punishment

The good news is that crime in the United States fell in the 1990s. Even so, individuals in America continually reported crime as the number one or two problem facing the country. In fact, though, it is not crime – generally – that is the problem in that society. Property crimes, for example, have fallen sharply since 1980.[14] One is now more likely to be robbed in Canada or Spain.

Instead, the issue is violent crime. It is true that there is evidence of a decline in violence, including homicides. The murder rate may have plunged by as much as 11 per cent in 1996 alone, with violent crime as a whole declining by 7 per cent in that same year. If such declines can continue or even be maintained, then violence will drop to below the levels that have plagued America in the last three decades.[15] Yet such figures must be kept in perspective. First, incidents of violent crime vary enormously throughout the country. Many midsize cities are, in fact, experiencing a surge in crime, including murders.[16] Second, even if the national rates of homicide decline can be maintained, America would still have a far higher rate than European and Asian countries maintaining such statistics. For instance, even with the 11 per cent drop in the USA, referred to above, the homicide rate would be 7.3 per 100,000 (the rate varied from 8 to 10 during the last three decades). Yet, in comparison, the following are the homicide rates per 100,000, in 1992, for other countries: Japan, 0.6; Great Britain, 0.7; Germany, 1; France, 1.1.[17] The point about violence in America can be put more concretely as follows: an individual is less likely to be burgled in Los Angeles than in Sydney, but that same individual is many times more likely to be murdered in the former city than in the latter (as much as twenty times more likely depending on which recent rates are compared).[18]

In contrast with America, many industrial democracies had huge increases in property crime from 1970 to 1990. Such growth has ranged from 177 per cent in Germany to 600 per cent in Italy. Yet during these three decades the homicide rate fell. In France, for example, theft has increased by five times between 1960 and 1990, but murder has decreased by one-third. It is suggested that the cases of increasing property crime in those countries reflect rising affluence (more property to steal), better police reporting, and a larger number of women working so that more homes are unoccupied for greater periods. At the same time, the much higher rate of murder in the United States is said to be accounted for by a combination of a highly violent illegal drug trade, large numbers of handguns, and a tradition among males to use extreme violence as a reaction to conflict.[19] The result is that 'the United States [is] clustered with other industrial countries in crime rate, but [is] head and shoulders above the rest in violent death.'[20]

Yet by failing to appreciate that crime generally is falling but that there remains a huge problem with violence – even if those rates are also declining – the United States has turned to policies that are expensive by many measures and that at the same time exacerbate the problem of crime. *The Economist*, not a soft touch on social problems, argues that '[Americans] are throwing their weight behind indiscriminate policies which, at huge cost, bludgeon crime as a whole but fail to tackle the problem of violence.'[21]

The reasons for and the effects of mandatory terms of imprisonment illustrate such controversial policies. Mandatory incarceration requirements denote a clear break from ideas of rehabilitation and, instead, are a clear embrace of concepts of 'just desserts' and deterrence. Responding to the alarms about the growth of crime (whatever the reality), many legislators have been attracted to mandatory prison terms as a solution: if the perpetrator is removed from the streets he cannot be committing crimes. Thus, for example, from 1984 to 1990 Congress altered federal sentencing laws so as to enact mandatory minimum sentences for various drug and firearm offences, including drug offences committed near schools; violent crimes (broadly defined); drug crimes involving the use of a firearm (the firearm triggers a mandatory sentence in addition to the sentence for the underlying offence); the possession of more than five grams of cocaine; and any degree of involvement in a drug conspiracy.[22] Even more extreme are the 'three strikes and out' initiatives that impose mandatory life sentences without parole on repeat offenders with little regard for the nature of the crime or the violator's record. While the announced target for the mandatory life sentence are violent offences, in some states such offences, counting as a 'strike,' include drunk driving, promoting prostitution, and petty theft.

These initiatives have been a leading cause of the exploding prison population. As of 1988, there were over 600,000 persons in federal and state prisons. That number represented a tripling of inmates during the previous fifteen years at a time when the general population was not increasing at anywhere near that rate.[23] Even so, the rate of incarceration continued to increase in the decade after 1988 even as crime fell. Despite a decline in the crime rate over the previous five years the number of those incarcerated rose.

In 1997 the number of people in prison increased by another 9 per cent. By June 1997 the total number imprisoned was 1,725,842. Thus, the incarceration rate nationally was in excess of 645 per 100,000 – more than double the 1985 rate of 313 per 100,000. Yet, as indicated, that latter rate already was almost three times more than that of fifteen years earlier.[24] Illustrative of this rush to imprison is the reaction of California voters. The prison population in that state grew by 400 per cent in the fifteen years before 1994. Nevertheless, voters that year overwhelmingly supported a referendum that required twenty-five years to life for anyone convicted of a third felony, even if the crimes included such offences as housebreaking.[25]

This impulse to lock up means that America now imprisons more people on a relative basis than any other country in the world except Russia. One example, using 1995 figures, will provide the contrast between the USA and other comparable societies.[26] In that year America had an incarceration rate of 600 per 100,000. The comparable rate for Canada was 115; for England 100. (The rate for Russia was 690; as mentioned above, the rate for the USA had climbed to 645 by 1997.) These skyrocketing rates of incarceration have had a devastating impact on those swept into the net. Especially affected are African-Americans. By mid-1995 the imprisonment rate for black men was nearly eight times higher than that for white males; the comparable rate for black women was seven times higher than that for white females.[27] There is evidence that some who supported imprisonment believed that it would help African-American communities by purging them of drug abuse. Instead, the 'developments are a classic example of the unintended and unfortunate consequences of insufficiently thought-out legislation.'[28]

Furthermore, prisons are costly. California built sixteen new prisons between 1984 and 1994, the direct cost of which exceeded $5 billion; with interest on bonded debt the cost could rise to as much as $10 billion. The estimated costs of proposed construction over the next decade would require a further $351 billion in federal funds. In addition to capital costs of the buildings there are the continuing expenditures for feeding, guarding, and housing prisoners.[29]

Yet such mandatory sentences do not appear to have been responsilbe for altering the rate of serious crime. Levels of crime have, indeed, fallen. Thus, it is tempting, particularly for advocates of imprisonment and robust proponents of deterrence, to assert that more individuals imprisoned for longer terms must equal less crime. However, it is unlikely that such decrease is the result of greater levels of incarceration. Crime also fell in the early 1980s, rose in the late 1980s, and fell again in the 1990s even as the prison population rose through the whole period. Similarly, the crime rates for states with career-criminal laws have stayed in line with those in the rest of the country.[30] What is more, crime has also fallen significantly in other societies that have not resorted to increasing the rates of imprisonment. Canada experienced an appreciable rate of decline in crime, including homicide, in the 1990s.[31] Yet, as indicated, its rate of imprisonment is almost six times lower than that in the United States.

In fact, even among experts, the reasons for the declining rates of crime are not clear.[32] Likely explanations for some of the decrease in crime are demographics and drugs. As for demographics, young men commit the largest number of crimes. When there are fewer of them there are fewer crimes. As for drugs, the appearance of crack in the 1980s sucked many individuals into drug use and trade and all the crimes that can accompany such activities. Crack consumption seems to be falling; thus other criminal activities, including killings, should abate.[33] Better policing methods in some cities and an upbeat economy have also contributed.[34]

In any case, one reason why 'three strikes and out' laws, in particular, will probably have little impact on violent crime is the difficulty of focusing on such perpetrators. Those who support such laws insist that they can decrease violence even if they apply to a small percentage of offenders because only a small percentage commit such deeds. Yet this argument breaks down because no one can confidently state the offenders who make up that percentage. At the same time, many who are imprisoned under these laws are involved with drugs. Perhaps there is – and should not be – enormous sympathy for such individuals despite the enormous expenditures and human costs involved in jailing them. The question remains how sending a crack user to prison for a long time responds to the very real problem of violent crime:[35] '[T]he anticrime crackdown is inefficient, diffuse in focus, and misses the opportunity to look beyond the category of criminal behaviour for the sources and control of the violence.'[36]

It is not that other solutions have not been proffered, from the discriminating use of early-intervention programs for children most at risk[37] to suggestions for generating norms that would bolster law-abiding behaviour in inner cities.[38] What is more, there is the critical issue of whether the money spent jailing those in the thrall of substance abuse would not be better expended on treatment programs or some other response.[39] The RAND Corporation has recently released a study assessing the effectiveness of mandatory minimum sentences for drug offences. It concluded that expenditures on treatment programs far outpaced even law-enforcement programs but clearly left in the distance longer prison terms as ways of reducing both the consumption of cocaine and cocaine-related crime: '[M]andatory minimums produce the smallest bang for the buck by far.'[40]

Yet constructive alternatives are mostly paved over in the rush to imprison. It may be that, at some point, these rates of incarceration that defy gravity may fall back.[41] Perhaps the decline in crime may enter public awareness and be matched by, finally, a sense of horror that such a sweep of confinement could have taken place in the land of the free. At the dawning of the new century there were some glimmers of hope.[42] Yet vengeance and an exaggerated sense of deterrence may be firmly ingrained whatever the actual effects. The 'punish-to-deter fallacy,'[43] the 'punitive paradigm'[44] may by now have permanently crowded out any other alternatives.[45]

Though not rigorously substantiated, there is anecdotal evidence of several unintended consequences of the 'three strikes and out' laws. The first is that such laws may actually contribute to violence on the streets. For instance, cornered offenders may try to shoot their way out rather than face life in prison.[46] A second is an increased burden on the court system: violators are unlikely to plead guilty when the automatic result must be a sentence of life in prison.[47] A third is subversion of the law by prosecutors, judges, and juries. When sympathetic instances arise prosecutors will not prosecute or judges and juries will not convict: 'You cannot tell human beings to do things they think are totally unfair. They won't do it. They'll figure a way out.'[48]

Yet another effect is one that has already been referred to: deflection away from other ways of dealing with violators and, even more profound, indifference to the underlying causes of crime. The problem that 'three strikes and out' initiatives are supposed to prevent is the early release of violent criminals. However, that problem might be better addressed, not by inflexible life sentences, but by shorter sentences for non-violent offenders, greater use of strictly supervised alternatives to prison in the case of such offenders and – with all the controversy it raises – the decriminalization of drugs.[49] At the same time, harsh prison sentences (and the prison space and expenditures such sentences require) would be reserved for those committing lethal violence.[50] More ambitiously, there would be the will to address basic conditions closely associated with lethal violence in America.[51] Three such circumstances are handgun availability and use, the staggering rates of lethal violence among African-Americans (as both perpetrators and victims), and the high incidence of 'stranger homicides' (victim and offender previously unacquainted).[52]

Instead, the *fable* of the deterrent effect of law – regardless of the reality, including patently undesirable impacts – has riveted the debates around mandatory jail terms, in general, and 'three strikes and out' initiatives, in particular, crowding out rational debate concerning alternatives. Joseph Biden, a leading Democratic, after voting with ninety other senators to impose life sentences on third-time violent offenders on federal property, had this to say: 'If someone came to the Senate floor and said we should barbwire the ankles of any one who jaywalks, I think it would pass.'[53] On the closely related initiatives of mandatory minimums Orrin Hatch, a leading Republican senator, confessed: 'Mandatory minimums are a political response to violent crime. Let's be honest about it. It's awfully difficult for politicians to vote against them.'[54]

So the drive to imprison continues, fuelled by a grasping at the idea of deterrence but also by a sense of resignation: 'It is as if all we can do is warehouse people until they die or are too old and decrepit to threaten anyone on the outside again.'[55] Meanwhile, these are the stark characteristics of the American system of criminal justice compared with the rest of Western industrialized society: highest per capita expenditures, highest per capita rates of imprisonment, yet, at the same time, the highest per capita rate of violent crime.[56] Lawrence Friedman, an insightful and balanced commentator, has, nonetheless, adopted an air of resignation to the torrent and any measures taken against it: '[T]he siege of crime may be the price we pay for a brash, self-loving, relatively free and open society.'[57]

There is yet another aspect of the American criminal-justice system that sets it far apart from other nations of a common heritage: capital punishment. This ultimate sanction is a special buttress for a system that is simultaneously so harsh even as it is so unsuccessful. The nation that is most absorbed by rights has persuaded itself that it may impose this deadliest expression of individual responsibility.

'Le signe spécial et éternel de la barbarie'[58]

The Causes of Abolition, The Effects of Popular Opinion

A study of the movement to eliminate capital punishment establishes three things about the impact of law: that international proclamations have an effect on the law of individual states; that substantial legal change can be effected and maintained despite lack of popular support; and that, in the United States, where the efforts at abolition have failed, the rate of murder and violent crime is, paradoxically, four to ten times higher than in countries which have abolished capital punishment. We will discuss the first two aspects here; the third we will examine in the next section.

Though some jurisdictions succeeded in eliminating it earlier,[59] the abolition of the death penalty is essentially a post–Second World War phenomenon. A critical stimulus was the international movement against it. The elimination of capital punishment had some endorsement as the *Universal Declaration of Human Rights* was being drafted in 1948. However, in the end there was only implicit recognition of the desirability of ending executions through the 'right to life' clause.[60]

Nevertheless, abolition of the death penalty gained momentum in the succeeding period. Those involved with developing international norms sought the restriction of its use by excluding a range of individuals who could be subject to it: juveniles, pregnant women, and the elderly. In addition, they promoted restricting its application to an ever-shortening list of serious crimes. Finally, they insisted on enhanced procedural safeguards in the instances where it remained available. Eventually, international law proclaimed capital punishment itself to be objectionable. Three international instruments were drafted that proclaimed the abolition of the death penalty: the first in 1983 and the other two at the end of the 1980s.[61]

The pattern since the end of the Second World War clearly favours a continuous march towards abolition:[62] during the decade from 1948 to 1957, six countries eliminated capital punishment; in the period 1958–1967, the figure climbed to eight; from 1968 to 1977, the total was fifteen; between 1978 and 1987 nineteen countries abolished capital punishment; and from 1988 to 1996 thirty-seven countries abolished the death penalty.[63] Meanwhile, countries retaining the sanction continue to feel the effects of international norms favouring abolition. Sometimes, this influence is direct; for instance, certain countries will not grant extradition if a fugitive, upon return, will be subject to the death penalty.[64]

A second impact of the abolition of the death penalty concerns the significance of public opinion. Chapter 4 discussed several ideas about the impact of law, including 'Law Acting in Concert with Social and Political Forces.' This hypothesis claims that the actual impact of a law will most closely correspond to its intended goal when that law and related social and political forces are aligned – the greater the alignment, the more likely that the law will have the effect that its proponents predict.[65] Yet the history of the abolition of the death penalty confronts the underpinnings of this model. In many countries where capital punishment has been eliminated such action has been taken in the face of seemingly widespread opposition. In the end, the fact that public-opinion polls continued to favour the death penalty did not stop legislators in such countries as the United Kingdom, Canada, and Germany from proceeding to eliminate it.[66]

Resentment among the electorate over abolition may continue for long periods. At the same time, there are countries like Germany where support for capital punishment has fallen appreciably (from about 74 per cent to about 26 per cent) during the years since its abolition.[67] In any case, in those countries where resentment does continue there is, nevertheless, general public support for the administration of criminal justice. Nor is there an instance, among Western industrialized nations (aside from America), where the death penalty has been reintroduced.[68] An American opponent of the death penalty has said, in speaking of successful efforts in other countries, that 'the relatively recent abolition of the death penalty has hardened into a broadly supported moral orthodoxy in short order.'[69] This may be an exaggeration. Yet opponents have not been successful in mobilizing mass opinion to demand reinstatement.

There are two explanations that respond to what, at first instance, appears to be such a threat to the core of 'Law Acting in Concert with Social and Political Forces.' First, there is some evidence that support for the death penalty among the populace may not be as strong as polling would indicate. These results come from the United States, where capital punishment exists and endorsement of it is widely thought to remain strong. When the question asked only permits respondents to indicate whether they favour or oppose the death penalty, support for it in the United States has been consistent. Indeed, it appears to have increased over recent decades, reaching in excess of 80 per cent of the population in some polls.[70]

However, that level of support falls drastically when certain other options are put to respondents. If life without parole and restitution to the victims' families is put as an alternative to the death penalty, there is much less support for the latter. Studies show that those favouring capital punishment drop by 32 to 62 percentage points when they are permitted to select the 'life/no parole/restitution' option.[71] On this basis some have argued that polls demonstrating support for the death penalty reflect not a deep commitment to that sanction but, instead, the desire of the public for a harsh punishment that will actually be imposed upon those convicted of murder.[72]

Second, it is arguable that abolition of the death penalty can be realized in the face of popular opposition because its elimination does not depend on any affirmative acts by those who do not support it. Capital punishment is carried out by officers of the state; it is eliminated by officers of the state. Thus, ordinary people cannot marshal their disapproval by evading or even directly refusing to carry out actions involved with implementing abolition. The ending of the death penalty can be contrasted with the prohibition of alcohol.[73] In the latter case, people disagreeing with the law could defy it by continuing to make, smuggle, and sell alcohol and by, of course, consuming it. However, those who disagree with the abolition of capital punishment are rendered passive even as they may object vehemently.

Whether these two responses are sufficient explanations of how a law can be enacted and enforced despite seeming widespread opposition in society is a matter of debate. In any event, the abolition of capital punishment stands, at first instance, as an example of the triumph of the expression and implementation of elite opinion over popular opposition.

Capital Punishment and American Exceptionalism

Despite the success of international norms in propelling the abolition movement forward there have been obstacles. Nowhere is resistance more conspicuous than in the United States. In spite of the qualification, expressed in the last section, about the precise meaning of the polls, the fact remains that support for the penalty has been robust in recent decades. It stood at somewhere between 65 and 80 per cent in 2000.[74] Moreover, there is nothing theoretical about the availability of capital punishment. It is used and, at least in some states, used with increasing velocity. It may be true that there is a worldwide movement to abolish the death penalty. But, so far as the United States is concerned, that movement may as well be on another planet. The USA is an outlier in terms of its embrace of executions.

Reviewing the history of the death penalty in the United States over the last decades reveals three aspects of such exceptionalism: attempts at abolition furnish a clear instance of the failure of litigation-based reform movements; capital punishment is employed erratically; and executions play a critical role symbolically in maintaining – and bolstering – a system determined to use punishment as a primary response to crime.

The Impact of Litigation

Discussing court challenges to the death penalty leads back to chapter 4 and the impact of litigation regarding social change.[75] On the one hand, there has been a prominent strand of opinion that holds that litigation and courts have a special role in transforming social and political issues. Nowhere is this strand stronger than in the United States, and it is perhaps strongest of all among progressives.

On the other hand, there is a second, contrary view holding that litigation is incapable of achieving substantial change, perhaps especially regarding progressive issues. Instead, litigation may galvanize opponents who are already aware of the issues and related developments. At the same time, in turning to the courts, progressive forces can exhaust sparse resources that might have been better spent in electoral, legislative, and administrative processes.

The accuracy of these two opposed depictions of the effect of litigation is a matter of debate, one pursued throughout this book. Yet the history of the death penalty in the United States over recent decades appears to offer a clear example supporting the second view, which insists that litigation will not bring about progressive reform; indeed, lawsuits may cause backlash that can result in outcomes quite contrary to those intended by the groups and individuals who turned to the courts. What is more, the failure of litigation in this context is thrown into relief by the fact that turning to courts to eliminate the death penalty, initially, seemed so effective.

In 1972, in *Furman v. Georgia*,[76] the Supreme Court of the United States brought the death penalty to a halt by striking down every statutory provision containing that sanction. In what has been called a 'badly orchestrated opera,'[77] each of the nine justices wrote his own opinion. The five-man majority was deeply split over the question of whether capital punishment was inherently unconstitutional or whether the laws that the court nullified contained flaws that, if corrected, could result in constitutional statutes imposing the sanction. Nonetheless, at least some abolitionalists were optimistic that – through the courts – the United States had joined the worldwide march for elimination. They believed that 'the inevitable had come to pass.'[78]

Moreover, there was cogent evidence that the Court was not defying the majority but, at least in some critical aspects, acting in concert with it. Over time fewer people had actually been executed: in 1933, 199; in 1950, 82; in 1967, 2; between 1967 and 1972 (the date of *Furman*) no one was put to death. Further, individual states had joined the international move towards abolition that had been gaining momentum since the Second World War: Alaska and Hawaii, in 1957; Oregon, in 1964; Iowa and West Virginia, in 1965 (Michigan, Maine, and Wisconsin having done so in the nineteenth century). Finally, public opinion before *Furman* had moved away from the death penalty: in 1936, 62 per cent appeared to favour it; by 1966, only 42 per cent did.[79]

Yet, soon after *Furman*, the reaction set in. There was popular and political backlash against the resolution of the issue by the Court. This reaction was exacerbated by the overconfidence of the attorneys who had brought the challenge in *Furman* regarding the impact of the decision.[80] Public opinion against the death penalty began to build, becoming a majority in the 1970s and, as indicated earlier, reaching almost 80 per cent by the end of the 1980s.[81] Positions have so hardened that the deterrent effect of the penalty is no longer the crucial determinant in terms of public opinion. Most proponents indicate that they would support the death penalty even if it were found not to deter (and most opponents say they would oppose it even if it did deter).[82] Three-quarters of the American public surveyed would still support the death penalty even in the face of proof that 1 per cent of those executed were innocent.[83] As public backlash against abolition grew, the legislators set to work, responding to *Furman*. Within two years, twenty-eight states had enacted new statutes containing the death penalty. Within four years (1976), thirty-five states had such enactments, with 460 individuals already sentenced to death.[84]

Once again, litigation was invoked, but this time with markedly different results. In 1976, in *Gregg v. Georgia*,[85] the Supreme Court reversed itself and upheld the constitutionality of statutes containing the death penalty. A critical determinant for the Court was public opinion favouring execution, particularly as evidenced by the legislative response to *Furman*. In the Justices' view that response indicated that 'a large proportion of American society continues to regard [capital punishment] as an appropriate and necessary criminal sanction.'[86] In 1977 executions resumed, with the pace picking up ever since. What is more, attempts to argue that the death penalty is imposed in a biased manner (a point pursued below) were unqualifiedly rebuffed by the Supreme Court in 1987 in *McCleskey v. Kemp*.[87]

The litigation that had once seemed so promising helped in the end to galvanize opposition and, then, to entrench results that were precisely the opposite of those intended.[88] Epstein and Kobylka, after analysing the various Supreme Court cases and the context in which they were brought, concluded that the Legal Defence Fund (LDF), the main sponsor of the litigation, had badly miscalculated: '*McCleskey* cemented the *Gregg* loss ... After coming out of *Furman* a doctrinal "winner," [the LDF] proved unable to maintain the momentum of legal change. In terms of its stated goal – abolition of capital punishment – the LDF, once close to victory, emerged as a legal "loser."'[89]

In the view of a leading academic opponent of capital punishment the litigation against the death penalty only solidified support for this sanction and stabilized its continuing existence. The Supreme Court cases permit the appearance of rationalizing the use of the death penalty even as the arbitrariness and discrimination surrounding its imposition continue. Thus, those who sought to bring capital punishment to an end through the courts have been the unwitting allies of enthusiasts for that penalty: 'The constitutional regulation of the death penalty can be viewed as a sobering lesson in unexpected consequences.'[90]

The Death Penalty and Its Erratic Employment

The imposition of capital punishment is erratic three times over: in terms of the states imposing it, its use within particular states, and the circumstances of the killing and the race of the victim.

A clear – and increasing – majority of states provide for capital punishment (38 as of October 1997).[91] What is more, its actual use is spreading. California, Delaware, Arizona, and Pennsylvania invoked it during the first half of the 1990s.[92] In January 2001 Oklahoma had set eight executions dates for that month.[93] Nevertheless, the 'Deep South' – the southeast states – has lead the way. As of February 1995, Arkansas, Alabama, Florida, Georgia, Louisiana, Missouri, North Carolina, Texas, and Virginia accounted for 226 of the 266 people executed since *Gregg* was decided in 1976. By contrast, as of that same date, more than a dozen states that provide for the death penalty had not executed a single person during the same period.[94]

Moreover, there is evidence of discrepancy of usage within those states insistent about invoking the death penalty. Texas is the leader in terms of sheer numbers and notoriety. It had executed – – as of October 1997 – 138 individuals, or about one out of three of all those put to death since *Gregg*. In 1997 alone it executed 37.[95] In 1998, under national and international glare, it killed a woman.[96] In 2000 there were 40 executions.[97] At the same time, within that state there has been wide discrepancy in terms of invoking the sanction.[98] Of the those put to death (as of February 1995), 37 had been from the Houston area, where the district attorney was a vocal proponent of the sanction. In contrast, during the same period, Dallas – with a population two-thirds that of Houston – had a more cautious district attorney: it executed only five criminals.[99] So goes the 'death belt' phenomenon: 'In southern Georgia, there are lots of death sentences; in northern Georgia, there aren't. In Tennessee, there are tons of death sentences in Memphis and East Knoxville, but not in Nashville.'[100]

Finally, capital punishment is imposed erratically in terms of the circumstances of the killing and of the race of the victim.[101] There has been a substantial body of research about the employment of the death penalty,[102] as well as controversy about the reliability of some findings.[103] Nevertheless, such studies have reached three main conclusions.[104]

First, disparities regarding capital punishment are most often related to the race of the victim. If the victim is white, then capital punishment is imposed more frequently regardless of whether the criminal is black or white. Second, bias can exist at points other than when juries decide to recommend the death penalty. Frequently disparities occur at an earlier point, as prosecutors decide whether to allow the accused to plead guilty to a lesser charge or, even, to ask for capital punishment.

Third, disparities are concentrated in 'middle ground' murders constituting about one-fifth to one-fourth of the total. On the one hand, the death sentence is rarely imposed in cases such as barroom brawls or crimes of passion. On the other, it is almost always invoked, regardless of race, when the killing is especially gruesome: multiple murders, torture, etc. However, for 'middle ground' killings, for example, the murder of a shopkeeper in a robbery, there is much more controversy among prosecutors and juries about the death penalty. It is in these cases that bias may be present. The overall disparity (black versus white) regarding when the death penalty is sought as a function of the victim's race is about 6 to 8 per cent. However, in the 'middle ground' cases the disparity is about two to three times that large.[105]

In 1990 the General Accounting Office reviewed 288 studies on race and capital punishment. It concluded that in 82 per cent of the studies the race of the victim influenced the probability of the accused being charged with capital murder or receiving the death penalty. The Office pointed to crucial gaps in studies that did not find such disparity. In contrast, the Office described the race of the victim as a 'remarkably consistent trend' through studies that varied in quality and scope.[106]

The Symbolism of Capital Punishment

What is the impact of the death penalty on American society? The answer to that question involves three basic points. First, its value as a deterrent is minimal or even non-existent. Second, and paradoxically, it has a symbolic effect mesmerizing Americans in their belief in punishment as the response to the plague of crime. Third, the death penalty (and punishment, more generally) provides a focus for a frantic, misplaced need for imposing responsibility in a society so otherwise absorbed by rights.

It is, of course, the case that capital punishment has a *specific* deterrence effect: executed murderers cannot kill again. However, that element of deterrence can clearly also be achieved in other ways: most prominently by requiring those convicted of murder to be sentenced to mandatory life sentences without any opportunity for parole. Abolitionists also point out that the alternative of life without parole has the additional advantages of being less costly (at least in many cases given the tortured process of appeals and delays) and, critically, of preventing the possibility of execution of the innocent.[107]

In terms of general deterrence, there have been several studies attempting to gauge the deterrent effects of capital punishment. There are methodological problems centred on its limited use: the United States is the only Western, industrialized nation that has it; its imposition, within that country, is largely confined to the states of the Deep South. That said, there appears to be widespread agreement, among both proponents and abolitionists, that, at the most, capital punishment (in American society) provides minimal deterrence.[108] One of the most outspoken advocates of the sanction acknowledges: '[W]e have no proof of the positive effectiveness of the penalty.'[109] A study by abolitionists in the late eighties, which carefully sifted through the relevant research,[110] concluded: 'There is room for debate only about whether the marginal deterrent effect is nil or very small in relation to total homicide volume.'[111] In any event, it argued that any small deterrence possibly achieved by capital punishment could be effected by other means.[112] A survey published in 2000 demonstrated that the dozen states that had chosen not to enact the death penalty did not have higher homicide rates than states with capital punishment. In fact, ten of those twelve states had homicide rates below the national average.[113] Yet, as indicated earlier, most people who support the death penalty indicate that they would do so even if it were found not to deter.

In some sense, whether the death penalty in fact deters is beside the point. America is a society determined to believe, regardless of the evidence, that the solution to violent crime is to force people to stop committing it. Such faith views the death penalty as the pinnacle of punishment, as the ultimate response to crime (though some might argue that life in prison is even harsher). 'The death penalty is concrete, it is forceful, and it is final (which nothing else seems to be); it is *something*, and being for it means that you insist that *something* be done.'[114]

Accompanying the *fable* of deterrence is the blood lust of retribution: murderers deserve to die and society should ensure that capital punishment is imposed.[115] What is more, the fact that any case involving the death penalty is likely to be extraordinarily protracted and, often, far more costly than incarcerating the criminal for life[116] seems to only enhance the idea of the value of the sanction: 'Whatever it costs is worth it.'[117] Such belief in the power of capital punishment permits proponents to urge that, if there is cogent evidence of bias in its imposition, the solution is to end disparities by increasing executions of the favoured group.[118] Such dark hope allows serious debate over what may be the ultimate obscenity: whether executions ought to be televised.[119] When the American Bar Association passed a resolution in 1997 calling upon states that have the death penalty not to impose it until greater fairness and due process can be assured, the U.S. House of Representatives' Republican Policy Committee circulated a document entitled 'How the ABA Became a Left-Wing Lobbying Group.'[120]

As indicated earlier, Texas executed a woman in 1998. Karla Faye Tucker – a young, white, articulate born-again Christian – became a media celebrity in the weeks before her execution as those of many stripes laboured to save her. When she was put to death, her execution was seen as a triumph by capital-punishment proponents.[121] In a very particular way, notions of equality in terms of race and gender had prevailed: a white woman had suffered the ultimate sanction. If someone as young, articulate, attractive, and repentant as Ms. Tucker could not attain clemency, few others of those convicted would be able to.[122] Reality and misplaced ideas dance about because outrage at crime demands to somehow be addressed, if only at the level of emotion. Writing about a certain district attorney, one of the most aggressive proponents of the death penalty, a journalist comments: 'To her, [capital punishment] doesn't offer society control over crime – she doesn't believe it's a deterrent – but instead gives the *feeling* of control demanded by a city in decay.'[123]

In all this swirl about the death penalty America rarely looks beyond its borders. Most studies on the effect of the death penalty, which conclude that it offers little or no deterrence, are focused on American society. Yet there is another way to gauge the effect of the death penalty: look at societies in which it is absent. When we do this we are presented with statistics perhaps even more damaging to the case for deterrence. In other Western industrialized nations (Europe, Canada, New Zealand, Australia), which do not have capital punishment, the rates for murder – and for violent crime generally – are anywhere from four to ten times lower. A relatively recent study scrutinized international data for any evidence that the presence or absence of the death penalty had an effect on homicide rates. It concluded that there is no evidence for any form of a deterrent effect.[124]

It will be immediately said by proponents of the death penalty that there is something different about the United States: race, decaying cities, and general poverty will surely be among the factors. Such societal aspects of 'American Exceptionalism' require the different approach to criminal issues that culminates in the death penalty. Yet there is another interpretation. There are variations among Western industrialized countries. However, generally, these societies spend much more than the United States creating a social safety net, developing social programs, and maintaining urban cores.[125] In addition, they are open to effective exercises in 'designing out'[126] and related issues (for example, regarding gun control).[127]

At the same time, these other societies have by no means jettisoned a respect for individual choice or a requirement of individual responsibility for anti-social acts. Nor do they deny a realistic role for deterrence in motivating choice, in underscoring responsibility. What they have done is recognize that choice and the circumstances in which that choice is exercised are linked. The nature of such connections need to be taken into account and continuously debated in forging and implementing sound social policy.

In the United States the extravagant confidence in punitiveness – a fable of the ability to require individual choice and responsibility – has blotted out other aspects of the debate.[128] America is, in many ways, a society now 'governed through crime.'[129] The consequences, the actual impacts are beside the point. A former assistant attorney general and special counsel to the US Senate Judiciary Committee is instructive on this point: '[T]he death penalty continues to monopolize center stage in the current debate over violent crime control. The emotional heat it gives off leads to a polarization of views which prevents consensus and compromise on other law enforcement fronts.'[130]

Some abolitionists believe that any chance for progress is dependent on those who oppose the death penalty demonstrating that there are credible alternatives to capital punishment to fight murder and violent crime generally. Such initiatives would include mandatory sentences and parole limitations, enhanced local law enforcement, and crime-prevention measures applied through social programs, job training, drug treatment, and so on. There were glimmerings of hope as the new century dawned. In 2000 there was some evidence that popular support for executions was decreasing; a study showed that two out of three convictions in death-penalty cases were overturned on appeal, mostly because of incompetent defence lawyers or because of police or prosecutors withholding evidence; and the governor of Illinois declared a moratorium on executions after thirteen men on death row in that state had been cleared because of new evidence.[131]

Yet the symbolic hold of capital punishment could be just too strong. Its capacity to deflect reasoned debate and political compromise may be unassailable:

> The idea that there might be some kind of reluctant accommodation between hard-liners and liberals, with the former relinquishing the death penalty in exchange for liberal support for other harsh crime control measures, might seem plausible in the abstract. But its plausibility rests on the false assumption that the real issue is crime control rather than the feelings of potency and security that accompany the use of governmental power in its ultimate form. On this deeper issue, there is no room for compromise.[132]

Conclusions

Traditionally there has been heavy reliance placed on deterrence to achieve compliance with the law. 'Thou shalt NOT ...' backed with some unpleasant consequence seemed as straightforward a way as any to get people to obey. Invoking deterrence also appealed to a sense of choice and responsibility for that exercise of choice.

Yet, as we saw in chapter 2, the effectiveness of deterrence has been called into question over the last several decades. For instance, the results of criminological research show for the most part that many crimes are committed on impulse without calculation of the consequences or are influenced by motivations not reachable by sanctions. As a result, any number of alternatives to deterrence have been put forward in several contexts: proactive measures that attempt to control the situations in which crime may occur, for instance, gun control; 'designing out' the underlying problem itself, for example, the English efforts in the 1960s to control suicide by eliminating carbon monoxide from gas for domestic use and so forth.

The point here is not to set deterrence against other alternatives in a win/lose battle. Alternatives have been shown to have their own various problems in achieving success: airbags prevent some injuries caused by car accidents even as they may be responsible for others. Rather, the claim is that responsible attempts to achieve better compliance examine the strengths and weaknesses of several approaches and carefully assess their effects when implemented. Such a multifaceted approach is the hallmark of crime prevention in most developed countries. The mix may vary substantially from nation to nation and rhetoric around rights and crime control does come into play. Nevertheless, in these societies there remains a commitment both to punish crime, especially violent crime, and to support policies that combat the social causes of crime – poverty, unemployment, poor education, and weak family and community structures being prominent among them. The test that is urged for the various approaches is a pragmatic one: 'Programs should be judged by whether or not they result in fewer crimes than would otherwise have occurred.'[133]

Yet in its approach to crime America is an outlier. Despite the fact that it has long relied upon deterrence (through punishment) to combat crime, it has the highest rate of lethal violence among Western nations. Though rates of such crime fell in the 1990s in the USA, they remain ahead of those in many other industrialized countries. At the same time, imprisonment rates have soared. Such rush to incarcerate sweeps many before it: some who are violent but many who are the hapless users of drugs or misfits in some other way. Moreover, at a time of austerity for the public it is ironic that there seems so much money to build jails. Meanwhile, sober and careful evidence of the cost-effectiveness of appropriate social programs in curbing crime is scarcely allowed to be a matter of policy debate, let alone implementation.

America's approach culminates in the death penalty. Alone among countries of a similar tradition the United States retains executions. The story of abolition in other counties raises important questions for us in terms of the ability of elites to pass and act upon laws despite a lack of public support. No such complexities plague America. There the use of the death penalty is increasing, public support for it is at an all-time high, and the Supreme Court has backed away from any arguments that executions are constitutionally invalid.

The potential of deterrence is exhausted with capital punishment. The evidence gives virtually no support to arguments that executions deter murders. All that remains are arguments based on vengeance. Capital punishment is the foundation for the edifice of punishment as the approach to crime in America. Imprisonment – and the ultimate sanction of death if necessary – is the solution. Underlying social and economic conditions are just other problems – or maybe just part of the price of a truly free society celebrating individual choice at every turning, whatever the reality. Still the society that is so absorbed by rights and freedoms also searches frantically for some offsetting expression of responsibility. In some warped way that quest finds an outlet: in punishment, in incarceration – and in death.

CHAPTER SIX

Smoking – and Waves of Cultural Antagonism

Smoking provides a dramatic instance of changes in public attitudes. A cigarette in hand was once thought to be glamorous, sophisticated, sexy, and who knows what else. Not so today. She who lights up is more likely to be thought of as a loser, an addict with a filthy, expensive habit dragging her down.

The cause for minority rights abounds in many areas. A conspicuous exception is the shrinking population of those in the thrall of nicotine. Here a plea for protection of the rights of smokers is – mostly – turned back with a mixture of pity and derision. Increasingly, the majority are insisting that smokers handle their obsession, as best they can, with little compromise for the lives of the smoke-free. With such change in attitudes has come a significant alteration in behaviour. The percentage of the population who smoke has dropped dramatically, in many countries, in the last several decades.

The question for this book, of course, is, What has law got to do with these changes? One can easily document a role for laws, in recent decades, designed to discourage smoking. Since consumption has fallen dramatically during roughly the same time, one could easily jump to the conclusion that smoking affords a clear instance of law's capacity to configure behaviour.

Yet careful consideration of the relevant questions invites a more searching inquiry. Did law 'cause' people to stop smoking (or to just not start)? Or was law largely a tag-along? Were changing individual and social attitudes the primary explanation for the drop in consumption, with law incidental to those attitudes?

Regulation of smoking provides an instance where policy-making backed by law has worked in the United States. A theme throughout

Yet there are some counter-trends as the lure of nicotine persists.[13] Statistics from the mid-1990s and beyond suggest that smoking among the young continues to a substantial degree and, in some instances, is back on the rise. Canada is a country noted for its success in suppressing the incidence of smokers. Nevertheless, the Canadian Institute of Child Health, in conjunction with UNICEF, published data which showed that 16 per cent of male fifteen year olds and 21 per cent of female fifteen year olds in Canada smoked daily in 1993–4. The prevalence of female smokers places Canada third out of twenty-two industrialized countries in that category.[14] Smoking rates among black teenagers in the USA, after substantially trailing that of other groups for some time, appeared to be rising in the late 1990s.[15] Cigar smoking, after falling steadily in the 1970s and 1980s, rose during at least some part of the 1990s. The cigar industry promoted the idea that its product was a safe substitute for cigarettes even as the facts establish that cigars can cause cancer and other deadly diseases.[16]

At the same time, in some non-Western and Third World countries smoking is dramatically increasing.[17] Such increases have occurred for many reasons. A prominent explanation is the aggressive marketing techniques that tobacco companies have employed.[18] They have turned to such strategies particularly in the largely unregulated markets (for tobacco) of eastern Europe and Asia and because of fears of declining markets in the United States.[19] Philip Morris, the world's largest tobacco company, increased its sales of cigarettes by nearly 80 per cent since 1990 even though its sales in the United States increased only 4.7 per cent during the same period.[20]

Thus, for those wishing to curtail consumption there is still much to be done. But how? And, what is the role for law?

Law and the Curtailment of Smoking

Changing Attitudes towards Regulation

Law and smoking for a long time did not have much to do with each other. Indeed, until recent decades official norms encouraged smoking in several ways from providing subsidies to farmers growing tobacco to distributing cigarettes to soldiers during war. There was a sprinkling of attempts at prohibition in America before the First World War, but these had little effect.[21] Any laws on the books restricting sales to minors only threw into relief the wide availability, including to teenagers, and the acceptance, indeed, desirability of smoking to relax, to socialize, to curb appetite, and so on.

Nonetheless, by the early sixties, doubts about tobacco were increasingly being voiced by the medical establishment, health-care advocates, and the media. A number of reports from prestigious agencies became ever more blunt in the cautions they issued about the harmful effects of nicotine.[22] Probably the most famous of these, at least in the United States, was the 1964 Surgeon General's Report. The message it delivered was clear: '[C]igarette smoking is a health hazard of sufficient importance in the United States to warrant appropriate remedial action.'[23]

As the warnings against smoking increased in number and intensity, so too did the efforts of the tobacco industry to resist the association between consumption and death.[24] Those responsible for the manufacture and sale of cigarettes adamantly denied both any causal connection between smoking and many diseases and that nicotine is addictive. However, few others credited such contentions.

It is theoretically possible that there is some other explanation that would establish that the strong association between smoking and so many diseases is not due to the noxious effects of nicotine. For example, it is conceivable that there is an as yet unknown genetic factor that triggers both the urge to smoke and diseases now linked to consumption of tobacco.[25] However, overwhelmingly, the scientific community rejects such other explanations and considers the association between various diseases and smoking to be well established.[26] Thus, in 1989, the US Surgeon General summarized twenty-five further years of studies and concluded that there were causal links between smoking and various cancers – lung, laryngeal, oral, and esophageal – as well as pulmonary diseases, heart disorders, and infant growth retardation.[27]

Further studies documenting the harmful aspects of smoking accumulated during the late 1980s and 1990s. Yet as late as 1994 senior executives of major tobacco companies were denying that cigarettes were addictive and disputing that they caused lung cancer and other deadly diseases. Finally, in 1997 a possible settlement of huge litigation claims (with certain immunities from future actions) was agreed to by the cigarette companies. (We will discuss that agreement in detail later.) The accord needed congressional approval and supporting legislation. In an effort to get the approval and have the legislation passed tobacco executives finally acknowledged the harmful and addictive aspects of tobacco.[28]

The recognition of the hazards of nicotine was accompanied by an entirely different attitude to regulation.[29] Over the last three decades and throughout the industrialized world non-smokers have increasingly pressed governments and their agencies to create official norms against the consumption of tobacco. And, if government wants to establish norms, at least in recent decades, it is primarily the law that it turns to.

Partly because of the strength of the tobacco industry and the obsession of smokers, partly because of the lesson learned in the 1930s regarding the prohibition of alcohol and black markets and smuggling, and partly because of fears regarding the effects on the millions dependent on nicotine, prohibition was not imposed, except in the case of children. Instead, governments tended to use several strategies to actively discourage smoking: banning advertising; requiring warnings on cigarette packaging; restricting the locations where smokers could indulge; and steeply increasing the price of the habit through substantial increases in taxation.

In addition, (mostly in the United States) there has been litigation. One set of lawsuits has sought – unsuccessfully – to establish that smokers may recover damages for the harm done to them by their addiction. More recently, there have been lawsuits by governments to recoup money that they have spent for the care of ill smokers. Finally, there have been claims by non-smokers for the harm they contend that they have suffered from ETS.

Grounds for Government Intervention

No one forces anyone to smoke or at least not in any obvious way. If that is the case, what is the basis for government intervention? Shouldn't individuals be permitted choice and, if that choice – even if it is unwise – is not harming others, why should governments meddle? Though several rationales for government action can be offered, they can, in essence, be captioned as follows: providing for informed choice; preventing costs to the state; and protecting non-smokers.

Informed Choice

The informed-choice rationale accepts that individuals should be able to make even harmful choices so long as they are, indeed, aware of the harms. The role of government under this rationale is to ensure that consumers are truly aware of the dangers of tobacco while allowing them to exercise choice. ('I understand smoking is harmful to me but I have decided that my enjoyment of it is greater than the risks. Leave me alone.') The notion of informed choice also supports restricting the sale of tobacco to minors on the grounds that, because of their age, they are not capable of true choice in terms of this dangerous substance.

However, some of those who oppose smoking would question the informed-choice rationale root and branch.[30] In doing so such advocates would point to the addictive properties of tobacco and argue that the ingestion of such a lethal and habit-forming substance calls into question the very idea of free choice. They push further by pointing to the insidious effects of advertising, which obscures the toxic aspects of tobacco and equates smoking, not with a dirty and expensive habit, but with glamour, talent, and physical appeal. Of course, many things are advertised that can be habit-forming or risky or both (from skydiving to potato chips to alcohol). Still anti-smoking advocates suggest that the magnitude of the harm caused by cigarettes and the strength of the addictive properties of nicotine set cigarette smoking apart and warrant its special treatment.

Those who defend tobacco or, in any event, assert the right to choose to smoke counter that, although smoking is habit-forming, the power of cigarettes is not such as to deny human will. They point to the fact that many who have formed a nicotine dependency have, nevertheless, stopped, albeit with some effort. There appears to be a 50 per cent quit rate among smokers (though the studies are unclear about several related issues, such as whether there is a segment of smokers who are particularly disposed to tobacco whether genetically or otherwise).[31] To put the issue another way, in America a recent National Survey on Drug Abuse found that almost three-fourths of respondents had tried smoking, but only about 30 per cent had smoked in the past month.[32]

As for advertising, defenders of the right to choose to smoke question its impact. They suggest, as we will see, that its primary effect (to the extent that it is effective) is in terms of inducing people to switch brands and not in persuading them to smoke in the first place. In any event, they argue that to deny the cigarette manufacturers the ability to advertise is to affront free speech.[33]

Costs to the State

The cost-to-the-state rationale focuses on the expense that the consumption of tobacco imposes on the public purse. This rationale is especially strong in countries such as Canada that have universal health care without user fees and without a private-care option. Thus, the health costs of disease are directly borne by the state. Moreover, in some cases, the burden of supporting individuals unable to support themselves because of diseases attributable to smoking must also be transferred to the public purse. This rationale promotes the complete elimination of smoking. It does not acknowledge any offsetting benefits such as those contemplated by the informed-choice rationale. Only the practical constraints of outright prohibition stand in the way of banning tobacco altogether.

Yet again, those who defend the right to choose to smoke raise a factual challenge in responding to this rationale for government intervention. They suggest that smokers already pay their way through the heavy taxes imposed on cigarettes.[34] Moreover, it has been argued that the burdens smokers impose on the state through their ill health are more than offset: they die young and, therefore, do not collect pensions, use the health-care system in old age (such demands can be very costly), or take space in nursing homes.

Protection of Non-Smokers

Finally, the rationale of protecting non-smokers focuses on how smoking can harm non-smokers through ETS (environmental tobacco smoke).[35] It can be invoked to buttress either the rationale for informed choice or that for costs to the state. In terms of informed choice, protection of non-smokers would stipulate that smokers must feed their habit in ways so as not to imperil the smoke-free. Thus, restrictions on where smokers may indulge (so as to shield non-smokers) override any claim to the 'right' to smoke anywhere in the name of freedom of choice. In terms of the costs-to-the-state rationale, protection of non-smokers suggests that smokers should be discouraged from burdening the health-care system by exposing the smoke-free to disease, the cost of which the system must then bear. In addition, smoking ought to be curtailed so that scarce health-care costs, otherwise consumed by diseased smokers, can be redeployed to care for other needs of those who do not indulge.

Again, those who defend the right to choose to smoke challenge the protection-of-non-smokers rationale on several grounds. They put in issue the extent to which ETS is harmful, pointing to the fact that studies indicate that prolonged and intense exposure to ETS can be harmful but are much less clear about intermittent exposure. As a result, defenders of smokers suggest that only in instances where non-smokers are being exposed to smoke on a continuous basis should there be any regulation. Those exposed intermittently may be able to argue for protection on the ground that smoke is a nuisance; but that is a far cry from suggesting that their well-being is imperilled and that the health-care system will be burdened.

The informed-choice rationale has been very effective in terms of prohibiting the sale of cigarettes to minors, regulating advertising, and making health warnings prominent. The cost-to-the-state rationale is propelling litigation in the United States to recover monies that governments have paid to care for ill smokers. At the same time, such litigation also tests the claim that smokers' early deaths offset any expenses that their illnesses otherwise impose. The protection-of-non-smokers rationale has supported regulation banning or at least restricting smoking in a variety of places, mostly on the ground that ETS is a nuisance if not also harmful. However, we shall see that such regulation of public places is testing the limits of the enforceability of the law in this context.

The Tools of the Law

The role of governments in the campaign against smoking is of interest on several levels. The most important, given the ambitions of this book, is the assessment of the impact of laws in terms of curtailment. This is a matter we will turn to momentarily.

Yet another focus of interest are the different policy tools available to governments and how, in this instance, they have been employed: governments of various stripe and in different countries have invoked regulation of marketing, taxation, restriction/banning of smoking in public places, and prohibition of sales to minors.[36] In addition, mostly in the United States, there has been litigation seeking to establish that smokers may recover damages for the harm done to them by their addiction. One tool that governments have not employed is outright prohibition of the sale and consumption of cigarettes. We begin with a discussion of this possibility that has not been used, other than in the important exception of minors.

Prohibition

At a theoretical level the easiest way to respond to the perils of tobacco would be simply to ban it. Such prohibition would plainly accord with

the costs-to-the-state and protection-of-non-smokers rationales discussed in the last section. This is so because, since neither of these
rationales recognizes a benefit to smoking, the most straightforward
way to alleviate its costs to health care, non-smokers, and so forth is to
ban tobacco. However, government involvement with a strong industry and the lessons learned from the prohibition of alcohol, taken
together, have been sufficient to curb any temptations to employ this
tool.

When governments finally began to intervene to curtail smoking
they found themselves in a contradictory position. On the one hand, a
critical mass of public opinion was pushing them towards considering
various legal measures to suppress smoking. On the other, they had
long been involved in supporting the tobacco industry and, in turn,
receiving revenues from it. Such assistance took several forms. In some
countries such as the United States and Canada, there were special
subsidies to farmers for growing tobacco.[37] In others, such as France,
the dominant producer and supplier (until recently) is state-owned.[38]
Then too, nearly all governments had placed some tax on the sale of
cigarettes; they were being pressured to take action against a significant source of revenue.

Further, the tobacco industry is a strong one. In Canada and the
United States a few cigarette manufacturers dominate the market and
have increasingly diversified their businesses. They are highly organized and coordinated. At the same time, they are important employers, advertisers, sponsors of sports, the arts, and charities, and large
contributors to political campaigns. Not an industry that would
readily accept its own demise.

At any rate, any temptation to invoke prohibition had also to face the
sorry record of attempts to ban alcohol in the United States in the nineteen thirties.[39] Prohibition fostered organized crime and aggravated
urban and rural division about the permissibility of drinking. In the
face of concerted opposition from the tobacco industry and the addictive powers of nicotine over those already smoking, banning appeared
too strong a step, one that was likely to do more harm than good.

The important exception regarding prohibition has been in the case
of minors. As we saw in the previous section, much of the claim of the
right to choose to smoke rests on the rationale of informed choice. But
a linchpin of informed choice is the capacity to choose. Law and society have long taken the position in many areas that children – just
because they are children – are incapable of independent choice

(regarding the forming of contracts, voting, drinking, and so forth). As a result, even robust supporters of informed choice draw the line with minors. They thus support restrictions of sales to children and of advertising that targets the underaged.[40]

As a result, some countries, such as Canada, have restricted the sale of cigarettes to minors. In the United States individual states ban the sale of tobacco to children. In addition, some states have recently enacted provisions holding children responsible for buying cigarettes, imposing a variety of penalties for doing so.[41]

Yet, here too, the ability of the state to achieve compliance with any form of ban is called into question. As discussed, one counter-trend to decreasing smoking rates is increasing consumption among teenagers. Moreover, smoking among minors is significant because it has been demonstrated that most adults who are in the thrall of a smoking habit started when they were teenagers. Very few individuals who try smoking as adults continue for any extended period of time; nine out of ten smokers start before they turn eighteen. What is more, those who start young are more likely, eventually, to suffer smoking-related illnesses, since the longer one has smoked the more likely it is that health problems will develop.[42]

The fact is that prohibition of sales and even the threat of punishment have not arrested smoking among teens; indeed, rates of consumption have, in fact, increased somewhat in the 1990s despite the ban on sales. Though there is some dispute about the strictness of enforcement on bans of sales to minors, studies of towns in the United States indicate that teenagers have little difficulty obtaining cigarettes: 70 per cent of underage youths who tried to buy tobacco said that they succeeded most of the time.[43]

As for advertising, many jurisdictions that have bans on selling cigarettes to youths also have prohibitions against advertising that induces the underaged to smoke. Yet cigarette companies long denied that they targeted minors, arguing that any aspects of their campaigns that appeared particularly attractive to youths are unintended and merely incidental to a strategy aimed at adults. The companies maintained that it was peer pressure and not anything they did which induced teenagers to begin to smoke.[44]

For almost as long a period anti-smoking activists hotly disputed this characterization by the cigarette companies. The most famous target of those opposed to smoking was Joe Camel. R.J. Reynolds, maker of Camel cigarettes, introduced in the United States in 1987 the character of 'Joe Camel.' This was a grinning, slick cartoon figure that anti-smoking activists claimed was intended to push teenagers towards smoking. The figure appeared not only on the packaging and in advertisements but also on T-shirts and other clothing under the theme 'smooth character.' Opponents pointed to figures that indicated that before the campaign Camel's share of the smoking market for minors was 3 per cent. After the campaign was introduced Camel's share rose steadily to 13.2 per cent in 1993.[45]

In early 1998, files of cigarette companies were released that established that R.J. Reynolds (among others) targeted teenagers. Memoranda from the 1970s into the late 1980s divulged concerted strategies to cultivate minors as purchasers. One 1975 memorandum stated: '[T]he [Camel] brand must increase its share penetration among the 14–24 age group, which have a new set of more liberal values and which represent tomorrow's cigarette business.'[46] Such revelations propelled the anti-smoking cause forward, especially regarding steps to cut underage smoking. It also finally demolished any vestige of a defence of 'Joe Camel,' which Reynolds, in an attempt to shield itself from the furor, had abandoned just months before.[47] In the proposed settlement of the tobacco litigation (which we will discuss in detail later)[48] the tobacco companies agreed to severe restrictions on advertising to minors. Whether or not the settlement will be finalized and what the effects of any such restrictions might be remain to be seen.

Regulation of Advertising and Marketing

One of the first things governments did when they began to intervene on the side of curtailment was to require cigarette packages to carry warnings about the dangers of smoking. Such labelling did not occur in isolation, but was linked to a tradition of governments requiring that hazardous products display warnings about their dangers. Starting with the comparatively mild and discreetly placed 'Smoking may be dangerous to your health,'[49] the cautions, in various countries, have become more prominent and more explicit; for example, 'smoking can kill you.'[50] Beginning in 2001 Canada required cigarette packages to carry an assortment of blunt warnings and graphic depictions of the horrors of diseases associated with smoking.[51] In addition, governments conducted their own anti-smoking campaigns in the media and elsewhere. Such campaigns, properly carried out, have been effective in depressing the rate of consumption.[52]

Subsequent to the initiatives concerning labelling, various countries in the 1980s restricted advertising. Typically, advertising and promotions on television and in newspapers and magazines have been banned. Some laws, as in Canada, also prohibit ads on billboards and transit posters and at points of sale. Further, there are sometimes restrictions of brand-name tobacco promotions of arts and sports events and their use on non-tobacco products (T-shirts, mugs, etc.).[53] As just discussed, these restrictions were particularly aimed at protecting youths from inducements to smoke. Some governments – moving on the offensive – began their own advertising campaigns warning of the deleterious effects of smoking.[54] In the United States the Food and Drug Administration (FDA) for the first time in 1996 asserted jurisdiction over cigarettes and other tobacco products. In doing so the FDA reversed a decades-old position. The goal of the FDA was to lessen consumption of tobacco by those under eighteen by means of a federal ban on the sale of tobacco products (to those under eighteen) and several restrictions on tobacco advertising. These initiatives were immersed in controversy concerning the FDA's jurisdiction. In early 2000 the Supreme Court ruled that the agency did not have such jurisdiction.[55]

How effective was the banning of advertising of cigarettes as an element of anti-smoking campaigns? Those detached from the partisanship around these issues have difficulty stating the impact with precision. At the same time, attempts to ban any form of communication will, at least in North America, run afoul of constitutional protection of free speech. The question of the effects of regulating advertising and the entanglements coming from claims of 'free speech' are explored below, where we look at the impact of all efforts regarding curtailing smoking. We will particularly focus on Canada, where attempts at banning cigarette advertising have been ambitious and, yet, where attacks on such bans, using the free-speech banner and litigation, have been effective.

Taxation

Many countries have invoked taxation as a tool in restricting consumption of cigarettes. At a theoretical level, a major rationale for using taxation is to transfer the cost of smoking from the public purse to those who produce and consume tobacco.[56] To this extent most countries have been very successful. The United States is, comparatively speaking, at a low level of taxes on cigarettes. Yet several studies argue that, even in that country, the taxes charged more than offset any costs imposed by smokers on the health-care system. One analysis, reported in 1996, suggested that smokers cost society an average of 33 cents a pack while paying 52 cents a pack in federal and state taxes.[57] The allegation that smokers pay (through taxes on tobacco) for any costs they otherwise impose on the public purse has been vigorously challenged.[58] Such allegations and responses to them are critical since, if it can be demonstrated that smokers pay their own way in terms of governmental expenditures on their behalf, the case for a claim by state agencies to recover such costs essentially evaporates.

Taxation can also be viewed as a practical alternative to prohibition. From this perspective smoking is not made the focus of the heavy hand of criminal law, with all the repercussions that may ensue. There is some controversy over the extent to which cigarettes are price-elastic, that is, how much price and consumption are directly related, so that raising the price of cigarettes will depress consumer purchases and, therefore, consumption.[59] However, most analyses suggest that elasticity exists, perhaps especially among teenagers.[60] Thus, taxes on cigarettes can be raised to such a level that smoking stops because the manufacture, sale, and consumption of it is uneconomical. To the extent that money is recouped to cover the public costs of smoking (even as the enterprise is ground to a halt), so much the better.

Taxation was incorporated into anti-smoking campaigns in several countries. However, the extent to which this tool was employed varied substantially. The United States employed it; Western Europe more so; Canada the most of all.[61] Yet if taxation is touted as a practical alternative to prohibition it can, if sufficiently onerous, produce unintended consequences akin to those resulting from prohibition. In important ways, such effects occurred in Canada. Such consequences will be pursued below, when we look at the impact that various forms of regulation of nicotine have had.

Restriction/Banning of Smoking in Public Places

Concern for non-smokers' comfort and the harm of ETS prompted several countries, most prominently Canada and the United States, to ban or drastically restrict smoking in public places. Other countries have followed suit, though in less-aggressive ways and, sometimes, with less concern about compliance.[62] Governments, within the scope of their legislative powers, have become aggressive in pushing smokers to indulge either outdoors or in the privacy of any homes tolerating the habit. Such initiatives included (at federal, state, and provincial levels) the banning of smoking on airplanes and in governmental buildings and, usually at municipal levels, the banning, or at least confining, of smoking in restaurants and bars.[63]

The evidence that exists suggests that, on the whole, compliance with these restrictions has been high.[64] When we turn to our discussion of impact we will see that obedience appears not to rest on the threat of sanctions so much as on a social consensus (shared to a great extent by those who indulge) that non-smokers ought to be shielded from ETS. At the same time, we will see that that consensus can be severely tested and cannot be pushed too far too quickly. Otherwise, governments can have defiance on their hands; the campaign against smoking can suffer setbacks.

Tort Litigation – An American Response

As with so many other complex issues, the United States has turned to litigation to forge policy regarding the liability of tobacco companies to smokers who become sick and die and, more recently, regarding the effects of ETS and for the recoupment of expenses borne by governments for the care of smokers. Other countries have turned to this particular form of legal policy-making much less frequently, if at all.[65] Chapter 4 discussed competing perspectives on the utility of using litigation to achieve progressive change.[66] Much of the litigation (to July 1999) claiming redress for harm done by tobacco provides evidence for those sceptical about the use of courts.

At a theoretical level, there are several reasons why litigation could be attractive as part of the campaign against smoking. Such reasons would include shifting the costs of smoking back to those responsible for the harm; raising the price of cigarettes (because of the shift back), thus discouraging consumption; and intensifying negative publicity, most prominently through a court finding of causal linkages between smoking and assorted diseases.[67] Yet, until very recently such lawsuits have failed.[68] A series of lawsuits brought by various state governments in the United States has resulted in a settlement. However, that agreement has been strongly criticized as inadequately restraining tobacco companies in marketing cigarettes and for pre-empting further legislative efforts in the states. In the shadow of that settlement, some municipalities have commenced tort litigation against gun manufacturers, seeking to hold them liable for the damage caused by the use of their weapons: desperate initiatives seeking to use lawsuits to forge policy.

Three Stages of Litigation: In the United States litigation regarding the effects of smoking has been described as having occurred in three stages.[69] The first comprised product-liability cases brought by individuals in the 1950s and 1960s. The two main theories upon which these claims were brought were breach of warranty (both express and implied) and negligence in the failure to warn of the addictive properties and sinister effects of tobacco.[70]

Cigarette companies asserted two defences in these cases. First, they contested the claim that tobacco caused the illnesses and damages suffered by the plaintiffs. Second, they asserted that, in any event, plaintiffs freely choose to smoke while aware of any dangers it might cause. Therefore, they were responsible for any harm that they suffered. As the public became more aware of the dangers of smoking, judges and juries were not sympathetic to the first defence, but, at the same time, this awareness buttressed the second one. No suits were successful in the first wave.

The second stage, during the 1980s, appeared to offer the prospect of recovery on behalf of an individual smoker when a federal court did hold cigarette companies liable in the *Cipollone* case.[71] This litigation encouraged other such suits to be filed. However, the verdict in *Cippollone* was overturned on appeal several years later, and the plaintiffs and their lawyers abandoned further steps in the case when the costs became overwhelming.[72] With the termination of the *Cipollone* litigation many anti-smoking activists concluded that there was little to be gained in bringing litigation on behalf of individual smokers.[73] There have, however, been some assertions of claims on behalf of smokers in class actions that focus on the addictive properties of nicotine and claim that cigarette companies conspired to hide the dangerous propensities of tobacco. None of these claims has been successful. They have either been dismissed at trial or have been overturned on appeal. However, in 2000, plaintiffs were successful in winning a jury verdict in Florida.[74] If that decision were to be upheld on appeal, very substantial sums could be awarded against the tobacco companies and the verdict could pave the way for other lawsuits.

That said, as late as 2000 not one cent had actually been recovered on behalf of smokers from cigarette companies. To succeed in these actions smokers need to convince judges and juries and appellate courts that their persistence in smoking resulted from a habit they were lured into by the tobacco companies. In sum, their claims rested on a claim of victimhood.[75] Despite the fact that 'victimhood' enjoys currency in other areas of the law, it has had little success in these lawsuits. In such actions the campaign against smoking was, in a sense, turned on smokers. After almost three decades of increasing publicity about the hazards of tobacco and evidence of huge numbers of smokers quitting, those claiming damages because they continued to smoke did not cross the critical threshold of sympathy necessary to be successful in litigation. Indeed, rightly or wrongly, smokers' claims of victimhood have, generally, not been responded to on any front. Unlike the case of alcohol, there are very few public or private treatment programs to assist smokers in combating and ending their addiction.[76] Rather, the norm that seems established and buttressed in any number of ways is 'Don't start.'

The third stage of litigation is a product of the 1990s. It has shifted the focus away from compensation for individual smokers. Instead, lawsuits have asserted two other kinds of claims for compensation. First, there has been litigation regarding the effects of ETS on those exposed to second-hand smoke on a continuous and intense basis. However, the 'rights' of non-smokers to be protected are to date (1999) quite unclear. Several courts have used the fact of a parent smoking as an element in determining custody of children or access to them.[77] The relevance of smoking in such custody cases is based primarily on the rationale that children are not capable, on their own, of protecting themselves from ETS. Other courts have held that to enforce such protective orders would invade a right of privacy of smokers to indulge in their own homes. In terms of employees, the right to be protected from ETS or to claim damages for harm caused by exposure to second-hand smoke is unclear. In 1997 a trial began in a class-action suit on behalf of flight attendants who claimed to have been damaged as a result of being exposed to second-hand smoke on a continuous basis during their employment.[78] The action claims the greatest amount of money sought to date against the cigarette companies. It is widely regarded as capable, if fully litigated, of substantially clarifying the extent of cigarette companies' liability for ETS.

The second kind of claim asserted in the 1990s has sought recompense for governments who have borne costs for the care and treatment of ill smokers, particularly in terms of Medicaid (America's health system for the poor). Such claims were led by Mississippi, followed by several other states. These actions were highly organized, had the force of government behind them, and were conducted by very talented and diverse counsel. The tobacco companies took them seriously.

The Tobacco Settlement: So seriously, in fact, that they entered into protracted negotiations, fuelled by the fact that a maverick company (Ligett) broke ranks and negotiated its own settlement. Such bargaining culminated in a huge and complex agreement in mid-1997. By its terms the states signing this settlement would grant the companies immunity from further actions by them. Individuals could still sue, but damages would be capped at $5 billion a year. In exchange the cigarette companies consented to a number of provisions, including the following:

- The payment of $368.5 billion over the next 25 years to compensate states for the costs of treating smoking-related illness, to finance nation-wide anti-smoking programs, and to underwrite health care for millions of uninsured children.
- Accepting responsibility for the reduction in smoking by teenagers up to 60 per cent in ten years, with penalties of $80 million for each percentage of the goal not met.
- The cessation of all advertising and marketing targeting underage smokers. All human and cartoon characters and Internet, movie, and television advertising would be banned. Cigarette companies would not sponsor sporting events or outdoor concerts and would not participate in give-aways of merchandise bearing cigarette logos.
- The industry would no longer challenge the jurisdiction of the Food and Drug Administration over its products. As a result, the FDA could regulate nicotine, including the acceptable levels of it in cigarettes.
- The deal would not limit criminal liability.

However, because of various provisions the agreement needed congressional approval (and supporting legislation) to be effective.[79] The ink was scarcely dry before critics of the deal began to cry foul.[80] One set of criticisms suggested that the entire settlement was misconceived and a capitulation to political pressure because, properly analysed, the states' cases would have revealed that the cigarette companies had no, or at least diminished, liability.[81]

Another set of criticisms worried that the deal was too lenient in terms of what was required from the companies and the controls put upon the industry.[82] For example, the accord made it clear that the FDA had the power to regulate tobacco and, therefore, could order levels of nicotine reduced in cigarettes. However, to do so the FDA would have to demonstrate that reduction of such levels would not create a black market in full-strength cigarettes. Moreover, the accord contained an obligation on the industry to reduce underage smoking by up to 60 per cent in ten years. However, one set of calculations indicated that the biggest penalty that the industry would have to pay would be $2 billion a year, an amount that could be recouped by raising the price of a pack of cigarettes by 8 cents. In any event, the industry could apply for a rebate of up to 75 per cent of the penalty if it could show that it had taken all reasonable available steps to curb smoking by minors.[83]

In addition, there was concern that the lawyers who had been hired to bring the cases – and who, in fairness, took the risks on a contingency basis – drove the settlement to get the highest fees possible (in terms of immediate and future monetary payouts by the industry) and not with a view to ending smoking.[84] Finally, in the wake of the possibility of a deal the shares in tobacco stock rose. Shares in tobacco companies had been trading at a discount for some time. The suggestion is that the settlement provided more certainty regarding the fortunes of the tobacco industry in America than did the vagaries of the political and litigation terrain up to the point of the accord. Even the maximum amount (which under the terms of the agreement was to be tax-deductible) paid under the accord would be dwarfed by the rise in stock values and the overall increase in business.[85]

That settlement eventually fell apart. In its place a multi-state deal was brokered in November 1998. That agreement did not require the participation of the federal government, and involved a smaller amount of money (about $206 billion). Therefore, the tax to be imposed would be less – about 35 cents a pack. There are also fewer restrictions on marketing. On the other side, tobacco companies were only protected from litigation brought by the participating states and not from litigation brought on behalf of individuals or by the federal government.[86] Meanwhile the federal government in late 1999 commenced its own civil litigation. The lawsuit charged the tobacco companies with fraud regarding the dangers of nicotine. It sought billions of dollars for reimbursement of funds spent by that government on smoking-related health care.[87]

The Hazards of the Tobacco Settlement: The November 1998 compromise (the multi-state agreement) has also been harshly criticized. The plan is not well designed to reduce consumption, particularly of the most harmful kinds of cigarettes: it contains fewer marketing restrictions than the other accord and the tax is imposed per pack rather than levied in proportion to the extent of danger of the cigarettes, for example, in terms of tar content. At the same time, the architects of the arrangement – lawyers – will receive gargantuan amounts out of the settlement. Estimates went as high as $16 million each for the 500 lawyers involved.[88] What is more, there is evidence that most of the states participating in the settlement are not using the funds they have received to combat smoking.[89]

That litigation (and its settlement) and tobacco lawsuits, generally, may have driven home the dangers of cigarettes. These lawsuits may have exposed the industry to all manner of negative publicity, particularly regarding the tactics that they employed to induce people to smoke, especially those underage.[90] Yet it may have been better for states to continue to fight in court, and to persist (by no means an easy path) until their legislatures passed enactments imposing a well-designed tax together with further, effective marketing restrictions. There is a track record here: regulation of tobacco is a proven instance where governmental activity has been successful, in the recent past, in battling levels of smoking.

More generally, there are overarching dangers in a broad-scale settlement that arises from litigation involving government and designed by lawyers collecting sky-high fees.[91] As the democratic process is subverted, a number of hazards await.[92] The 'victory' of a settlement may impose ill-designed terms that do not accomplish their goals.[93] An agreement may, as a practical (and, depending on its terms, legal) matter, take the steam out of other initiatives (education, restrictions of smoking in public places, effective restrictions on advertising, and so forth) that may be vital in suppressing even farther the consumption levels. 'No sane system would invite lawyers to design bad taxes by stealth in exchange for a fat cut of the proceeds. Insane or not, this is the turn that American product-liability law has now taken.'[94]

Meanwhile, outside the USA the lure of litigation beckons at the expense of pushing forward with policies that could be much more effective. The province of Ontario (Canada), urged on by several factors, including the US settlement, announced that it would sue for loss sustained for health care and related costs in helping smokers. That action was launched even though advisers to the government were publicly adamant that such litigation, even if successful, would play a marginal role in the war against smoking ('suing the tobacco industry is not to be confused with tobacco control.')[95]

The tobacco litigation and any settlements it achieves send out a signal that the hard, hard work of popular politics should be bypassed in the fight against smoking and in other areas. Inspired by the example of the tobacco litigation, some US cities, abetted by enterprising tort lawyers, are commencing lawsuits against gun manufacturers for the havoc wreaked by arms (though some states have outlawed such suits).[96] America does need a sane policy on gun control (a matter discussed in chapter 2).[97] However, attempting to forge such a response through litigation, in the shadow of the tobacco settlement, is yet another erosion of popular politics in the Republic. Such politics should be capable of making and implementing a policy on gun control. Yet just now, there are few indications of that ability.[98] The worry is that tort lawsuits as a substitute will only make matters worse. Such litigation – whatever the outcome – is yet another desperate attempt in America to stitch together policy through the courts, however chancy the results.[99]

The Law, Attitudes – and Impact

'The Rising Wave of Cultural Support'

Chapter 4 discussed a number of ideas about the impact of the law. One of these was titled 'Law Acting in Concert with Social and Political Forces.' This hypothesis claims that the actual impact of a law will most closely correspond to its intended goal when that law and related social and political forces are aligned – the greater the alignment, the more likely that the law will have the effect that its proponents predict.[100] Another idea discussed in chapter 4 is 'Law as Deflection.' This idea asserts that law often shifts attention away from underlying social, political, or economic problems that it was meant to redress. As a result, law can actually exacerbate rather than assist problematic conditions to which it was meant to respond. One variant of 'Law as Deflection' is captured in the work of 'normativists.' Although they vary in their perspectives and the topics upon which they focus, those interested in 'normativity' share in common a scepticism about the capacity of law to alter behaviour directly. Instead, they insist that norms, existing or altered, have a critical role in achieving policy goals. It is not that law is irrelevant. Rather, norms can be a significant determinant in attaining the ends one seeks to achieve through law.

An example of both 'Law Acting in Concert with Social and Political Forces' and 'normativity' is the results of the campaign against smoking. Laws aimed at suppressing smoking, imposing high taxes upon it, and regulating the public spaces where smokers can indulge all buttressed developing norms relating to smoking – converting it from being viewed as a glamorous indulgence to being seen as a dirty, deadly addiction. A surfing analogy ('a rising wave of cultural support'), used by one set of commentators, is quite descriptive. It is a depiction not only of law's role against smoking but also of the 'law acting in concert' hypothesis generally:

> Like surfers, legislators and corporate officials who wish to change every-day social norms must wait for signs of a rising wave of cultural support, catching it at just the right time. Legislate too soon and they will be swamped by the swells of popular resistance. Legislate too late and they will be irrelevant. Legislate at the right moment and an emerging cultural norm, still tentatively struggling for authority – such as that condemning involuntary exposure to tobacco smoke – acquires much greater moral force.[101]

One response to this perceived close interaction between law and developing norms is to suggest that the result is obvious and unremarkable. Yet, a priori, it is as plausible that curtailment of smoking by elites and anti-smoking activists results in relevant legislation as it is that anti-smoking laws bring down the rate of consumption.[102] Moreover, if we look beyond the United States and Canada, the experience in other societies indicates that the relative success of anti-smoking campaigns in these two countries was by no means preordained.

In some countries, such as Japan, there appears to be little desire to combat smoking.[103] At least, in part, the population may have been lulled into a false sense of security about their susceptibility to the poisons of nicotine. Similarly, as discussed earlier in this chapter, there is evidence that smoking is on the rise in third world nations and in eastern European countries.[104] In these countries tobacco companies have become even more aggressive in their marketing techniques, in part to offset declining sales, actual and anticipated, in the North American markets.

Also remarkable are countries such as France, where there has been a government-sponsored campaign against smoking that mirrors, at least in some critical ways, those in Canada and the United States. However, the French initiatives were much less successful, at least up to the mid-1990s. It is, of course, possible that the campaign in France could take hold at some point and do so in fairly rapid order.[105]

The French experience, compared with that of Canada and the United States, is evidence of another idea discussed in chapter 4: 'National Styles of Regulation – "American Exceptionalism" I.'[106] This hypothesis claims that there may be significantly different ways in which societies use law and implement it. A critical aspect of this potential difference is the role of law in the United States compared with other countries, particularly other Western industrialized nations. Several studies, in a wide range of areas, all point in the same direction: the United States' form of regulation is highly legalistic, contentious, and costly compared with that of other such societies. The French experience offers evidence that laws, about essentially the same subject, can have markedly different impacts in different countries. At the same time, an analysis of the regulation of smoking demonstrates that in America it has worked.

France came to using law later than Canada and the United States. Only in 1976 did it require cigarette packages to carry – ambivalent[107] – warnings about the dangers of smoking. It has banned tobacco advertising from television, radio, billboards, and movies. Further, while not curtailing the activities of the state-owned tobacco consortium SEITA, the French government did raise taxes on tobacco considerably.[108] This last measure turned out to have revenue-enhancing consequences because consumption did not decline.

Smoking among French elites has remained at high levels. Generally, consumption rates, in comparative terms, have greatly exceeded those in Canada and the United States, at least for several years.[109] Meanwhile, educational campaigns were ill financed and bans on movie ads and prohibitions on smoking in government facilities were largely ignored.[110] Why? And why for a country that, in many ways, is far more regulated than the United States and, even, Canada.[111]

The explanation lies not with the laws themselves but with the difference in the relevant norms and the comparative support for those norms.[112] This account returns us to the ideas of the 'normativists' discussed in chapter 4.[113] Norms characterizing smoking as a harmful, dirty addiction became far more entrenched in Canada and the

United States than they did in France during roughly the same period. Why?

One explanation that has been offered is the presence in the United States (and Canada) of 'a cultural disposition strongest in the educated classes but with wide support throughout the middle and working classes, to decry the ingestion or inhalation of chemical substances that are thought to be the causes of disease.'[114] In contrast, in France there is 'fierce popular resistance to moralistic social control of individual beliefs and lifestyle choices.'[115] However misdirected such resistance may have been in this case, the campaigns and laws to discourage smoking were judged to reflect such controls.[116]

Anti-smoking laws in France were the product of elite accommodation and only a section of the elite at that. France's chief pressure group was a loose alliance of academics and doctors who treated smoking as a public health issue rather than waging an anti-tobacco company campaign.[117] Campaigns to enact such laws were nowhere near the product of popular agitation that they were in Canada and the United States.[118] The non-smokers' rights activists who asserted themselves popularly and in the voice of the law had no real counterpart in France, in any event, until recently.

Laws in the United States and Canada focused on suppressing smoking and on regulating public spaces, for those who do smoke, were successful both in sharply curtailing the rate of smoking and in achieving compliance with stipulations concerning where it could take place. These laws were supported by and interacted with a 'rising wave of cultural support.' Such laws and the cultural support of them reflected 'the broadest range of social meaning regulation'[119] In France, at least until the late 1990s, similar enactments had little effect on smoking rates and their attempts to regulate where smokers could indulge were widely flouted. For such laws there was little cultural surf and more a calm sea of indifference.[120]

The Quandaries of Advertising: The Case of Canada

Of all the laws targeting nicotine, in many ways the most controversial have been those that ban the advertising of tobacco. These laws are contentious: on the one hand, because they run afoul of free-speech concerns, especially in Canada and the United States with their constitutionalized protections, and, on the other, because there are serious questions about the effectiveness of advertising and, therefore, the case for its banning.

For a number of reasons Canada is a good country to focus on in terms of the impact of laws regulating smoking. Canada initially lagged behind the United States. However, by 1991 it was close to, if not leading the world, in restricting cigarette marketing, in deterring use through taxation, and in directly regulating cigarette use.[121] Yet such aggressive policies, in turn, were the subject of reaction. In this section we will look at the Canadian laws banning advertising and their entanglements with free-speech issues. In the next section we will look at the unintended consequences of the very high taxes imposed on cigarettes and on the regulation of smoking in public places. There we will examine what may be the limits to laws that have otherwise been effective in curtailing smoking.

The Effects of Advertising?

There is a widespread belief – perhaps particularly among anti-smoking advocates – that cigarette advertising is very effective in promoting sales. Common sense suggests that it must have an impact; otherwise why would corporations, with a hard eye on the bottom line, do so much of it? Yet, as we will see, the impact of advertising is not so clear. So, for a book focused on the consequences of law, it is especially interesting that, in this instance, there are also important issues raised about the effects of some of the activities that the law has regulated.

It is not clear that corporations, in fact, spend a great deal on advertising, though the dollars spent and the significance of advertising expenditures are controversial.[122] In most product areas, advertising expenses represent a small percentage of total expenses in producing and marketing a product. For instance, in 1990, tobacco companies, in the United States, spent approximately 4 cents in advertising for every dollar of sales. This amount is consistent with advertising for sales, generally, in that country; hospitals, for instance, spent about 5 per cent.[123]

Second, corporations maintain that advertising can have an impact, but a limited one. In the context of smoking, the claim is that its main consequence is to shift smokers from brand to brand. Major advertising for a brand may only yield 3 per cent of the cigarette market, but that may be quite sufficient for profitability.[124] Third, there may be no clear direct benefit to advertising. Yet corporations may do so because they fear – in this consumerized society that they have helped to create – what will happen if they stop. For example, investors in tobacco companies may be deterred if they are not greeted by an aggressive, slick sales pitch in the marketing of the company's products.[125]

Several commentators, including those who support curtailment of smoking, suggest that 'commercial advertising for cigarettes as well as for other products normally has only slight effect in persuading people to change their attitudes or behaviours.'[126] Likewise, the evidence is mixed regarding the impact of educational campaigns to deter smoking.[127] What is more, a large number of econometric studies to model the effects of aggregate advertising on aggregate tobacco sales or consumption find either no overall relationship or a small (but statistically significant) positive relationship.[128]

Results from 'natural' experiments are also hard to evaluate. That is to say, there are countries that have banned advertising where smoking has declined. However, in virtually all these nations banning was accompanied by other anti-smoking measures, such as raising taxes. Therefore, it is difficult to demonstrate what effect, if any, banning has had.[129] Nevertheless, a British report done in the early 1990s analysed the effects of advertising bans in Canada, Finland, New Zealand, and Norway. The World Health Organization, quoting the report, concluded: 'Though there are qualifications ... the current evidence ... indicates a significant effect. In each case the banning of advertising was followed by a fall in consumption which cannot be reasonably attributed to other factors.'[130]

Many of those opposed to smoking might recognize the difficulty of establishing a direct link between prohibiting advertising and the suppression of smoking rates. Yet they point to one area where surely advertising has had some effects by the cigarette companies' own admission: the recruiting of underage smokers. We have canvassed the pertinent facts, in the earlier discussion in this chapter, surrounding underage smokers and advertising by cigarette companies. Briefly, the companies denied that advertising targeted teens and, in any event, insisted it was peer pressure that induced minors to smoke. On the other side, anti-smoking activists pointed to the fact that nine out of ten smokers started underage; thus recruitment of minors was absolutely essential to the continued thriving of the industry. In addition, they alleged that cartoon characters, such as R.J. Reynolds' 'Joe Camel,' presented cigarettes as an attractive activity for teenagers.

In the context of the tobacco settlement documents came out that suggest the anti-smokers were essentially right: memoranda over at least fifteen years reveal a concerted effort to recruit teens. For example, as recently as 1988, R.J. Reynolds planned to use billboards and posters to aggressively promote its products in areas where minors gather, such as fast-food restaurants and video-game arcades. Moreover, a 1986 memorandum of that company discussed ways to attract admittedly 18 to 24 year olds ('younger adult smokers') by using 'peer acceptance/ influence to provide the motivations for target smokers to select Camel.'[131]

In the fray around the tobacco settlement Reynolds abandoned its 'Joe Camel' campaign. As indicated, as part of the accord the cigarette companies agreed to cease all marketing and targeting of underage smokers and to take responsibility for a reduction in teenage smoking and pay fines if the use of cigarettes by minors did not decline.

In any event, even if evidence of the effects of banning advertising can be characterized as uncertain, there remain powerful arguments permitting advertising bans as part of a government's campaign against smoking. Studies may find only a small (but statistically significant) relationship between tobacco advertising and sales. However, that relationship is positive. Moreover, while governments banning advertising usually combine the prohibition with other anti-smoking devices, the fact is that, together, these measures can result in curtailment of smoking. The fact that one cannot precisely attribute an impact to prohibiting advertising does not deny the possibility that banning, in conjunction with other measures, can result in the curtailment of smoking.[132]

Finally, it can be forcefully argued that there are very few benefits that may be denied by such efforts.[133] We know that tobacco kills. Even if banning advertising only has a marginal impact, its costs do not interfere with a product that has any social utility.[134]

The Supreme Court of Canada, Smoking – and Free Speech

Nevertheless, once 'free speech' is invoked things can take quite a different turn. There are endless debates in the literature about how basic free speech is to democracy. Suffice it to say here that responsible commentators immediately agree that it is fundamental. The problem arises in trying to answer basic questions about free speech such as What constitutes speech? Should corporate actors be entitled to its protections? Under what circumstances can governments interfere with speech in attempting to promote other, fundamental goals?[135]

In 1995 free speech locked horns with the ban on tobacco advertising in the Supreme Court of Canada.[136] The ban lost. Whether free speech won depends very much on one's point of view. The majority focused on the lack of clear evidence that advertising induces people to start (or not cease) smoking. Based on this lack of evidence, they then separated lifestyle advertising (designed to increase overall consumption) from brand-name advertising (encouraging brand loyalty or, conversely, brand switching.) The former can be banned because of the 'common sense' connection between advertising and consumption. However, in the absence of significant evidence establishing a link, banning the latter was an excessive curb on the right of corporations to engage in free speech. (The issue of how, practically, one can distinguish between lifestyle and brand-name advertising is an important one; not, however, pursued here.)

The decision created a stir and pleased scarcely anyone. Anti-smoking advocates were up in arms.[137] They charged that the decision demonstrated the Court's lack of sensitivity to complex issues of social policy, perhaps particularly of a progressive cast.[138] Simultaneously, commercial-free-speech enthusiasts criticized the Court for its narrow majority and its lack of robust enthusiasm for the rights of corporations.[139] The controversy, itself, was important. The Court's decision may have far-reaching implications in terms of what elements of free speech are fostered in Canada and the extent to which corporate interests come to dominate the way free speech is understood in Canada.[140] The judgment was also further evidence that progressives who see courts as a promising alternative to recalcitrant politicians and a dulled citizenry will, mostly, face disappointment.[141] In this instance, 'rights' were successfully invoked by corporations to shield campaigns that induce individuals to enter the thrall of a poisonous addiction.

Immediately after the decision the tobacco companies seemed conciliatory. Media stories appeared suggesting that the enthusiasm that even cigarette companies have for advertising was on the wane.[142] One media expert was quoted as saying, 'I don't think the manufacturers are going to antagonize the public or the legislators. It's not worth it.'[143]

Yet not long thereafter another round in the tobacco wars was initiated. Part of the appeasement the cigarette companies offered was a code of self-regulation regarding promotion of tobacco products in terms of ad placement, use of media, not directing efforts at underage smokers, and so forth.[144] However, within a year of the Supreme Court decision, anti-smoking activists were charging that the companies, freed from legal constraints, were no longer abiding by the code.[145] Violations, it was alleged, ranged from placing ads within two hundred metres of schools to using people in lifestyle commercials. Organizations, such as the Canadian Cancer Society, were up in arms[146]; they urged new legislation based upon a poll revealing that 71 per cent of Canadians believed that, notwithstanding the Supreme Court of Canada judgment, smoking advertising should be banned.[147]

The government did introduce a bill and insisted that it had drafted it with a careful eye on the Supreme Court's ruling. Nevertheless, critics howled that the bill contained the same restrictions (if not worse ones) that had been struck down, with but a little window dressing added.[148] After much rancorous debate the bill was passed in the spring of 1997. However, a section banning the promotion of cultural and sports events by cigarette companies had particularly caused upset, especially among the organizers of such events who worried about replacing lost sponsorship dollars. In addition, the same poll that had established that a clear majority of Canadians wanted advertising banned also revealed that a slim majority, nevertheless, believed that cigarette companies should be able to sponsor events. As a result, the Act suspended, until the fall of 1998, the coming into effect of the sections banning sponsorship. After the legislation was in force, the tobacco companies continued to try to drum up sympathy around the sponsorship issue. Meanwhile the government continued to reiterate its support for all of the Act.[149] Still it danced around the question of whether there might be some room for flexibility, perhaps through establishing a public fund to cushion the loss of sponsorship by sports and cultural groups.[150] (One might surmise that a basis for such flexibility would be as a quid pro quo from the tobacco companies that they would not attack the constitutionality of the legislation.)

A study written in 1993, and referred to earlier in the chapter, compared initiatives in Canada, France, and the United States. The authors specifically addressed the challenge to the advertising ban then working its way up to the Supreme Court of Canada. They were confident that anti-smoking had developed too great a momentum to be deterred if the challenge was successful: '[T]he tobacco companies' legal victory ... will have come too late. The highly publicized legislative struggle over [various anti-smoking acts] legitimated further public and private anti-cigarette measures, and further delegitimated cigarette smoking in Canada.'[151]

This quote is largely accurate in terms of what has happened in the wake of the 1995 decision. As we have seen, in our discussion in chapter 4, backlash against court victories can, ultimately, result in the litigation assisting the losers more than the winners. Such an outcome galvanizing opposition against a court's pronouncement can be an important impact of litigation.[152] And such reaction appears to be a primary outcome of the Canadian Supreme Court's decision. Thus the decision, though a 'loss' in court for anti-smoking activists, may ultimately aid the war on tobacco. However, more generally, the precedent of recognizing 'rights' that protect corporate activity in peddling lethal substances is surely a setback for governmental policy that supports progressive politics.

Too Much of a Good Thing?

Smoking is on the decline. If the overall trends of the last two decades continue, at least in Canada and the United States, there may be few who indulge. Nevertheless, despite the decline, there remain two major concerns. First, there is the worry that the downward trend may stall. So, smokers will increasingly be found among the poorer, the less educated, and the young (who then may persist in smoking). What is more, those better educated and better off may lose interest in curtailing the habit, especially if they are shielded from the effects of second-hand smoke. Second, even if decline continues, millions of people in the meantime will get sick and many will die from the consequences of tobacco.[153]

Still, more law may not be the answer. Law may, indeed, have ridden a 'rising wave of cultural support,' but that wave may also have important limits – perhaps because many people who favour a smoke-free environment do not feel comfortable about coercion or, in any event, any more coercion than is necessary to shield them from the effects of others smoking. Instead, there may be a critical mass of opinion that believes that, in the long run, the way to conquer tobacco is, indeed, through informed choice: people deciding for themselves – nudged along by social pressure, by high taxes, by restricted areas for smoking, and by education – that the habit is just too dangerous, that any pleasures from smoking are vastly outweighed by its perils.

Perhaps we have now arrived at something of a delicate balance that raises the issue of unintended consequences (discussed generally in chapter 3).[154] A law, as implemented, may have effects quite different from those intended, at least by its advocates. If tobacco companies are too aggressive regarding the peddling of an addictive toxic substance, they face backlash that actually operates in favour of the anti-smoking forces. For the reason recounted in the last section, a good example of such unintended consequences, operating to the detriment of tobacco companies, may be the wake of the 1995 Supreme Court of Canada's decision regarding cigarette advertising. That decision may have done the tobacco companies more harm than good.

On the other hand, if anti-smoking activists are too aggressive in their efforts to curtail smoking, such actions may send the populace the other way in terms of smoking and their attitudes toward it.[155] Illustrations of such setbacks for those opposed to smoking are provided by Canada's efforts to suppress smoking by substantially raising taxes and by local efforts in both Canada and the United States to eliminate smoking altogether in bars and restaurants.

Canada, Tax Increases – and Unintended Consequences

As indicated earlier, by the early 1990s Canada was a world leader in using law to restrict tobacco.[156] A critical aspect of this policy was the imposition of very high taxes. Canada was not unique in using taxes to hike the price of tobacco to discouraging levels, and these measures appear to have contributed substantially to the curbing of smoking.[157] Indeed, there seems to be something of a consensus between cigarette companies and anti-smoking activists that pricing is the main way to discourage the underaged from smoking. (After such basic agreement the two sides part company: cigarette companies point to the importance of pricing to fend off efforts to control advertising and marketing; anti-smoking activists want to jack up prices in addition to employing other strategies to suppress cigarette consumption.)[158]

In any event, such tax increases in Canada produced significant unintended consequences. To begin with, some smokers simply turned to rolling their own cigarettes to offset costs while maintaining consumption. Consumption of fine-cut tobacco rose 29.4 per cent from 1985 to 1989.[159] Further, and of critical importance, the United States did not impose such high taxes. The American and Canadian economies are integrated in many ways. Because of the longstanding and peaceful relations between the two countries, moreover, there are many points of entry that are unguarded. What arose, therefore, was an active black market in smuggled cigarettes.

Contraband tobacco going between Canada and the United States is not the only instance of cigarette smuggling. There is increasing evidence of large amounts of cigarettes being smuggled in many countries to avoid tax, as well as evidence that cigarette companies, at the least, do nothing to discourage such activities.[160]

Nevertheless, for the reasons just mentioned, smuggling between Canada and the United States became acute. Such tobacco, not burdened by tax, could be sold much more cheaply. Estimates suggest that at its height, black-market traffic in cigarettes constituted twenty per cent of the market.[161] After several manoeuvres the Canadian government decided that it had no other choice and substantially lowered taxes to undercut the black-market advantage.

Almost immediately Canadian cigarette exports, most of which were smuggled back into the country, dropped by over 70 per cent.[162] At the same time, there is evidence that overall consumption increased.[163] However, the degree of consumption is unclear, since some of the increase in the rates is accounted for by the shift from illegal to legal consumption.[164] In any event, Canada continues to have a problem with smuggling – between provinces – because of lack of uniformity across the country in the extent that cigarettes are taxed.[165]

The Canadian experience with high taxes suggests that there can be too much of a good thing. Taxes can be effective in lowering consumption. But this does not mean that the higher the taxes, the lower the consumption. At some point, those determined to smoke will create demand that some market – legal or illegal – will supply. This demand for cigarettes does not negate the need for price increases but, rather, suggests the need for realism about the limited effectiveness of raising prices and the attendant costs (e.g., smuggling) in doing so. Such realism also urges greater uniformity in taxing policy regarding cigarettes (between countries and within countries where states and provinces possess such powers) and in measures to prevent complicity by the cigarette industry in smuggling. Such lessons need to be grappled with as opinion within the USA and the World Health Organization urges price increases to combat smoking.[166]

Bans in Restaurants and Bars – and Backlash

Yet another example of a setback for the anti-smoking campaign occurred regarding efforts to eliminate smoking in restaurants and bars. Two prominent instances of the ensuing battles occurred in Toronto and in California.

Before 1997 Toronto had a smoking bylaw that permitted smoking in 50 per cent of a restaurant, in a segregated area. That year the city banned all smoking in all bars, restaurants, coffee shops, and bowling alleys unless they had enclosed, separately ventilated smoking rooms. These were the toughest anti-smoking bylaws in Canada. However, the regulations caused unprecedented defiance from the Ontario Restaurant Association over the issue of lost jobs. Evidence of popular opinion was contradictory, but one poll, taken after the bylaw had come into effect, indicated that 70 per cent of those polled thought that the bylaw went too far.[167] Six weeks after the bylaw came into force the City retreated and passed amendments allowing smoking sections of between 10 and 25 per cent of overall floor space. The mayor was heard to remark: 'There was broad disrespect for [the] bylaw. It didn't work the way we hoped it would.'[168] Controversy continues regarding the scope and application of the bylaw.[169] At the same time, a campaign to encourage restaurants to voluntarily go smoke-free and to promote that status with patrons appears to have enjoyed considerable success.[170]

California has one of the lowest percentages of smokers: Only 18 per cent of the population smokes. A 1995 law banned smoking in offices, restaurants, and public buildings in California. Bars were exempt until January 1997. Shortly before the exemption was to expire there was such a protest that another one-year exemption was granted. Finally, the law came into effect in January 1998. However, it has been met with widespread defiance.[171] Litigation has been commenced to nullify the ban and widespread confrontation has been promised by those opposed to the prohibition.[172]

The examples provided by Toronto and California do not suggest that more local initiatives seeking to eliminate smoking in public places are doomed to failure. The general 1995 provision in California banning smoking in public places has been accepted and, as indicated, that state has one of the lowest smoking rates. Rather, the argument here is that regulation of smoking in public places illustrates the balance that must be struck between the majority's desire to avoid smoke and its tolerance for what remains a legal activity.

The Suppression of Smoking – Law and Norms

Some anti-smoking activists may believe that such tolerance is misplaced, but whether it is or not is, ultimately, beside the point. The fact is that that those charged with regulation must judge well the public temperament. If proposed regulation tips too heavily against tolerance, enacting a law can set off reactions that harm the anti-smoking cause, at least in the short run.[173] Such judgments are difficult. Still, they need to be made. And those making them should not cling to undue optimism about the power of law.

This discussion of attitudes and strategies for curtailing smoking returns us to the ideas of the 'normativists,' discussed earlier (in chapter 4 and in this chapter). Normativists want to focus on what they assert is the critical role of norms in terms of the effectiveness of law. Not surprisingly, some normativists have seized upon the issue of the curtailment of smoking: it seems to illustrate the vital role for norms in allowing law to achieve underlying policy goals.[174]

As a result, one normativist, as part of a larger discussion of techniques for altering social meaning (thus altering norms, thus altering behaviour, thus achieving ultimate policy goals), has applied that analysis to anti-smoking campaigns. The following are some important concepts in such an analysis and their application to efforts against tobacco:

- tying: smoking was successfully tied to unhealthy behaviour;
- ambiguation: non-smoking signs assist non-smokers in preventing smoking because the signs draw upon individuals' desire to conform with rules;
- inhibition: certain acts, such as smoking among the young were forbidden, thereby weakening social support for the behaviour itself;[175]

Such analysis is very helpful, particularly in placing the campaign against smoking in the larger context of the discussion of the role of norms and the effectiveness of law. However, this analysis is essentially retrospective. It focuses on what has worked and then, after the fact, tries to explain why it worked. It says little about the tough choices that lie ahead in terms of such issues as the rise in teenage smoking, the resurgence of cigars, raising taxes while guarding against smuggling, limiting advertising campaigns promoting cigarettes, further restrictions of smoking in public places, and the complicated role of litigation.

Moreover, this and related analyses may be too optimistic in their accounts of norms as the undergirding of changes in behaviour. For some time there appeared to be at least one example where an advertising campaign was quite successful in suppressing smoking among teenagers, admittedly for very specific reasons. It is the case that smoking among white teenagers has not declined for over a decade, and indeed, as indicated earlier, there is evidence that it is on the increase. In 1993 22.9 per cent of white teenagers smoked and this figure had not changed for a decade (and has moved up somewhat since). Meanwhile, the percentage of Afro-American teenagers who smoked in 1993 was only about 4.4, a number four times smaller than ten years earlier. During that time a concerted effort was made in the black community to persuade teenagers not to smoke. Part of that campaign involved overtones of the connection of the tobacco crop to slavery and of the enslaving power of cigarettes and their (white) companies. One poster in the Harlem subways showed a skeleton resembling the Marlboro man lighting a cigarette for an Afro-American child. The caption was 'They used to make us pick it. Now they want us to smoke it.'[176]

Normativists seized on the low rates of smoking and the ad campaign as proof of how norms in a particular community can be nurtured so as to produce any number of desirable results. It turns out that as the 1990s closed there was evidence that smoking among black teenagers has increased sharply.[177] Why this increase has occurred is not clear: some accounts indicate that there is now a widespread belief among teenagers that cigarettes can prolong the effects of marijuana use.[178] In any event, a cherished example regarding the deployment of norms seems to be dissipating.

All of this is not to argue against the importance of norms and their relationship with law in terms of behaviour generally and smoking in particular. However, that relationship is a complicated one. Looking back we may see how law and norms interacted to suppress smoking. Looking ahead, with a view to using law and norms to curtail consumption even further, the prospect is much more challenging. As insitutions, such as the World Health Organization, urge an international treaty on tobacco regulation they need to contemplate that complex interaction. Obtaining agreement for that treaty will be difficult. Its effective implementation in a variety of cultural contexts will be harder still.[179]

Conclusions

Could the decline in smoking have been brought about in the absence of changes in the law? Probably not. Would the diminishing rates of smoking have occurred without changing attitudes and norms towards cigarettes? Almost certainly not.

Smoking provides an excellent example of the interaction between the effects of law and altering attitudes in bringing about change in behaviour. In this regard two aspects stand out.

First, without education of the public concerning the harms and the addictive quality of nicotine and, most important, without the acceptance by the public of the reality of those harms, the laws designed to bring about curtailment would have had little effect. Thus, widespread belief that cigarettes were toxic was the critical foundation for any laws aimed at cutting smoking. To this extent it could be said that knowledge provided the sufficient basis for people to quit (or to not start at all); law then nudged the process along by repeatedly warning of the dangers, by preventing teenagers from simply sliding into smoking, by discouraging the practice through high prices, and by establishing that smoking should occur in ways that would not harm non-smokers or, even, cause them annoyance.

Second, law enjoyed a measure of success because of the multi-pronged strategy that it employed: regulation of advertising; promotional campaigns warning of the hazards; taxation; prohibition of sale to minors; lawsuits claiming damages for harm done as a result of smoking; and restriction of smoking in public areas. As we have seen, each of these strategies had limitations and, indeed, when relied on too heavily, at times actually caused setbacks; for example, the tax hike in Canada and its contribution to the sharp increase in smuggling. However, the advantage of a multi-pronged strategy is that no one of the prongs has to work all the time in order for the strategy, overall, to be successful. Indeed, with regard to private litigation, that prong has had no success, including in claiming damages for smokers. The 1998 US 'Tobacco Settlement' raises troubling questions regarding law's effects on suppressing rates of smoking. The agreement also sets a desperate precedent for invoking litigation as a policy-making tool to control other dangerous items such as guns.

One prong was not employed: prohibition (with the exception of teenagers). We will never know what would have occurred if nicotine had been banned. This uncertainty allows some anti-smoking activists to contend that things would have been very different (and so much better) if the heavy hand of the law had been invoked. In fact, however, the more plausible suggestion is that the absence of prohibition paved the way for the gradualism that works – admittedly over time and with difficult judgments and compromises along the way. A mere sampling of questions that policy and law makers need to confront include the following: How high can taxes be without causing undesirable results such as the development of black markets? Should there be a differential in taxes based on the degree of toxicity in particular brands of cigarettes? How tight can the restrictions be on smoking in public places without causing backlash, even among non-smokers? Should cigarette companies be required to advertise the toxic levels of cigarettes and, if so, will such campaigns lead smokers to use 'safer' brands? Should anti-smoking campaigns be more targeted: at teenagers? at those with less education?

The war against smoking and its harnessing of law suggests one instance in which patience is, indeed, a virtue: '[P]erhaps all the agitation by antismoking advocates is alarmist, seeking inappropriately strong government initiatives when such action may not be all that critical. Patience may accomplish the objectives of virtually all the perspectives on the smoking problem'[180] Still, the patience required is not the one that simply does nothing.

It is the patience that makes and implements policy in diverse democracies with many forces at play. It is the patience that recognizes that law can be effective in bringing change, but a period of time is required and problems will be encountered for which more law may not be the solution. An overly aggressive use of legalization may not speed up the process and might actually impede it. Patience in this law-saturated age? Imagine.

CHAPTER SEVEN

The Environment – Sunshine or Apocalypse?

Environmentalism provides a clear example both of the growth of law over the last decades and of its effectiveness when buttressed by social and economic forces. Of all the 'movements' for change occurring as a result of the tumult of the sixties, environmentalism may have enjoyed the broadest support, including from the upper classes. A man may ignore the sting of sexism, a white the burden of racism, the rich the cries of the ghetto. But we are all part of the environment; the affluent not the least so, as they frolic on their recreational properties.

As with other areas where law has regulated controversial issues, those battling over the environment have confined themselves, too often, to theoretical arguments. So the evidence about the effectiveness of law is not as systematic as good policy formulation requires. Nevertheless, a recent and thorough study of the United States' experience establishes that there is substantial evidence that laws to protect the environment have been effective. To be sure, not as successful as the assurances that some of the architects of these laws so confidently provided; much remains to be done regarding issues of both over- and under-regulation.[1] Yet, generally, such laws have yielded results that justify the costs that they have imposed.

Still there are strong claims to the contrary. Here we see a strange convergence of critics of the law on both the left and the right. On the one hand, there is a strand of environmentalists who either ignore the facts or treat any disparity between the goal of environmental laws and what they have achieved as failure. The solution? Either much more regulation without regard to costs or effectiveness or, to the contrary, a pronouncement that law is a failure and that it must be avoided.

On the other side are venerators of free markets – and no market can be free if it is burdened by regulation. These celebrants make their own claims about the ineffectiveness of laws to protect the environment. They can point to failures or, at least, to instances where the costs of regulation substantially exceed any benefits. The fallacy is that these individual situations are generalized to condemn virtually all legal standards. What is more, conservatives gain momentum by underscoring progressive critics' claims about the failure of environmental regulation; this is the convergence referred to earlier. Free marketers argue that when even environmentalists pronounce the laws as not working there is no way that their costs can be justified. The solution is obvious: repeal most ecological regulation.

We will examine the effectiveness of law in safeguarding the environment by looking closely at a study, referred to earlier, of some aspects of environmental law in the United States. That report demonstrates that, generally, the benefits of such laws do outweigh their costs. In addition, that study, and related ones, also establish that enforcement through governmental regulation and administrative agencies is more effective than resorting to litigation in the courts.

Further, we will examine the capacity of individual countries to engage in effective regulation in the face of economic interdependency. It is received truth among many environmentalists and proponents of free trade that trade and protection of the environment are diametrically opposed: more of one means less of the other. Ecologists believe that when free trade and environmental laws collide, the latter will be the loser. In this depiction free trade represents a significant limitation on law and its ability to have its desired effects: in this case, regulation in individual countries designed to improve the environment. However, there is some good evidence to support the claim that expansion of free trade and stricter environmental regulation can be mutually reinforcing.

A study of the impact of law regulating the environment provides a clear example of the way law can draw upon political and social consensus to be effective. Such outcomes are not instrumental: there are many problematic effects produced by such laws in terms of both under- and over-regulation. Yet, overall, public support of the environment and laws protecting it have advanced in mutually supporting ways. A study of some important aspects of environmental regulation in the United States indicates that that country has shared in such benefits. But, as with so many areas, America is an outlier in its use of law to protect the environment. The USA, more than other countries, relies on litigation as part of legal strategies to safeguard the natural world. Yet, as in many other areas that we have examined, litigation by and large has yielded disappointing results, including when compared with outcomes produced by regulatory authorities.

The effects produced by law negate sweeping critiques from both the right (in terms of those advocating unrestricted, free markets) and the left (in terms of those who are against the use of law) regarding regulation used to protect the environment.[2] Environmental regulation has not put a stranglehold on the economy. What is more, there is evidence that protection of the environment and market economies can satisfactorily coexist. Conversely, pollution laws are not a licence to degrade; environmental regulation is not a barrier to achieving some ecological utopia, however that might be attained. The positive outcomes produced by such regulation and the legitimate and substantial role that law needs to play in shielding the environment have to be acknowledged. Failure to do so may allow popular (and expert) opinion to be swayed by attacks from extreme viewpoints regarding the very fundamentals of such protection.

The Rise of Environmentalism and the Growth of Law

There is rarely one defining moment for transformations in society. Yet if such a point had to be fixed for the modern environmental movement, it might well be the publication of Rachel Carson's *Silent Spring*.[3] The book was a sobering, eloquent documentation of the many ways in which pesticides, especially DDT, were wreaking havoc. Published almost forty years ago, it was a clarion call to America and other Western societies to protect nature and safeguard human welfare.

Silent Spring, though, is largely venerated in retrospect. When published it was derided, in magazines like *Time*, as alarmist; *Newsweek* charged its author with 'paranoid fears.'[4] Nevertheless, that book came to have an enormous influence because 'the material, cultural, and political circumstances'[5] were ripe for the United States and the West, generally, to embrace forces that would be stamped as 'environmentalism.'

As early as the 1950s the foundation for modern environmentalism was laid by the controversy over radioactive fallout from nuclear-testing in the atmosphere. During the 1960s prosperous and educated Americans became increasingly worried about the quality of their life. There was attention to preserving the wilderness, long a focus of those interested in safeguarding nature. In addition, urban America became focused on key elements of the environment in city life: air, water, and soil.

Many factors contributed to such attention. A prominent one was dissent over the war in Vietnam. Television graphically depicted the suffering that conflict was causing, including the loss of life and devastation of nature caused by chemical warfare. Parts of the anti-war movement fuelled parts of environmentalism.[6] Revulsion at the mayhem of battle, including the use of chemicals to kill and maim and to destroy the landscape, buttressed protests against environmental poisons such as radioactive wastes, polychlorinated biphenyls, and sulphur dioxide. While memberships in established groups such the Audubon Society and the Sierra Club grew appreciably, more protest-oriented groups sprang up, focusing on such issues as air and water quality and the blocking of offshore drilling. The biologist René Dubos urged, 'Think globally, act locally.' In 1970 Earth Day was born.[7]

Such activity, continuing into the 1970s and 1980s, laid the foundation for a turning to law. Our previous discussion of the battle against tobacco provided an instance where transforming norms and legal regulation moved roughly together to suppress smoking to a significant degree in many countries.[8] The campaign to protect the environment is another example of legal regulation and developing norms moving in generally the same direction to achieve significant aspects of compatible goals.

Legal activity designed to safeguard the environment predated the 1970s. Yet that decade witnessed the coming into its own of the US Environmental Protection Agency, an institution with an ambitious mandate. At the same time, politicians in favour of governmental intervention warmed to the task, inflating public expectations about the capacity of law beyond reasonable limits. For example, in 1971 Senator Edwin Muskie assured that the 1972 Federal Water Pollution Control Act would virtually eliminate water-borne pollution by 1985.[9] This was an unsupportable boast given the clear limits of the statute.[10]

Nevertheless, Congress passed an array of environmental-protection legislation, including the Clean Air Act (1970), the Clean Water Act (1972), and the Endangered Species Act (1973). Other legislatures, throughout Western Europe, in some of the states in America, and in other countries took similar initiatives.[11] In this regard, the Canadian experience is instructive.

In step with other industrialized countries, the Canadian response to the legacy of environmental ills brought about by chemical, and energy-intensive, industrial and agricultural production, resource exploitation, and short-sighted waste-management choices has been largely a legal one. Since the late 1960s, volumes of new laws and regulations attempting to 'protect the environment' have been added to the legal inventory. Over this time, the approach of environmental law has changed, becoming more sophisticated technically, to reflect an altered view of the underlying issues of concern and gradually accommodating broader perspectives.

Before the 'modern' era of environmental law, Canadian law dealt with what would now be called environmental issues in limited ways. Public health issues such as drinking-water quality, air pollution, and sewage treatment were addressed, to the extent that they were at all, by individual municipalities under the oversight of provincial governments. Common-law actions (such as for nuisance) were available to private litigants seeking to protect the integrity of their property or their health. Federal involvement was limited to protecting water quality under its fisheries jurisdiction.[12] These traditional zones of responsibility reflected the perception of environmental issues as involving isolated events, local in impact, with a limited role for governments.[13]

The modern era of environmental law in Canada dates from the 1950s, when governments first started coming to terms with water and then air pollution. This era has been characterized as progressing through three stages: symbolic regulation, preventative regulation, and cooperative problem solving.[14]

The first stage, symbolic regulation, was reactive to the 'gross' pollution problems that had developed with post-war industrialization. Although the impacts of pollution were still considered to be localized, the widespread extent of occurrence caused first provincial governments and then the federal government to step in and regulate the industrial sources. The problem was seen as a technical one necessitating a technical solution, which influenced the kind of regulation adopted.[15] Impacts on water were treated separately from those on air and land, and each medium was treated as having the capacity to assimilate a certain level of pollution.[16]

With this 'command and control' approach, the onus was on the regulator to limit pollution through the establishment of standards which are then enforced through negotiations, administrative orders, and prosecutions.[17] In the absence of standards, an industry could continue to discharge any quantity of any substance into the environment so long as demonstrable harm was not created.[18]

The second stage, preventative regulation, was characterized by greater emphasis on the prevention and control of environmental problems through the establishment of more complex licensing schemes for industry, greater monitoring requirements, and environmental-impact assessment before approval for new projects. With greater scientific understanding, the focus of concern shifted away from instances of 'gross' pollution toward the more insidious impacts of toxic substances, particularly persistent bio-accumulative ones such as dioxins, and from local to more regional and even global impacts. Environmental-assessment processes required consideration of a broader range of environmental problems. For example, some processes included consideration of land use and degradation of habitat and accounting for the social and cultural impacts of major developments, all before project approval.

Regulation of the command-and-control type continued, but more and more stringent standards were set, a more consistent approach to compliance was adopted,[19] and liability for environmental harm was expanded for those whose business carries such types of risk.[20] Pollution control continued to emphasize 'end-of-the-pipe' treatment of wastes and little attempt was made to integrate standards and licensing across all media. Participation in regulation began to open up to a broader range of voices. Environmental-assessment processes across Canada were perhaps the most open administratively, but even the making of new policies, statutes, and regulations was opened to broad consultation.[21] The only area from which the public was still often excluded was that of the licensing of industry.

The third stage, which continued into the 1990s, cooperative problem solving, was characterized by a search for new approaches to try to improve the chances of success in achieving environmental protection. The underlying links between environmental quality and economic well-being were broadly recognized, largely as a result of the work of the Brundtland Commission.[22] One response, in Canada, was the establishment of Roundtables, at the national, provincial, territorial, and municipal levels, comprising of representatives from numerous sectors, to plan ways of reworking government and private institutions to put the recommendations of the Brundtland Commission and other initiatives into practice.

Regulation is now more complex than ever, with a growing emphasis on priority toxic substances, 'cradle-to-grave' management, cross-media standards, and pollution prevention. Many problems are now recognized as having regional or global reach and an 'ecosystem approach' is now recognized as necessary.[23] Governments are shifting some responsibility onto polluters to undertake audits, disclose all toxic releases, and develop toxic-use reduction plans.[24] In addition, there is now better coordination among the provincial and federal governments and, increasingly, coordination between Canada and other nations on trade in chemicals and wastes, transportation of hazardous goods, transboundary pollution impacts, harmonization of standards, and so on.[25]

Overall, Canadian environmental law has mushroomed over the last twenty-five years. It has grown in sophistication and complexity as scientific understanding has given us a better, though still incomplete, picture of human impact on the natural environment and in turn on our own health. Governments first got involved because of the concerns raised by the environmental movement in the 1950s and 1960s that resonated with the public. But governments have been selective about which concerns were addressed: for example, Canadian governments have not systematically addressed issues of population, conservation of resources, economic structure, or discriminatory impacts. Canadian environmental law is primarily directed at controlling pollution from point sources.

Furthermore, governments have not shifted the onus onto polluters or others responsible for environmental degradation to demonstrate their 'safety' before being allowed to operate. The onus is still predominantly on the public, and governments as their agents, to bear the risks until the proof is there to limit or stop a particular activity.[26] A focus on pollution prevention, requiring industry to rethink the need for highly polluting products and processes and to redesign industrial processes, is very recent and is not yet reflected in enforceable legal instruments.

More generally, during the 1980s and into the 1990s the threat of global ecological stress received increasing attention. There were dire threats issued about the 'coming anarchy.'[27] A principal source of that mayhem would be caused by a degraded Third World. Yet the havoc would spread over the globe in terms of such issues as significant climate change and ozone depletion. Allegations that 'free trade' would downgrade national efforts to protect the environment added to such alarms as the generation of wealth and a safe environment were seen as inevitable opponents.[28] (We will return to such contentions later in this chapter).[29]

Yet another aspect of environmentalism has been the opposition it has generated. Doubters held themselves out not as being opposed to a healthy environment but as being against the costs and burdens of laws claimed as necessary to its protection. By the 1980s conservative politicians, reacting to the alarm bells of debts and deficits, openly questioned the value of existing programs and mounted concerted opposition to new initiatives. Law in the name of the environment was indicted on the grounds of being expensive to administer, paralysed by litigation, and prone to delay by bureaucratic tampering: 'a classic case of meddling government run wild.'[30]

During that decade, the Reagan administration in the United States substantially curtailed the budget of the Environmental Protection Agency. While not formally dismantled, the EPA's efforts were substantially curtailed.[31] By the 1990s conservative elements were calling for outright repeal and abolition of many laws and programs.[32] In some instances, governments openly encouraged business to set out the terms of legal regimes that a sector was prepared to tolerate.[33] Some laws were actually repealed. In addition, government austerity cut funds for the enforcement of many of those that remained.[34] By the second half of the 1990s new legal initiatives were rarely heard of, let alone realized. Yet there was also some evidence, as the nineties closed, that broadsides against the environment were abating, including under the Clinton administration.[35]

Attacks by fiscal and philosophical conservatives were not the only challenge issued to environmentalism and accompanying legal regulation. Other interests, of a more progressive cast, questioned that same agenda. Such perspectives frequently characterized environmentalists as tending to be white, middle to upper middle class, and too often unconcerned with the implications of such protection for poorer, particularly minority, citizens. As early as the 1970 Earth Day, Whitney Young, the head of the Urban League, urged that 'the war on pollution ... should be waged after the war on poverty is won.'[36]

One result has been tension between environmentalists and those worried about impacts on jobs. The threat to economic stability – and growth – in the drive for ecological protection has sometimes pitted advocates of such regulation against unions and other groups (including those representing minorities) who have felt economic pressures particularly acutely.[37] Another development has seen those representing disadvantaged groups attempting to shape environmentalism in ways conducive to their interests. Prominent in such efforts is the activism of women. It could be that this presence hinges on the claim by some eco-feminists that 'femaleness' tends toward a harmonious relationship with nature. Or perhaps there are other factors. It may be that many women are closer to the daily life of their neighbourhood and are, therefore, better positioned to recognize threats to their families, especially children.[38]

In any event, environmentalism in Western countries had, by the 1990s and into the new century, become a complex phenomenon. Its values were part of the calculus of choice in virtually all spheres of action. Yet there was political currency in curtailing its influence. At the same time, the movement, by this point, was being subjected to challenges by other forces seeking to harness law and other resources of the state to achieve their ends. In short, environmentalism was unambiguously part of numerous policy agendas and a conscious presence in daily life.

Throughout all the furor, overall support for the environment and government action to protect it remained high.[39] Voters broke rank with the conservative governments they had elected with regard to safeguarding the environment.[40] Publications, even those decidedly market-oriented, continuously reminded readers of the need for government regulation to protect the environment as a public good.[41] The public in many countries increasingly rejected the premise that protecting the environment necessarily required sacrificing the economy.[42]

Sunshine or Apocalypse?: Accounts of Environmentalism

In the mid-1990s there appeared a spate of books purporting to take stock of the effects of environmentalism. Whether designed to be popular accounts or of a more scholarly cast, a number of them received substantial attention in the press. Such publicity reflected a curiosity about what, if anything, had been achieved by all this social, organizational, political, and legal activity.

Such works tended to take strong – and dramatically divergent – positions on the effects of the environmental movement. On the one hand, there was the view that environmentalism, and its harnessing of law, had achieved spectacular successes. This stance was exemplified by Easterbrook's *A Moment on the Earth: The Coming Age of Environmental Optimism*.[43] He argued that environmental laws over twenty-five years were a 'stunning success,' yielding trends in the United States and Europe that were 'for the most part, positive.'[44] He further claimed that environmentalists, by not recognizing the successes, were harming their own cause: they were playing into the hands of opponents of regulation, who could urge that if, by environmentalists' own accounts, regulation was not working then it was surely not worth the cost it imposed.

On the other hand, there was also an outright pronouncement of failure despite all the expenditure of time, energy, and resources. This 'failure' view then divided into polarized reactions. One response suggested that even more drastic measures had to be taken to protect the environment.[45] In 'The Coming Anarchy' Kaplan argued that environmental threats as well as demographic pressures, combined with the collapse of traditional nation states, would bring on a period of chaos.[46] The leaching toxins of a degraded ecology would spread strife, first, in developing nations, then, inexorably throughout the globe: 'The political and strategic impact of surging populations, spreading disease, deforestation and soil erosion, water depletion, air pollution, and possibly, rising sea levels in critical, overcrowded regions ... will be the core foreign-policy challenge from which most others will emanate.'[47]

A second reaction, responding to the alleged failure, claimed that such disappointments were a signal to give up on regulation and to bank on market forces to achieve whatever environmental standards there ought to be.[48] Part of this stance disputed the extent of degradation. In any event, restoring the earth was largely a matter of applying methods that had degraded it: what technology had done it could undo; what economic growth had caused more economic growth could fix.

A third reaction provided a clear example of one of the ideas about the effects of law discussed in chapter 4 – 'The Ineffectiveness of Law.'[49] One strand of this idea contends that law, rather than being a catalyst for progressive change, is in fact an impediment barring groups and individuals from paths that could lead to fundamental alterations in society. A variant of this strand – 'deep ecology' – has found expression within debates on the environment.[50]

Deep ecology scorns instrumentalist claims about the effects of law, especially regarding the environment ('Conservative jurisprudence, which sees law as being both the most appropriate and most effective instrument of social change, is in need of rethinking').[51] What is more, 'rights' to protect the environment are a concoction of 'shallow ecologists' and must be eschewed ('Attempts to rectify or heal our world situation through the use of legal rights are met with great suspicion by deep ecologists').[52] Indeed, law is viewed mostly as a cover for environmental degradation as the lawyers and consultants who are involved fatten their wallets ('[E]nvironmental regulation has become nothing more than a licensing system for polluters. In addition, it is a booming business, lining the pockets of law firms').[53] Law, in terms of the environment in particular, and in terms of progressive reform in general, should be sidelined ('[T]his focus on the law is one of the reasons the traditional environmental movement is in deep trouble. The law is dangerous to social movements').[54]

In contrast to the foibles of law, deep ecology commands a 'fundamental reconsideration of the relationship between ourselves and the world.'[55] Rights are rejected; 'rightness' is claimed ('a need for a proper and healthy relation between persons and nature.')[56] Are specific solutions offered? Not really ('Deep ecology does not lend itself to blueprints for action').[57] Instead 'personal insights'[58] loom large. As a result, one might start 'an organic garden, or ... [might] heavily insulat[e] one's home, shu[n] factory farmed products or participat[e] in grassroots political protest and action; no party line has to be followed.'[59]

What can one say? The intentions of deep ecologists may be good. But reading such works one remembers a point made earlier in this section about the right playing off the naysaying of the left. In this depiction 'deep ecologists' and free marketers become strange bedfellows – but bedfellows nonetheless. For if environmental regulation is a drag on growth and entrepreneurship, is nothing more than a licensing system for polluters, and is impeding a 'deep' relationship between ourselves and nature – who needs it?

The Impact of Environmental Laws

As we have just seen, those debating the ramifications of environmental regulation frequently get caught up in theoretical arguments and rhetorical exchanges about, on the one hand, the efficacy of law and, on the other, its costs. At the same time, the facts – establishing what have actually been the effects of law – have often been sidelined. Germany and the United States are generally acknowledged to be world leaders in laws to protect the environment.[60] Yet a study attempting to compare the effectiveness of such laws in both countries faced formidable challenges in obtaining reliable and comparable data regarding results: 'Twenty years of environmental policy-making have failed to build up a strong knowledge base that would permit intercountry comparisons and an analysis of the impact of past policies.'[61] Similar conclusions have been voiced regarding the lack of knowledge concerning the outcomes produced by environmental regulation in Canada.[62]

What is more, there are ever-present questions about what 'impact' means in the conduct of environmental regulation. Questions regarding compliance loom large. Beyond these issues are ones dealing with stipulating and measuring the effects of any law or set of laws. Reduction of the emission of pollutants is an outcome that is critical. The expenditures required to achieve such reduction is another. But apart from these obvious benchmarks are other 'effects' such as increase in green space, enhancement of parks, effective disposal of garbage, and largely unquantifiable results, such as enhanced enjoyment of public spaces.

Then, too, there are complicated issues around the law and other social forces. When pollution, however measured, is reduced, at acceptable costs, can we attribute this decrease to law or has the result been brought about by some complex interaction of law, public norms in support of the environment, and other forces, such as the market? When law deserves at least some of the credit, are there different kinds of law, of decision-making processes, that are more effective than others: for example, litigation to protect the environment versus the actions of regulatory authorities?

Is it possible to come to some reasonable assessment of the outcomes produced by various legal efforts to protect the environment? We will attempt to answer this question in two ways. First, by looking at a detailed evaluation of important aspects of environmental regulation in the United States. Second, by examining the impact of international agreements liberalizing trade on environmental regulation and vice versa. Here the available evidence questions the assertion that free trade limits the effectiveness of environmental laws, curtailing their impact in terms of protecting the environment.

The Environment in the United States

In America the environment became one area where the fascination with law and its ability to shape social issues led to heated debates and to spectacular claims about law's effects. During the 1980s alarm caused by the prospect of being held responsible for environmental injury became so great that insurance to protect against such liability often became unobtainable.[63] Moreover, whatever the reality, there was chronic worry about the effects of environmental regulation on economic growth and development.[64]

In addition, some critics, offering a more balanced view, pointed to substantial problems regarding both under- and over-regulation of environmental risks. Of note here is Breyer's (now a Justice of the Supreme Court) 'vicious circle' pertaining to risk regulation generally.[65] This sorry state of affairs comes about through the interaction of three factors: public risk perception, Congressional action and reaction, and uncertainties in the technical regulatory process. The public exerts pressure on Congress because of perceived risk. As a result, Congress pressures agencies to regulate. The regulatory process begins with frequent uncertainty (and ensuing controversy) regarding risk assessments. As the public learns of such uncertainties through a sensationalist media, it becomes more anxious and increases pressure on Congress: thus the 'vicious circle.' The fallout is 'tunnel vision of agencies' – which single-mindedly pursue goals to the point where the outcome is more harm than good; 'random agenda selection' – whereby agencies respond to public opinion in an undisciplined fashion; and 'inconsistency' – among different agencies in the assessment of risks and implementation of regulations.[66]

Nonetheless, a recent wide-ranging study, to be discussed shortly, rejects charges that environmental law has been, generally, ineffective and argues that many of the heated debates about law's role have been misdirected. It and related studies suggest that legislative and administrative enforcement require, in some instances, significant alteration. Nevertheless, such enforcement is a much more promising route to protect the environment than court-based litigation, especially tort actions. This study is important, especially for our purposes, for it speaks directly to the effectiveness of law in protecting the environment, comparing the outcomes of litigation and of regulatory actions.

The Dewees Study

Dewees, Duff, and Trebilcock sifted through a legion of studies, mostly from the United States but also from Canada, to evaluate the impact produced by environmental regulation.[67] Their more general purpose was to test the efficacy of tort law in achieving three goals ascribed to it by different theorists: deterrence, compensation, and corrective justice (the morally culpable must restore their victims to a pre-injury state).[68] To this end the authors compared the impact of litigation with that of regulatory requirements for five kinds of accidents: automobile, medical, product-related, environmental, and workplace. Their broader conclusions regarding the effectiveness of torts, in general, were discussed in chapter 4.[69]

The problems covered by the study included injuries to the environment, to persons, and to property caused by the discharge of air and water pollution from fixed or mobile sources such as factory smoke stacks, sewers, and automobiles and by the discharge and disposal of solid and liquid wastes.[70] The study's more specific conclusions on the effects of law in protecting the environment can be summarized as follows. Tort litigation has contributed only modestly to environmental protection, primarily in problems of soil contamination and severe local water pollution by isolated sources. Its limitations are inherent in the lack of clarity as to the source of many pollutants and the uncertainty of science regarding their effects.

Regulatory intervention is flawed. However, it is the better instrument for deterring pollution the effects of which are uncertain. This is so because regulation can provide greater certainty for both polluters and victims regarding their rights, on the one hand, to emit pollutants and, on the other hand, to enjoy a clean environment. Moreover, the regulatory process (compared with judicial fact-finding procedures) provides a better forum for debating the evidence regarding the effects of pollutants. Finally, the financial impact of erroneous tort liability may be even greater than the financial impact of misdirected regulation because of the retrospective liability inherent in the former.[71]

Deterrence: The deterrent effect of tort law is largely confined to certain kinds of environmental problems. In the case of most air and water degradation there is scientific uncertainty whether the pollution causes actual harm and, if so, in what amount. Even where there is pollution, it is almost impossible to establish that an individual has been harmed to a specific degree by the discharge from a given source. Even in cases where an individual can demonstrate specific harm from emissions from a particular source, the harm is often so small that litigation is not worthwhile.

However, when such difficulties can be addressed, tort litigation can deter; that is, it has been effective where a large amount of pollution is discharged from an isolated source, resulting in harm in a substantial amount to individuals or their property. There has been successful litigation regarding intense local pollution problems, such as lead pollution from a smelter that results in serious disease to individuals in the immediate area and emissions into groundwater, that cause increased disease for those drinking that water.

Moreover, the contamination of the ground, groundwater, or sediment of a river or lake by toxic materials has given rise to liability for the costs of cleanup. It is easier to win a lawsuit involving contaminated land or water because the costs of cleanup form a benchmark for measuring damages despite the fact that it may be impossible to prove that any individual contracted a disease as a result of the pollution. This kind of liability has been grounded in common law and some has arisen in the United States under the Superfund established under CERCLA.[72]

Those responsible for creating toxic substances are taking greater care in handling and disposing of them as a result of the threat of both common-law and statutory liability. At the same time, the CERCLA program has also caused excessive cleanup and litigation costs and rendered some land unusable until liability for possible past contamination can be resolved.

Finally, some pollution abatement has resulted in response to public demand. Such is the case either because firms wish to be perceived as environmentally conscious or because they want to avoid retaliation for environmental damage when they are required to seek approval from public bodies for rate increases, building permits, or zoning changes.[73]

In comparison with tort litigation, government regulation at the local, state, and federal levels has resulted in considerable reductions in pollution discharge. This reduction would not have occurred in the absence of regulation. Between 1970 and 1988 the US population increased by 20 per cent, coal use increased by 53%, and GNP by 66%. Nevertheless, traditional air emissions – 'criteria pollutants' – have declined significantly since 1970: lead is down by 96%, particulates decreased by 63%, and the others have declined by more than 25% (except oxides of nitrogen, which have increased slightly). In addition, there have been smaller but still substantial reductions in airborne concentrations of the same pollutants. Such reductions are attributable to specific governmental programs and represent 'a major success for regulation.'[74]

Water pollution has declined by smaller amounts and improvement in water quality has been more modest. Some measures of ambient water quality have improved because of both federal and state regulation since 1970, even though non-point pollution sources have not been substantially regulated. Concentrations of toxic substances have decreased in some bodies of water as a result of bans on, or at least regulation of, the discharge of those substances. Thus, even though the impact of regulation on the quality of water has not been as great as on air, 'again it is clear that regulation has registered some significant emission reductions.'[75]

Nevertheless, an economic analysis of the regulatory system yields mixed results. This is because many programs and their implementation have imposed costs greater than necessary to achieve the desired environmental result.[76] The degree of regulation of stationary air-pollution sources through the late 1980s could be justified through a cost-benefit analysis. However, the costs of automobile emission controls seem to exceed those benefits. In the case of water pollution, the costs of regulations through the 1980s seem to have considerably exceeded the benefits, though it is a question whether all such benefits have been fully acknowledged (in part because they may be difficult to quantify).[77]

Compensation: Tort law performs poorly as a means of compensating victims of environmental harms. Many individuals suffer marginal increases in risks for some diseases because of exposure to a variety of environmental harms and some may develop diseases from such exposure. Yet few recover because of tort litigation or its threat.

A significant problem is that most victims cannot be distinguished from those of non-environmentally-caused diseases or conditions. Therefore, the extent of such undercompensation cannot be ascertained; lawsuits are rare. In situations where individuals do recover from environmental harms, they do not recover the full amount of their losses. Again, there is the issue of causation: damage because of pollution can come from many sources and it is often difficult to establish the source of any particular harm. When property is harmed by toxins and there is litigation, there is often insufficient recovery for complete cleanup either because of legal limitations or because of the defendant's inadequate assets.[78]

Government-mandated compensation for environmental harms is minimal. The *Price-Anderson Act*[79] stipulates compensation for injuries arising from nuclear power plant accidents while, at the same time, limiting liability. CERCLA provides compensation for cleanup costs. However, in most cases the government is the plaintiff and there is no provision for recovery for personal injuries. The *Oil Pollution Act*[80] of

1990 does provide for cleanup of oil spills and for compensation of victims. However, there can be significant issues of causation.

The authors conclude that creating an administrative mechanism to provide personal compensation would be difficult. This is because of the likelihood that only a small fraction of the incidence of any particular disease is caused by environmental pollution and because of the problems in respect of individual causation.[81]

Corrective Justice: Tort law performs no better with respect to corrective justice than it does with deterrence. Only a small fraction who suffer harm are compensated by the wrongdoer. In most instances the individual whose disease was caused by pollution cannot be distinguished from those whose diseases were caused by non-environmental sources. The required cause-and-effect relationship cannot be established.[82]

Administrative alternatives also do not perform well in terms of corrective justice. For example, the *Price-Anderson Act* requires the nuclear industry to carry liability insurance and the federal government may have residual liability. Nevertheless, that legislation limits total liability. In any event, so many decisions are involved in nuclear power development that it may not be possible to identify the parties responsible if a major incident were to happen.

Both CERCLA and the *Oil Pollution Act* provide compensation for victims. However, CERCLA's joint and several strict liability is inconsistent with corrective justice. Some parties may be held liable for more than the full cost of their activities. At the same time, others may pay for little or none of the damage that they have caused.[83]

Conclusions and Comment: Dewees' conclusions, regarding all three goals of tort, are unambiguous. There is 'no alternative to government regulation to control most pollution discharges; there is no other instrument that can perform this function adequately.'[84] At the same time, the authors maintain that there are several ways in which regulation can be improved.

First, legislation that bans all harm from pollution without regard to the costs imposed should, in most instances, be altered to permit balancing of costs and benefits. At the same time, there are many difficulties, in specific contexts, with a cost-benefit approach. We will return to such problems in a moment.

Second, if local pollution is not a serious problem, then greater use should be made of market-oriented regulatory policies such as marketable pollution permits and effluent charges. Such instruments are able to lessen the cost of pollution control and quicken the pace at which such control proceeds.[85] Critics of such permits object to them on several grounds, including that converting pollution into a commodity removes the moral stigma that ought to be associated with such environmental degradation.[86] Nevertheless, Dewees maintains that substantial benefits stemmed from marketable pollution permits in the United States during the 1980s.

Third, where regulations capture the appropriate stringency there should be private enforcement of those regulations. Victims should be assisted in claiming redress. In this regard, they could be allowed to keep some portion of the fines recovered.

Dewees does not advocate special regimes to compensate victims of general air and water pollution. For most situations the per capita risks are very small. As a result, compensation would require a tax on everyone with receipts payable to virtually everyone; amounts might be dependent on location of residence and workplace. Such a program would be costly and would not accomplish much. At the same time, in those cases where risks are large and causation is clear, tort litigation is available.

Damages for land that has been contaminated should be addressed though lawsuits based on nuisance and negligence. Where the defendant may have insufficient assets to compensate those who have been harmed, there could be a public cleanup fund financed by a tax on the activity responsible for the damage. The cleanup of past contamination, where there is no solvent party who can be held responsible, should be financed publicly. Yet the claim on such funds may substantially exceed their availability. Thus, care must be taken to determine which sites ought to be cleaned up and which should be sealed off. Moreover, there must be reasonable standards to define a 'clean' site because of the limits on funds.[87]

Still, the recommendations of the Dewees study are, themselves, not free from difficulties. A clear instance of such problems arises respecting actually implementing any cost-benefit analysis with regard to proposed regulation. As indicated above, Dewees places great reliance on cost benefit analysis to avoid errors of regulation, particularly over-regulation. Yet, as reviewers of this study have noted, advocating careful cost-benefit analysis in the abstract is one thing. Actually ascertaining all costs and benefits, determining their magnitude, and weighing them off against each other dispassionately in a concrete situation is quite another.[88]

One of the authors of the Dewees' study (Trebilcock) has attempted to respond to the question of how best to implement cost-benefit analysis in practice.[89] His fundamental point is that the political process must be disciplined by 'technocratic tools such as the use of science in risk assessment and cost-benefit analysis in risk management.' Yet the political process must, in turn, discipline these technocratic tools: 'Key social decisions cannot be made solely by unaccountable experts. Not only would the results be anti-democratic, they would likely be inefficient as well.'[90]

As a result, Trebilcock takes on the challenge of the design of credible risk-regulating institutions that incorporate technocratic tools and make appropriate use of experts while still allowing room for meaningful public participation. In responding to this challenge he offers a detailed set of recommendations addressing such issues as mandatory risk assessment, notice-and-comment period, peer review, mandatory cost-benefit analysis, and the role of the courts (essentially confined to policing procedural requirements).[91]

Of particular interest are the decisional criteria advanced. Consistent with the conclusions of another study,[92] this one recommends three criteria: first, maximize expected values; second, avoid catastrophes; and third, dismiss remote possibilities.[93] In addition, a fourth criterion is advanced: adopt equitable regulations. This factor is necessary because 'our considered judgments about justice are often incapable of being captured in a cost-benefit analysis' and because, more specifically, 'differential imposition of risks on citizens threatens to violate both their basic liberties and their legitimate expectation that government fashion policies and institutions that work to the greatest advantage of the least advantaged groups in society.'[94]

These recommendations offer a thoughtful starting place for applying risk assessment and cost-benefit analysis in a way that takes advantage of the best of both technology and politics.[95] Particularly compelling are the four criteria offered to guide the various aspects of the processes used for decision-making in this context. Yet intractables must be faced. Trebilcock himself insists that 'there are still the practical limitations we have repeatedly referred to: the difficulties of identifying all possible costs and benefits, and even if identified, problems in valuing them.'[96]

Environmental Litigation

The Dewees study is persuasive in establishing the effectiveness of administrative regulation compared with tort litigation. However, tort lawsuits are not the only kind of litigation regarding environmental issues. Two other types of civil litigation are actions to achieve constitutional recognition of right to a healthy environment and actions to ensure that administrators and agencies carry out their functions regarding environmental regulation.[97]

As part of turning to law and along with so many other movements of the 1960s and 1970s, environmentalists sought to enhance their efforts at protection by resort to the language and claims of 'rights.' Such recognition was not necessarily court-based. Environmentalists in several jurisdictions sought recognition of an environmental 'bill of rights.' In some instances they were successful, though such 'bills of rights' were limited to legislation (that is, were not actually enshrined in constitutions) and, sometimes, relegated court-based litigation to a subsidiary role in terms of enforcement.[98]

Nevertheless, many legal environmentalists, especially in America, were eager to adopt a litigation-based strategy to enshroud the environment in the protective mantel of rights recognized and enforced by the courts. There were several reasons for this:[99]

- There was claimed to be a direct parallel between efforts to protect the environment and the struggle for recognition of civil rights. What *Brown v. Board of Education* had done for Afro-Americans, the right case, or at least series of cases, would do for the environment.
- These environmentalists, by and large, accepted a 'dynamic court' view. In this depiction courts were seen as more responsive and less biased than the legislative or executive branch. In addition, courts could overcome popular ignorance and indifference and bureaucratic inertia. At the same time, lawsuits were held out as simpler compared with other forms of political activity.
- Courts were coming to play an increasing role in setting and implementing the public-policy agenda. The environment needed to be part of the litigation terrain so as not to be left out. Moreover, there was some evidence of judicial receptivity to environmental claims.[100]

Attempts to achieve constitutional recognition of a healthy environment in the United States have been a failure. There are mainly two reasons for such lack of success.[101] First, the courts, constrained by precedent and the dominant legal culture, are not likely to act as 'crusaders.' The creation of a constitutional right to a clean environment would have required a significant break with existing law. Second, environmentalists had not built the kinds of precedent that might, in any event, lead the courts to take such a step.[102]

Litigation in the United States to ensure that administrators carry out their functions respecting regulation has produced mixed results.[103] There were some substantial successes in terms of the courts ordering agencies to comply with procedural requirements such as the filing of environmental-impact statements. However, courts were mostly deferential to agencies' decisions on the merits. Thus, courts had little impact on the substance of environmental policy.[104] What is more, courts have significantly curtailed 'citizens suits' to enforce environmental laws.[105] Such restrictions have occurred because judges have imposed strict standing requirements. These decisions stipulate that plaintiffs must go beyond claims that they are seeking to defend some aspect of the environment and to show that they, themselves, have suffered injury as a result of the alleged harms. Thus, the occasions for even bringing lawsuits to protect the environment (let alone achieving any substantive results) have been diminished.

In addition, despite claims to the contrary,[106] courts appear to have had little effect on increasing public opinion in favour of the environment, generating media coverage of relevant issues, otherwise increasing membership in environmental organizations, and pressuring legislators to act. For example, regarding the last aspect, much environmental legislation predated major court actions and, conversely, there is no indication that courts played a significant role in legislation that launched the environmental decade.[107] In sum, 'environmental litigation, as a strategy for producing a clean and healthy environment, achieved precious few victories.'[108]

The Dewees study's conclusions and the review, just presented, of attempts to constitutionalize environmental rights and to use judicial review of agencies' decisions suggest, again, that claims about the effects of litigation have been exaggerated. The misplaced faith in litigation is especially clear with regard to the environment because of Dewees' conclusions about the comparative efficacy of the legislative and administrative processes. Thus, the environment provides yet another opportunity to examine the idea presented in chapter 4 that there is something different about the effects of litigation compared with the outcomes produced by other forms of law – in particular, that litigation can bring about significant social change only in limited circumstances.[109] In this instance, a study of the environment leads to the conclusion that litigation is clearly less effective in producing the intended results.

Studying litigation to protect the environment also illustrates another idea discussed in chapter 4 regarding national styles of regulation. The suggestion is that different societies use law in different ways. Thus, conclusions about the effect of law in one society – however reliable for that society – have to be applied with caution to other countries. More specifically, America is an outlier in its reliance upon litigation and the discourse of rights in the formulation of public policy.

Again, this claim about 'American exceptionalism' is borne out in the case of the environment. For example, studies of the United States and Germany,[110] the United States and England,[111] and the United States and Canada[112] all document that, in terms of environmental protection and policy formulation, America relies to a substantially greater degree than those three other countries on court-based litigation and the adversarialness that accompanies it. What is more, the review in this section suggests that greater reliance on litigation does not produce better results within American society in terms of shielding the environment.

However, it is also the case in this instance that it is not clear that the other national systems (relying less on litigation) produce better results or, even if they do, that such outcomes occur because of decreased reliance on courts. For example, the study examining the United States and England concluded (in 1986) that there was no clear evidence that 'either nation's environmental policies have been significantly more or less effective than the other's.'[113] The study of Germany and the United States suggested that greater use of litigation by the former would bring greater accountability to decision-making regarding the environment.[114]

Results produced by litigation on behalf of protection of the environment in the United States have been disappointing compared with those stemming from the legislative and administrative processes. America is an outlier in the extent to which it relies on court-based litigation, and its attendant adversarialness, to protect the environment and to formulate policy. Yet, obviously, societies that rely on litigation to a lesser extent do not necessarily end up with better results with regard to safeguarding the natural world. What is crucial is public support for environmental protections matched with effective regulation.

That said, many of those who have looked at achieving more effective environmental regulation urge that there should be more flexibility and less of the confrontation that is so much the hallmark of environmental regulation – and law generally – in the United States.[115]

Such flexibility indicates no less a commitment to protecting the environment. Rather, 'in the majority of circumstances, the use of multiple rather than single policy instruments, and a broader range of regulatory actors, will produce better regulation.'[116]

The Environment and International Trade

Whatever the concerns about the environment in any one country, there is increasing worry about international implications.[117] Fears about the deterioration of the ozone layer and the effects of global warming are but two instances of ecological concerns that can be responded to only through multilateral action.[118] Conversely, there are worries that concerted action among nations to halt degradation can be undone because of the irresponsibility of a handful of countries.[119]

A particular aspect of this international focus on environmental issues is the impact of trade agreements. The nub of concern is that such agreements will require the dilution of national standards because such regulation is seen as impeding the free flow of goods.[120] Among other concerns, it is feared that these standards will impose cost burdens on the production of goods, making them less marketable. In addition to other consequences, it is believed that the demands of free trade will negate domestic legal efforts at ecological protection. The environmental laws of any particular nation will be blunted both within and outside of its borders. When free trade and domestic laws to protect the environment meet, the former will limit and confine the latter. Thus, free trade will be a severe constraint on the impact of law and its effectiveness in protecting the environment. Put more elaborately, this fear has three aspects.[121]

First, the expansion of domestic regulations, including for the environment, in combination with reduction of other forms of trade restrictions, most notably tariffs, has resulted in the increase of the importance of such protective regulations as non-tariff barriers. Thus, it is feared that agreements to liberalize both regional and international trade are trying to dilute these regulations as obstacles to trade.

Second, environmental regulation cannot be accounted for only in national terms. As with many other areas of public policy, such regulation is being influenced increasingly by forces outside individual countries. International agreements are one development that affects national regulatory standards.[122] Yet the role of trade agreements in enhancing the regionalization and even globalization of regulation is still more important. Countries are increasingly exporting and importing standards as well as goods. Agreements and the trade that they are meant to facilitate are conduits permitting such forces as producers, interest groups, and governments to influence regulation in the affected countries. Thus, a number of the debates about environmental regulation that, in the past, took place within nations are now taking place among them.

Third, organizations working on behalf of the environment are now actively participating in the shaping of trade policy. In contrast to producers or workers, these non-governmental organizations (NGOs) are not interested in the economic impact of trade policies but, instead, are focused on how such policies have an impact on the quality of the environment in particular countries. In many instances, NGOs have transferred their suspicion of domestic markets to global ones. One result of this transfer are alliances between some producers, seeking protection from trade liberalization, and NGOs, resisting such liberalization on the grounds that it will dilute regulation.

These three aspects are making the relationship between regulation and trade increasingly subject to conflicts. On the one hand, those seeking free trade wish to confine regulations on the ground that they interfere with the international flow of commerce. There is fear of 'eco-protectionism' – the justification of trade barriers on environmental grounds. On the other hand, environmentalists insist that trade agreements must not limit regulation. They allege that liberalization of trade will dilute both their own nation's standards of regulation and those of the countries who exchange goods and services with their own.[123]

Yet Vogel has recently argued that enhancement of trade and protection of the environment are not inevitable opponents.[124] He insists that the enhancement of trade and of agreements to facilitate it frequently does not weaken regulatory standards but, instead, buttresses them. He argues that, on balance, both global and regional economic integration has increased at the same time that environmental and consumer regulatory requirements have become stronger. Or, to put the point more strongly in terms of the effects of free trade, he insists that such liberalization 'has, on balance, contributed to strengthening national regulatory policies, especially for traded goods and ... for domestic production standards as well.'[125]

Environmentalists' fears can be summarized in terms of a 'race to the bottom' or 'Delaware effect.' States in America have the power to charter corporations and are required to recognize each other's ability to do so. Because of this competition there has been some loosening of requirements by those states seeking to attract companies. In this regard, Delaware is thought to lead the way with conditions most conducive to the interests of management. Transferred to the context of international trade, the apprehension is that the 'Delaware effect' will lead nations to lower environmental requirements in order to facilitate commerce.

In contrast, however, there has, in fact, been a 'race to the top' or 'California effect.' Named after the state that has been a leader in environmental regulation, this effect refers to the role that wealthy 'green' jurisdictions can play in promoting strict regulatory standards and compliance with them. Within the American economy, California's relative size and affluence has helped drive many American environmental regulations upward. Within the European Union, Germany's relative size and wealth has contributed to strengthening regulatory standards and to encouraging compliance.

The 'Delaware effect' notion asserts that strict regulation will result in competitive disadvantage. That may be the case in other areas, for example, regarding labour standards. However, the costs of complying with stricter consumer and environmental standards have not been so great as to force political jurisdictions to lower such standards in order to keep domestic entities competitive.

Instead, in the case of many environmental and consumer regulations, more stringent requirements have been a source of competitive advantage for entities within the regulating jurisdictions. There have been examples to the contrary: for instance, in the USA the automobile emission standards of the 1977 Clean Air Amendments were modified as a response to the automobile industry's competitive difficulties; in the early 1980s automobile safety requirements were delayed for similar reasons.[126] Nevertheless, when wealthy nations, like Germany and the United States, stipulate more onerous standards, their trading partners are, generally, forced to comply with them so as to retain their export markets. Such compliance frequently encourages NGOs in the exporting country to claim similar requirements for products in the domestic market. Internationally-oriented producers are more inclined to accede to such claims since their exports to greener markets already comply.

However, there are important qualifiers to the 'California effect.' First, the role of greener markets in raising the regulatory standards of their trading partners is mostly limited to product standards. Trade liberalization, by itself, is not as likely to reinforce regulations relating to how goods and natural resources are produced.

Second, there must be substantial economic integration for the 'California effect' to occur. In this regard, the stronger the role of international institutions in terms of the promotion of trade, the greater the leverage of rich states over the regulatory powers of trading partners.[127]

The European Union's support for a single European market has enabled Germany to enjoy such suasion regarding the environmental policies of other member states. In contrast, the GATT (now the World Trade Organization [WTO]) is a much weaker institution. Unlike the EU, it does not have any legal mechanisms that enable its most powerful members to strengthen the regulatory standards of other signatories. Thus, greener nations such as America have had much less influence on the environmental policies of trading partners.

The North American Free Trade Agreement (NAFTA) occupies a middle position between the EU and the GATT. It resembles the EU to the extent that it does subject national standards to extra-national inspection. A signatory can be disciplined either for failing to enforce regulatory standards or for lowering such requirements in order to attract investments. However, the inspecting institutions established by NAFTA have much less authority to compel uniform standards than do comparable institutions under the EU.

Not surprisingly, Vogel's position has generated controversy. He is given full credit for posing and answering the question of under what conditions trade liberalization and environmental protection will work together: nations with a strong impact on the world economy that also support strict environmental standards and effective international institutions that promote the acceptance among other nations of these higher strictures. However, he is criticized for ignoring the crucial question of how to transform influential trading nations who, at present, do not have strong ecological protections. For instance, he refers to Japan as being indifferent to leading the greening of Asia without attempting any suggestions about how this position might be altered.[128]

Vogal has also been taken to task for presenting insufficient data to establish his contentions, particularly regarding the relationship of increasing trade and environmental protection in less-developed countries.[129] Critics worry that the relationship between developed and developing nations will follow a pattern more like the one set by

GATT's tuna-dolphin decision. In 1991 GATT nullified US trade restrictions on tuna caught in a manner that also ensnared a substantial number of dolphins. The decision limited the regulatory powers of a nation over products produced outside its jurisdiction. The fear is that the wave of the future regarding trade between richer and poorer nations will look like the result of the tuna-dolphin controversy: if the protections of a wealthy nation impede a primary industry of a less-affluent country, those regulations will have to go.[130] Further substantiation of such apprehensions came from a more recent WTO ruling. In that instance, the WTO judged that the USA was wrong in prohibiting shrimp imports from countries that fail to protect sea turtles from entrapment in the trawls of shrimping boats.[131]

Finally, even as there is agreement with the outcomes posited by Vogel, there are arguments raised about the causes of such results. Thus, it is contended that the 'California effect' does not arise from trade liberalization. Rather it occurs 'as a result of the affirmative regulatory activity characteristic of a higher degree of structural integration than that found in most free trade agreements ... [A]s international institutions acquire more active rule-making powers, it is that affirmative authority, not the constraints imposed by trade liberalization, that has the capacity to offset the deregulatory effects of trade liberalization.'[132]

Yet Vogel may not be nearly as deterministic as at least some of his critics would paint him. Indeed, he concludes his book by emphasizing that the effect of free trade on domestic efforts to regulate the safeguarding of the environment is by no means predetermined. The capacity for liberalization of trade to strengthen regulation on behalf of the environment depends on the realization by wealthy nations and their policy-makers that trade can be a positive influence on standards and their willingness to see this influence realized: 'To date, increased economic integration has, on balance, contributed to strengthening national regulatory policies, especially for traded goods and – in the case of the EU and, to a lesser extent NAFTA – for domestic production standards as well. Whether or not it continues to do so depends on the preferences of the world's richest and most powerful nation states.'[133]

In any event, the point here is that efforts to increase international trade are not inevitably a limit on the effectiveness of domestic law. The circumstances under which free trade and individual countries' legislation to protect the ecology can be compatible pose challenging but not insurmountable problems. The search for that compatibility will be 'one of the great themes of economic integration in the 21st century.'[134]

Conclusions

A study of the environment provides a clear example of law and altering societal views acting together in mutually supporting ways. Without the changed attitudes regarding the environment, the many green
laws would not have been passed or, if passed, would have produced
more problematic results. Since these laws were passed and enforced,
it is impossible to say what the state of the environment would be
without such legal regulation. Yet careful analysis of (mostly American) studies suggests that the progress that has been made has
depended to a significant extent on law and its enforcement; however,
the role played by litigation, at least in the United States, has been disappointing. At the same time, there is a strong basis for arguing that
regulation and market forces are not inevitable foes in terms of ecological protection. Studies regarding free trade and the environment make
this possibility clear: laws to protect the environment can be effective
even as free trade increases.

Is it possible to reconcile this – cautiously – positive assessment of
the effects of laws to protect the environment with the gloomy scenar-
ios that are continuously presented? Not entirely. However, there are
several factors, under two broad headings, that can be highlighted to
explain much of the divergence.

First, in terms of the actual effects produce by environmental regulation there are these elements:

- The slow pace of regulation, on the one hand, and the continuous
  discovery of new environmental problems, on the other, means that
  there will be some important pollutants unregulated at any given
  time.
- Zero is the only rate of emission of a pollutant that guarantees no
  environmental degradation. A regulatory program that reduces
  emissions by 75 per cent may, indeed, be successful. Yet for persistent toxins this may not be adequate.
- Much of regulation responds to effects on human health. Nevertheless, many ecologists emphasize that, to prevent the planet from
  being blighted, more attention must be given to irreversible damage
  to ecosystems.[135]

Second, environmental regulation is awash in extravagant statements:

- Proponents of a regulatory program are prone to make pronouncements that lead to unrealistic expectations about what that program – or others – can accomplish.

- Unrestrained advocates of the market are anxious to decry environmental regulation just because it is regulation.
- Extreme positions taken by some environmentalists suggest that any kind of compromise is connivance and, in any event, that law is nothing but a smokescreen for degradation.
- The environment is a presence on policy agendas and a fact of everyday life – we are, all of us, in that sense environmentalists. Thus, the media and popular publications readily report on such extravagant statements, but often at the expense of covering sober and even-handed evaluations.

There should be no complacency on issues regarding the environment or respecting law's role in this matter. What there needs to be is continuous monitoring and evaluation of the effects produced by regulation. The approach should be flexible and pragmatic, using a number of strategies. Those amenable to persuasion regarding ecological protection and the part to be played by regulation should be wary of salvos from all directions. They should, instead, be 'taking the facts seriously'[136] to better protect the environment, to use law most effectively.

CHAPTER EIGHT

Pornography – Fractured Protests, Harms(?), and Unstoppable Technology

[I]t has become clear that although everyone knows hard-core pornography when they see it, they see it in strikingly different places, and so no one really knows it at all.[1]

Erotica celebrates sexuality as an integral part of our common humanity; pornography, it is said, exploits and degrades. Yet if anything was ever in the eye of the beholder – including over time and cultures – it is what constitutes these two sides of the same coin.[2] What arouses some may offend others. That which repels a segment of the population may, to those differently inclined, explore sensual terrain long forbidden. Yet another vantage point insists that the dangers of pornography – to the extent there are any – scarcely ever come from sex at all and almost always come from violence.

Attempts to control pornography in the latter part of the twentieth century have been fraught with controversy. Efforts to prevent children from being exploited in any way by pornography enjoy a wide measure of support. However, the relationship between women and pornography has generated bitter debate. Women are the supposed victims of much pornography. Yet the evidence of harm caused them by sexual imagery is inconclusive at best. Feminists are deeply divided in terms of the circumstances under which pornography should be regulated, if at all. Meanwhile, the coming of the Internet may place the suppression of the obscene beyond the effective reach of legal regulation. The World Wide Web may provide one conclusive answer to questions regarding the impact of law: minimal in the face of unstoppable and pervasive technology.

Analysis of pornography differs from the other case studies we are examining. Those on capital punishment, smoking, the environment, and affirmative action all focus on enacted and enforced laws and their impact. The debate over pornography focuses much more on *its* effects and on the claims of proponents of regulation concerning the impact law could have. Nevertheless, we will look at one instance – in Canada – where a law has been interpreted (by the Supreme Court) consistent with the goals of those who believe that pornography does harm, damaging women in particular.

An analysis of obscenity permits us to assess several of the ideas regarding the impact of law discussed in part 2. First, we will focus on the question of whether pornography is, in fact, a problem or, in any event, one that the law should address. Here the emphasis will be on whether it 'causes' harm and, if so, whether law can be invoked to effectively suppress such objectionable effects. (Debates about defining social phenomena as problems and questions regarding issues of causation were examined, at a general level, in chapter 3.)

Second, this chapter affords a chance to examine an idea discussed in chapter 4 regarding the effectiveness of law: national styles of regulation.[3] Debates focused on using law to regulate or suppress pornography are widespread.[4] However, they are especially prominent in the United States and Canada. Meanwhile, some societies have largely abandoned attempts at such regulation, except for pornography that involves children or that is, otherwise, accessible to them. In some instances (such as some Scandinavian countries), the high status of women (including low incidence of violence against them) and minimal laws targeting pornography coincide.

Third, the Supreme Court of Canada's recognition of 'harm' as a constitutional justification of laws aimed at pornography permits us to examine two other ideas discussed in chapter 4: first, that law has a capacity to (re)constitute social relations and, second, that the impact of law produced by the judiciary may vary substantially from that of legislatures.[5] Evidence of the effects of the Court's ruling is not systematic but is, nevertheless, indicative. Such evidence suggests that important consequences of the ruling are substantially at odds with the announced goals of many of those who hailed the decision. In these circumstances, what the regulation of pornography is reconstituting and the effects produced become unclear and problematic, to say the least. A major fear is that the fights over invoking law to suppress sexual depictions deflect attention from the proliferation of violent ones. Are we far too upset about the former and far too complacent about the latter?

Finally, we look at the limits imposed by ever more sophisticated technology on compliance with law (a topic that chapter 2 focused upon). The issue of the regulation of the Internet, especially as it relates to pornography, affords a specific opportunity to examine the limits placed on law's capacity to effectively regulate behaviour because of technological developments. At the same time, there is the possibility of control of the Internet by other aspects of technology and through self-regulation and market forces. Here we will return to another idea discussed in chapter 4: the complicated role of norms in regulating behaviour.[6]

Before we take up these four issues a brief canvassing of theoretical approaches to pornography will provide an important context for understanding why this subject is so controversial.

Theoretical Approaches to Pornography

In discussing theoretical approaches to pornography it is most useful to concentrate on liberalism, moral conservatism, and feminism, especially anti-pornography and post-structuralist feminism. It is these approaches that have most fuelled the debates in the last two decades.

Contemporary debates about pornography almost always begin by addressing liberal ideals for society. There are many strands of liberalism, but they hold in common the primacy of individuals and the need for their autonomy in society. Such individualistic independence rests upon a number of values. Three of these loom large in a discussion of pornography: the 'harm principle,' freedom of expression, and privacy. All three values, at least as traditionally articulated, buttress contentions that any regulation of pornography should be kept to a minimum.

John Stuart Mill advanced the harm principle as the basis of state action in a society guided by liberal ideals: 'the only purpose for which power can be rightfully exercised over any member of a civilized community against his will, is to prevent harm to others.'[7] The attractions for liberals of the harm principle is apparent, since it argues for a sphere of autonomy in which individuals are free to engage in any behaviour they believe conducive to their own interests, limited only by the obligation not to inflict injury on others. Even if one accepts the attractiveness of liberalism in this context, the question that nevertheless immediately arises is, What constitutes 'harm'? Almost all human conduct affects the interests of others to some degree. Thus, the 'harm' principle is not self-executing but, rather, gives rise to all manner of debate about what actions should be proscribed. Nowhere are the debates more intense than over the application of the harm principle in the context of pornography. A first position on pornography, resting on one conception of liberalism, holds that if someone wants to produce pornography and someone wants to consume it, they should be able to strike a bargain to do so. The answer simply comes quickly back is that they cannot because pornography 'harms,' most particularly women, in any number of ways. Yet, as we shall see, that answer simply ignites a debate regarding the effects of pornography.

A second tenet of liberalism that is fundamental in this context is freedom of expression. It is asserted that freedom of expression bolsters liberal values in three ways: by promoting the search for truth, by facilitating participation in the political process, and by enhancing individual self-fulfilment.[8] Such purposes, in turn, reflect liberal assumptions about individuals, society, language, and expression. Perhaps most importantly they arise out of the view that freedom of expression is a 'negative' right, one that shields the individual from interference from other individuals and the collectivity (represented most prominently by governments). The classic problem posed by freedom of expression is that, unqualified, it is bound to infringe on the interests of others. In the case of pornography, unbounded liberalism asserts that characterizing any communication as sexual, degrading, violent, or whatever is beside the point. It is all 'speech,' and as such it must be 'free' or democracy will be imperilled. The response to this view pits one fundamental right against another: 'free speech' is infringing upon equality (of women) and, to that extent, must give way.

Finally, liberalism places great store on the value of privacy and the capacity to draw distinctions between private and public acts and values. In this conception, actions and values that can be characterized as private have an especially strong claim for protection against state interference. Thus it is asserted that; at the very least, a distinction should be drawn between private consumption of pornography (videos, magazines, etc.) and public exhibitions involving pornographic material. Yet the public/private distinction has encountered much difficulty, particularly regarding how, if at all, a boundary can (or should) be drawn between what constitutes the private, as opposed to the public, realm. In particular regarding pornography, it is argued that the privileging of so-called private acts just conceals the harm done to women, something that has a pre-eminent claim to be of public concern.

Moral conservatism (unlike liberalism) is far less concerned with staking out neutral territory where individuals can seek their own destiny in terms of contractual arrangements, consumption of pornography/erotica, and the like. Instead, such conservatism maintains that there are moral principles that need to be adhered to by a society if it is to endure. Such principles may not be capable of justification as inherently right and immutable. Nevertheless, to permit widespread disregard of them will result in the loss of society's cement and thus lead to social disintegration.[9]

These conservatives (especially the religious right) take a basic position: pornography is bad and ought to be so regarded. Indeed, it ought to be suppressed simply because it is offensive. In addition, it in fact harms because it is subversive of sex, which ought to be heterosexual, monogamous, procreative, and expressed within the confines of marriage. It is a fact that marriage as an institution is breaking down, at least as reflected in the rising divorce rate. The latter is associated with the increased economic independence of women. Yet for moral conservatives these two phenomena (escalating divorce rate, increased economic independence of women) are both linked to pornography and its debasement of marriage and of the appropriate roles of men and women within that institution.

Until the last decades, conflict about the public display of the sexual was dominated by liberals and civil libertarians and their commitment to free speech, on the one hand, and by moral conservatives and their struggle to suppress erotic/pornographic display, on the other. However, in recent years a claim by a strand of feminism that pornography is an ideology of sexual domination and violence has come to prominence and played a major role in the courts and legislatures and in shaping public opinion. The foremost advocate of this position is a legal academic, Catherine MacKinnon. Anti-pornography feminists profess to put aside any moral qualms about pornography even as they sometimes ally themselves with moral conservatives in battles to criminalize or otherwise regulate it. Instead, they mainly focus on confronting the liberal tenets that underwrite pornography's availability: the harm principle, freedom of expression, and privacy.

It is claimed that pornography harms women because it invades their fundamental right to equality. It does this by promoting the subordination of women. In its extreme form it incites violence as a means of terrorizing women into compliance: '[P]ornography is the theory, and rape is the practice.'[10] In any event, pornography is at least complicit in the most offensive aspects of a sexist, male-centred culture. The message of the obscene is that men are active and powerful while women are passive and accepting – objects, not subjects. Thus, men are thereby convinced that women are inferior and need not (or should not) have equal rights. Pornography is 'the essence of a sexist social order, its quintessential social act.'[11]

Anti-pornography feminists insist that to the extent that freedom of expression (in its application to pornography) collides with women's equality, the former must yield.[12] Moreover, such feminists argue that pornography does not, in any event, merit protection as freedom of expression because it is not speech at all but, rather, vile action: 'Pornography is not an idea any more than segregation or lynching are ideas, although both institutionalize the idea of the inferiority of one group to another.'[13] In any event, freedom of expression and its emphasis on negative liberty, to the extent it can be reflected in pornography, is also challenged: '[T]he market place of ideas is literal: those with the most money can buy the most speech, and women are poor.'[14] This depiction of freedom of expression as a negative right, and one to be exercised through market forces, allows pornographers to flood society with their 'speech' as women are kept silent.

Feminists opposed to pornography also attack claims of privacy regarding the consumption of pornography head on: to claim protection of privacy regarding pornography is to conceal the harm it does to women and their equality. Thus, it is contended that those opposed to censorship become fixated on questions of causality and standards of proof regarding pornography and its relation to violence against women. Such fixation leads to claims that its consumption, at any rate, should be a private matter. In other words, lack of proof of causation means no regulation, which, in turn, results in giving pornographers a free hand in objectifying and vilifying women while shielding themselves behind the screen of privacy.

Yet feminism is not monolithic. Marxist feminists argue that the best response to sexism is not to become embroiled in contests over pornography but, rather, to concentrate on the obliteration of capitalist values and structures that cradle such beliefs and acts. Another strand warns of trying to use legal measures to change society and, instead, urges employing education and other processes of socialization said to be more successful over the long haul. Yet another group, the sex radicals, maintain that sex should be regarded as a site of unmodified pleasure and agency and that all pornography/erotica ought to be viewed as an aid to the creative, disruptive, empowering force of sexual pleasure.[15]

A sustained challenge to anti-pornography feminists has come from those who employ post-structural analysis to question the fundamentalist claims of those feminists opposed to pornography. This challenge claims that insights about power, sexuality, and social construction suggest that female sexuality is too complicated to finally categorize pornography as either a means of domination of women or as a site of pleasure and freedom. Specifically, anti-pornography feminists are charged with fundamentalism regarding its meaning. Instead, what is required is a grappling with complexity: 'The feminist view à la MacKinnon is that "pornography is a form of forced sex" ... [but] pornography and sexuality must be understood as a terrain of struggle and contradiction.'[16]

Even within post-structuralist feminism there are different emphases placed on the implications of a more nuanced and complicated approach to the meaning pornography entails. One strand claims that pornography does have an impact that is negative but that is not direct and linear. The obscene is 'enigmatic and contingent,' so that its harm is not 'physical or directly observable.' Rather, pornography underscores patriarchy. It 'works from within by constituting our subjectivities.'[17] Thus, pornography's sexist messages do need to be challenged. However, censorship is not the solution. Instead, the indeterminacy of pornographic messages suggests possibilities for transforming both them and the right to freedom of expression.

Another strand of post-structural feminism emphasizes the contradictory effects of pornography and, more generally, of sexuality. In this depiction, sexuality is both a site of pleasure and agency and one of domination and danger. Moreover, sexualities can change, and one of the means of change is pornography: '[O]ur sexualities are complex and contradictory, always in the process of being constituted and reconstituted through a multiplicity of discourses, one of which is pornography.'[18] As a result, this strand of post-structural feminism is adamantly opposed to censorship for two reasons. First, censorship of pornography inhibits the search by women for ways to express the complexities of sex and stifles their sexual agency. Second, the power to censor will be turned on marginalized groups, including women generally, but especially feminists, gays, and lesbians. Such fears are especially pronounced in Canada. There, in the wake of a decision upholding a criminal provision permitting censorship on the grounds that pornography 'harms,' there is evidence that 'gay and lesbian sexualities, sadomasochistic sexuality, and other alternative sexualities all continue to be a major target of obscenity law.'[19] We will pursue the implications of events in Canada momentarily.

In any event, according to this strand of post-structural feminism, being against censorship law does not mean that there is no role for law. Instead, this view asserts that workers in pornography (and prostitution) could be protected by decriminalizing pornography and all aspects of prostitution and by then applying existing laws that protect other employees regarding conditions of work – for example, employment standards, human rights, occupational health and safety, and workers' compensation laws. Thus, a role for law in achieving change is not rejected: '[W]e simply reject its role in bringing about such change through the repression of representations.'[20]

Does Pornography Harm?

A central question, then, regarding pornography is whether it harms. We have seen, from the preceding discussion, that claims about harm can essentially be reduced to three points: the corruption of morals; violence against women, particularly of a sexual nature; and the subordination of women.[21] In addition, there is a fourth critical point to be examined regarding harm: is the danger in pornography (if there is danger) not sex but, rather, violence?

The Corruption of Morals

This claim about the effects of pornography is most closely identified with an element of the right: one might say the moral, religious right. The contention is that sex exists to beget children within the confines of marriage. Any depiction of sex that suggests otherwise undermines its acceptable purpose and leads to corruption, that is, the breakdown of the institution of marriage: '[F]or conservatives, pornography, like prostitution, is an agent of corruption, subverting the nuclear family and the patriarchal authority based in it by sanctioning those old devils, licentiousness and vice.'[22]

Even if such representation of sex is only mildly explicit, it still has dark power: '"[S]oft-core" pornography breeds sexual dissatisfaction and helps break up marriages.'[23] Needless to say, gay and lesbian sexuality, women showing any pleasure or exercising any control in sexual activity, or women and men enjoying sex just because it is sex are all beyond the pale. This contention is fiercely adhered to by those who believe it. Typically, the position is simply asserted as self-evident, with no need of verification: '[C]ommon sense tells us pornography is bound to contribute to sexual crime ... It seems ludicrous to argue "bad" books do not promote bad behaviour.'[24] In any event, whether the decline of marriage (to the extent that it is declining) can be characterized in any way as a form of corruption is highly debatable.

Moreover, it is unclear what pornography has to do with any instability in the institution of marriage. Some who adhere to this view allege that marriages will be corrupted because consumption of pornography is associated with masturbation.[25] (The focus of the effects of pornography is nearly always men.) Yet there appears to be no evidence that males, as a whole, prefer masturbation to intercourse. In any event, consumption of pornography is scarcely a precondition of masturbation.

It is true that many marriages are breaking down – and, indeed, more and more couples choose not to marry at all. There are several reasons for these phenomena. A primary one is the enhanced status of women and their increased economic strength. Many would consider these changes alterations for the good. In any event, women can now elect to marry (or not) or to continue (or discontinue) a marriage to an extent unimaginable even a generation ago. Whether the stability of the institution of marriage contributes to or detracts from a civilized and humane order is a subject upon which – not unexpectedly – there are differing opinions. Yet it is a debate for which the issue of pornography seems to have little relevance, despite the adamant protest of the religious right.

Violence against Women

The claim that pornography causes violence against women fuels much of the contemporary campaigns for regulation and suppression. In its unqualified form that claim alleges that pornography is a 'crucial element' causing such violence; the link 'is considerably stronger than for cigarette smoking and cancer'; and there should be no doubts that 'anybody disputes the data.'[26] Those who hold this view assert that the obscene brings about these pernicious results both aphrodisiacally and ideologically.

The aphrodisiacal qualities of pornography increase male sexual excitement, creating pressure for an outlet. This pressure leads to rape and other forms of sexual assault. Yet such pressure could also lead to other forms of release – consensual sex and masturbation. Indeed, it is arguable that by facilitating masturbation, pornography may actually decrease, not increase, the incidents of rape. The ideological aspects of pornography signal that women liked to be raped or, in any event, that their choices just do not matter. Such messages are not the product of conspiracy but, rather, reflect common fantasies, at least when directed at men: the strong, aggressive male; the beautiful, admiring female.

So it is possible to argue that pornography both aphrodisiacally and ideologically incites rape. But does it, in fact, do so? On this question there is plenty of evidence, of three different types, regarding the effects of pornography. Overall the evidence is inconclusive. Each type of evidence suffers from different frailties.

First, there are continuous allegations that those who commit crimes of sexual violence are enthusiastic consumers of pornography.[27] A cross-state study in the United States found a strong positive correlation between the circulation of soft-core pornographic magazines (the only kind for which such figures are available) and the incidence of rape. The correlation persists when certain sociological factors are introduced. In any event, the authors doubt that the relationship is a causal one.[28] Still other studies have tended to establish the opposite. When rapists have been compared with a non-rapist control group it has been found that the control group has had earlier and more exposure to pornography as adolescents and more recent exposure to pornography as adults than did rapists. In addition, there is some evidence through self-reporting studies, that prior attitudes about women are a better predictor of rape than is exposure to pornography.[29] What is more, eliminating alcohol (unlikely as that may be) might curb more sexual assaults than banning explicit sex.[30]

Second, laboratory experiments, mostly with male college students, have been conducted to ascertain whether exposure to pornography induces aggressiveness towards women or disregard for their desires.[31] Clearly, there are difficulties in stating confidently that what happens in a laboratory of students is indicative of what happens in real life.[32] ('There can be few things more contested, even from within its own theoretical framework, than the relevance of the controlled and contrived social-psychological laboratory experiment to human action in the world at large.')[33] That said, most of the studies conclude that *only* when pornography is *violent* does it have the predicted impact. The central importance of violence rather than sex is a matter we will return to below.[34] One study concluded that exposure to highly arousing erotica did lead to increased shock levels being administered to another person (the experimenter's stooge) who had angered the subject earlier.

Yet the same material also led to positive behaviour towards the stooge if the previous interaction had been friendly.[35]

The third type of evidence compares the effects of pornography over time in the same and different societies. First, over the last decades pornography has become much more widely available. Such dissemination is attributable to several factors, including the video recorder. If pornography causes rape, one would expect the incidents of sexual violence to have increased. In addition, because of much stronger public norms against such acts one would expect a greater willingness to report these crimes. Yet such incidents and their reporting have fallen, not risen.[36]

Second, some studies have explored the linkage between the availability of pornography and sex-crime rates by comparing societies. In the late 1960s, Denmark repealed its pornography laws. The repeal was followed by a sharp drop in sex crimes. However, the question of whether there was any causal relation has become deeply controversial.[37] Other studies conclude that pornography correlates with increased crime in other countries such as Japan, where all crime rates, including those for sex crimes, dropped after pornography restrictions increased. It is hard to see how the availability (or non-availability) of pornography should be related to overall rates for crime. In any event, pornography in Japan is especially violent so the results, to the extent they can be stated confidently, may say more about violence than they say about sex.[38]

Thoughtful commentators caution about drawing confident conclusions from these cross-societal studies. Instead, they urge more careful investigation involving random sampling, accurate consumption rates, and multivariate research. At the same time, these commentators tend to think that the available data are even less conclusive than are laboratory experiments in demonstrating that non-violent pornography is linked to violent crime against women.[39]

The Subordination of Women

Quite apart from inciting men to rape (if it does do that), pornography could contribute to the subordination of women. ('Dachau brought into the bedroom and celebrated.')[40] Pornography supposedly does this by devaluing them and signalling that discrimination and harassment are acceptable, perhaps even what women really want. This charge concerning the pernicious effect of pornography is levelled at all of it, from the most sexually violent to *Playboy*. Indeed, some feminists believe that *Playboy* may be one of the most harmful forms.[41] This is so because the magazine gives the appearance of consent to participate to what is, in fact, a coercive relationship.[42]

The inequality of women is a problem that must be addressed. Yet it is doubtful that attempts by law to eliminate *Playboy* would have much impact on this issue. Male attitudes of superiority were more strongly entrenched before the advent of *Playboy*, and they flourish in societies – Islamic cultures, for example – that attempt to suppress all forms of erotica, let alone anything that could be characterized as pornographic. As we have seen, feminists opposed to anti-pornography crusades argue that women do not need more censorship but, rather, more sexually explicit material produced by and for women. Moreover, there is need for more open discussion of all sexual issues, coupled with the struggle against women's subordinated social, political, and economic status.[43]

At the other extreme from fundamentalist Islamic countries and their attitude to pornography is Denmark. It was the first Western country to repeal most regulation of pornography. A similar course was followed in Sweden.[44] In those societies women enjoy equal status and have achieved economic[45] and political power[46] that may well be the highest in the world. Indeed, at least as far as Western societies are concerned, the proliferation of pornography and the rise in the status of women are, generally, positively correlated. For example, there are some studies comparing states in the USA in terms of the availability of pornography and measures of gender equality. Generally, these studies run counter to claims that pornography encourages discrimination against women. One study of the relationship between circulation rates of soft-core pornography and levels of gender equality established a positive correlation between equal opportunities for women in employment, education, and politics and higher circulation rates of pornography.[47] Another study concluded that states with a preponderance of Southern Baptists (members of the same religion as the anti-pornographer and politically right-wing preacher Jerry Falwell) had the highest levels of inequality between men and women. The conclusion of that study was not that pornography led to more positive attitudes towards women's equality but, rather, that other factors like greater (or lesser) social tolerance likely explained the relationship. Also of interest in terms of violence (rather than sexual explicitness) being linked to the subordination of women was the study's finding that gender inequality correlated with the presence and extent of legitimate violence in a state (as measured by the numbers of people trained to work in the military; the use of corporal punishment in schools; government use of violence; and mass-media preferences for violence, as in circulation rates of the magazine *Guns and Ammo*).[48]

There is another puzzling aspect to this charge (regarding the subordination of women) that makes the strange alliance between some feminists and the religious right on these issues stranger still. If pornography of all shades subordinates women, why do moral conservatives wish it suppressed? In fact the religious right claims quite the opposite. It alleges that pornography promotes sexual freedom and with it the free, 'liberated' woman who denies her 'essential' nature. Is it possible that pornography can have such diametrically opposed effects simultaneously?

Yet another way to examine this charge of subordination is to admit its possibility but wonder why pornography is especially singled out. Popular culture more generally – television, magazines, videos, music – may be much more responsible for depictions of the inferiority of women: *Playboy* is the theory, but *People* is the practice. If this is the case, focusing on pornography, whatever its effects, deflects attention away from the more insistent problem: finding ways to alter images of women in the popular media. Such attention also claims a power for law that it may not possess.[49] In the end, depictions in the media may not be a matter that law can (or should) control. Rather these depictions reflect situations and roles that require fundamental social change.[50]

Is Sex the Problem?

A number of those who have studied the impact of pornography maintain that it can have anti-social effects. However, they believe that what makes a depiction pornographic is not sex but violence: 'The present focus on the visual dangers of titillation, copulation, and autoeroticism would be better turned toward mutilation, corpses, and autopsies.'[51]

In this view, the depiction of even 'hard core' sex has few negative effects, including regarding the three forms of harm just discussed. It is violence that is the culprit. Such violence may include sexual depictions, but is by no means limited to them. Thus, from this perspective vociferous complaints against *Playboy* deflect and confound the issue when *Robocop II, The Wild Bunch*, and *Texas Chainsaw Massacre* ought to be targeted.

Laboratory experiments support the contention that the villain is violence.[52] Some psychological experiments have established that men watching violent pornography are more likely to score higher on measures of aggression and to display, at least temporarily, more calloused attitudes towards women. There are three important points arising out of such research. First, it was those subjects who said, *before* watching the violent pornography, that they were likely to commit rape if they could get away with it who demonstrated more calloused attitudes after watching it. Second, violence rather than sexual explicitness correlated with the increase in calloused attitudes and higher measures of aggressiveness towards women (established after using non-pornographic films involving violence against women). Third, counselling subjects after they had watched violent pornography that all rape is harmful led to lower rather than higher expressions of calloused attitudes towards women in all subjects. Such an effect persisted for at least six months, offering some evidence of the power of anti-sexist education.[53]

In any event, as anyone who watches any amount of television or browses in a local video store knows, there is plenty of graphic violence widely available. Indeed, there is evidence that violence and male dominance has sharply increased in R-rated videos while such scenes have decreased in X-rated films.[54] One study (in 1980) concluded that violent images in magazines like *Playboy* and *Penthouse* did increase from 1 to 5 per cent between 1973 and 1977. However, a 1985 study found a decline after 1977, with well under 1 per cent of such material containing violent imagery. What is more, there was no increase in violent sexual imagery in 'adult' videos from 1979 to 1983 according to another study done in the United States. A 1990 US survey reported between 3.3 and 4.7 per cent of violent imagery in a random sample of pornographic films and another 7 per cent of s/m or bondage imagery with women submissive in pornographic magazines, but 9 per cent with men submissive. Moreover, heterosexual men list violence as the least titillating aspect of pornography and have become less, rather than more, tolerant of it.[55]

If violent images are linked to violent acts we have a huge problem. Such depictions are all around us. Meanwhile, the focus on sex that underlies virtually all definitions of pornography may simply be irrelevant and may deflect attention away from the real dangers. Equally confounding may be current definitions (including by those feminists who support regulation) that start with sex and then add a measure of violence. Uncertainties remain, including in terms of our understanding of issues of causation, the nature and extent of the problem, and acceptable solutions.[56] Still, violence may hold the pernicious key: 'We do not yet know whether the addition of sex to graphic violence has a more harmful impact, but we can safely look for the source more within the violence than the sex as such.'[57]

Canada Experiments

The Supreme Court of Canada and 'Harm': R. v. Butler

Chapter 4 discussed the assertion that litigation can bring about social change and criticism of that idea. As part of that analysis the question was raised whether a significant expansion of the role of courts regarding complex social and political issues would alter the underlying conditions of a society. Such possible changes were discussed using Canada as an example. Since 1982 it has an entrenched bill of rights that has greatly expanded the role for courts regarding an array of issues. An instance of the changed role for the judiciary and the complications that can result is provided by a discussion regarding the Canadian Supreme Court's treatment of pornography and the aftermath of that decision.

Many feminists seeking to suppress pornography, or at least regulate it, believe that the key is to shift from an analysis exclusively focused on the morality of sexual explicitness. Instead, the focus should be on the harm to women's equality done by pornography. Nevertheless, such analysis retains sexual explicitness as the ingredient triggering the damage. This approach, these feminists maintain, converts debate over pornography from focusing on 'free speech' to highlighting gender equality.

Such arguments have, generally, not been accepted in the United States. A few attempts to enshrine such views in legislation have been struck down by the courts.[58] Reaction to the 'harms' of pornography and what should be done have largely been confined to debates in the political arena, the media, and the academy. Thus, American society may be exhibiting the correct stance regarding these issues. Widespread discussion regarding these questions is encouraged. A rush to legalize the 'harms' of pornography and to provide 'solutions' to them is not.[59] (Attempts to regulate pornography on the Internet are discussed below.)[60]

However, in *R. v. Butler*[61] the Supreme Court of Canada accepted much of this harm analysis. The legislation under attack was a Criminal Code provision (s. 163) that made producing, distributing, and possessing obscene material an offence. Essentially, the statute makes something obscene if its 'dominant characteristic' is 'the undue exploitation of sex, or of sex and ... crime, horror, cruelty and violence.'[62] Note that the section adopted the traditional focus on sex. Violence is a possible appended ingredient but cannot, itself, render material obscene.

The Court found that the legislation clearly infringed freedom-of-speech guarantees. Nevertheless, it upheld the legislation, under section 1 of the Charter,[63] by finding that the provision advances the substantial and compelling purpose of preventing harm to women. In doing so, the Court characterized the empirical evidence on the connection between exposure to pornographic imagery and acts of violence against women as 'subject to controversy.'[64] Instead, it appealed to common sense and deference to parliamentary judgment to make the connection between the restriction and the prevention of harm.

As for common sense, the Court asserted a presumption about connections: 'It is reasonable to presume that exposure to images bears a casual relationship to changes in attitudes and beliefs.'[65] Further, it maintained that this presumption is widely held by the community: 'A substantial body of opinion ... holds that the portrayal of persons being subjected to degrading or dehumanizing sexual treatment results in harm.'[66] Regarding deference to Parliament, the Court concluded that the government ought to have 'a margin of appreciation to form legitimate objectives based on somewhat inconclusive social science evidence.'[67] Thus, 'Parliament was entitled to have a "reasoned apprehension of harm" resulting from the desensitization of individuals exposed to materials which depict violence, cruelty, and dehumanization in sexual relations.'[68]

As a result, the question of obscenity was no longer that of regulating public morality. Rather, the regulation of the pornographic was to be focused on avoiding harm, especially damage to women. The test for determining obscenity would be based on classifying pornography according to three categories:

- explicit sex and violence – always characterized as obscene
- explicit sex without violence but with elements that are degrading and dehumanizing – characterized as obscene if found to cause harm

– explicit sex, with no violence, no depiction of degradation and dehumanization, and no dipiction of children – generally not found to be obscene.

The three classifications were to be made reflecting the community-standards test set out in a previous Supreme Court case: that is, what Canadians would tolerate other people being exposed to.[69] Finally, there would be the possibility of an artistic defence regarding a determination of whether or not the representation was unduly exploitative of sex.

When the Court rendered its judgment, feminists of the pornography-harms persuasion hailed the decision as a breakthrough. Catharine MacKinnon, the prominent American feminist so associated with anti-pornography campaigns, had helped write an intervenor's brief in support of the law. She declared, in a front-page story in the *New York Times*: 'This makes Canada the first place in the world that says what is obscene is what harms women not what offends our values.'[70] Yet such cheering may be misplaced.

The Court talked about curbing pornography that harms. It used violence, particularly against women, as the example, but did not limit its discussion to that instance. To the contrary, it talked about harm as coming from anti-social conduct, described as 'conduct which society formally recognizes as incompatible with its proper functioning.'[71] Such a description of 'harm' leaves a great deal of room for several applications, including a very conservative one. Also, such language can bolster attempts to suppress any material seen to undermine 'a moral view about the roles of men and women, the importance of the nuclear family and the nature of sexuality and sexual relations.'[72]

The heated debates about what constitutes pornography, the effects of pornography, and whether the effects (whatever they are) depend on sexual or violent representations cannot, to say the least, be characterized as yielding a common understanding. The Supreme Court's embrace of the assertion that pornography does harm, while leaving what constitutes such objectionable results as 'wild cards,'[73] did little to calm matters in Canada. Instead, it left several questions about law and the regulation of the erotic/pornographic in its wake. Further, for at least some feminists, the decision has become a clear illustration of one idea about the effect of law discussed in chapter 4. That idea was 'law as deflection,' the thrust of which, as articulated by some progressives, is that law can do more harm than good and should be resorted to, if at all, with extreme caution in aid of change. One of the leading proponents of this idea has said: 'Pornography is an issue which clearly reveals the limits of law in terms of feminist strategy.'[74] The aftermath of the *Butler* decision provokes thought regarding the accuracy of this idea.

The Impact of Butler

It is difficult to say what the impact of *Butler* has been. It is a relatively recent decision and no systematic study has been undertaken of its consequences. Nevertheless, a number of strands have surfaced related to the broad themes we are exploring regarding impact.

We can start by reminding ourselves that in examining the aftermath of *Butler* we are looking at the impact of judge-made law. Again, we are testing the hypothesis that the effect of litigation on social and political issues may be different from that of other kinds of law (from the legislatures or administrative processes). These different consequences are attributable to institutional characteristics peculiar to courts: their independence (or, from another perspective, their lack of accountability), win-lose outcomes emanating from judges that may cause more intense reaction, constrained enforcement mechanisms, and so forth. At the same time, there are two opposed elements to the claim that court judgments have a particular sort of impact.

On the one hand, it is contended that judicial decisions are more effective in reshaping social and political issues. This is because the independence and tenure of judges and the principled nature of their decision-making equips them to respond to the rigidity of bureaucracies, the deal-making of politics, and the intolerance of the majorities. On the other hand, it is argued that the very independence of judges removes them from the political mainstream and constrains them. Because courts have limited tools of enforcement, serious problems can arise in terms of their judgments being implemented, particularly those that involve complicated and costly remedies. Finally, involvement by courts in complex social and political issues may cause the political and administrative processes to withdraw from 'hot potatoes' instead of struggling to reach generally accepted and long-lasting solutions.

Both of these opposed elements are represented by *Butler*. There is no question that *Butler*, on its face, reshaped the law. What is more, the Supreme Court did what the legislature would, or could, not do. However, as we will discuss below, *Butler* may have produced consequences substantially at variance with those sought by those invoking 'harm' to defend the criminal regulation of pornography. What is more, there is little evidence that the pornography meant to be suppressed by *Butler* has, in fact, diminished in availability.

The strands of *Butler* can be traced back about ten years earlier. Then there had been a government-appointed study – the Fraser Committee Report[75] – into pornography. This report reached several conclusions, but most important, for our purposes, was the contention that, in a competition, freedom of speech must yield to equality. The Fraser Committee accepted that there was no 'consistent and conclusive' evidence that pornography caused 'demonstrable harm.'[76] Nevertheless, it asserted that '[o]ur approach is characterized by acceptance of the egalitarian argument that impairment of a fundamental social value can properly be regarded as a "harm" meriting legislative control.'[77]

Yet, whatever the merits of this shift from freedom of speech to equality that the Fraser Committee represented, the suppression of pornography never garnered wide popular support. There were no politicians with a major public profile who championed the cause. Attempts by a few newspapers to sound the alarm did not result in widespread response. In Quebec, where there is generally more sexual tolerance, the pornography debates in the rest of Canada looked 'like the tortured dances of an exotic tribe.'[78] Indeed, in terms of Canada generally, the Fraser Committee itself reported a remarkable fact: only 1 per cent of Canadians considered pornography to be a major issue.[79] The minimal indication of concern among Canadians is at variance with polls in the United States, taken at about the same time, which reported significantly higher levels of popular concern regarding pornography.[80] The discrepancy may have occurred because the survey cited by the Fraser Committee permitted people to characterize the extent to which pornography was an issue. When asked, 59 per cent agreed it was *a problem* (though not as significant as other social and economic issues). However, only 1 per cent were prepared to indicate that it was a *major* issue. The Canadian finding was a reproof, at least in that country at that time, to feminist anti-pornographers' vehement insistence that there was substantial concern regarding the menace of smut.

With such wobbly support for anti-pornography efforts it is no surprise that two legislative attempts at reform were unsuccessful. In the second attempt Canadian librarians rebelled, balking at the potential dangers of the new laws to a range of books they saw themselves as guarding. In addition, the right suddenly withdrew its support from the same bill, fearing that it would be too permissive. The bill did fail and, at that point, further attempts at legislative reform were halted.

Nevertheless, a few years later, *Butler* enshrined through litigation the approximate position of the Fraser Committee. Thus, those supporting anti-pornography efforts could claim that the courts had triumphed over the indecisiveness of legislative politics. But with what effect? No systematic study has been done, so firm conclusions are impossible. Still, at least three developments can be pointed to suggesting that *Butler* has had little impact on its targets while creating uproar in other areas: consequences for purveyors in pornography, greater surveillance of certain forms of erotica/ pornography, and divisions within feminism.

First, peddlers of explicit sex and violence were not very upset by the decision. In fact there is evidence that they were quite relieved by it. For *Butler* settled bounds and fences within which they could operate while clearly legitimating much of what they sell.[81] Far from being blunted, the sale of pornography appears to be flourishing, 'booming in Canada as never before.'[82] At the same time, arguments that violence rather than sexual explicitness is the villain have been largely submerged in the wake of that decision. Anyone who watches television can attest to the fact that violent images are the stock in trade of many popular programs, including those aimed at children. Yet fights over sexually explicit pornography have occupied the terrain, even as images of shootings, knifings, and other forms of terror surround us.

Second, in contrast, certain kinds of erotica have come under greater surveillance. The big losers in the wake of *Butler* appear to be gays and lesbians and the artistic community.[83] Critics of *Butler* challenge claims of anti-pornography feminists that the case represents a radical departure from the history of moral regulation that has so strongly influenced the control of erotica/pornography in the past, particularly in Canada. Those opposed to *Butler* argue that the decision and its aftermath has much to do with regulation of sexual immorality: 'While the specific content of sexual immorality may have changed, the object of the law has not.'[84] There is no question that harassment of homosexual publications is nothing new and certainly took place before the *Butler* decision. Yet there are good indications that judgment provided the authorities with a new springboard for focusing on unconventional sexual practices.[85] For example, anything that can be construed as sadomasochistic may be targeted – even 'a dopey Hollywood sex comedy.'[86] What is more, there are continuous allegations of general harassment extending to the seizure of books on university reading lists.[87] The following are further examples of the 'breadth of post-*Butler*' censorship (admittedly drawn from sources strongly opposed to the decision):

- Bookstores selling controversial gay and lesbian books and magazines have been prosecuted, with some convictions (and some successful appeals from those convictions).
- Material is routinely censored by Canada Customs officials, who are empowered to prohibit importation of the obscene. However, at the end of 2000 the Supreme Court did attempt to establish new standards for seizure by customs officials. The Court's decision arose out of activity by such officials targeting gay and lesbian literature.[88]
- Toronto's funding to gay and lesbian artists has been threatened and, in some instances, actually revoked.
- In Alberta the funding for lesbian visual art has been threatened.
- The Reform party attacked the National Film Board for 'promoting a homosexual and lesbian lifestyle' (a collection of gay-positive videos) and protested the use of government funds to produce a Canadian AIDS Society safe-sex pamphlet.
- The CRTC (Canadian Radio-television and Telecommunications Commission) warned a Halifax radio station that it must stop broadcasting sexually explicit materials after complaints were brought about gay and lesbian issues being covered.
- *X-tra! West*, a gay and lesbian publication, has been banned in parts of British Columbia.[89]

Finally, the fight over pornography may have done little for conditions of inequality for women, while deflecting attention away from those very conditions. More time and energy spent on fights over pornography and its effects has meant less time devoted to other critical issues such as education, child care, and the political empowerment of women.[90] This fight has certainly divided the feminist community, anti-pornography feminists, civil libertarians, and post-structural feminists. At the same time, a large part of the lesbian and gay community has been alienated from many feminist claims.[91]

Those who believe in the constitutive aspects of law persist in the assertion that the struggle against pornography that invokes law will be transformative: 'The liberal democratic tradition thus provides the symbolic resources to struggle against all forms of subordination; it offers a discourse that enables the production of new social and political subjectivities and new ways of governing.'[92] Maybe. Or perhaps the fights over pornography demonstrate how deeply divisive and deflective claims to legal regulation can be when, at least in Canada, these contretemps appear to proceed with little popular base. Or, even worse, maybe those who rail against sexual images unwittingly provide a front behind which violent ones flourish. Such depictions abound and may be the real problem: seeping into popular consciousness; telling us to accept violence as part of day-to-day life, as reality and images blur.

The Limits of the Law?: Pornography and the Internet

As technology becomes ever more powerful it may blunt the force of law in any number of ways. Our very sense of what can be (and should be) regulated (and how) may be significantly altered as technology substantially changes the ways in which goods and services can be produced, supplied, and consumed.

One example of how technology may transform an act and the controversies surrounding it is the development of the abortifacient RU 486. This pill should permit women, themselves, to induce an abortion within the first weeks of pregnancy. If it fulfils expectations, RU 486 and related substances will permit the termination of pregnancies, in the early stages, to be largely a private matter. (Most abortions are performed in the first months of the pregnancy and public support for the availability of the procedure is highest when abortions are performed at such an early stage.) Thus, with wide availability of this pill, many abortions may be removed from the scrutiny of anti-abortion protestors. Much remains to be seen about the use and effects of this form of termination of pregnancies.[93] However, it could be that the performance of the procedure would no longer provide nearly as many occasions for pitched battles, outside abortion clinics and so forth.[94]

A more immediate example, for our purposes, of the possible limits of the law in the face of technological developments is the Internet and its capacity to disseminate material, including pornography. The Internet was created under the threat of nuclear war. It now thrives as creative anarchy defying any central regulatory authority. 'The [Inter]net interprets censorship as damage and routes around it.'[95] In the end, perhaps this world-wide form of digital communication can be tamed by law's command. Yet such compliance will not easily be achieved nor, on balance, may it be desirable.[96]

The Internet began as a project of the Pentagon. The goal was to a permit scientists working on military contracts to share computers and other resources. The main technical advantages of the Internet come from its military origins. Splitting data into small packets that are able to take different routes to their destination makes it difficult to eavesdrop on messages. Moreover, this 'packet-switched' network was designed to resist destruction even by a nuclear attack: if one route were to be destroyed, packets could simply travel along another left intact. By the same token, these technical strengths are resistant to the command of law, particularly if the law is limited to enforcement in a few countries.

What started as a Pentagon project has grown through widely available personal computers and modems into a truly worldwide link through which thousands of separate networks and millions of users in virtually every country in the world are connected. By the 1990s 'cyberspace' had dawned with the coming of the World Wide Web. A combination of software and connection of documents has permitted users to travel the network with pictures, sound, and video by pointing and clicking a mouse. The Internet has become a new medium based on broadcasting and publishing, but with interactivity as still another dimension.

Yet the Internet's virtue of widespread use and the availability of millions of pieces of information, opinions, and images has, for some, become its vice.[97] Who knows what messages of hate, of destruction, and of obscenity course through its paths inviting consumption by the willing and, worse, affronting those who stumble unsuspecting on these dark materials. The stereotypes frequently waved about evoke images, on the one hand, of neo-Nazis using the Internet to spread their vile messages and, on the other, of little Jane (while eagerly trying to find information for her dinosaur project) stumbling upon graphic depictions of highly unconventional sex.

Nevertheless, the extent of the dark side of the Internet may be exaggerated.[98] *Time* magazine (3 July 1995) published a cover story entitled 'Cyberporn!' That story summarized the results of a study purporting to have found that 83.5 per cent of newsgroup pictures on the Internet were sexually explicit. *Time* subsequently published a clarification citing 'damaging flaws' in the research. In any event, even if the statistic was correct it has been estimated that, in terms of all sources of Internet traffic, sexually explicit material would still make up only about one-third of 1 per cent: a proportion considerably lower than could be found in many video stores or on many television channels.[99]

Still, those advocating regulation argue that there is something different about the Internet and its accessibility, particularly by children, that must be addressed. Books and videos can be placed in areas with controlled access and sold only to those who can comply with proof-of-age requirements. The contents of a television program can almost always be known beforehand (TV guides, etc.) and can, in any event, be relatively easily monitored. However, the Internet is not so easily managed. Any material can, of course, be deliberately searched for, but obscenities can also be stumbled upon quite inadvertently while one looks for something else.

Whatever the arguments for regulation, there have been plenty of warnings for government to stay clear, particularly in these early stages of the Internet's development. Many of these admonitions come from those who are generally suspicious of governmental regulation of economic forces.[100] Nevertheless, at least some of those who are sceptical accept that, in principle, there are a number of activities for which there is a case for regulation. For example, there is no obvious reason why a libel should be treated differently just because it appears on a web site rather than in a newspaper or why the rules of sales tax that apply to mail ordering should not apply with equal force to electronic commerce.[101]

However, those countenancing some form of government control hasten to point out there are peculiarities about the Internet that raise questions about the effectiveness of any regulation. First, intrinsic to the Internet is its ability to transcend borders: thus Finland can scarcely dictate what is available in Australia. Moreover, some suggest that individual nations should not attempt to police this unbordered space: governments cannot 'credibly claim a right to regulate the net based on supposed local harms caused by activities that originate outside their borders and that travel electronically to many different nations.'[102] Second, regulation has often differentiated between public and private communications. Yet the Internet is both a private conduit, for messages between individuals, and a public one.[103]

Despite these doubts there already have been attempts to regulate the Internet. In the United States the main effort was focused on the dissemination of pornography. In February 1996 Congress passed the *Communications Decency Act*, criminalizing the knowing use of an 'interactive computer system' to transmit or display to a minor 'any comment, request, suggestion, proposal, image, or other communication that, in context, depicts or describes, in terms patently offensive as measured by contemporary community standards, sexual or excretory activities or organs.' The Act applied not only to the originator of the offending communication, but also to anyone who knowingly permitted a telecommunications facility under his or her control to be used for such an activity, irrespective of whether 'the user of such service placed the call or initiated the communication.'[104] The legislation provided for substantial fines and imprisonment. How such sweeping provisions would have been enforced and at what cost remains a matter of conjecture. The Act never went into effect because of a stay issued by a lower court. In June 1997 the Supreme Court struck it down as a violation of the First Amendment and its protection of free speech.[105] Congress responded with a pared-down version directed at shielding children from pornography on the Internet. However, at the end of the 1990s that legislation was also being challenged in the courts.[106]

Other countries little troubled by the constraints of free speech still find themselves wrestling with technological limitations in censoring the Internet. China's biggest service provider has been ordered to block at least one hundred sites. In most uncensored systems, a service provider links users via a 'gateway' to Internet addresses. The Chinese service providers block access to certain 'undesirable' sites, including *Playboy*. This embargo is accomplished by blocking the address of each site. Yet such efforts can be ineffective for at least three reasons.[107]

First, routers are not designed to filter content. As a result, if a country programs large numbers of routers to block certain addresses, bottlenecks can be created that could dramatically slow the flow of data. Second, users can outsmart the blacklisting of sites. One way to do this is 'spoofing' – fooling the censor: for example, by using a web site called 'The Great Canadianizer.' This site adds stereotypical Canadian conversational quirks, such as the word 'eh,' while transferring Web pages. This 'Canadianized' Web page enables the user to slip around blacklist barriers, since the 'Canadianized' Web page has a different address. Third, users can bypass the censors by accessing the Internet long-distance through an overseas service provider or through locally accessed on-line services like CompuServe.

Hope has been expressed that effective control of Internet content will come from market-induced self-regulation. Not surprisingly, such expectations are promoted by those who are generally doubtful about the effectiveness of economic regulation: 'Thus can a little technology, backed by a global network, replace a lot of government.'[108] The assertion is that markets have incentives to regulate themselves, competing to provide consumers with ways to protect themselves (and their children) from offensive material. One system that apparently is very efficient in terms of 'do-it-yourself-censorship' is the Platform for Internet Content Selection (PICS),[109] which labels documents and then permits those in charge of individual systems to take various actions, from prohibiting access to an unlabelled document to allowing access to any document that is not explicitly forbidden. There is concern, however, that such filtering, especially by organizations, could impose a form of censorship on ultimate (adult) users of which they are not even aware. Any filtering done should be explicitly acknowledged so that consumers are aware, at a minimum, that they are receiving edited communications.[110]

There are indications, for example, by regulators in Canada[111] and by the OECD,[112] that agencies are being cautious about how and when the Internet will be subject to regulation. Meanwhile, those who are interested in general in the potential of self-regulation and of norms to buttress acceptable conduct (ideas discussed in chapter 4) look to the Internet.[113] If it is the case that governments cannot (or will not) invoke law to enforce standards, then other forms of shaping conduct, including the norms of cyberspace, have an extraordinary opportunity to demonstrate their potential (and risk revealing their ineffectiveness).[114]

Still, such calls for self-regulation, 'normativity,' and consumer filtering of material may sidestep a fundamental point. Some would argue, including with regard to pornography, that some forms of communication should simply not be available at all: they are so harmful they should be entirely suppressed. Such a stance returns us to the philosophical arguments that we canvassed at the beginning of this chapter. It is not just the consumption of certain materials but also their very production that must be proscribed. Yet technology may leave such a position with currency only in terms of intellectual debate. With inventiveness willing distributors and receivers can link up: 'Governments can make it very difficult for citizens to access "undesirable" materials such as pornography or political criticism. But with ingenuity, users can nearly always find ways to bypass the censors.'[115]

Most laws can, of course, be evaded to some extent. Evasion does not, itself, negate a law's validity. Moreover, just as the technology of cyperspace is rapidly changing so, too, could the very forms of regulation change to respond effectively to the many issues raised by the 'structural plasticity' of virtual reality.[116] That said, the question remains whether cyberspace will permit the flouting of regulation to such a degree that the very capacity of government to enforce its laws is put into question. Arguments promoting the corralling of pornography by law may pass into history. The anti-pornography movement may be to the Internet what the Luddites were to machinery: passionate but unavailing protesters in the face of unstoppable change.

Conclusions

The link between pornography and the subordination of women remains unclear. At the societal level there are examples where, if anything, they are inversely correlated. The countries of fundamentalist Islam ban 'it' and those societies are notorious for the subordinated status of women. Some Scandinavian countries regulate 'it' in only limited ways and women in those societies enjoy very high (if not the highest) status in terms of sexual equality. What is more, there is scant evidence (based on simulations) for the claim that pornography, in terms of sexual explicitness, incites violence. The clearest evidence there is (in terms of laboratory experiments and related studies) suggests that it is the depiction of graphic violence that produces the strongest sexual aggression in those who witness such displays.

At this juncture the position taken in America regarding fights over the 'harms' of pornography may be appropriate. In the midst of such divisiveness regarding the effects of pornography US courts have declined to accept the 'harms' analysis. Instead, the shifting terrain regarding the impact of pornography is unfolding though widespread debate.

Chapter 4 looked at six major ideas about the influence of law. One idea examined the way in which law can (re)constitute social, political, and economic relations. In this depiction law's effects are rarely direct. Instead, law can be used to mobilize reform and articulate new rights that can lead to transformation in terms of specific problems. A second idea focused on the effects of litigation compared with other forms of law and on the specific question of whether litigation can bring about social change.

Law *can* reconstitute social and political relations. However, it is most unlikely that it can do so when there is so little agreement about the nature of the problem or any solutions. This lack of consensus – in terms of both defining the malady and providing answers – is most prominent among feminists, the groups most focused on the inequality of women. It is small wonder then that the Supreme Court of Canada's decision in *Butler*, largely accepting a 'harms' analysis, has produced results inconsistent with reformers' goals. In this instance the preconditions for court orders to be effective are not present. Instead, the most prominent outcome of *Butler* may have been to splinter feminists and other progressive forces even further over questions of women's inequality and gay and lesbian rights. There may, indeed, be (re)constitutive effects of invoking law in this context: progressive issues have been set back. Meanwhile violent depictions, perhaps the real villains, flourish on the sidelines as the spotlights focus on the wars over sexual images.

If the regulation of pornography is fraught with disagreement in the real world, in the virtual one it is not even feasible, at least for the near future. Cyberspace tests the limits of law, especially in terms of compliance. Whether and how effectively the Internet can be regulated by national or international agreement, through market forces, by self-regulation, or by some combination of several influences, remains an important but unanswered question as the new millennium dawns.

CHAPTER NINE

Discrimination, the Law – and Blacks in America

Combating discrimination has been one of the most conspicuous uses of law in post–Second World War societies. Repulsed by the spectre of the Nazis and fuelled by a commitment to treat minorities better, most conspicuously blacks in America, many Western societies became convinced that discrimination could be eradicated by the force of law. Indeed, the wellspring of the rights movement that wove its way into the fabric of societies in the 1970s and 1980s was the optimistic belief that minorities could best be protected by arming them with fundamental entitlements enshrined in law.

Yet all discrimination is not banned. The fact is that we differentiate all the time: we prefer the beautiful to the homely, we prize intelligence and pity the stupid, we refuse to sell our house to someone who will not meet our price, we insist on marrying those of the same religion – or of no religion. Despite the folly of any of these preferences in any particular circumstances, the law is silent: most of us would be dismayed at the prospect of having it any other way.

Instead, regulation prohibiting discrimination focuses on a particular sort of conduct that differentiates. The target of such laws is the exercise of choice based on characteristics irrelevant to the decision to be made – so-called 'invidious' forms of discrimination.[1] Thus, in the workplace and in education, laws against discrimination (ignoring, for the moment, the debate around affirmative action) place merit on one side and characteristics such as race, gender, disability, and religion on the other: merit is relevant to the decision to be made; the characteristics just listed are not. In commerce and housing it is the ability to pay that is to be determinative; race, gender, and so forth should be extraneous to the exchange.

There is a substantial consensus about the desirability of such laws at a general level (though we shall discuss prominent challenges to even such basic agreement). Yet, a discussion of specifics soon reveals an enormous amount of controversy. For example, there is substantial debate over whether prohibition of discrimination should be confined to instances where there is proof of intent to harm, that is, 'disparate treatment,' or whether such banning should also extend to statistical forms of discrimination regardless of intent, that is, 'disparate impact.' Most prominently, there is a firestorm over attempts to rectify past wrongs by requiring that individuals from designated groups, who have suffered injustice, be given some degree of preference through 'affirmative action.'

A discussion of regulation seeking to combat discrimination gives rise to many of the major themes of this book. First, is there a problem – in any event, one that can (and should) be remedied by law? As already indicated, there is a strong consensus about the need for laws to battle discrimination. What does this consensus tell us about the ability of law to change attitudes over time and across changing social conditions? Second, what is the evidence of the impact of laws prohibiting discrimination? Even more contentious is the question, What are the outcomes produced by affirmative action? Is there a framework for evaluating any evidence that exists? Third, can we differentiate between the impact of litigation and other forms of law regarding the effects of prohibitions against discrimination?

These questions are important ones for assessing all forms of prohibited discrimination. We will focus on one area where there have been concerted attempts at such evaluation: the situation of blacks, particularly regarding employment and education, in the United States. There have, of course, been efforts in other countries to combat discrimination. However, it is the USA that is most preoccupied with anti-discrimination laws and with controversies regarding their impact. That preoccupation is particularly focused upon the situation of Afro-Americans.

This focus of the USA on civil rights protected by law and on the outcomes produced is further evidence of 'American exceptionalism' regarding the invoking of law. The bitter legacy of slavery and of segregation (bolstered by law) has driven efforts to protect the civil rights of blacks as a prime means of securing equality for Afro-Americans. There is evidence that law has been effective in combating discrimination in some areas. Yet many questions remain unanswered regarding its impact. Nowhere is the debate more intense than concerning the effects of affirmative action – a particular American experiment. Civil-rights laws driven by litigation and affirmative-action programs are an inadequate substitute for solutions to the underlying conditions of inequality between blacks and whites. The intractable difficulty is that such conditions are unlikely to be effectively addressed anytime soon.

The Pervasiveness of Disparity – The Presence of Discrimination?

A discussion of discrimination returns us to a point made in chapter 3. That chapter addressed issues regarding how to assess outcomes of a law or series of laws. One such issue is a preliminary concern about whether the law is directed to a phenomenon that is, in fact, a problem or, in any event, one that the law ought to respond to. Discrimination raises such quandaries directly. Some surveying the relevant terrain see human action deeply flawed by the scars of bigotry. Others look at the same picture and see rational explanations (often produced by markets and their relentless pursuit of efficient outcomes) for the outcomes being scrutinized.

Minorities in many societies suffer. Yet perhaps no hardship stands out as much as that of segments of the black population in America. The plight of such individuals is underscored not just in terms of their own dismal state but also in contrast to the rich and powerful society of which they are a part.[2] Much progress has been made in terms of some dimensions of black life in the United States.[3] The black middle class has expanded significantly over the last decades.[4] It has been suggested, for instance, that income differentials between whites and blacks are negligible for young, college-educated, two-earner married couples.[5] Yet as Henry Louis Gates, Jr has observed: 'We need something we do not yet have: a way of speaking about black poverty that does not falsify the reality of black achievement; a way of speaking about black advancement that does not *distort* the enduring realities of black poverty.'[6]

For those blacks trapped in urban ghettoes it is the effects of poverty that speak volumes. As *The Economist* stated a few years ago: 'The slums in America's great cities are shameful. They are a damning indictment of the richest country in the world. The problems that fester in them are not peripheral: they constitute America's main domestic challenge today.'[7] The problems start at birth. A black baby is twice as likely to die before its first birthday as is a white newborn. Then, half of all black children – compared with 16 per cent of white – live in families headed by a woman. The median income for black families (however constituted) is 56 per cent that of whites. As a result, nearly a third of all blacks – as opposed to 10 per cent of whites – live below the poverty line, including 45 per cent of all black children (compared with 15 per cent of white children). Blacks are more than twice as likely as whites to be jobless. The approximately thirty-one million blacks in America form about twelve per cent of the population, but represent nearly half of those in prison. Or, to view the stygian landscape another way: at the beginning of the 1990s black men made up a mere 2.5 per cent of all college students – with that proportion probably declining – but formed 40 per cent of the population in prisons.[8] A report published in 2000 established that black (and Hispanic) youths are treated more severely at all stages of the juvenile justice system.[9]

Of more specific concern are issues relating to blacks and education. Progress has been made in narrowing the education gap between blacks and whites. For instance, blacks have secured significant gains in graduating from colleges and universities. In 1995 they received a record number of PhD's. True, Afro-Americans continue to earn most of their PhD's in education and the social sciences. Still, blacks went from 319 science and engineering doctorates in 1987 to 557 in 1995.[10]

Yet blacks, on the whole, continue to perform poorly in the school system. They are still under-represented in higher education relative to their numbers and their rate of graduation from high school. Further, those who get to college have higher dropout rates than do other groups. Moreover, there is a gender gap: black males do not do as well as black women (and other minority members) in terms of rates of enrolment in higher education.[11]

The causes of such poor educational performance are linked to the dismal state of the lives of a segment of the black population.[12] They include low wages and joblessness among black males, the high percentage of black children living in houses headed by single female parents, inappropriate academic evaluation and placement, linguistic differences between blacks and whites, cultural differences and deprivation, the physical deterioration of neighbourhoods, and the lack of contact between poor black children and exemplary role models.[13] Such problems are so severe that a growing number of educators, most prominently among blacks, are suggesting that efforts to bring about integration in schools be replaced by efforts to remedy the dismal quality of education for Afro-Americans even if in segregated schools.[14] Thus, despite some significant progress, a recent commentary entitled 'America's Caste System: Will It Change?' still seems dangerously close to the mark in discussing relations between blacks and whites.[15]

Yet documenting such discouraging statistics about blacks is one thing; demonstrating that discrimination is responsible for these situations is quite another. The debates about the extent of discrimination as the cause of grim social circumstances tends to pit market believers against those arguing that the very structure of society is configured (even if unconsciously) against the interests of minorities.[16] Such debates are intense and illustrate a point made in chapter 3: that keeping facts and values separate is not as easy as is suggested by optimistic accounts of the capacity of empirical investigation to determine the effects of law.[17]

At one level there are plenty of examples of differential treatment of Afro-Americans that is difficult to explain other than by the workings of discrimination – and, of course, despite laws prohibiting such actions. As recently as 1994, 13 per cent of whites in America answered 'yes' to the statement that most blacks had 'less ability to learn.'[18] In 1996 one-sixth of whites still favoured laws making interracial marriages illegal.[19]

A recent study documented practices applying to the buying and selling of new cars. Trained testers using common negotiating scripts purchased new cars from dealerships in Chicago. The results were disturbing in terms both of race and of gender. Compared with white men, white women and black men and women had to pay substantially more for cars.[20] In the world of sports, where productivity can be measured with some accuracy, studies establish that blacks are often paid less than whites when productivity is held constant.[21]

Even national television has contributed to chronicling the everyday nature of prejudice. On ABC's 'Prime Time Live,' hidden cameras captured repeated examples of marketplace discrimination committed against a well-dressed and articulate black man compared with a white counterpart. The program showed a salesman snubbing a black, while a white customer was served immediately. Yet the salesman did not even acknowledge the presence of the Afro-American; he simply stood around throughout the lengthy sequence.[22] Rationales for some of such conduct can be advanced: for example, a heightened fear of shoplifting by the black because Afro-Americans do commit crime at a higher rate than whites. Even such a rationale, if otherwise justified, may itself be based on prejudice: field experiments have demonstrated that white shoppers spontaneously report shoplifting at a higher rate when the perpetrator is black than when he or she is white.[23]

One study has been especially clear about demonstrating the prejudice of employers in Chicago against black males who were seen as unstable, uncooperative, and dishonest. These attitudes are not the product of reactions only to race: '[R]ather it is race in a complex interaction with employers' perceptions of class and space, or inner-city residence.'[24] Nevertheless, the results of the interviews conducted for the study suggest that employers reject blacks more often because they view them as low-income persons more likely to steal, as products of ineffective inner-city schools, and as members of work-averse subcultures. In addition, holding other factors constant, employers avoid hiring minorities for jobs, emphasizing the importance of verbal and mathematical skills and academic achievement.[25]

Other studies seeking to establish prejudice have generated more unclear results about its existence. In the early 1990s in Washington, Chicago, and Denver researchers from the Urban Institute assessed employment discrimination through the audit method, that is, by having matched pairs of testers (male college students who, theoretically, had identical qualifications but were of different races) apply for advertised jobs.[26] Those studies found that there was virtually no evidence that blacks ever received special treatment over ostensibly equally qualified white applicants.[27] Thus, the study refuted allegations that black candidates are inevitably swept up in the employment sweepstakes – powered along by civil-rights laws and affirmative action.

On the other hand, the results of the studies did establish discrimination against blacks, but the magnitude of that discrimination is uncertain. The clearest evidence of such discrimination came from the Washington portion of the study.[28] There the white member of the pair was favoured over the black partner almost 20 per cent of the time, while the black was favoured only 5 per cent of the time. However, in the Chicago portion, blacks and whites were treated the same 86 per cent of the time (either both were offered the job or neither was). Whites were favoured over blacks 10 per cent of the time; blacks were favoured over whites 5 per cent of the time. In the Denver portion, blacks and whites were treated the same way 78 per cent of the time. In cases of disparity the margin of difference between blacks and whites was small: blacks were favoured over whites in 10 per cent of the cases, while whites were favoured in 12 per cent of the cases.[29]

In another study in the early 1990s, the Federal Reserve Bank of Boston conducted an extensive investigation of lending practices for mortgages. The study concluded that racial discrimination in the banking industry was still widespread. A survey of mortgage applications in the Boston area found that banks rejected about 11 per cent of white applicants, and about 29 per cent of non-white applicants, for a gap of 18 per cent. This raw disparity was analysed in terms of relevant economic and demographic data (including applicants' income, net worth, marriage status, and credit history) in order to explain any rational basis for the discrepancy. However, even after such analysis there remained an 8 per cent gap that could not be accounted for.[30]

Nevertheless, other analyses of the same data yielded far different conclusions. Some critics of the study sampled part of the survey data and found what they contended was improbable or inconsistent information in 57 per cent of the rejected mortgage applications. For example, five applicants were turned down for government-subsidized mortgages because they earned too much to qualify. Eliminating such cases shrank the rejection rate gap to 3 percentage points. When two other factors were adjusted for – lenders' ability to verify information on applications and their standards for credit risks – the gap in rejection rates disappeared completely.

Fury accompanied the debate about how to interpret the relevant data. The academic opponents descended into sniping and name-calling. The study was the subject of a lengthy article in the *New York Times*, which reported that its senior author had lost her appointment to the Federal Reserve Board because of the controversy surrounding it.[31]

The point here is not to resolve the contest between these heated and, in some ways, very technically laden positions. Rather, it is to use that study and the debate that engulfed it to illustrate two opposing points. First, deprivation, even as the product of deep and enduring economic patterns, does not itself mean there has been discrimination. It can be exceptionally difficult to differentiate between the impact of discrimination by race – clearly illegal – and discrimination based on purely economic factors – how lending institutions serve capital markets.[32] Second, the bitter legacy of slavery and of segregation has condemned many black Americans to live in inner cities, to consume fundamental goods (such as education and health care) of inferior quality, and to be excluded from the institutions of power. What appears as 'economic factors,' from one perspective, looks, from another angle, like the pernicious workings of pervasive discrimination.

Such clashes regarding whether a set of occurrences constitute discrimination are intensified by what has been called the 'paradox of integration.' As blacks and whites interact on an array of fronts, the opportunities for conflict multiply. In a poll in 2000 only 18 per cent of whites responding thought that 'too little [had] been made' of problems facing black people, in marked contrast to 51 per cent of blacks responding.[33] Whites tend to focus on the real progress that has been made to end discrimination, while blacks' attention is concentrated on the deprivation that remains: 'What exists, then, is a serious mismatch in racial perception of change. Most middle-class whites feel, correctly, that things have gotten much better not only in the objective socioeconomic condition of blacks but in their improved attitude toward blacks. The typical black person perceives and experiences the situation as either having not changed or having gotten worse.'[34]

Normative Debates Regarding Laws against Discrimination

Perhaps precisely because there can be such controversy regarding both what constitutes discrimination and what effects are produced by anti-discrimination laws, some address such issues by resorting to extreme philosophical positions. At the one end there is an unqualified libertarian insistence that individuals are free to associate with each other on mutually agreeable terms for whatever reasons, absent the use of fraud or coercion. Thus, government intervention that prohibits certain kinds of relations and, further, requires that there be contracts with certain kinds of individuals constitutes illegitimate force on the part of the state. Instead, employers, for instance, should be free to discriminate or not, to act affirmatively or not, as they prefer.

At the other end is an unqualified insistence on collectivism rather than individual rights. The status of groups (rather then specific transactions between individuals) has priority. Government has an obligation to intervene to assist disadvantaged sectors. As a result, anti-discrimination and affirmative-action regulation are judged successful to the extent that they promote the interests of the intended beneficiaries.

Yet there are several philosophical perspectives that can be usefully brought to bear on debates concerning 'invidious' discrimination. Such perspectives reveal complexities around discrimination and reactions to it that are paved over by the positions staked out by the extremes of libertarianism and collectivism. These other perspectives address autonomy, utilitarianism, efficiency, distributive justice, and communitarianism.[35]

In large measure autonomy theories directly clash with anti-discrimination laws. Such theories stress the right of the individual to choose, unconstrained by other conceptions of the good. To the point in this context: if an individual chooses not to interact with another because of race, sex, or religion, that is her business. It is not the business of government to require her to do otherwise.

Even some holding this position acknowledge that there can be two important exceptions to such strong claims against governmental interference. First, if initial property rights have been obtained through an unjust taking, then rectification of this injustice should occur. However, there are problems with applying this principle, if only because group A's unjust taking from group B in the recent past may have been proceeded by B's previous unjust taking from others. Yet many black Americans can make a good claim. Slavery precluded any prior unjust taking on the part of those enslaved and a host of discriminatory state policies after abolition compounded the deprivation of their descendants.

The second exception is the 'harm principle.' Here the argument is that, when A does not hire B or serve B because of invidious discrimination, B's ability to pursue various goals is frustrated. Thus B's autonomy is harmed. Moreover, third parties may not be directly implicated in the interaction (or non-interaction), but they may suffer what they consider to be grave moral offence.

However, for many adherents to autonomy theory this application of the harm principle is a non-starter. For them the entire foundation of autonomy theory is its emphasis on negative notions of liberty such that the state or third parties are not entitled to interfere with individual choice. Granted, such choice must not impact directly on others. At the same time, the 'do not impact' restriction simply does not involve a positive duty to take affirmative action to assist others in exercising what happens to be their choice.

In contrast, utilitarian theories can support the overriding of individual preferences if a course of action would, on balance, promote the general welfare. Thus, it can easily be seen how utilitarian theories could support anti-discrimination legislation. Too much so, perhaps. If a society comes to be dominated by anti-discriminators, there may be a temptation to rectify past wrongs even if other interests (i.e., white able-bodied males) are sidelined. Some would suggest that such a utilitarian calculus has found expression in various affirmative-action policies.

Yet the theory could also lead to opposite results. If utilitarian theory rests upon an assessment of what is best overall, this means that minority interests can be sidelined precisely in order to achieve that common purpose. So what exactly does such theory say about the need for and desirability of legislation to protect the civil rights of minorities? Various ideas have been advanced to prevent conclusions favouring non-action by the state – or worse – passage of legislation having discriminatory effects. Yet all these ideas involve ruling out certain kinds of preferences based on distinctions for which there is unlikely to be agreement.

Efficiency theories are highly dubious regarding the desirability of civil-rights legislation. They urge that, in competitive markets, such regulation is unnecessary. Individuals or firms who engage in discriminatory practices will deprive themselves of profits and will, over time, be overtaken by individuals or firms who do not discriminate and who, therefore, reap profits from the non-discriminatory transactions. At the same time, such laws impose burdens such as administrative and error costs. Finally, firms may engage in substitution strategies (such as relocating) in order to avoid the reach of the laws. Such ploys may cause even further efficiency losses. In contrast, in competitive markets, there are incentives for employers to develop techniques to target and hire the most capable employees.

However, it has been contended that anti-discrimination laws, in fact, assist in forcing markets to competitive positions by eliminating the 'disequilibrium condition' of discrimination. Proponents of such a position suggest that there is empirical evidence demonstrating such effects of civil-rights laws – a matter pursued in the next section. In any event, some go even further and suggest that without anti-discrimination laws even competitive markets may not eliminate the disequilibrium caused by discrimination. This failure to extinguish the effects of discrimination may occur because of persistent adverse selection, which may be rational for an individual employer but which, overall, is socially inefficient.

Statistical proxies are an example of adverse selection that may perpetuate conditions of disequilibrium. For instance, suppose Afro-Americans, on average, are less well qualified (because of educational and other disadvantages) than whites are, on average, for a particular sort of job. Employers may then use race as a proxy for hiring. This use means that even individual blacks who exceed the average are unlikely to be hired. Moreover, over time blacks will have fewer, not more, incentives to invest in the resources necessary to improve their qualifications.

Distributive-justice theories, particularly those with a social-contract emphasis, stress equality of opportunity. Therefore, these theories support anti-discrimination regulation – though to varying degrees, depending upon the goals to be achieved by such laws. Probably the most famous version of these theories is the one espoused by Rawls.[36] He suggests that individuals consider themselves to be cloaked by a veil of ignorance such that they are unaware of their race, class, sex, and so on. In this situation Rawls contends that three principles of justice would be unanimously endorsed: equal liberty; equal opportunity; and 'difference,' that is, the allocation of all primary goods should be to the greatest benefit of the least advantaged (with equalities tolerated only to the extent that they are, nevertheless, consistent with the allocation to the least advantaged).

Though Rawls's conception of justice is supportive of anti-discriminatory regulation, the extent to which theories of distributive justice can be invoked to support the reach of such laws is generally unclear. These quandaries are illustrated with reference to affirmative action. At one level it is possible to invoke distributive justice to support such programs. This is so because such theories emphasize the need for better distribution of life's goods in the future regardless of how such inequality was brought about. Yet affirmative action tests the limits of distributive justice. Far-reaching forms of affirmative action require disadvantaged groups to be hired even if, on assessment of individual merits, they are not as well qualified.

Such programs generate consequences at odds with the ultimate goals of distributive justice. First, individual members of the community, most prominently able-bodied white males, are singled out to bear the brunt of any corrective action. These individuals may be completely innocent of any discriminatory acts. Moreover, especially in employment contexts involving entry-level positions, they may, themselves, be relatively powerless. Second, particularly in the case of education programs, the beneficiaries of these programs may be the better-endowed members of the targeted groups. Third, affirmative-action programs, by definition, will not reach non-targeted groups who are, nonetheless, disadvantaged (poor white males or gay white males, for example).

Communitarianism clearly supports anti-discrimination regulation. Though there are many variations, a central idea of communitarianism is that individuals are not products of unfettered personal choice but are created as part of a large social and cultural body. The capacity of all to participate in that body is essential. Hence, anti-discriminatory laws are justified as measures to prevent the exclusion of minorities from participation. Communitarian theories, under certain circumstances, support affirmative action. However, arguments advanced in favour of such programs by communitarianism mirror distributive rationales, just discussed, and suffer from the same frailties.

Assessing the Impact

Since the debates about discrimination often take place at an abstract and polarized level, those seeking a middle course frequently plead for careful evaluation of the effects of regulation in order to ground the discussion. They are right in calling for more studies. Yet attempts to assess the costs and benefits of such regulation and to ascertain outcomes of various programs can also implicate fundamental values; such attempts can, themselves, generate heated debate. At one extreme are those who question the very concept of merit. Choices purporting to be made on the basis of ability are viewed as little more than ill-disguised racism and other forms of oppression. Thus, attempts at measuring the effects of invidious forms of discrimination versus decisions based on merit are bound to yield illegitimate results drawing false distinctions.[37] Law, whatever its weaknesses, must be invoked to combat such exercises of raw power. At the other extreme are calls for outright abolition of laws against discrimination.[38] It is asserted that such regulation imposes administrative costs and allocative dislocations. Any benefits cannot be established separate and apart from changing social and economic conditions, including the effects of education.[39]

There are few comprehensive examinations of the effects of anti-discrimination laws in the United States. Despite the centrality of these laws the actual outcomes that they produce are remarkably under-investigated, at least in any systematic fashion. There are significant methodological difficulties in any such studies: the outcomes produced by anti-discrimination laws and other factors such as education, changing attitudes, and market forces interact in many complicated ways.[40] Yet debates over civil-rights laws are often driven by ideological positions rather than by attempts, however difficult, to ascertain the outcomes that have been produced.

There are a number of evaluations of specific aspects of civil-rights laws that do shed some light on the effects of such regulation. Many of the most important studies available do focus on the effects of anti-discrimination laws on the situations of Afro-Americans. Here we first look at one attempt to provide a framework for evaluation of one of the most important efforts at regulation in the United States in terms of employment, Title VII. Next we examine evidence of the capacity of anti-discrimination laws to improve the level of employment and wages for blacks. There is then a discussion of the lightning rod for debates regarding programs to combat the effects of discrimination: affirmative action. We will examine a recent, broad-ranging study of the effects produced by affirmative-action programs in higher education. Finally, we conclude by looking at the impact of litigation on civil-rights issues; in particular, the legacy of *Brown v. Board of Education* regarding educational issues.

A Framework for Evaluating Title VII

An important reaction to the uncertainties left by theoretical debates about anti-discrimination is to assess the actual costs and benefits of regulations. The hope is that the philosophical clashes regarding such laws will recede in the face of demonstrations concerning the concrete advantages and disadvantages resulting from such regulation.

Yet how are such effects to be ascertained and measured? What benefits and costs are to count and how are their outcomes to be evaluated? Most would immediately realize the complexity of the task at hand. Many might pronounce the enterprise undoable, abandoning it for theories and abstract models, perhaps especially those pitched at extreme views. Others, recognizing the complexities, suggest that we ought nevertheless attempt such assessments with a view not to ending theoretical debates but to informing them and exposing both the strengths and weaknesses of positions.

One such attempt is advanced by Donohue,[41]specifically in the context of markets for employment and the effects of Title VII of the *Civil Rights Act*,[42] which proscribes discrimination in that context. His effort is largely in reaction to the criticism of anti-discrimination laws advanced by the Chicago School with its unremitting advocacy of free markets and its warnings about the tamperings of governmental regulation.[43] Donohue's reaction focuses on how the Chicago School emphasizes – theoretically – the burdens of anti-discrimination laws. He concedes that there are costs and that these burdens must be taken into account. However, he insists that the benefits conferred by such regulation must be fully recognized and their effects ascertained. At the same time, he also recognizes the controversy over what he wants to count as benefits and over the measures of them he wishes to employ.

Donohue's efforts illustrate clearly the complexities of even establishing what should count as costs and benefits in deriving a framework for evaluating the outcomes produced by anti-discrimination laws, particularly in this case Title VII. At the same time, they emphasize the need to grapple as comprehensively as possible with such costs and benefits. Whatever the imprecisions of Donohue's efforts, they are an effective rebuttal to those in the Chicago School who wish only to underscore the theoretical costs of such laws.

Regarding costs, Donohue suggests four factors: the frequency with which firms are sued and the costs of such litigation; the administrative costs of enforcing anti-discrimination laws; the higher costs of selecting a workforce prescribed by Title VII; and the productivity losses that would follow from misallocation of labour. In terms of the frequency and the costs of litigation and the ensuing administrative costs, Donohue (admittedly using some estimates) demonstrates that very few firms are actually sued and that the costs are very small compared with the overall American economy.[44] However, compliance costs (to select a workforce prescribed by Title VII) are greater than litigation costs. Relying on a prior study of the costs of governmental regulation,[45] Donohue puts these costs at $6.5 billion.

Donohue concedes that, generally, free labour markets will generate a more productive workforce than those that are regulated. Hence, markets regulated by Title VII will suffer some loss of productivity. However, he insists that account must be taken of three countervailing factors.

First, any discrimination based on the animus of the employer could impair productivity (even though the total monetary and psychological wealth of the discriminator may be maximized). Second, freedom from discrimination could improve the attractiveness of the workplace, thus generating productivity gains not otherwise achievable. Third, anti-discrimination law is designed to eliminate unreliable proxies based on such characteristics as race or gender. The excluding of such proxies results in more accurate hiring decisions in terms of qualifications and, therefore, greater productivity. At the same time, the costs of selection (without proxies) is already factored into compliance costs.

Nevertheless, despite these three offsetting factors, there remain productivity costs caused by having less homogeneous workforces and from hiring, promoting, or not firing less qualified workers (in order to avoid litigation or to comply with affirmative-action requirements). There appears to be general agreement that there is enormous uncertainty in establishing these costs. Donohue estimates them to be in the order of $7.5 billion a year, for a total cost imposed by Title VII of about $15 billion. Moreover, he acknowledges that informed critics of Title VII would estimate the costs to be substantially higher, as much as $80 billion a year.

His starting point regarding benefits is to insist that anti-discrimination laws (in the employment context) confer more than economic advantages on individuals, important as those benefits may be. Many Americans who abhor discrimination, even if they themselves will not be its victims, receive intangible benefits from these laws' statement against prejudice. At the same time, such laws impose symbolic costs on those who are offended by such governmental intrusion even if they never have to bear the tangible costs of such measures. As a result, such symbolic benefits and costs have to be accounted for – though how remains a difficult question.

Donohue concedes that, given the absence of empirical data and the difficulty of assessing Title VII's utility, widely varying estimates of the costs and benefits may be asserted. What he insists on is that the market alone cannot be relied upon for optimal social welfare regarding the elimination of discrimination. The public-good dimension of Title VII is a significant component of its value. Yet the public-good aspect, precisely because it is shared so widely, could not reach its optimal level through the market.

Conversely, Donohue argues that to repeal Title VII would lead to fierce racial strife. As a result, he contends that even if Title VII could be shown to be costly, by generally accepted standards, society might support it, nonetheless, in order to forestall cataclysm. What is more, Title VII represents the path of moderation. It rejects arguments that interference with the market is too high a price to pay even to battle the evils of discrimination. At the same time it steers away from rigid preferential hiring to combat the gulf that continues to exist between blacks and whites.

As emphasized earlier, Donohue scarcely provides a precise statement of the costs and benefits of regulating discriminatory behaviour. Indeed, he is the first one to admit such vagaries. The important point is that such unknowns exist on both sides of the question: anti-discrimination laws do impose unquantified costs even as they bestow critical, if imprecisely determined, benefits. Such imprecisions should not prevent systematic attempts to assess outcomes. Yet the complexities in doing so need to be openly acknowledged.

Evidence Regarding Anti-discrimination Laws and Employment Opportunities for Blacks

There have been some major studies that cast important light, in a broad sweep, on the effects in the United States of such regulation on blacks and economic progress through enhanced employment opportunities. Before examining these studies it is important to draw a critical distinction. Anti-discrimination laws aid individuals (blacks and otherwise) who have suffered discrimination to obtain redress. That impact is clearly a benefit to victims and is part of the rationale advanced in defences of anti-discrimination regulation such as those provided by Donohue in the previous subsection of this chapter. Nevertheless, aside from providing for redress of individual grievances, a prime purpose of these laws is to narrow discrimination or even eliminate it so as to produce employment benefits generally for those protected, in this case blacks. Thus, regarding that purpose, a critical question is whether anti-discrimination laws have had an impact in improving black employment levels and wages relative to those of whites.

A number of scholars have attempted to answer that question in the United States with respect to Title VII. Their studies isolate three periods that are particularly important: 1940–50, 1965–75; and 1980–9. The first (1940–50) is a period of relative growth in economic status for blacks that can be explained by patterns of migration from the south. The second (1965–75) is the period of growth that can largely be attributed to the effects of Title VII. The third (1980–9) represents a period of stagnation, and even decline, for groups of unskilled workers in which blacks are disproportionately represented.[46]

With limited exceptions,[46] the Chicago school has long taken the position that anti-discrimination laws were both unnecessary and unsuccessful at providing economic benefits for blacks. A 1989 article contended that 'the racial wage gap narrowed as rapidly in the 20 years prior to 1960 (and before affirmative action) as during the 20 years afterward. This suggests that the slowly evolving historical forces we have emphasized ... – education and migration – were the primary determinants of the long-term black economic improvement.'[47]

Yet certain studies, admittedly by moderate supporters of anti-discrimination laws, call such a stark conclusion into question. Heckman and Payner have demonstrated a dramatic surge in black employment in the textile industry of South Carolina beginning in 1965.[48] This opening of employment for blacks is in marked contrast to conditions from 1910 (when employment data first became available) into the 1960s. During this period blacks were almost totally excluded from such employment despite the fact that, since the skill requirements for the positions were modest, the explanation for their exclusion could not be that there were insufficiently qualified Afro-Americans. This denial of opportunity persisted even in the face of tight labour markets during the Second World War.

There were, however, gains by blacks (in economic standing relative to whites) between 1940 and 1950 (the first period). These gains are explained by the 'Great Migration,' in which large numbers of Afro-Americans moved from the South to the North to take jobs in industry. Jim Crow laws had a negative impact, while state civil-rights laws in the North may have contributed somewhat to induce immigration. However, there is no evidence that any laws exerted a strong effect on the improvement of the economic standing of Afro-Americans during this period.[49]

In contrast, the rapid increase in black employment in 1965 coincided with the coming into effect of Title VII and President Johnson's Executive Order 11,246 providing for affirmative action on behalf of blacks by federal government contractors. The upsurge in black hiring was identical in timing and magnitude generally for all areas studied, regardless of the variation in demand. Moreover, Heckman and Payner eliminated a number of other explanations for the breakthrough. As a result, they concluded that anti-discrimination laws were responsible for eliminating barriers to black employment.

In addition, another study contends that the sizable gains in black employment in the decade from 1965 to 1975 (the second period) cannot be fully explained by patterns of migration and improvements in education.[50] Migration is not the explanation (unlike the period 1940–50) because these gains were achieved largely in the South, whereas any shift in location by blacks during this period was to the North. Moreover, the steep decline in the rate at which Afro-Americans migrated from the South after the passage of Title VII buttresses the contention that these anti-discrimination provisions did help to improve their economic status. There was improvement in the quality and quantity of education for blacks by 1965. But this improvement had been steady and long-term – not at a pace that would explain sudden improvement in employment. Moreover, such gains in employment were achieved across all cohorts of black workers, even among the oldest workers and regardless of when they were educated.[51]

Finally, enforcement of Title VII was not fully in place until the mid-1970s. Nevertheless, it has been argued that the law had its effect by clearly indicating that the federal government would act to end segregation. In addition, the law was largely welcomed by the textile industry in which many blacks found jobs. This industry was in fierce competition with other countries such as Taiwan. The law paved the way to a new source of labour and the industry took the opportunity.[52]

From 1980 until 1989 (the third period) an entirely different phenomenon became apparent. After 1980 there is virtually no relative improvement of wages earned by blacks. However, the explanation appears to have little direct connection with race. For many groups of unskilled workers, both black and white, real wages stagnated or even declined. Nevertheless, blacks are more heavily represented among unskilled labour because of such factors as historical patterns of discrimination and inadequate schooling.[53]

Another analysis by Bloch generally agreed with the analysis of black employment by Heckman and Payner and others just described. Bloch went on to point to (in 1994) an even starker fact: 'Despite almost thirty years of anti-discrimination and affirmative action regulation in the United States, the unemployment rate of blacks has remained twice that of whites.'[54] Bloch attributes this dismal result to four factors.

First, federal policies appear to have resulted in the redistribution of blacks from small and medium-sized firms to large employers and federal contractors subject to these policies, but without improving the level of Afro-American employment overall. Second, there are incentives for employers to reduce their exposure to litigation by avoiding hiring minority, female, and other workers. This incentive exists because employees are far more likely than applicants to file discrimination suits and are likely to receive higher damage awards when such actions are successful. Third, the applicable laws cannot generally assist those who do not discover job opportunities. Such problems of discovery can arise for blacks, Hispanics, and Amerindians because they have lower rates of entrepreneurship than whites and Asian-Americans, and thus their job-recruitment networks are not as efficient. Generally, unemployment rates and entrepreneurship are strongly but negatively correlated across groups. Fourth, employers favour screening criteria that exclude minorities out of proportion to their presence in the general population.

Bloch's response is to turn from anti-discrimination laws as a key ingredient in combating lack of jobs among Afro-Americans and, instead, to explore other avenues to increase work opportunities.[55] As a result, he advocates such policies as curtailing the applicability of minimum-wage laws and of occupational licensing, and the lowering of taxes on businesses. He argues that adopting his recommendations would expand opportunities for employment and entrepreneurial activity, including for minorities. More specifically, he advocates a set of policies for inner cities, especially regarding young blacks. Such strategies would tackle difficult issues such as drugs and crime, the mismatch between available workers in inner cities and jobs in suburbs, and minority business formation.

However controversial Block's alternatives may be, they underscore the suggestion that discrimination laws may have limited impact in further narrowing the gap between blacks and whites. Heckman, one of those who demonstrate the effects of law in assisting black economic progress in the second period (1965–75), is much less optimistic about the capacity of law to secure advances in the 1990s. The economic boom of the 1990s has alleviated black poverty to some extent.[56] Specifically, the economic surge has provided more jobs for unskilled workers, especially black males.[57] Such work is particularly welcomed because it appears to be a factor in terms of falling crime rates, as more young black males are gainfully employed. Yet being equipped with appropriate skills appears to be key, especially for sustained economic progress for blacks. As Heckman and a co-author comment: '[T]he available economic evidence strongly suggests that the law is unlikely to have a major influence on aggregate racial disparity in the 1990s. Basic economic forces such as the decline of manufacturing industries and the increasing return for skilled labor relative to unskilled labor will play a much more prominent role in shaping black relative economic status.'[58]

The Benefits of Affirmative Action – and Its Capacity to Deflect

The Consensus Regarding Anti-discrimination Laws – The War over Affirmative Action

There is war over affirmative action in the United States. No other society has attempted to the same extent as the United States to solve problems of disparity, especially regarding blacks, by establishing programs that give preference to members of groups who have suffered discrimination in the past. No other society has been engulfed in such controversy regarding such programs. There is evidence that such programs can be effective at comparatively little cost. Yet, whatever benefits they bestow, these programs are a poor substitute for tackling the underlying causes of disadvantage.

The convulsions over affirmative action are in strong contrast to the consensus around the need for basic anti-discrimination laws. Of course, as noted already, an exception to this consensus are theorists of the Chicago School, who basically argue that properly competitive markets will eliminate discrimination; laws meant to do so are simply another example of governmental tampering.[59] Yet such arguments against anti-discrimination laws have not found a receptive audience. There have been no organized efforts to have the provisions repealed. Instead, proponents of such regulation point to the existence of the prevailing consensus as compelling evidence of the law's utility and note that such regulations are producing wide-ranging social benefits, particularly in terms of promoting racial harmony.[60]

Indeed, one outcome of the heated debates about affirmative action is that they throw into relief the amount of agreement there is about the need for legislation protecting civil rights. It may be the case that fear of social conflagration was a primary motivating factor propelling the passage of original civil-rights legislation in the United States.[61] Yet thirty years on such legislation is an example of how law and social attitudes can interact to provide underlying support for the goals a society seeks to achieve.

An index constructed to gauge the approval of the goal of racial equality and the need for an active role by the federal government in promoting that end suggests that the public was much more supportive of the goal in the early 1980s than it had been in the late 1960s, though even then the support was quite high.[62] Moreover, substantial majorities are now committed to core civil-rights values, agreeing that discrimination still exists and that there should be laws to protect its victims.[63] In a recent poll (December 1997) a large majority (69 per cent) of all those polled affirmed that it was 'necessary to have laws to protect minorities against discrimination in hiring and promotion.'[64] In 2000, 74 per cent of those polled (78% of whites; 58% of blacks) agreed that the country had made real progress in reducing racial discrimination.[65]

At the same time, Americans, regardless of race, stress the importance of individual hard work and ambition in improving one's lot. From 1983 to 1992 about two-thirds of respondents consistently agreed that 'people get ahead by hard work.' Over 80 per cent said that 'ambition' is essential or very important for 'getting ahead in life,' as opposed to coming from a wealthy family (20%) or having well-educated parents (39%). Blacks are also committed to the notions that individual attainment in education and hard work will result in them getting ahead. A 1991 Gallup Poll found that 68 per cent of blacks (and 69% of whites) agreed that 'African-Americans should focus most of their energy on improving [their] education.'[66]

Such attitudes are not supportive of affirmative-action programs. Public reaction to affirmative action tracked for over a decade reveals that a majority of people are opposed and that opposition is probably growing. When the *New York Times*/CBS News Poll began asking about racial preferences in 1985 Americans were evenly divided about the desirability of such programs.

However, opinion turned sharply against such programs in the late 1980s and remained negative through 1997. In 1997, to the question 'Do you believe where there has been job discrimination in the past, preference in hiring and promotion should be given to [black] [women],' 37 per cent answered 'yes' in the case of women and 35 per cent answered 'yes' regarding blacks, with the rest answering 'no' or 'don't know.'[67] In polls where the question posed does not refer to specific past discrimination (as does the *Times*/CBS Poll) support for affirmative action has been even lower. Conversely, if the question mentions affirmative action but indicates that the program would not impose 'rigid quotas,' support, in some polls, has been higher.[68] Among the possible beneficiaries of affirmative action, blacks tend to support affirmative-action programs, sometimes by substantial margins.[69] Yet, other possible beneficiaries of such programs are less supportive: Latinos, women, and Asians (with the latter two yielding a clear majority that are opposed).[70] Two students of race relations in the United States suggest bitter, unintended consequences of affirmative action, which 'is so intensely disliked that it has led some whites to dislike blacks – an ironic example of a policy meant to put the divide of race behind [Americans] in fact further widening it.'[71]

Still, even regarding affirmative action, the majority (that seems to reject it so clearly) cannot, in most instances, bring itself to agree with the outright termination of such programs. As indicated earlier, in the

1997 *New York Times* / CBS Poll only about a third of those polled supported affirmative action. Yet only 12 per cent indicated that such programs should be 'ended now.' The rest thought they should be either
'phased out over the next few years' (40%) or 'continued for the fore-
seeable future' (41%).[72]

As we saw in earlier in this chapter, the theoretical justifications for
affirmative action are complex and controversial.[73] Little wonder then
that scarcely a day goes by without the media reporting on some initiative to repeal or limit some form of affirmative action, typically on the
grounds that such programs prefer one race over the other; or they
negate merit by requiring groups to be hired by quota; or they dilute
standards for admission to educational programs, leading the beneficiaries of such dilution to ultimately fail or drop out in disproportionate numbers.[74] Meanwhile, supporters issue dire warnings about the
effects of eliminating such programs, particularly those addressing
issues in employment and education, charging that without such
action the workforce and higher education will return to being bastions of white able-bodied male privilege.[75]

In addition, such debates are now much more the stuff of daily popular politics and election campaigns. Opposition to affirmative action
is not, by and large, led by corporate America, where there has been
acceptance of such programs[76] and even some innovative voluntary
initiatives to bring diversity to the workforce, including at senior levels.[77] How effective these programs have been, particularly in terms of
minority women, remains a question.[78] Even in electoral politics the
issues are complicated and results are divided: in 1996 the electorate in
California voted to ban affirmative action; in 1997 the citizens of Houston, Texas, voted to uphold it.[79]

Debates over affirmative action have become even more complicated
given the range of positions that are now taken. There is a growing set
of critics of affirmative action who do not object to affirmative action
itself but, rather, the characteristics that are now targeted: gender, race,
disability, and so forth. Instead, they suggest that the driving characteristic behind any such initiative should be socio-economic status.
These critics argue that economic disadvantage cuts across race, gender, and so on and would, therefore, be much less divisive. At the same
time, programs based on need would be more equitable by not favouring (say, for admission to law school) a black female from an upper-
middle-class family while ignoring a white male from a poor one. In
addition, there is substantial evidence that a majority of Americans

would support affirmative-action programs, at least regarding educa-tion, if they were based on need.[80] In contrast, supporters of 'tradi-tional' affirmative action argue that focusing on socio-economic status does not, at least in the case of blacks, capture the cumulative effects of discrimination wrought by the history of slavery and by official acts to promote segregation and the inferior status of blacks.[81] Moreover, though proportionally more blacks than whites live in poverty, in abso-lute numbers poor whites greatly outnumber poor blacks. Thus, the concern is that whites applying for assistance based on need would swamp black applicants, especially when the number of positions in a program was limited. As a result, critics continue to argue for pro-grams targeting race.

Among all anti-discrimination laws and programs the least that is known may be about the effects of affirmative action. To the extent there has been progress there has been little effort to assess the separate effects of affirmative-action programs from civil-rights laws, enhanced educational opportunities, and responsive markets.[82] There have been few efforts to assess such factors as the effects of backlash arising from the belief that certain groups, whatever their historical plight, are now being preferred. Similarly, there have been few attempts to gauge the impact on targeted groups regarding how affirmative action affects their image of self and their motivation. Few measurements have been taken of the results upon those who are not eligible for these programs even though they have done no wrong themselves. Instead, most debates about affirmative action operate at a highly ideological, 'cos-mic' level[83] – even as both advocates and critics claim very concrete outcomes.[84] ('Facts have never played much of a role in the affirmative action debate ... At the same time, the lack of a developed factual record is fully consistent with the ideological nature of the debate, which sharply reduces the incentives for collecting data that may turn out not to support one's desired position.')[85]

We do know that *ending* affirmative-action programs in education can have substantial impact on at least some beneficiaries. Opponents are achieving success both in courts and in politics in terminating such programs. In 1996 the Fifth Circuit Court invalidated an affirmative-action program at the University of Texas Law School, rejecting all rationales for using race as even a factor in admission decisions.[86] Also in 1996 California voters approved Proposition 209, which prevents any 'preferential treatment' on the basis of race, sex, and so forth. Those promoting diversity had substantial fears that ending affirmative action in educational institutions would have substantial impact on the composition of the student body. They were right and wrong.

The experience at the University of California at Berkeley and at Los Angeles (UCLA) regarding admission of the freshman class for the 1998 academic year is instructive in terms of the aftermath of the termination of such programs. Berkeley and UCLA are among the most selective public universities in the country. In fact, the ending of affirmative action had no effect on certain groups. Women were essentially unaffected. Officials let it be known that they had not, in any event, taken sex into account in terms of admissions because of the large number of women applying. Likewise, the percentage of Asian-Americans actually increased slightly at both UCLA and at Berkeley, at least in the short run.[87]

However, results were very different for African-Americans, Mexican-Americans, Hispanic-Americans, and American Indians. Initially, fears were eased because minority applications rose after affirmative action was ended, allowing university officials to hope that the pool of these minority applicants would be sufficiently large to sustain the numbers admitted under the preferential program.[88] Nevertheless, results in terms of admissions were, in fact, substantially at odds with those produced by affirmative action. At UCLA, admissions of individuals belonging to the groups just listed fell from 19.8 per cent in 1997 to 12.7 per cent in 1998. At Berkeley the results were even worse. Such admissions fell over 50 per cent: in 1997 they stood at 23.1%; in 1998 they were at 10.4%.[89] More specifically, in terms of legal education, a similar set of results in terms of decline in admissions is being experienced at the laws schools of Berkeley and UCLA.[90]

These results in terms of the minority groups elicited predictable responses. Those supporting affirmative action decried the shrivelling of diversity at elite institutions. They charged that such results sent a 'message of despair':[91] that the doors of opportunity were closed for certain groups in America even as the classrooms in these bastions would grow more insensitive to the plight of those not present.[92] Opponents pointed to such results as confirming how pervasive were the effects of affirmative action at these institutions. At the same time, they insisted that such drops in admissions were painful but short-term adjustments to a world where harder striving and acceptance of performance standards will eventually yield real equality.[93] What is more, critics of affirmative action were quick to point out the effects of 'cascading.' This term refers to students not admitted to elite institutions because of the ending of affirmative action who proceed to enrol in less selective colleges and universities. Thus, in California many of the rejected applicants, after the termination of affirmative action, 'cascaded' from the most selective campuses of the University of California (Berkeley, UCLA) to less demanding ones (Santa Cruz, Riverside). The point that critics were making was that rejected applicants were still pursuing higher education, possibly at institutions that were more committed to improving the educational system as a whole and its response to the needs of minorities, particularly blacks.[94]

Affirmative Action as Deflection: *The Shape of the River*

We have already emphasized the lack of evidence regarding affirmative-action programs that are, at the same time, immersed in controversy. Nevertheless, a recent study does document the effects of affirmative action in elite colleges and universities. It does demonstrate that affirmative action can produce substantial positive effects. It also underscores how few people, among minorities, benefit from such programs even as more pervasive solutions to the problems of a poor public-education system remain largely ignored.

In *The Shape of the River: Long-Term Consequences of Considering Race in College and University Admissions*, W. Bowen, a former president of Princeton, and D. Bok, a former president of Harvard, have assessed the effects of affirmative-action programs using the College and Beyond (C&B) database created by the Mellon Foundation (at present headed by Bowen).[95] The database records the academic and institutional records of 90,000 entering students in 28 selective colleges and universities for the years 1951, 1976, and 1989. This material has been supplemented by surveys of students in the years since their graduation or leaving of college. The survey covers critical aspects of their experience in college (retrospectively) and their lives since: further education, occupation, income, marital status, civic participation, and so forth. In addition, another survey permitted comparison with control groups that parallel in age the two earlier entering classes. The study confines itself to the effects of such policies on blacks. It, therefore, says little about the impact on other beneficiaries such as Hispanics or Latinos. However, the focus of this, in any event, massive study is understandable. Afro-Americans are central to debates about the need for and effects of affirmative-action programs. The study is also confined to the most elite institutions. Yet, it is at those institutions that such programs are most widespread precisely because of the competition to be admitted. In contrast, nearly 60 per cent of America's institutions of higher education have no reason to practise affirmative action because they admit virtually everyone with the basic qualifications who applies.[96]

The Shape of the River clearly establishes the advantages of affirmative-action programs for the few who benefit from them and for the larger university communities that have such programs. In sum, the study demonstrates, on a comparative basis, that students who gain admission to colleges with the help of racial preferences take a wide range of courses, graduate from college at very high rates (though not as high as their white counterparts), and pursue lucrative careers that include high levels of community involvement. They also report great satisfaction with their college experiences. Moreover, other students are accepting of such programs and benefit from having a diverse student body.

Nor do such programs interfere with the prospects of other applicants to any appreciable extent. The study estimates that if the programs were eliminated the chances of admission for whites would improve by only about 1.5 per cent. Such minimal impact on whites does not, itself, deal with philosophical objections to any negative effects on their chances for admission.[97] At the same time, admission policies at these elite institutions, particularly the private ones, have never been based solely on academic achievement. The Bowen/Bok study documents that factors such as athletic prowess and whether a close family member graduated from the institution also come into play in the decision-making process. In that context racial diversity becomes one other of those factors. One reviewer of the book observes, in terms of the findings: 'If one came upon an investment option that demonstrated such potential, one would be hard pressed to reject it.'[98]

In sum, the study demonstrates that graduating from an elite college or university greatly improves the earning power of blacks and enhances the leadership roles that they assume. Graduates of the elite colleges and universities in the survey earn well above the national average. Black graduates from the institutions in the survey, especially black males, trail their white counterparts. However, both male and female graduates still do much better than the national averages. For example, the earnings of a black male graduate of a C&B institution were 82 per cent greater than those of all black holders of BA degrees.[99]

Black male graduates were particularly active in civic and cultural organizations. Such activities were particularly pronounced for those who ultimately became professionals. For C&B graduates who became doctors, twice as many Afro-Americans held civic leadership roles as compared with their white counterparts.[100] For those who became law-yers the corresponding figures were 21 per cent for blacks and 15 per cent for whites.[101] Such involvement helps to meet arguments that affirmative action does not benefit the larger community and, in partic-ular, that beneficiaries of affirmative action are anxious to distance themselves from their roots as they enter more elite circles.

Thus, *The Shape of the River* goes a long way, at least in the context of higher education, in establishing that affirmative action can produce positive results for individuals who are benefited by such programs and for the universities that engage in such procedures. Other studies regarding affirmative-action programs in law and medical schools have reached similar conclusions.[102] Whether these results can per-suade courts to uphold such programs, as a matter of principle, remains to be seen in the face of litigation attacking affirmative action on many fronts.[103]

Yet even those who are persuaded by the findings of the Bowen/Bok study should realize how limited are the effects of even successful pro-grams.[104] These programs assist only a handful of blacks at privileged institutions: '[T]he stakes in the university affirmative action debates are ... about the constitution of the American elite.'[105] Such initiatives do not respond to the problems that haunt a large segment of black youth. They do nothing regarding a bad public educational system. Nor do they respond to disruptive social and family conditions and the deplorable state of inner cities in which many public schools most operate: 'A worse childhood than in the Balkans.'[106] A comprehensive worldwide comparison of education standards – the Third Interna-tional Mathematics and Science Study – found that out of 21 countries America ranked 16th in general science, 19th in maths, and last in physics.[107] In Cleveland, at the end of the 1990s, the number 14 signi-fied the woes of public education. Only 1 in 14 public-school students graduated with all the minimum proficiency scores demanded by the city at the time that they should. Pupils stood a 1-in-14 chance of being a victim of crime in any year at school. The public school system achieved none of the 14 performance criteria set by the city.[108]

A society riveted on wars over affirmative action is unlikely to tackle the problems that have led to such measures. Thus, the real problem that affirmative action poses is that it is a solution that is no solution at all. It is a response that is capable of generating heated debates and much acrimonious litigation. Such programs deflect attention away from the underlying problems, undermine any political will to tackle those challenges, and are a lightning rod for racial tensions. Yet developing educational and training opportunities for blacks (and everyone) trapped in rotting urban cores is critical: 'Extending and vastly improving education in the ghettos, from very early Head Start Programs, to financial incentives for students, teachers, and successful schools, to expanding apprentice programs that combine classroom instruction and on-the-job training, are the directions to be followed for children and school-age youth.'[109]

The hope is that proponents of affirmative action would realize that it can accomplish comparatively little and that large gains will only come from generally improved social, educational, and employment conditions. Opponents would recognize that the best way to undercut the case for affirmative action would be to support concrete policies that would lead to these general improvements. Thus, the pressure for affirmative action would decrease as sound policies took hold. Alas, the chances of easing such pressure and implementing such policies in the near future are remote. At the beginning of his administration President Bush (the younger) cast himself as a leader in education.[110] A good intention. But what of the results?

The Impact of Litigation: The Legacy of Brown v. Board of Education

One of the questions chapter 4 asked was whether litigation can produce significant social change.[111] The record regarding civil rights is mixed. There are instances where such litigation has been 'successful,' but the results produced are inadequate in terms of the problems to be addressed. Conventional opinion holds that it was the courts, most prominently through Brown v. Board of Education[112] that were the catalyst for the civil-rights movement. Yet a recent set of opinions challenges that assertion and assigns Brown and subsequent decisions a much less significant role in terms of the recognition and implementation of civil rights. In any event, the main point to be derived from a discussion of litigation regarding civil rights is how little impact it has had in terms of addressing underlying problems. Such limited effects are illustrated by a discussion of litigation regarding educational issues, especially desegregation, over the last decades.

At least according to popular lore, litigation to protect civil rights would appear to provide a clear example of the effectiveness of courts in achieving change, particularly regarding progressive reform. Even the most uninformed are likely to have heard of *Brown v. Board of Education*, to know the legend of how in one fell stroke the Supreme Court of the United States ended the shame of segregation. Yet there is recent work that suggests that the impact of *Brown* has been seriously overstated. A well-known sceptic regarding the capacity of courts to effect social change is Rosenberg.[113] The most controversial example he tackles is the aftermath of *Brown*. He contends that in the ten-year period after that decision (1954–64) virtually nothing occurred to end segregation in public schools (or other discriminatory practices regarding voting, transportation, and accommodation). As late as 1964, ten years after *Brown*, only 1.2 per cent of black children in the south attended school with whites.[114] Instead, Rosenberg argues, it was only after the enactment in 1964 of the *Civil Rights Act* that any real progress was made towards desegregation; and it is the case that by 1971 85.9 per cent of black children in the South were attending desegregated schools. (The quality of the education they were receiving is a matter pursued below.) Rosenberg asserts, therefore, that it was not the Supreme Court but, rather, Congress and the executive branch that effected desegregation.[115]

Yet even if his account of what caused desegregation were to be accepted, an entirely different response to him would be to argue that it was the decision in *Brown* that propelled the awakening of civil rights. More specifically, the contention would be that *Brown* altered the way race relations were viewed so that the legislation and other government action that did begin to end discrimination ensued: *Brown* may have not been the immediate cause, but it was the ultimate one. Rosenberg also refutes this argument. His research, examining the structure of civil-rights organizations to press reaction and public-opinion polls, found no evidence that the judgment mobilized concern for civil rights or was influential in molding opinion. To the contrary, he alleges that after the ruling the press did not devote more attention to civil-rights issues, that organizations did not use *Brown* as a basis for fundraising or membership recruitment, and that civil-rights legislation of the 1950s and 1960s proceeded with few references to the decision.[116] What did occur was the galvanization of opposition by a hard core familiar with attempts to promote civil rights, including through the courts, so that after *Brown* there was growth in the membership and activities of pro-segregation groups such as the White Citizens Councils and the Ku Klux Klan.[117]

Still, if some have been at fault for making sweeping assertions about the efficacy of litigation, issue has been taken with Rosenberg for being too unqualified in the other direction. Sunstein, in reviewing *The Hollow Hope*, points out that the principles of *Brown* may have been deeply internalized by blacks so as to profoundly alter their sense of entitlement.[118] He suggests that, if in fact the decision was rarely mentioned in the press, this may have been because the Court's ruling was so patently right that people did not see it as necessary to constantly refer to it. Further, Martin Luther King did refer to Supreme Court decisions and to the Constitution and from this Sunstein suggests it is possible to conjecture that *Brown* must have been a nurturing, if unmentioned, moral force. Others contend that careful historical research reveals that there was a relationship, if a complicated one, between the decision and the activities of civil-rights groups and other forces.[119]

A close reading of Rosenberg indicates that his main target is the claim that *Brown* specifically effected change regarding civil rights. He acknowledges that after Congress and the Executive took action in the 1960s the courts did play an important role in the struggle to realize the promise of civil rights.[120] Other studies support the contention that courts have assisted the furtherance of black progress in some areas. Court decisions appear to have contributed to the positive effects of anti-discrimination laws regarding employment of blacks and their earnings.[121] (Anti-discrimination laws and employment issues were discussed earlier in this chapter.)[122] Acting in conjunction with social and political forces is also a role consistent with the one that courts appear to have played in the 1930s in improving segregated schools. They allied themselves with the NAACP and certain philanthropic efforts to improve black education.[123] Rosenberg acknowledges that courts can bring about change when they are acting in conjunction with other political institutions and social forces. The problem for those wishing to use the courts to promote change is that this conjunction too rarely occurs. Meanwhile, critical resources can be expended that might have been better spent in other ways, including in the political process.

Whatever the contribution of *Brown* and related decisions, those examining judicial activity regarding educational issues and the plight of blacks in the last three decades of this century report decidedly mixed results. A study examining civil-rights litigation, in several areas (including education) from the late 1960s to the late 1980s, concluded: '[That] litigation ... should be seen as ... extremely complex, problematic and contingent both on external events and intra-organizational developments.'[124] There is evidence that some state courts have produced 'dramatic results' regarding the equity and adequacy of school finance systems.[125] However, even the author of a study investigating the effects of such decisions was not able to specify the conditions under which such results will occur.[126]

In any event, the deplorable state of public education, particularly in many inner-city schools, remains. Judicial decrees and remedies have left that problem largely untouched. One of the high hopes of reformers using litigation was that desegregation, often implemented through court-ordered busing, would end the plight of black children in inferior schools. As late as 1984 a major critique of the school system argued that even more aggressive techniques should be employed to bring about desegregation of public education.[127]

Yet the effects produced by desegregation have been disappointing at best. Judicial fiats, particularly involving busing, can cause much public resentment. Even more importantly, desegregation does nothing, in itself, to provide access to quality education and may, in certain circumstances, actually work against that goal:

> [T]here is little evidence that changing a school's racial composition *alone*, while leaving the educational program unchanged, has any appreciable impact on the academic performance of minority students, and there is nearly unanimous consensus that it does not benefit white academic performance. Likewise, there is little evidence that increasing choice by itself, among schools that have few differences in educational programs, would have any impact on academic outcomes.[128]

It seems obvious that to have a good education a child must have access to good educational programs. However, an exhaustive study of the effects of court-ordered desegregation emphasizes that that apparent point has been obscured by those insisting that desegregation must occur at any price. Of course, desegregation is an important goal. However, litigation, the language of the law, and unyielding antagonists have so narrowed the terms of the debate that desegregation, including through busing, has been turned into *the* issue in much litigation alleging discrimination. Meanwhile, the overarching question of access to quality programs has been largely sidelined. The study just referred to observes: 'The conclusion that improved academic performance requires improved educational programs may seem to belabor the obvious, but perhaps only to readers who have not been exposed to the decades-old argument advanced by many supporters of school desegregation, in which racial balance alone is somehow supposed to correct educational deficiencies that may exist in predominantly minority schools.'[129]

Another study of court-based reform efforts over the last three decades regarding educational issues, in general, comes to much the same conclusions: litigation – even when successful – can so narrow the terms of the debate as to deflect attention away from the underlying problems and the solutions to them. Litigation, focused on educational issues, resulted in a shift in goals from access to quality programs to 'a racial numbers game ... whose basic object was distributing black and white students randomly throughout the school buildings of a system ... Equal educational opportunity for black children ... was no longer the objective or the legal right to be realized, and was seldom even discussed.'[130] This relentless pursuit of numbers has had many untoward effects, including putting into jeopardy the viability of historically black colleges, which make important contributions to the development of the Afro-American middle class and to stable communities.[131]

Even as Sunstein takes issue with Rosenberg for being too unqualified in his conclusions, he nevertheless recognizes the vigour of *The Hollow Hope* as a force in bringing up short those who simplistically draw conclusions about the impact of litigation: '[H]e has shown that there is room for much uncertainty about this matter [of consequences]. In any case, he has put into question the assumption of people who now believe ... that litigation is an especially promising approach to social reform.'[132] Yet it may be asserted, notwithstanding the work of Rosenberg and others, that in America there was no choice but to turn to the courts regarding civil rights: the racism, the caste system were just too embedded. Social attitudes and popular politics may have had to be forced along a path that only an independent judiciary could clear. This is possibly so. But as we have seen already in this book, when courts intervene to a significant degree public policy formation can pay a steep price. A cumbersome, adversarial, litigious approach to complex social problems may create some possibilities for change. It is more likely, however, that the range of responses will be constrained, that the positions advocated will become polarized.

Conclusions

The support for civil-rights laws in contemporary America is a dramatic example of the interaction of norms and law. Racism has not been eradicated. However, there is a strong commitment to combat prejudice with law. By 1997, 69 per cent of those asked agreed that it was 'necessary to have laws to protect minorities against discrimination in hiring and promotion.' Developing norms and laws have combined to promote a strong public ethos against racism. Such consensus is an enormous accomplishment considering the prevalence of segregationist practices and attitudes and the assumption of the inferiority of blacks that prevailed in the United States less than five decades earlier.

Other impacts of anti-discrimination laws on the lives of Afro-Americans are less clear. It is not that the condition of blacks has not changed appreciably. Rather, it is very difficult to isolate the effects of law as opposed to other factors such as education, a changing job market, shifts in population, and alterations in public attitudes, particularly between blacks and whites. A black middle class has emerged, taking its place economically, politically, and socially in the life of that country. At the same time, blacks remain disproportionately poor. A substantial segment of Afro-Americans are trapped in poverty, many in the rotting cores of the inner cities. Have civil-rights laws alleviated the plight of blacks and can they continue to do so in the future? There is far too much rhetoric and far too few systematic attempts to get at the facts in attempting to answer this question.

Studies of the effects of Title VII, banning discrimination in employment, suggest that that law had a substantial impact in promoting the economic status for black for about a decade (1965–75). However, these analyses also suggest that the largely stagnating economy for unskilled workers, a group in which blacks are disproportionately represented, has meant that Title VII has had little impact in improving economic conditions for Afro-Americans in the 1980s and 1990s. Thus, development of skills, backed by educational and training programs, would appear to be key in pushing more blacks into the stable, possibly middle-class, workforce.

The war over affirmative action is unlikely to end anytime soon. Indeed, attacks on such programs are likely only to intensify on the political front and in the courts now that opponents have had the whiff of victory in such states as California and Texas. At the same time, a massive study of affirmative action in higher education has demonstrated that many negative allegations against such programs are unfounded. *The Shape of the River* establishes, among other things, that blacks admitted to college under affirmative action do not suffer from feelings of inferiority, do graduate at high rates, do take up lucrative careers, and are very active as community leaders. Moreover, such programs do not appreciably lessen the chances of admission for whites and, by and large, affirmative action does not cause resentment among them.

At the same time, affirmative action in higher education benefits only a handful of students at the most elite colleges and universities. Such programs do not respond to the problems of an inadequate public school system and the problems of poverty and social dysfunction that plague the lives of a disproportionate segment of blacks. Affirmative action deflects attention away from these very issues and fans racial tensions. Anti-discrimination laws enjoy a large measure of popular support. By and large the opposite is the case for affirmative action.

Many of the same points regarding affirmative action can be made with regard to civil-rights litigation on behalf of Afro-Americans. As with affirmative action, at least some litigation can be demonstrated to have been 'successful' in terms of its immediate goals. However, as with the effects of affirmative action, the results of litigation have done little to meet the underlying problems. The role of the courts, including the landmark *Brown v. Board of Education* case, in bringing about the recognition and implementation of civil rights has been challenged. In any event, the results of litigation in the past three decades on behalf of blacks have been disappointing. Lawsuits to force desegregation of schools are illustrative. Many of these suits have been successful and many more black children now attend integrated schools. But the underlying problem is the quality of education that they receive. Litigation has had very little impact on that issue. Instead, such litigation has converted issues regarding education of black children into a pursuit of numbers in the name of racial balance. At the same time, efforts to improve the quality of public education for black youth (and for all children) have been muffled.

America has much to be proud of in terms of its record of civil rights backed by law. The record is the more impressive given the despicable conditions that once existed for blacks in America. Yet the possibilities of making more progress are uncertain. A public will to tackle problems of poverty, broken urban cores, and dysfunctional families, buttressed by a variety of programs (backed by law where appropriate), is necessary. In that light affirmative action should be seen for what is: a limited, stop-gap measure that must not be allowed to impede real change. Yet America is largely addressing such issues through a style of law that has been apparent in other areas we have examined: adversarial, litigious, and far too dependent on lawyers and courts. Thus is the way paved for much wrangling and for much disappointment in the results.

PART FOUR

Conclusions

Conclusions: The Consequences of Law, the Limits of Litigation, the Need for Pragmatism

The last decades have witnessed enormous change – in technology, through the globalization of economies, and in politics, to name but a few of the sources of such transformation. The role of law has been key in many of these transitions. It has been called upon to tackle a host of social, political, and economic issues. There are more laws, more lawyers, more writing about law, and more litigation and alternatives to it.[1]

An American Story

Nowhere is this appetite for law more apparent than in the United States. America is the land of the law, in terms of a particular form of legalization. The Republic is the society of detailed legal rules, deterrence as the means to achieve compliance, individualism, and adversarialness driven by the engine of litigation.[2] Other nations have increasingly turned to law and do regulate some issues more than the United States. Accessibility to health care, social-welfare entitlements, and workplace issues are examples of areas that other societies have legalized to a greater degree. Yet the United States stands apart. The extent of America's reliance on courts to address significant areas of policy makes it exceptional as the land of the law and certainly as the land of litigation. The USA is also the most examined society in terms of law and its impact. Most comparative studies also focus on America as they attempt to shed light on the effects of law in other societies.

The Republic's loose party structure in politics, the presence of an array of interest groups, its highly individualistic philosophy, and a legal fee structure that encourages assertion of claims in court have all contributed to a turning to litigation and to looking to judges to shape significant policy issues. Beyond these factors has been the growth of rights. The American courts, inspired by an entrenched bill of rights and prompted by many claims of injustice in the decades following the Second World War, were active in fashioning a list of entitlements. Such 'rights talk' reverberated in the legislatures, in the media, and on the streets to create a set of expectations of law and particularly the courts. Beyond rights there was a need to address a sea of crime, particularly that involving violence. America's propensity to seek compliance through deterrence became linked to punishment as a response. The Republic's reliance on litigation led it to use prosecutions and the sanctions meted out by courts as a prime response to wrongdoing. A misplaced search for responsibility in the surge of rights settled upon imprisonment as a response to individual wrongdoing. Incarceration became key. America now imprisons by far the greatest number of individuals per capita in the Western world. Atop the courts, the lawyers, and the criminal law, as the response to crime, sits the death penalty. The resurgence of capital punishment is a misdirected affirmation that in the land of rights there can be responsibility – responsibility imposed ultimately by law. Other nations of a similar tradition have forsaken this ultimate sanction. America imposes it in determined isolation.

This turning to law, in the USA, has multiple causes. The receding of institutions traditionally relied upon to regulate human behaviour is one important reason.[3] Schools, churches, voluntary associations, and the family wield less influence in shaping behaviour. Participation in politics – in terms of party membership or in the fundamental act of voting – is on the wane as dissatisfaction with government and lack of faith in its ability to tackle problems runs high.

A second reason for the growth of legalization is that law is displacing politics across the political spectrum.[4] Towards the left side there is the claiming of rights and the invoking of law to curb outcomes otherwise dictated by the market. The very notion of individuals participating in society has been transformed. The central act is no longer voting but making claims as a 'rights regarding citizen': '[R]ights-consciousness places the courtroom alongside the polling place in the practice of public life.'[5] Towards the right side of the spectrum is the desire to blunt personal behaviour that is seen to be objectionable, to punish and to deter wrongdoing. Here the heaviest machinery of the law, the criminal process and the courts, is hauled out in the hope that people can be made to conform.

The Impact of Law and Its Complexity

What have been the consequences of this turning to law? The mission of this book has been to gather together what is known about the effects of law. Probably more questions have been raised than have been answered. This is not surprising. A central purpose has been to demonstrate how complex is the task of ascertaining the outcomes produced by law. That demonstration of complexity carries with it a cautionary note. A law can be a powerful instrument for regulating behaviour. Yet its effects are often not nearly as straightforward as either its proponents or detractors would claim. Law, therefore, ought to be employed cautiously, with a commitment to monitor, as clearly as possible, its outcomes. It should be invoked in a manner that recognizes that approaches should be altered when the effects produced suggest another course of action. It should be employed pragmatically.[6]

Law can be effective in achieving the goals set for it. The impacts produced, however, are often not nearly as direct as instrumentalist claims suggest. Sometimes unintended consequences complicate matters significantly. However, the suppression of smoking, the protection of the environment, and the backing of civil rights[7] – areas where law in the United States has played a prominent role – provide three important instances of the utility of law. Yet the successes have not been as swift and as sure as advocates would like. What is more, difficult questions arise, in the case of civil-rights laws, regarding how much more improvement can be made to the economic conditions of blacks (as opposed to the protection of the civil rights of individual Afro-Americans). Yet the changes in these three areas have been significant and the role of law conspicuous. Such results indicate the potential of law and are a retort, on the one hand, to those who advocate only market solutions and, on the other, to those who insist that turning to law only deflects attention from underlying problems.

The answers to the question of how law has produced outcomes in these areas and the precise extent of its influence are uncertain. Shifting attitudes in public opinion provide part of an answer. A span of fifty years, from the ending of the Second World War to the dawning of the new millennium, encompasses substantial changes in public opinion regarding civil rights, protection of the environment, and attitudes toward smoking. Such alterations are linked to broad-based approval or, at any rate, to an acceptance of a role for law in realizing changes in these areas. But which is the chicken and which the egg? Is it law that causes these shifts in public opinion or is it changing public attitudes that lead to changes in behaviour that law then reflects?

At some point there needs to be a convergence between what law dictates and what people will support. The coming together of law and public attitudes can be imperfect; they can both lead and follow one another regarding important details. But at some critical phase they both need to be moving in the same direction. Activists across the political spectrum, employing multiple strategies (including litigation), can do much to lay the groundwork so that the link between law and public attitudes occurs. But agitation alone is not enough. Sooner or later a law needs the foundation of public opinion on which to rest. The surfing analogy, quoted in the discussion of smoking (chapter 6), describes, more generally, both the relationship of law and of public opinion and the difficulties of policy-makers knowing the critical phase at which to act:

> Like surfers, legislators and corporate officials who wish to change everyday social norms must wait for signs of a rising wave of cultural support, catching it at just the right time. Legislate too soon and they will be swamped by the swells of popular resistance. Legislate too late and they will be irrelevant. Legislate at the right moment and an emerging cultural norm, still tentatively struggling for authority – such as that condemning involuntary exposure to tobacco smoke – acquires much greater moral force.[8]

This quote also underscores the complex relationship between law and norms. There are charges that the growth of law has crowded out the sources of norms – churches, schools, the family, and so forth – so that, increasingly, the only guide to conduct is what is legalized. There is indeed evidence of this imperialism of law. Yet such allegations are often overblown. Norms remain critical in structuring behaviour. The unqualified claims of instrumentalism are wrong. Law cannot just work its will. It needs to connect to public attitudes and sources of other rules of conduct in order to achieve its goals. This is why the work of the 'normativists' has potential. They insist on examining the role of norms and how they may be linked to regulation in any particular area in order to maximize the likelihood of achieving underlying goals.[9]

The challenge for policy-makers, as the surfing quote expresses, is knowing when and how to make the necessary links. The regulation of smoking is a particularly good example of that challenge. Law has been successfully invoked, in countries such as Canada and the United States, in the campaign to suppress smoking.[10] Yet what to do next, in terms of employing law, raises difficult questions. The practical issues regarding the imposition of higher taxes are illustrative. It is generally agreed among anti-smoking advocates that raising taxes is – in theory – an effective counter to smoking. Moreover, public attitudes are now generally receptive to government initiatives to curtail consumption of tobacco. Still, in Canada, increases in taxes produced the unintended and undesirable consequence of the smuggling of cheaper cigarettes from the United States. The black market in tobacco became so significant that the government was forced to lower taxes so as to remove the incentive for the contraband.[11] Raising taxes may, indeed, be a good strategy for suppressing smoking; the mood of people is generally receptive to such initiatives. But, in the real world, tax increases must be imposed in a context where there are few other sources of tobacco. Law and norms discouraging smoking can shape behaviour; but people are not saints. Smokers may be encouraged to quit as the price of tobacco rises through the imposition of taxes and as an anti-smoking atmosphere continues to develop; but cheaper cigarettes – legal or illegal – make a hefty pull in the opposite direction.

The areas of pornography and affirmative action tell a different story than the ones recounted by the comparative successes of regulation regarding smoking, the environment, and civil rights. There has been enormous agitation by advocates around the issues of pornography and affirmative action. Yet regulation regarding these two issues has not met with broad-based approval and has produced outcomes that can, at best, be described as mixed.

There are vociferous charges that pornography causes harm to women.[12] Yet, however that allegation is understood, the evidence is unclear. Part of the complexity is caused by the possibility that any harm resulting from pornography arises from the depiction of graphic violence not from explicit sexual acts. In this area we looked to Canada because of the success of the 'harm' argument in that country's courts. Yet the Canadian Supreme Court's acceptance of the 'harm' test has not suppressed sexually explicit materials, has deeply divided groups committed to women's equality, and seems to have contributed to the seizure (and prosecution) of gay and lesbian and other unconventional sexual material.[13] What is more, the coming of the Internet and its capacity to transmit information and images from all parts of the world

may place the dissemination of pornography (and all sorts of information) beyond the effective reach of the law.[14] It (whatever 'it' is) may be
distasteful and offensive. Children should certainly be kept away. Otherwise it is questionable how many legal resources should be expended
on this issue.

Affirmative action is well intended – and deeply resented.[15] What
public support there once was appears to be decreasing. Such programs are being assailed in the courts and in the realm of popular politics.[16] The actual effects of affirmative action are little known – as if the
antagonists in this strife-riven debate have too much at stake in their
ideological positions to dare to assemble the facts. A major study, *The
Shape of the River*,[17] does establish that affirmative action has achieved
most of its goals in higher education regarding blacks (the focus of the
analysis).[18] Yet that study also demonstrates how limited are the effects
of affirmative action. In the context of higher education such programs
assist only a handful of blacks at the most elite colleges and universities; almost 60 per cent of institutions of higher education in the United
States have no reason to practise affirmative action since they admit
virtually everyone, with the basic qualifications, who applies. Such
programs do little to remedy the basic problems of a bad public-school
education system, particularly in rotting urban cores where many
Afro-American children (and other disadvantaged kids) must struggle.
The acrimonious fights over affirmative action deflect attention and
resources away from these more pervasive problems.

While public support may be a necessary condition, it is not always
a sufficient one for law to achieve its underlying objectives. The especially punitive aspects of the criminal-justice system in the USA appear
to be widely supported by the populace. Public support for the death
penalty has reached new highs. If the purpose of these laws is to feed
an appetite for vengeance then they may be doing their job. To the
extent that the goal of these laws is to suppress crime, however, the
American variety cannot be counted a success.[19] Crime, including that
of a violent nature, is on the decline. But the reasons for the decrease
are not closely linked to America's harsh imprisonment policies.
Meanwhile these drastic measures are responsible for the incarceration
of substantially more individuals per capita than in any other nation in
the world except Russia. At the same time, despite this decrease,
America remains besieged by serious crime. In comparison, crimes,
including those of violence, have decreased in other countries, including neighbouring Canada. Yet these nations did not have as much vio-

lent crime to begin with, imprison nowhere near the number of people per capita as does the USA, and have, for some time, renounced capital punishment.

The explanations for such harsh measures, which are at the same time so unsuccessful, are complicated. Lack of effective regulation of guns is a factor. Faith in deterrence as part of the style of American law is surely another. Deterrence is an important but limited element in achieving compliance with any law. Yet the American style of regulation places more faith in the capacity of deterrence than do other approaches. Much of this faith is misplaced; for example, in the ability of tort litigation to modify behaviour. Moreover, this misdirected confidence can engender a lack of flexibility regarding other possibilities for achieving compliance, for example, regarding administrative schemes. Yet another factor contributing to America's dismal record in addressing crime is that society's yearning for a sense of responsibility in the midst of insistent rights claiming. Such a desire may be misdirected. It may be misapplied. But criminal punishment – imprisonment, executions – expresses the law's ability to impose responsibility even as it confers all those rights.

The Limits of Litigation

Quite apart from questions of the impact of law in general there are questions regarding the influence of different kinds of law. An issue that has captured much attention in the last decade is the effect of litigation. This matter has been particularly debated in the United States because of the significant role that courts are assigned in the American approach to law.[20] The issue is also important in other societies, particularly ones like Canada, that have recently expanded the judicial role, often through an entrenched bill of rights.[21] Constitutional issues are not the only way that courts can exert substantial influence. Civil litigation, particularly tort lawsuits, carry the potential for courts shaping issues of social policy. Judicial review of administrative action is yet another area where the courts can exercise significant sway. Finally, as we have seen, courts can play a decisive role regarding crime, particularly if the approach to the control of wrongdoing is driven by deterrence and punishment.

The question of the impact of litigation on social policy has largely been directed to progressives. It is they who have placed hopes in the courts to bring about the changes on their agendas, claiming that such changes could not have been achieved in the legislatures. It is they who have most sought judicial recognition of rights as the pathway to betterment, particularly for minorities who, it is argued, could not seek redress through a politics dominated by majoritarian interests.

What is the evidence regarding the impact of litigation? That question should be answered in two ways: first, in terms of the effects of litigation regarding specific issues and, second, in terms of the impact of litigation regarding the forging of public policy generally. The first way of answering the question is of particular interest to Americans because that society relies on litigation so heavily. The second is of particular interest to societies contemplating an expanded role for the courts.

Effects of Litigation regarding Specific Issues

The last decade has witnessed more sceptical stances about the capacity of litigation to bring about change regarding specific issues. This scepticism has not led to crisp answers concerning the effects of litigation or even about how such impacts should be assessed. It has put in issue theoretical and instrumental claims about the capacity of litigation to bring about change and to shape behaviour. Those assertions now appear far too optimistic regarding the capacity of court decisions to alter, by themselves, significant social, political, and economic conditions. Other institutions in society need to promote such change. The significance of courts, other institutions, public opinion, the participants in litigation, and their various interactions are all a matter of debate in terms of effecting change. What is clear is that the effects of litigation will only be ascertained through a more careful study of such factors. Meanwhile relying on courts to forge and implement specific goals is now viewed as a much more hazardous option than the optimistic accounts of litigation's capacity to effect change once suggested. Progressives' assertions of the capacity of lawsuits to achieve reform have especially been put in doubt. The five areas examined – capital punishment, smoking, the environment, pornography, and discrimination against blacks – illustrate the dubious effects of relying on courts to forge and implement policy.

As discussed, in three of these areas – suppression of smoking, safeguarding of the environment, and protection of civil rights – law has enjoyed a measure of success in achieving goals set for it. Yet little of such success is attributable to litigation. In the case of smoking litigation has played a minimal role, at least until very recently, in the efforts to use law to suppress tobacco consumption.[22] (Meanwhile the litigation in Canada must surely give progressives pause. Tobacco companies have used the newly entrenched right to free speech to have legislated curbs on cigarette advertising struck down.[23]) In the case of the environment, litigation – tort and other lawsuits – has been much less effective than have regulatory efforts at achieving legal protection of the environment.[24] (More generally, claims on behalf of tort litigation regarding its effectiveness for deterrence and the provision of compensation for victims have been demonstrated, in several areas, to be wide of the mark.)[25]

In the case of civil rights, particularly those of blacks, litigation to protect those rights has undoubtedly made a contribution. However, the effects of such lawsuits in bringing about improvements in the conditions of disadvantaged Afro-Americans, a critical goal of the civil-rights movement, have been disappointing. Lawsuits regarding the quality of education black children are receiving are illustrative here.[26] When the civil-rights movement gathered momentum after the Second World War most of America's schools were segregated. Now none are, legally, and most are not, in fact. Litigation has played an important role in this transformation. However, the overarching goal of the movement was to improve the educational opportunities for blacks. Yet civil-rights lawsuits became focused on desegregation while sidelining questions of how to improve black educational opportunities.

Debates focusing on pornography have come to centre on arguments regarding whether it causes harm, particularly to women. The evidence of harm, however defined, is uncertain at best. Yet a strand of feminism is adamant that sexually explicit pornography produces such objectionable outcomes. The Supreme Court of Canada in the 1990s essentially agreed. However, as discussed earlier, the aftermath of that court's decisions indicates that sexually explicit material in Canada has not been curtailed.[27] Meanwhile there has been a crackdown on gay and lesbian publications and other material on unconventional sex practices. Whether the seizure (and sometimes prosecution) of such material is worse now than before the decision is debatable. In any event, the widespread perception that it is and the very question of employing law and litigation to address debates about pornography have deeply divided the feminist, gay and lesbian, and other progressive communities. At the same time, the riveting of attention on the suppression of sexually explicit material by law has deflected attention away from what may be the more dangerous element – displays of graphic violence.

The campaign against capital punishment provides a clear example of litigation not achieving its intended goal and, instead, contributing to diametrically opposed results. Litigation in the 1970s was successful in having the US Supreme Court nullify legislation authorizing capital punishment because of vagaries in how the sentence was imposed. However, that decision, along with other events, produced a strong backlash in the public mood and in the legislatures.[28] Support for capital punishment increased; states reinstituted it and began to impose it at an accelerated pace. Subsequent court cases rejected arguments regarding the unconstitutionality of the death penalty and its discriminatory imposition. Not only was such litigation unsuccessful, but the Supreme Court cases helped cement support for capital punishment. These decisions give the appearance of rationalizing executions even as the arbitrariness and discrimination surrounding their imposition continue. Thus, not only did such lawsuits fail; they also provide a striking example of unintended consequences for those who promoted them.

The Effects of Litigation on Forging Public Policy

The other way of examining the consequences of litigation is to ask what effects courts have generally on the forging of public policy. What outcomes are produced when litigation is assigned a significant role regarding complex social, political, and economic issues? The inquiry here concerns differences in degree. Many court decisions in all sorts of societies reflect some sort of policy. Courts in common-law countries are capable of effecting policy decisions by applying (and altering) various judicial rulings or by creatively interpreting statutory provisions in a host of areas.

Nonetheless, it is the courts of the United States that have been involved most extensively in policy formation. It is litigation that is looked at to address all manner of policy issues. It is the claiming of rights, in many contexts including in lawsuits, that drives the search for answers to many of that society's intractable problems. The courts in the USA are involved because of their capacity to entertain constitutional issues but also because of other kinds of litigation such as tort lawsuits and judicial review of administrative decision making.[29]

What are the implications of this expansive role for judges in American society? As with so many other issues regarding consequences that we have examined, the answer to this question is not straightforward. The allegation is that such judicial activity crowds out other forms of policy-making. Popular politics is sidelined and the willingness of legislators to tackle difficult issues diminishes. Such marginalization occurs, particularly regarding progressive issues, as various groups and organizations to the left of the spectrum insist upon expending efforts on litigation. As a result, popular politics, to the extent that it engages policy issues at all, becomes dominated by solutions dependent on market forces and driven by individualistic ideology.

The evidence suggests, however, that such charges need to be qualified. Suppression of smoking, safeguarding of the environment, and backing of civil rights are three significant areas where legislators have acted and their laws have enjoyed substantial success. Moreover, in each of these areas the record of the courts in promoting such policies was mixed at best. Yet the courts' decisions did not prevent the applicable laws from achieving their policy goal. Litigation was not a barrier to public support of such policies.

Still, the charge that lawsuits crowd out other forms of government policy-making remains. Litigation and its capacity to bypass other institutions of government and to blunt public opinion are powerful magnets for an array of issues. The adversarial and individualistic foundations of lawsuits buttress similar values in popular politics. The turning to courts may not be responsible for the erosion of government. But the shift to the work of judges is a response to the dissatisfaction with politicians and the sense of drift regarding public policy. Such dissonance in politics and people's reaction to it is not unique to America. There is deep questioning in many countries about the institutions of government even as the desirability of democracy, itself, is confirmed.[30] The point is a comparative one. Yet in the Republic the courts are viewed as an obvious alternative to the foibles of popular politics.

An eloquent but disturbing account of this move to the courts as a reaction to the decline of popular politics is Schudson's *The Good Citizen: A History of American Civic Life*.[31] As the title suggests, the book recounts the different understandings of what has constituted desirable roles for individuals in public life at different periods of the Republic. The colonial period was associated with a citizenship founded on social hierarchy; the nineteenth century emphasized mass political participation; the Progressive Era's ideal was the informed citizen. What is most relevant for our purposes is Schudson's assertion that the latest era is that of the 'rights-regarding citizen.' In this depiction the decline in voting, the lack of trust in government, and the dissatisfaction with popular politics are indicators, not of the decline of public life but, rather, of its transformation: 'Rights and rights-consciousness have become the continuous incitements to citizenship in our time.'[32]

The Good Citizen is important for all sorts of reasons. Schudson is very compelling when he reminds us that what has been called the 'long civic generation' has probably never existed in America and that every era has had its sceptics warning about the dissipation of public life. He reminds us forcefully that, not so long ago, the very conception of citizenship did not include women, blacks, and other minorities. Rights have clearly had a role in creating space for the excluded to take their place in public life. Moreover, even as Schudson insists on this new characterization of citizenship, he underscores the fact that the transformation to 'rights-regarding' is not, itself, the answer to democracy's discontents.

Yet he enshrines the centrality of rights and of courts as the vehicle for their recognition. As he does this he engages in an exercise linked to the themes of this book. He asks what effects has this turning to rights produced in terms of citizenship and a sense of community, and examines seven measures: voter turnout; trust in government; social capital; quality of public discourse; disparity between rich and poor; access of least-advantaged groups to political power; and the reach of state-guaranteed rights. He concludes that 'there is clear decline on one measure' (voter turnout); 'clear progress on two others' (access of least-advantaged groups to political power and reach of state-guaranteed rights); 'a mixed verdict on three' (social capital, quality of public discourse, disparity between rich and poor); and 'one measure is ... far too faulty a concept to use' (trust).[33]

There is much to be said for using these measures and for Schudson's analysis. Yet he is surely wrong regarding some of the conclusions he reaches. Just the rise in the income of the top 1 per cent of individuals since 1997 was estimated (in 1999) to exceed substantially the total earned income of the bottom 20 per cent of individuals. Wealth is distributed even more unequally than income. In 1999 it was more concentrated among the top 1 per cent and top 20 per cent than at any time since the Depression.[34] How do these figures add up to a 'mixed verdict' on the (growing) disparity between rich and poor?[35]

Beyond taking issue with any of Schudson's conclusions regarding the measures he uses, we can note that he is curiously uninterested in other obvious manifestations of public life and of commitment to community. Where does he take account of the state of urban cores? Of education? Of the levels of crime? Of the numbers in prison? Of the imposition of the death penalty? Of availability to basic health care? Of welfare entitlements? Of access to basic housing? He is right to salute the growth of state-guaranteed rights and their contribution to human dignity. But he seems little interested in the ways that other democracies, of a similar tradition, have secured these and other advances without being awash in 'rights talk,' without making the 'commons a barren place.'[36]

The ideal of rights is noble. Whether a society should so immerse itself in rights and in going to court that the very concept of citizenship, the very notions of what constitutes public life become embodied in 'rights regarding' individuals is a question that needs urgent attention. Any such discussion is probably too late for American society. Its commitment to lawsuits is just too strong. A society that believes an appropriate response to crime are torts suits against gun manufacturers has likely gone too far down the litigation path.

Other societies still have time: even countries, like Canada, that have entrenched rights and embraced courts as the new Solomons. The formidable challenge is to achieve the promise of rights, to harness the advantages of litigation while not debilitating popular democracy and the other institutions of government. Careful examinations of the impacts of litigation would be a good start in meeting that challenge.

A Final Note – Pragmatism

Pragmatism. Assessment. Flexibility. Three important words when invoking law.

In ending I have no list of crisp points to offer regarding the influence of law and its interaction with society. I doubt that anyone has, save perhaps those who view law's working from an unyielding ideology. For many reasons there is great need for pragmatism when turning to law. Books have been written on the meaning of pragmatism. A dictionary definition states that the 'pragmatic' 'relate[s] to the affairs of a community' and 'is concerned with practical consequences or values.'[37] A study of the impact of law indicates that societies of the new millennium will turn to it to mediate all manner of issues. That resort to law needs to be accompanied by flexibility and curiosity about the outcomes that are produced. Law's employment should carry with it a willingness to change and adopt different approaches when the results suggest another course of action.

Of course, the use of law is embedded in a host of values that inevitably clash. My urging of pragmatism in law's employment is matched by my attraction to a similar approach in politics. A commitment to moderation, a flexible approach to the use of society's institutions with an open mind regarding the effects produced, is the prescription offered here. Whether such an approach will have a strong voice in law – and in politics – as the new era dawns is a good question. Those interested in the answer need to observe closely American society and its many ventures with legalization. They may not wish to emulate the Republic. Yet they can learn a great deal from the land of law. All the while, they should remember that the spirit of the law, like the spirit of liberty, needs to be 'not too sure that it is right.'[38]

Notes

Introduction

1 From his famous Spirit of Liberty speech as quoted in G. Gunther, *Learned Hand: The Man and Judge* (New York: Alfred A. Knopf, 1994), 549.
2 W.A. Bogart, *Courts and Country: The Limits of Litigation and the Social and Political Life of Canada* (Toronto: Oxford University Press, 1994).
3 M. Schudson, *The Good Citizen: A History of American Civic Life* (New York: The Free Press, 1998).

Chapter One: So Decried, So Demanded

1 L. Friedman, 'I Hear Cacophony: Herzog and the *Republic of Choice*,' *Law and Social Inquiry* 17 (1992): 159, 162.
2 Ibid., 163.
3 P. Ewick and S. Silbey, *The Common Place of Law: Stories from Everyday Life* (Chicago: University of Chicago Press, 1998), 35 (emphasis in original).
4 See chapters 3, 'The Complexities of Assessing Impact,' and 4, 'Six Ideas about the Impact of Law – America the Outlier.'
5 For an excellent historical study of workplace health and safety laws and their impact see E. Tucker, *Administering Danger in the Workplace: The Law and Politics of Occupational Health and Safety Regulation in Ontario 1850–1914* (Toronto: University of Toronto Press, 1990).
6 D. Vogel, 'The "New" Social Regulation in Historical and Comparative Perspective,' in T. McCraw, ed., *Regulation in Perspective: Historical Essays* (Cambridge, Mass.: Harvard University Press, 1981).
7 B. Bresner et al., 'Ontario's Agencies, Boards, Commissions, Advisory Bodies and Other Public Institutions: An Inventory (1977),' in *Government Regu-*

lation: Issues and Alternatives (Toronto: Ontario Economic Council, 1978), 207–75.

8 See C. Sunstein, *After the Rights Revolution: Reconceiving the Regulatory State* (Cambridge, Mass.: Harvard University Press, 1990); J. Evans et al., *Administrative Law: Cases, Text, and Materials*, 4th ed. (Toronto: Emond Montgomery, 1995), 1–5.

9 C. Booker and R. North, *The Mad Officials: How the Bureaucrats Are Strangling Britain* (London: Constable and Company Ltd., 1994), 9–11.

10 J. Adams, *Risk* (London: UCL Press Ltd., 1995), 206.

11 Booker and North, *supra* note 9, 213–15.

12 I. Ayres and J. Braithwaite, *Responsive Regulation* (New York: Oxford University Press, 1992), 11–12.

13 Ibid.

14 Ibid.

15 See this chapter, 'Crime and Punishment,' p. 46.

16 See R. Abel, 'Lawyers in the Civil Law World,' in R. Abel and T. Lewis, eds, *Lawyers in Society: The Civil Law World* (Berkeley: University of California Press, 1988).

17 M. Galanter, 'Law Abounding: Legalisation around the North Atlantic,' *Modern Law Review* 55 (1992): 1, 4, citing R. Abel, *The Legal Profession in England and Wales* (Oxford: Basil Blackwell, 1988).

18 B. Curran, *Supplement to the Lawyer Statistical Report: The U.S. Legal Profession in 1985* (Chicago: American Bar Foundation, 1986); W. Glaberson, 'Lawyers Contend with State and Federal Efforts to Restrict Their Rising Power,' *New York Times*, 5 August 1999, A15.

19 D. Stager and H. Arthurs, *Lawyers in Canada* (Toronto: University of Toronto Press, 1990), 149; J. Melnitzer, 'Size of Ontario Bar Grows 30 Per Cent,' *Law Times*, 29 March–4 April 1999, 1.

20 Galanter, *supra* note 17, 4.

21 Ibid.; for Canada, see Stager and Arthurs, *supra* note 19, 149.

22 E.g., M.J. Mossman, '"Shoulder to Shoulder": Gender and Access to Justice,' *The Windsor Yearbook of Access to Justice* 10 (1990): 351; and J. Hagan, M. Zatz, B. Arnold, and F. Kay, 'Cultural Capital, Gender, and the Structural Transformation of Legal Practice,' *Law and Society Review* 25 (1991): 355.

23 Galanter, *supra* note 17, 5–6.

24 O. Lippert, 'Consumer Demand for Legal Services,' *Canadian Lawyer*, November/December 1996, 14.

25 Ibid.

26 Ibid., 16.

27 See, for example, the works cited below in notes 71, 72, 73.

28 W. Novak, *The People's Welfare: Law and Regulation in Nineteenth-Century America* (Chapel Hill: University of North Carolina Press, 1996), ix.

29 Vogel, *supra* note 6, 158–9.

30 Ibid., 162.

31 M. Schudson, *The Good Citizen: A History of American Civic Life* (New York: The Free Press, 1998), 265.

32 Galanter, *supra* note 17, 6.

33 Ibid.

34 G. Engle, 'The Legislative Process Today,' *Statute Law Review* (1987): 71.

35 Galanter, *supra* note 17, 7.

36 Ibid.

37 Ibid.

38 Consultative Group on Research and Education in Law, *Law and Learning* (Ottawa: Social Sciences and Humanities Research Council of Canada, 1983), 82.

39 Galanter, *supra* note 17, 7.

40 Ewick and Silbey, *supra* note 3, xi.

41 Galanter, *supra* note 17, 7. This part of chapter 1 is obviously indebted to the Galanter article.

42 Schudson, *supra* note 31, 264–73.

43 Galanter, note 17, 13.

44 I. Jenkins, *Social Order and the Limits of Law* (Princeton: Princeton University Press, 1980), 215.

45 D. Dewees, M. Trebilcock, and P. Coyte, 'The Medical Malpractice Crisis: Comparative Empirical Perspective,' *Law and Contemporary Problems* 54 (1991): 217.

46 Ibid., 250 n. 76.

47 All statistics taken from Galanter, *supra* note 17, 8 and sources cited.

48 Statistics taken from ibid., 8 and the sources cited.

49 F. Zemans and P. Monahan, *From Crisis to Reform: A New Legal Aid Plan for Ontario* (North York, Ont.: York University Centre for Public Law and Public Policy, 1997), 19.

50 Ibid., 20.

51 J. McCamus et al., *Report of the Ontario Legal Aid Review: A Blueprint for Publicly Funded Legal Services*, vols. 1–3 (Toronto: Ontario Legal Aid Review, 1997); *Legal Aid Services Act*, S.O. 1998, c. 26.

52 Galanter, *supra* note 17, 11.

53 O. Fiss, 'Against Settlement,' *Yale Law Journal* 93 (1984): 1073 and 'A Solution in Search of a Problem,' in R. Macdonald, *Study Paper: Prospects for Civil Justice* (Toronto: Ontario Law Reform Commission, 1995), 205.

54 N. Tate and T. Vallinder, eds, *The Global Expansion of Judicial Power* (New York: New York University Press, 1995).

55 J. Griffith, *The Politics of the Judiciary*, 4th ed. (London: Fontana Press, 1991); C. Harlow and R. Rawlings, *Pressure through Law* (London: Routledge, 1992).

56 L. Tribe, *God Save This Honourable Court* (New York: Random House, 1985), xviii, 111, 139–40, quoted in A. Hutchinson, 'Charter Litigation and Social Change: Legal Battles and Social Wars,' in R. Sharpe, ed., *Charter Litigation* (Toronto: Butterworths, 1987), 358.

57 O. Fiss, 'Against Settlement,' *supra* note 53, 1089.

58 P. Atiyah, 'Tort Law and the Alternatives: Some Anglo-American Comparisons,' *Duke Law Journal* (1987): 1002, 1018.

59 J. Leo, 'The Age of Litigation,' *U.S. News and World Report*, 30 March 1992, 22, as quoted in S. Lipset, *American Exceptionalism: A Double-Edged Sword* (New York: W.W. Norton and Co., 1996), 270.

60 A. Gold, 'The Legal Rights Provisions – A New Vision or Déjà Vu,' *Supreme Court Law Review* 4 (1982): 108, quoted in C. Manfredi, *Judicial Power and the Charter* (Toronto: McClelland and Stewart, 1993), 27.

61 J. Whyte, 'On Not Standing for Notwithstanding,' *Alberta Law Review* 28 (1990): 347, 351 (emphasis in original).

62 L. Friedman, *The Republic of Choice* (Cambridge, Mass.: Harvard University Press, 1990), 74. He has continued to develop these and related ideas in *The Horizontal Society* (New Haven: Yale University Press, 1999).

63 For a harsh review and response see D. Herzog, 'I Hear a Rhapsody: A Reading of *The Republic of Choice*,' *Law and Social Inquiry* 17 (1992): 147 and L. Friedman, 'I Hear Cacophony,' *supra* note 1. See also J. Kaplan, [Review] *Harvard Journal on Legislation* 27 (1990): 613.

64 Friedman, *The Republic of Choice*, *supra* note 62, 61.

65 Ibid., 62–3.

66 Ibid.

67 See this chapter, 'Rights and Transformation.'

68 Friedman, *The Republic of Choice*, *supra* note 62, 65.

69 Ibid., 65–8.

70 Ibid., 206.

71 W. Olson, *The Litigation Explosion: What Happened When America Unleashed the Lawsuit* (New York: Truman Talley-Dutton, 1991).

72 P. Howard, *The Death of Common Sense: How Law Is Suffocating America* (New York: Random House, 1994).

73 M. Glendon, *A Nation under Lawyers: How the Crisis in the Legal Profession Is Transforming American Society* (New York: Farrar, Straus, and Giroux, 1994).

74 P. Compos, *Jurismania: The Madness of American Law* (New York: Oxford University Press, 1998).

75 D. Farber and S. Sherry, *Beyond All Reason: The Radical Assault on Truth in America* (New York: Oxford University Press, 1997).

76 Galanter, *supra* note 17, 1.

77 P. Howard, *supra* note 72.

78 For a thoughtful account of the issues raised by Howard that also underscores the imprecision and overgeneralization of the book, see D. Wirth and E. Silbergeld, 'Risky Reform,' *Columbia Law Review* 95 (1995): 1857.

79 P. Howard, *supra* note 72, 3–4.

80 Ibid., 11.

81 Ibid., 10–11.

82 This paradox is not new. Shakespeare made much of similar contradictions: see, for example, *Measure for Measure*; this point is discussed in R. Macdonald, *Study Paper on Prospects for Civil Justice* (Toronto: Ontario Law Reform Commission, 1995), 8.

83 Glendon, *supra* note 73, 262.

84 Ibid., 268.

85 For a review pointing out just how sweeping – and, in ways, dangerous – are the claims of Glendon, see S. Levinson [Review] *Journal of Legal Education* 45 (1995): 143.

86 Glendon, *supra* note 73, 280, quoting A. de Tocqueville, *Democracy in America*, ed., J. Mayer, (New York: Doubleday Anchor, 1969), 268.

87 Ibid., 281, quoting de Tocqueville, *Democracy in America*, 264.

88 Ibid., 282–3.

89 F. Fukuyama, *Trust: The Social Virtues and the Creation of Prosperity* (New York: The Free Press, 1995). He has continued with these and related ideas in *The Great Disruption: Human Nature and the Reconstitution of Social Order* (New York: Free Press, 1999).

90 See F. Zakaria, 'Bigger than the Family, Smaller than the State,' *New York Times Book Review*, 1; T. Maxwell, 'Trust: The Social Virtues and the Creation of Prosperity,' *Denver Journal of International Law and Policy* 25 (1997): 423; A. Sanderson, 'Trust [book review],' *Choice* 33 (1995): 660; P. Green, 'Trust [book review],' *The Nation*, 25 September 1995, 318; 'Trust [book review],' *The Economist*, 2 September 1995, 79.

91 'The End of Economics,' *The Economist*, 2 September 1995, 79.

92 Fukuyama, *supra* note 89, 269–325.

93 *The Economist*, *supra* note 90, 79–80.

94 R. Putnam, 'Bowling Alone: America's Declining Social Capital,' *Journal of Democracy* 6 (1995): 65. See also R. Putnam, 'The Strange Disappearance of Civic America,' *American Prospect* 24 (1996): 34.

95 R. Putnam, *Bowling Alone: The Collapse and Revival of American Community* (New York: Simon & Schuster, 2000); M. Talbot, 'Who Wants to Be a Legionnaire?' *New York Times Book Review,* 25 June 2000, 11.

96 Putnam, 'Bowling Alone,' *supra* note 94, 70.

97 Ibid., 68–9.

98 M. Levi, 'Social and Unsocial Capital: A Review Essay of Robert Putnam's *Making Democracy Work,' Politics and Society* (1996): 45, 47, quoting remarks of Putnam during the Roundtable on Trust, American Political Science Association meetings, Chicago, September 1995.

99 Lipset, *supra* note 59, 281, quoting Putnam.

100 Ibid., 281.

101 H. Konig, 'A French Mirror,' *The Atlantic Monthly,* December 1995, 95.

102 R. Bibby, *The Bibby Report: Social Trends Canadian Style* (Toronto: Stoddart, 1995); R. Bibby, *Mosaic Madness: The Poverty and Potential of Life in Canada* (Toronto: Stoddart, 1990); R. Macmillan, 'Changes in the Structure of Life Courses and the Decline of Social Capital in Canadian Society: A Time Series Analysis of Property Crime Rates,' *Canadian Journal of Sociology* 20 (1995): 51.

103 Putnam, 'Bowling Alone,' *supra* note 94, 70–3. See also N. Lemann, 'Kicking in Groups,' *The Atlantic Monthly,* April 1996, 22–6; and Lipset, *supra* note 59, 276ff.

104 S. Carter, *The Culture of Disbelief: How American Law and Politics Trivialize Religious Devotion* (New York: Basic Books, 1993).

105 Chapter 8.

106 Lemann, *supra* note 103, 26.

107 Levi, *supra* note 98, 51–2.

108 Schudson, *supra* note 31, 297–300.

109 Ibid., 8. See also Friedman, *The Horizontal Society, supra* note 62.

110 D. Black, *The Behavior of Law* (New York: Academic Press, 1976), 117.

111 Friedman, *The Republic of Choice, supra* note 62, 56.

112 G. Gilmore, *The Ages of American Law* (New Haven: Yale University Press, 1977), 110–11.

113 Lipset, *supra* note 59, 282, quoting the statistic in the text from a variety of sources.

114 'He Believes in Government, So Why Doesn't America?' *The Economist,* 24 January 1998, 19.

115 See chapter 4, 'The Ineffectiveness of Law,' p. 133.

116 Schudson, *supra* note 31, 255–64.

117 P. Williams, 'Alchemical Notes: Reconstructing Ideals from Deconstructed Rights,' *Harvard Civil Rights – Civil Liberties Law Review* 22 (1987): 401, 431.

118 S. Sunstein, 'Rights and Their Critics,' *Notre Dame Law Review* 70 (1995): 727.

119 M. Glendon, *Rights Talk: The Impoverishment of Political Discourse* (New York: The Free Press, 1991), 7.

120 J. Handler, *Social Movements and the Legal System: A Theory of Law Reform and Social Change* (New York: Academic Press, 1978). For a contemporary group of essays on lawyering in the 'public interest,' see A. Sarat and S. Scheingold, eds, *Cause Lawyering: Political Commitments and Professional Responsibilities* (New York: Oxford University Press, 1998).

121 S. Scheingold, 'Constitutional Rights and Social Change: Civil Rights in Perspective,' in M. McCann and G. Houseman, eds, *Judging the Constitution: Critical Essays on Judicial Lawmaking* (Boston: Scott, Foresman / Little Brown, 1989), 87.

122 M. Minow, 'Interpreting Rights: An Essay for Robert Cover,' *Yale Law Journal* 96 (1987): 1860, 1876, 1880 [footnotes omitted].

123 A. Hutchinson, *Waiting for Coraf: A Critique of Law and Rights* (Toronto: University of Toronto Press, 1995).

124 S. Holmes and C. Sunstein, *The Cost of Rights: Why Liberty Depends on Taxes* (New York: W.W. Norton and Co., 1999), 24–5.

125 Novak, *supra* note 28, 'Conclusion – The Invention of American Constitutional Law.'

126 Scheingold, *supra* note 121, 85.

127 A. Hacker, 'The War over the Family,' *New York Review of Books*, 4 December 1997, 34, 35.

128 R. Hughes, *Culture of Complaint: The Fraying of America* (New York: Oxford University Press, 1993).

129 Ibid., 31, quoting Pat Robertson.

130 S. Walker, *The Rights Revolution: Rights and Community in Modern America* (New York: Oxford University Press, 1998).

131 Schudson, *supra* note 31, 309.

132 Quoted in F. Siegel, 'Nothing in Moderation,' *The Atlantic Monthly*, May 1990, 108, 110.

133 Hughes, *supra* note 128, 29, quoting Václav Havel.

134 R. Posner, *Sex and Reason* (Cambridge: Harvard University Press, 1992), 434.

135 D. Polsby, 'The False Promise of Gun Control,' *The Atlantic Monthly*, March 1994, 57.

136 Chapter 2, 'Designing Out the Problem,' p. 70.

137 A. Walinsky, 'The Crisis of Public Order,' *The Atlantic Monthly*, July 1995, 39.

138 See the discussion in chapter 5, 'Punishment – and Capital Punishment.'
139 See 'Crime and Punishment' and 'Crime in America: Violent and Irratio-
    nal – and That's Just the Policy,' *The Economist*, 8 June 1996, 17 and 23,
    respectively, and M. Howard, 'In Defence of Prisons,' *The Economist*,
    22 June 1996, 56.
140 W. Kaminer, 'Crime and Community,' *The Atlantic Monthly*, May 1994, 111;
    and Kaminer, 'Federal Offense,' ibid., June 1994, 102.
141 Posner, *supra* note 134, 442.
142 Ibid., 441–2: 'Some combination of aggressive and explicit sex education
    from an early age, provision of contraceptives to teenagers, conditioning
    generous maternity and child welfare benefits on the mother's having
    established herself in the job market, solicitous attention to fetal and neo-
    natal health needs, and an end to discrimination against homosexuals
    may be the essential elements of a realistic (and inexpensive) program for
    dealing with our national blights of teenage pregnancy, teenage parent-
    hood, and sexually transmitted AIDS.'

Chapter Two: Compliance with Law

  1 C. Tuohy, 'Achieving Compliance with Collective Objectives: A Political
    Science Perspective,' in M. Friedland, ed., *Sanctions and Rewards in the
    Legal System: A Multidisciplinary Approach* (Toronto: University of Toronto
    Press, 1989), 179.
  2 See, below, the discussion of corporate crime in 'How Best to Deter' and
    the discussion of rewards in 'Alternatives to Deterrence.'
  3 K. Hawkins and J. Thomas, 'The Enforcement Process in Regulatory
    Bureaucracies,' in K. Hawkins and J. Thomas, *Enforcing Regulation* (Boston:
    Kluwer-Nijhoff Publishing, 1984).
  4 Tuohy, *supra* note 1, 179.
  5 R. Paternoster et al., 'Perceived Risk and Social Control: Do Sanctions
    Really Deter?' *Law and Society Review* 17 (1983): 457.
  6 L. Friedman, *Crime and Punishment in American History* (New York: Basic
    Books, 1993), 13.
  7 Ibid., 457–9.
  8 Ibid., 458 (emphasis in the original).
  9 R. Cotterrell, *The Sociology of Law: An Introduction*, 2nd ed. (London: But-
    terworths, 1992), 142–3.
 10 Ibid., 143.
 11 F. Haines, *Corporate Regulation: Beyond 'Punish or Persuade'* (Oxford: Clar-
    endon Press, Oxford, 1997), 5.

12 Ambrose Bierce, as quoted in B. Fisse and J. Braithwaite, *Corporations, Crime and Accountability* (Cambridge: Cambridge University Press, 1993), 15.

13 D. Vaughan, 'Rational Choice, Situated Action, and the Social Control of Organizations,' *Law and Society Review* 32 (1998): 23, 29.

14 Haines, *supra* note 11, 5–6.

15 B. Hutter, *Compliance: Regulation and Environment* (Oxford: Clarendon Press, 1997).

16 I. Ayres and J. Braithwaite, *Responsive Regulation: Transcending the Deregulation Debate* (New York: Oxford University Press, 1992), 35–41.

17 J. Braithwaite, 'Responsive Business Regulatory Institutions,' in C. Coady and C. Sampford, eds, *Business Ethics and the Law* (Sydney: The Federation Press, 1993), 83.

18 Haines, *supra* note 11.

19 Cotterrell, *supra* note 9, 143–4.

20 H. Ross, *Deterring the Drinking Driver: Legal Policy and Social Control*, rev. ed. (Lexington, Mass.: Lexington Books, 1982).

21 P. Cook, 'The Economics of Criminal Sanctions,' in Friedland, *Sanctions and Rewards, supra* note 1, 63.

22 D. Kahan, 'Social Influence, Social Meaning, and Deterrence,' *Virginia Law Review* 83 (1977): 349, 379.

23 See, generally, A. Polinsky, *An Introduction to Law and Economics* (Boston: Little Brown, 1983) and R. Posner, *Economic Analysis of Law*, 5th ed. (New York: Aspen Law and Business, 1998).

24 R. Posner, *Sex and Reason* (Cambridge: Harvard University Press, 1992), 393–4.

25 Ibid., 393–4, citing I. Ehrlich, 'Participation in Illegitimate Activities: An Economic Analysis,' in G. Becker and W. Landes, eds, *Essays in the Economics of Crime and Punishment* (New York: National Bureau of Economic Research, distribution by Columbia University Press, 1974), 868.

26 Ibid., citing F. McLynn, *Crime and Punishment in Eighteenth-Century England* (New York: Routledge, 1989), 106–9 and A. Clark, *Women's Silence, Men's Violence: Sexual Assault in England 1770–1845* (New York: Pandora, 1987), chap. 3.

27 Ibid., citing R. Mehdi, 'The Offence of Rape in the Islamic Law of Pakistan,' *International Journal of Sociology of Law* 18 (1990): 19.

28 D. Dewees, D. Duff, and M. Trebilcock, *Exploring the Domain of Accident Law: Taking the Facts Seriously* (New York: Oxford University Press, 1996).

29 Ibid., 413.

30 Ibid., 413.

31 Ibid., 417, discussing P. Weiler, *Medical Malpractice on Trial* (Cambridge: Harvard University Press, 1991).

32 Ibid., 419.

33 Ibid., 414.

34 M. Friedland, 'Rewards in the Legal System: Tenure, Airbags, and Safety Bingo,' *Alberta Law Review* 31 (1993): 493.

35 Ibid., 493.

36 Ibid., 495, citing M. Heumann and T. Church, 'Criminal Justice Reform, Monetary Incentives, and Policy Evaluation,' paper delivered at the annual Law and Society Association meeting, Vail, Colorado, June 1988) (unpublished): 'The results of these incentives are ambiguous.' See also T. Meares, 'Rewards for Good Behavior: Influencing Prosecutorial Discretion and Conduct with Financial Incentives,' *Fordham Law Review* 64 (1995): 851.

37 Friedland, *supra* note 34, 496–8.

38 Ibid., 498–9.

39 Ibid., 495.

40 Friedland, *Sanctions and Rewards, supra* note 1, 4.

41 For a nuanced account of both the potential and the limits of rewards, see R. Howse, 'Retrenchment, Reform or Revolution? The Shift to Incentives and the Future of the Regulatory State,' *Alberta Law Review* 31 (1993): 456.

42 *Canada Health Act*, R.S.C. 1985, c. C-6.

43 For example, R. Stewart, 'Madison's Nightmare,' *University of Chicago Law Review* 57 (1990): 335; R. Howse et al., 'Smaller or Smarter Government,' *University of Toronto Law Journal* 4 (1990): 498; S. Rose-Ackerman, *Rethinking the Progressive Agenda: The Reform of the American Regulatory State* (New York: Free Press, 1992).

44 J. Hanson and K. Logue, 'The Costs of Cigarettes: The Economic Case for Ex Post Incentive-Based Regulation,' *Yale Law Journal* 107 (1998): 1163, 'IV. Choosing among Regulatory Approaches,' 1263–81; J. Handler, *Law and the Search for Community* (Philadelphia: University of Pennsylvania Press, 1990), 46–9.

45 Howse, 'Retrenchment, Reform or Revolution?' *supra* note 41, 459.

46 R. Brown and M. Rankin, 'Persuasion, Penalties, and Prosecution: Administrative v. Criminal Sanctions,' in M. Friedland, ed., *Securing Compliance: Seven Case Studies* (Toronto: University of Toronto Press, 1990), 348.

47 R. Brown, 'Administrative and Criminal Penalties in the Enforcement of Occupational Health and Safety Legislation,' *Osgoode Hall Law Journal* 30 (1992): 691.

48 Haines, *supra* note 11.

49 M. Friedland et al., *Regulating Traffic Safety* (Toronto: University of Toronto Press, 1990), 151–2.

50 C. Ram, 'Living Next to the United States: Recent Developments in Cana-
    dian Gun Control Policy, Politics, and Law,' *New York Law School Journal of
    International and Comparative Law* 15 (1995): 279, 282.

51 See ibid. and 'America and Guns,' *The Economist*, 4 April 1998, 16. The mat-
    ter has grown more complex as the Supreme Court has held that federal
    gun-control legislation can unduly intrude on the power of the states and
    any such legislation would be unconstitutional: *Printz v. United States* and
    Mack v. United States 117 S.Ct. 2365 (1997) and L. Greenhouse, 'Justices
    Limit Brady Gun Law as Intrusion on States' Rights,' *New York Times*,
    28 June 1997, 1. For efforts at gun control, at the federal level, as recently as
    June 1999 see editorial 'New Showdown on Gun Control,' *New York Times*,
    9 June 1999, A30, and J. Dao and D. Van Nutta, 'N.R.A., Thriving under
    Attacks, Mobilizes to Fight New Gun Curbs,' *New York Times*, 12 June 1999,
    A1, A10.

52 W.A. Bogart, *Courts and Country: The Limits of Litigation and the Social and
    Political Life of Canada* (Toronto: Oxford University Press, 1994), chap. 7,
    'The Courts and Two Models of the Criminal Law.'

53 S. Jacobs, 'Toward a More Reasonable Approach to Gun Control: Canada as
    a Model,' *New York Law School Journal of International and Comparative Law* 15
    (1995): 315, 332–4.

54 F. Zimring, *American Youth Violence* (New York: Oxford University Press,
    1998).

55 Friedman, *supra* note 6, 459.

56 J. Lott, *More Guns, Less Crime: Understanding Crime and Gun-Control Law*
    (Chicago: University of Chicago Press, 1998). See, in particular, chapter 7,
    'The Political and Academic Debate,' where the author replies to academic
    critics of his work, especially his statistical analysis.

57 'Do Guns Mean Crime?' *The Economist*, 13 January 2001, 76, discussing
    studies by H. Dezhbakhsh and P. Rubin and by M. Duggan.

58 Friedland et al., *Regulating Traffic Safety, supra* note 49, 152.

59 W. Gray and J. Scholz, 'Does Regulatory Enforcement Work? A Panel Anal-
    ysis of OHSA Enforcement,' *Law and Society Review* 27 (1993): 177.

60 N. Brooks and A. Doob, 'Tax Evasion: Searching for a Theory of Compliant
    Behavior,' in Friedland, *Securing Compliance, supra* note 46, 154–5.

61 Gray and Scholz, *supra* note 59.

62 Brooks and Doob, *supra* note 60, 157, citing D. Kahneman, P. Slovic, and A.
    Tversky, eds, *Judgment under Uncertainty: Heuristics and Biases* (Cambridge:
    Cambridge University Press, 1982).

63 Gray and Scholz, *supra* note 59.

64 Brooks and Doob, *supra* note 60, 157, citing R. Cialdini, *Influence: Science and
    Practice*, 2nd ed. (Glenview, Ill.: Scott Foresman and Co., 1988).

65 D. Dewees, 'The Effect of Environmental Regulation: Mercury and Sulphur Dioxide,' in Friedland, *Securing Compliance, supra* note 46, 354.

66 Ibid., 386.

67 Ibid., 386–7.

68 R. Clarke and P. Mayhew, 'The British Gas Suicide Story and Its Criminological Implications,' *Crime and Justice: An Annual Survey* 10 (1988): 79.

69 P. Cook, *supra* note 21, 63.

70 For a similar approach in the environmental context see R. M'Gonigle et al., 'Taking Uncertainty Seriously: From Permissive Regulation to Preventative Design in Environmental Decision Making,' *Osgoode Hall Law Journal* 32 (1994): 99.

71 Friedland, *Securing Compliance, supra* note 46, 9.

72 Friedland et al., *Regulating Traffic Safety, supra* note 49, 152.

73 For a discussion of the idea that social problems can behave like infectious agents, see M. Gladwell, 'The Tipping Point,' *The New Yorker*, 3 June 1996, 32.

74 W. Haddon, 'On the Escape of Tigers: An Ecologic Note,' *American Journal of Public Health* 60 (1970): 2229; T. Christoffel, 'The Role of Law in Reducing Injury,' *Law, Medicine and Health Care* 17 (1989): 7.

75 For example, S. Peltzman, 'The Effects of Automobile Safety Regulation,' *Journal of Political Economy* 83 (1975): 677.

76 For example, G. Wilde, 'Risk Homeostasis Theory and Traffic Accidents: Propositions, Deductions, and Discussion of Dissension in Recent Reactions,' *Ergonomics* 31 (1988): 441.

77 For a developed treatment of the argument that, generally, the effects of safety improvements give rise to riskier behaviour, including regarding driving, see J. Adams, *Risk* (London: UCL Press Ltd, 1995).

78 Friedland et al., *Regulating Traffic Safety, supra* note 49, 19–20.

79 M. Valpy, 'Let's Sue over Airbags,' *Globe and Mail*, 10 April 1997, A19.

80 M. Wald, 'New Rule Seeks to Reduce Danger from Car Air Bags,' *New York Times*, 15 March 1997, A7.

81 Friedland et al., *Regulating Traffic Safety, supra* note 49, 152.

82 J. Donohue and P. Siegelman, 'Allocating Resources among Prisons and Social Programs in the Battle against Crime,' unpublished, 25 July 1996.

83 Ibid., 3.

84 Ibid., 37–40.

85 Ibid., 4.

86 Ibid., 68–9.

87 L. Windlesham, *Politics, Punishment and Populism* (New York: Oxford University Press, 1998), 11.

88 Ibid., 224, citing statistics from *The Sentencing Project* (Washington, DC, 1997).

89 F. Butterfield, ' "Defying Gravity": Inmate Population Climbs,' *New York Times*, 19 January 1998, A10.

90 E. Schlosser, 'The Prison–Industrial Complex,' *The Atlantic Monthly*, December 1998, 51.

91 Friedland, *Securing Compliance*, *supra* note 46, 18: 'Carefully designed further studies may offer some guidance as to which of these techniques are the most effective. Until that is done, our judges, administrators, and policy-makers will be basing their actions on ... hunches and guesswork.'

92 S. Christianson, *With Liberty for Some – 500 Years of Imprisonment in America* (Boston: Northeastern University Press, 1998), ix.

93 Cotterrell, *supra* note 9, 141–2.

94 Ibid., 141 citing J. Tapp and L. Kohlberg, 'Developing Senses of Law and Legal Justice,' *Journal of Social Issues* 2 (1971): 27, 65–91.

95 Ibid., 142 citing W. Kurtines and E.B. Greif, 'Development of Moral Thought: Review and Evaluation of Kohlberg's Approach,' *Psychological Bulletin* 81 (1974): 453–70; and R. Irvine, 'Legal Socialization: A Critique of a New Approach,' in D. Farrington et al., eds, *Psychology, Law and Legal Contexts* (London: MacMillan, 1979), 69–89.

96 Cotterrell, *supra* note 9, 142, citing C. Gilligan, *In a Different Voice: Psychological Theory and Women's Development* (Cambridge, Mass.: Harvard University Press).

97 Kahan, *supra* note 22, 354.

98 See chapter 4, 'Ineffectiveness of Law,' p. 133.

99 Cotterrell, *supra* note 9, 151–7. Critiques by the left of such internalization are pursued in chapter 4, 'Law Acting in Concert with Social and Political Forces,' p. 120.

100 R. Lempert, 'A Resource Theory of the Criminal Law: Exploring When It Matters?' in B. Garth and A. Sarat, eds, *How Does Law Matter?* (Evanston, Ill.: Northwestern University Press, 1998).

101 For example, see J. Staddon, 'On Responsibility and Punishment,' *The Atlantic Monthly*, February 1995, 88.

102 J. Grusec, 'Sanctions and Rewards: The Approach of Psychology,' in Friedland, *Sanctions and Rewards*, *supra* note 1, 109.

103 Ibid.

104 J. Hagan et al., 'Family Violence: A Study in Social and Legal Sanctions,' in Friedland, *Securing Compliance*, *supra* note 1, 392.

105 T. Tyler, *Why People Obey the Law* (New Haven: Yale University Press, 1990), 5.

106 Ibid., 7.
107 Ibid., 97.
108 Ibid., 156–7.
109 Ibid., 101.
110 Ibid., 107.
111 See H. Ross, 'Book Review: *Why People Obey the Law*,' *American Journal of Sociology* 96 (1991): 1055; L. Hamilton, 'Understanding Legal Compliance,' *Michigan Law Review* 89 (1991): 1778.
112 Tyler, *supra* note 105, 45.
113 'Diminished Deference – How Perception of Injustice Influences Compliance with Law,' in *Researching Law* 2, vol. 11, 4 (Fall 2000) (Chicago: American Bar Foundation), discussing a study by J. Nadler.
114 Tyler, *supra* note 105, 148.
115 A. Sarat, 'Authority, Anxiety, and Procedural Justice: Moving from Scientific Detachment to Critical Engagement,' *Law and Society Review* 27 (1993): 647, 656ff.
116 Robinson, 'Moral Credibility and Crime,' *The Atlantic Monthly*, March 1995, 72.

Chapter Three: The Complexities of Assessing Impact

1 A. Lewis (moderator), 'The First Amendment, Under Fire from the Left,' *New York Times Magazine*, 13 March 1995, 40.
2 T. Cook and D. Campbell, *Quasi-Experimentation: Design and Analysis Issues for Field Settings* (Boston: Houghton Mifflin Co., 1979).
3 R.G. Collingwood, *The Idea of History* (Oxford: Clarendon Press, 1946), cited in J. Chandler et al., *Questions of Evidence: Proof, Practice, and Persuasion across the Disciplines* (Chicago: University of Chicago Press, 1994).
4 See the media coverage of the new sensitivity to issues of causation through historical counterfactuals: W. Honan, 'Historians Warming to Games of "What if,"' *New York Times*, 7 January 1998, B7.
5 M. Poovey, *A History of the Modern Fact: Problems of Knowledge in the Sciences of Wealth and Society* (Chicago: University of Chicago Press, 1998).
6 See chapter 8.
7 See this chapter, 'Surprise – Unintended Consequences,' p. 99.
8 See chapter 9, 'The Pervasiveness of Disparity – The Presence of Discrimination?' p. 279.
9 Ibid.
10 See this chapter, 'Surprise – Unintended Consequences,' 99.
11 See chapter 5.

12 See chapter 2, 'Designing Out the Problem,' p. 70.

13 See chapter 8.

14 See chapter 6.

15 A. Hunt, *Explorations in Law and Society: Toward a Constitutive Theory of Law* (New York: Routledge, 1993), 214.

16 Ibid., 214–15.

17 Poovey, *supra* note 5, 8.

18 D. Nelken, 'Beyond the Study of "Law and Society"'? – Henry's *Private Justice and O'Hagan's The End of Law?' American Bar Foundation Research Journal* [1986]: 323.

19 A classic example that Nelken cites is L. Friedman and S. Macaulay, eds, *Law and the Behavioural Sciences*, 2nd ed. (Indianapolis: Bobbs-Merrill, 1977), chap. 3, 'On the Impact of Law on Society,' and chap. 4, 'On the Impact of Society on Law.'

20 A model that itself is under attack: see 'You Can't Follow the Science Wars without a Battle Map,' *The Economist*, 13 December 1997, 77.

21 M. McCann, 'Causal versus Constitutive Explanations (or, On the Difficulty of Being So Positive ...),' *Law and Social Inquiry* 21 (1996): 457, 459; see also B. Garth and A. Sarat, 'Studying How Law Matters: An Introduction,' in Garth and Sarat, eds, *How Does Law Matter?* (Evanston, Ill.: Northwestern University Press, 1998), 1, comparing 'instrumental' approaches and 'constitutive' approaches. Chapter 4 of this book addresses those approaches directly: see 'Instrumentalism,' p. 114, and 'Law (Re)Constituting Social and Political Relationships,' p. 126.

22 The most illustrious proponent of this position may be D. Black: see *The Behavior of Law* (New York: Academic Press, 1976) and *Sociological Justice* (New York: Oxford University Press, 1989).

23 Nelken, *supra* note 18, 325.

24 Ibid. Nelken cites examples of this position in E.P. Thompson, *Whigs and Hunters* (Harmondsworth, Eng.: Penguin; New York: Pantheon Books, 1975) and D. Kairy, *The Politics of Law: A Progressive Critique* (New York: Pantheon Books, 1982).

25 P. Ewick and S. Silbey, *The Common Place of Law: Stories from Everyday Life* (Chicago: University of Chicago Press, 1998), 22.

26 McCann, *supra* note 21, 460.

27 Ibid., 460.

28 Ibid., 462.

29 Ibid., 463–4.

30 See chapter 4, 'Law as a Resource for (Re)Constituting Social and Political Relationships,' p. 126.

31 M. McCann, *Rights at Work: Pay Equity Reform and the Politics of Legal Mobilization* (Chicago: University of Chicago Press, 1994), 15.

32 R. Cotterrell, *The Sociology of Law: An Introduction*, 2nd ed. (London: Butterworths, 1992), 13–14.

33 E. Mertz, 'A New Social Constructionism for Sociolegal Studies,' *Law and Society Review* 28 (1994): 1243, 1261.

34 A. Sarat, 'Off to Meet the Wizard: Beyond Validity and Reliability in the Search for a Post-Empiricist Sociology of Law,' *Law and Social Inquiry* 15 (1990): 155, 165.

35 Cotterrell, *supra* note 32, 4.

36 See chapter 4, 'The Impact of Litigation Regarding Social Change – "American Exceptionalism" II,' p. 144.

37 G. Rosenberg, *The Hollow Hope: Can Courts Bring about Social Change?* (Chicago: University of Chicago Press, 1991), 107–9 (discussing issues of causation in the context of the influence of courts upon civil rights).

38 Cook and Campbell, *supra* note 2, 9–37.

39 Ibid., 91–5.

40 Rosenberg, *supra* note 37.

41 C. Frankfort-Nachmias and D. Nachmias, *Research Methods in the Social Sciences*, 5th ed. (New York: St Martin's Press, 1996), chap. 7, 'Measurement.'

42 F. Zimring, 'Methods for Measuring General Deterrence: A Plea for the Field Experiment,' in M. Friedland, *Sanctions and Rewards in the Legal System: A Multidisciplinary Approach* (Toronto: University of Toronto Press, 1989), 99.

43 L. Ross et al., 'Determining the Social Effects of a Legal Reform: The British "Breathalyser" Crackdown of 1967,' *American Behavioral Scientist* 13 (1970): 493, 494.

44 R. Lempert, 'Strategies of Research Design in the Legal Impact Study: The Control of Plausible Rival Hypotheses,' *Law and Society Review* 1 (1966): 111.

45 Cook and Campbell, *supra* note 2, 50–70.

46 Ross, *supra* note 43, 494–5; Lempert, *supra* note 44, 122–32.

47 Lempert, *supra* note 44, 120, drawing upon an example in A. Rose, *Theory and Method in the Social Sciences* (Minneapolis: University of Minnesota Press, 1954).

48 Ibid., 122–32.

49 Ibid., 131.

50 Ibid.

51 D. Campbell and J. Stanley, *Experimental and Quasi-Experimental Designs for Research* (Boston: Houghton Mifflin, 1966), 47.

52 The example of gun control and related methodological difficulties deter-

mining impact are illustrated by the following debate: C. Britt et al., 'A Reassessment of the D.C. Gun Law: Some Cautionary Notes on the Use of Interrupted Time Series Designs for Policy Impact Assessments,' *Law and Society Review* 30 (1996): 361; D. McDowall et al., 'Using Quasi-Experiments to Evaluate Firearms Laws: Comment on Britt et al.'s Reassessment of the D.C. Gun Law,' *Law and Society Review* 30 (1996): 381; C. Britt et al., 'Avoidance and Misunderstanding: A Rejoinder to McDowall et al.,' *Law and Society Review* 30 (1996): 393.

53 Britt et al., 'A Reassessment of the D.C. Gun Law,' *supra* note 52, 365.

54 W. Charemza and D. Deadman, *New Directions in Econometric Practice: General to Specific Modelling, Cointegration, and Vector Autoregression* (Lyme, N.H.: Edward Elgar Publishing, 1997); G. Maddala, *Introduction to Econometrics* (New York: Macmillan Publishing, 1988); and D. Pyle and D. Deadman, 'Assessing the Impact of Legal Reform by Intervention Analysis,' *International Review of Law and Economics* 13 (1993): 193.

55 Britt et al., 'A Reassessment of the D.C. Gun Law,' *supra* note 52, 369.

56 L. McCain and R. McCleary, 'The Statistical Analysis of the Simple Interrupted Time-Series Quasi-Experiment,' in Cook and Campbell, *supra* note 2.

57 Britt et al., 'A Reassessment of the D.C. Gun Law,' *supra* note 52, 369.

58 Ibid., 370.

59 Ibid., 371.

60 Cook and Campbell, *supra* note 2, 70–80.

61 Rosenberg, *supra* note 37, 455.

62 E. Tenner, *Why Things Bite Back: Technology and the Revenge of Unintended Consequences* (New York: Alfred A. Knopf, 1996), 255.

63 Ibid., xi.

64 Mertz, *supra* note 33, 1246–8.

65 For example, see M. Gerson, ed., *The Essential Neo-Conservative Reader* (Reading, Mass.: Addison-Wesley, 1996); in particular, see the foreword by J. Wilson.

66 Tenner, *supra* note 62, 270.

67 J. Wilson, 'Foreword,' to Gerson, *supra* note 65, vii–viii.

68 W. Safire, 'No Pol Will Tell You,' *New York Times*, 26 September 1996, A11. See also, generally, the debates over raising the federal minimum-wage laws in 1996: e.g., D. Rosenbaum, 'Much Bluster over 90 Cents,' *New York Times*, 30 April 1996, A1.

69 D. Card and A. Krueger, 'Minimum Wages and Employment: A Case-Study of the Fast Food Industry in New Jersey and Pennsylvania,' *American Economic Review* 84 (1994): 772, 776–7. This study has, itself, been heavily

criticized: see 'Of Magic, Myth, and the Minimum Wage,' *The Economist*, 30 September 1995, 94.

70 R. Howse, 'Retrenchment, Reform, or Revolution? The Shift to Incentives and the Future of the Regulatory State,' *Alberta Law Review* 31 (1993): 455, 472, citing W. Streek, 'Comment on Ronald Dore, "Rigidities in the Labour Market,"' *Government and Opposition* 23 (1990): 413, 420.

71 Ibid., 472.

72 U.S. Constitution, Amendment XVIII.

73 For a discussion of prohibition and its impact, see Cotterrell, *supra* note 32, 55.

74 Ibid., 55.

75 Ibid., 55–6.

76 A. Sinclair, *Prohibition: The Era of Excess* (Boston: Little, Brown, 1962), 249.

77 J. Griffith, 'Is Law Important,' *New York University Law Review* 54 (1979): 339, 355.

78 F. Dobyns, *The Amazing Story of Repeal: An Exposé of the Power of Propaganda* (Chicago: Willet, Clark and Co., 1940).

79 J. Gusfield, *Symbolic Crusade: Status Politics and the American Temperance Movement* (Urbana, Ill.: University of Illinois Press, 1963).

80 Ibid., 1.

81 For example, D. Canon, *Race, Redistributing, and Representation: The Unintended Consequences of Black Majority Districts* (Chicago: University of Chicago Press, 1999) and C. Wichmann, 'Ridding FOIA of Those "Unanticipated Consequences" Repairing a Necessary Road to Freedom,' *Duke Law Journal* 47 (1998): 1213. See also R. Posner, 'The Decline of Law as an Autonomous Discipline: 1962–1987,' *Harvard Law Review* 100 (1987): 761, 770–1.

82 T. Franck, *The Power of Legitimacy among Nations* (New York: Oxford University Press, 1990) and 'Legitimacy in the International Systems,' *American Journal of International Law* 82 (1988): 705.

83 L. Pal, 'Speak Loudly and Carry Small Sticks,' *Literary Review of Canada*, September 1995, 15–16.

84 K. Nossal, *Rain Dancing: Sanctions in Canadian and Australian Foreign Policy* (Toronto: University of Toronto Press, 1994).

85 M. Miyagawa, *Do Economic Sanctions Work?* (New York: St Martin's Press, 1992), 206–7.

86 Nossal, *supra* note 84, 267.

87 Ibid., 265.

88 Ibid.

89 J. Dashti-Gibson et al., 'On the Determinants of the Success of Economic Sanctions: An Empirical Analysis,' *American Journal of Political Science* 41 (1997): 608 (analysing data collected in Hafbauer et al., *Economic Sanctions Reconsidered: History and Current Policy*, 2nd ed. (Washington: Institute for International Economics, 1990).

90 Ibid., 616–17.

91 Ibid., 613.

92 Nossal, *supra* note 84, 267.

93 S. Carrol, *No-Fault Approaches to Compensating People Injured in Automobile Accidents* (Santa Monica, Calif.: Institute for Civil Justice, 1991), 1.

94 M. Trebilcock, 'Incentive Issues in the Design of "No-Fault" Compensation,' *University of Toronto Law Journal* 39 (1989): 19, 28–9.

95 Ibid.

96 M. Gaudry, 'The Effects on Road Safety of the Compulsory Insurance, Flat Premium Rating and No-Fault Features of the 1978 Quebec Automobile Act,' appendix to *Report of the Inquiry into Motor Vehicle Accident Compensation in Ontario* (Osborne Report) (Ontario: Queen's Printer, 1988) and R. Devlin, 'Liability versus No-Fault Automobile Insurance Regimes: An Analysis of the Experience in Quebec,' paper presented at Canadian Economics Association meeting, Windsor, Ontario, 3 June 1988.

97 Trebilcock, *supra* note 94, 29.

98 R. Devlin, 'Liability versus No-Fault Automobile Insurance Regimes: An Analysis of the Experience in Quebec,' PhD thesis, University of Toronto, 1988.

99 D. Dewees et al., *Exploring the Domain of Accident Law* (New York: Oxford University Press, 1996), 22–6.

100 Ibid., 26.

101 Ibid.

102 L. Weitzman, *The Divorce Revolution: The Unexpected Consequences for Women and Children in America* (New York: The Free Press, 1985), xii; but see H. Peters, 'Marriage and Divorce: Informational Constraints and Private Contracting,' *American Economic Review* 76 (1986): 437.

103 See R. Peterson, 'A Re-evaluation of the Economic Consequences of Divorce,' *American Sociological Review* 61 (1996): 528; L. Weitzman, 'The Economic Consequences of Divorce Are Still Unequal: Comment on Peterson,' *American Sociological Review* 61 (1996): 537; and R. Peterson, 'Statistical Errors, Faulty Conclusions, Misguided Policy: Reply to Weitzman,' *American Sociological Review* 61 (1996): 539.

104 H. Jacob, 'Another Look at No-Fault Divorce and the Post-Divorce Finances of Women,' *Law and Society Review* 23 (1989): 95.

105 M. Glendon, *A Nation under Lawyers: How the Crisis in the Legal Profession Is Transforming American Society* (New York: Farrar, Straus and Giroux, 1994), 275–6.

106 Ibid., 276.

107 For example, see L. Bradford, 'The Counterrevolution: A Critique of Recent Proposals to Reform No-Fault Divorce Laws,' *Stanford Law Review* 49 (1997): 607 and R. Gordon, 'The Limits of Limits on Divorce,' *Yale Law Journal* 107 (1998): 1435.

108 Dewees et al., *supra* note 99, 427–8.

109 Tenner, *supra* note 62, xi.

Chapter Four: Six Ideas about the Impact of Law

1 For example, see R. Cotterrell, *The Sociology of Law: An Introduction*, 2nd ed. (London: Butterworths, 1992), a work that is particularly good regarding the history of ideas about the influence of law; see also C. Auerbach, 'The Relation of Legal Systems to Social Change,' *Wisconsin Law Review* (1980): 1227 and R. Abel, 'Law as Lag: Inertia as a Social Theory of Law,' *Michigan Law Review* 80 (1982): 78.

2 For example, see this chapter, 'Law Acting in Concert with Social and Political Forces' (p. 120), for Marx's ideas about law.

3 For example, see chapter 8, 'Theoretical Approaches to Pornography' (p. 25) for a discussion of John Stuart Mill and the 'harm principle.'

4 For a thoughtful account of the history of ideas in the USA regarding law see S. Feldman, *American Legal Thought from Premodernism to Postmodernism: An Intellectual Voyage* (New York: Oxford University Press, 2000).

5 M. Galanter, 'The Radiating Effects of Courts,' in K. Boyum and L. Mather, eds, *Empirical Theories about Courts* (New York: Longman, 1983), 127.

6 I. Jenkins, *Social Order and the Limits of Law* (Princeton: Princeton University Press, 1980), xi.

7 J. Griffiths, 'Is Law Important?' *New York University Law Review* 54 (1979): 339, 343.

8 Ibid., 347.

9 R. Summers, *Instrumentalism and American Legal Theory* (Ithaca: Cornell University Press, 1982), 30.

10 H. Lasswell and M. McDougal, 'Legal Education and Public Policy: Professional Training in the Public Interest,' *Yale Law Journal* 52 (1943): 203.

11 Griffiths, *supra* note 7, 372, n. 74 (citations omitted).

12 Lasswell and McDougal, *supra* note 10, 232.

13 Ibid., 291–2.

14 Summers, *supra* note 9, 29.

15 Ibid., 20.

16 For example, see Jenkins, *supra* note 6, xi: '[W]e regard it as able to decide and effect anything at all ... [W]e think of it as an autonomous and self-sufficient force upon which the rest of the social order depends but which itself depends upon nothing.'

17 D. Nelken, 'Legislation and Its Constraints: A Case Study of the 1965 British Rent Act,' in A. Podgorecki et al., eds, *Legal Systems and Social Systems* (London: Croom Helm, 1985), 74.

18 Ibid.; D. Nelken, *The Limits of the Legal Process: A Study of Landlords, Law, and Crime* (Toronto: Academic Press, 1983) and 'The "Gap Problem" in the Sociology of Law: A Theoretical Review,' *Windsor Yearbook Access to Justice* 1 (1981): 35.

19 Nelken, *supra* note 17, 85.

20 D. Trubek, 'Back to the Future: The Short, Happy Life of the Law and Society Movement,' *Florida State University Law Review* 18 (1990–1): 1, 42.

21 D. Trubek and M. Galanter, 'Scholars in Self-Estrangement: Some Reflections on the Crisis in Law and Development Studies in the United States,' *Wisconsin Law Review* [1974]: 1062, 1067–8, n. 16, quoting Justice William O. Douglas.

22 Griffiths, *supra* note 7, 350–1.

23 Trubek and Galanter, *supra* note 21, 1072.

24 Ibid., 1074.

25 Griffiths, *supra* note 7, 350–1, citing D. Trubek, 'Toward a Social Theory of Law: An Essay on the Study of Law and Development,' *Yale Law Journal* 82 (1972): 1; and Trubek and Galanter, *supra* note 21.

26 Trubek, *supra* note 20, 37–8.

27 Trubek and Galanter, *supra* note 21, 1092.

28 Griffiths, *supra* note 7, citing R. Pozen, *Legal Choices for State Enterprises in the Third World* (New York: New York University Press, 1976).

29 C. Rose, 'The "New" Law and Development Movement in the Post-Cold War Era: A Vietnam Case Study,' *Law and Society Review* 32 (1998): 93.

30 'Reassessing Reform – Structural Complications in Exporting and Importing the Rule of Law,' *Researching Law* 1, vol. 11, 4 (Fall 2000) (Chicago: American Bar Foundation), discussing work of B. Garth and Y. Dezalay.

31 T. Ginsburg, 'Does Law Matter for Economic Development? Evidence from East Asia,' *Law and Society Review* 34 (2000): 829.

32 P.S. Atiyah, 'Tort Law and the Alternatives: Some Anglo-American Comparisons,' *Duke Law Journal* [1987] 1002, 1018 and cf. B. Markesinis, 'Litiga-

tion-Mania in England, Germany, and the USA: Are We So Different?'
Cambridge Law Journal [1990]: 233.

33 D. Dewees and M. Trebilcock, 'The Efficacy of the Tort System and Its Alternatives: A Review of Empirical Evidence,' *Osgoode Hall Law Journal* 30
(1992): 57; R. Epstein, 'The Social Consequences of Common Law Rules,'
Harvard Law Review 95 (1982): 1717.

34 D. Dewees, D. Duff, and M. Trebilcock, *Exploring the Domain of Accident
Law: Taking the Facts Seriously* (New York: Oxford University Press,
1996).

35 Ibid., 414.

36 Ibid., v.

37 Ibid.

38 G. Robertson, 'Informed Consent in Canada: An Empirical Study,' *Osgoode
Hall Law Journal* 22 (1984): 139; see also J. Wiley, 'The Impact of Judicial
Decisions on Professional Conduct: An Empirical Study,' *Southern California
Law Review* 55 (1982): 345, but cf. D. Givelber et al., '*Tarasoff*, Myth and Real-
ity: An Empirical Study of Private Law in Action,' *Wisconsin Law Review*
[1984]: 443.

39 *Reibl v. Hughes*, [1980] 2 S.C.R. 880.

40 For example, the General Counsel to the Canadian Medical Protective
Association contended: 'No legal event in the last fifty years has so dis-
turbed the practice of medicine as did the decision of the Supreme Court of
Canada in *Reibl* v. *Hughes*'; quoted in Robertson, *supra* note 38 n. 5, 140. The
author of a leading book on torts, himself a judge, opined: 'The ultimate
effect of [the case] should be medical practitioners who are even more sensitive, concerned and humane than they now are. Moreover, the doctor-
patient relationship should be improved greatly by the better communication between doctors and their patients' – Justice Linden in *White v. Turner*
(1981), 120 D.L.R. (3d) 269, 290 (Ont. S.C.) quoted in Robertson, *supra* note
38, 140.

41 G. Robertson, 'Informed Consent Ten Years Later: The Impact of *Reibl* v.
Hughes,' *Canadian Bar Review* 70 (1991): 423.

42 For example, D. Givelber et al., *supra* note 38, 443; but cf. Wiley, *supra* note
38, 345.

43 Similar remarks could be made regarding efforts at tort reform in the USA:
papers on Institution see. e.g., P. Born and K. Viscusi, 'The Distribution of
the Insurance Market Effects of Tort Liability Reforms,' and T. Campbell et
al., 'The Link between Liability Reforms and Productivity: Some Empirical
Evidence,' in M. Baily et al., eds, Brookings, *Economic Activity* (Washington:
Brookings Institution, 1998), 55 and 107 respectively.

44 P. Bell and J. O'Connell, *Accidental Justice: The Dilemmas of Tort Law* (New Haven: Yale University Press, 1997).

45 Dewees et al., *supra* note 34, 414.

46 B. Ackerman, *Reconstructing American Law* (Cambridge, Mass.: Harvard University Press, 1984).

47 Ibid., 109.

48 L. Kalman, *The Strange Career of Legal Liberalism* (New Haven: Yale University Press, 1996).

49 See chapter 9.

50 Jenkins, *supra* note 6; R.A. Samek, 'A Case for Social Law Reform,' *Canadian Bar Review* 55 (1977): 409.

51 Jenkins, *supra* note 6, 371.

52 Ibid.

53 I. Ayres and J. Braithwaite, *Responsive Regulation: Transcending the Deregulation Debate* (New York: Oxford University Press, 1992); R. Cheit, *Setting Safety Standards: Regulation in the Public and Private Sectors* (Berkeley: University of California Press, 1990); B. Hutter, 'Regulation: Standard Setting and Enforcement,' *Law and Society Review* 27 (1993): 233.

54 Jenkins, *supra* note 6, 133–5.

55 Ibid., 135.

56 L. Barnett, *Legal Construct, Social Concept: A Macrosociological Perspective on Law* (New York: A. de Gruyter, 1993), ix.

57 Abel, *supra* note 1.

58 A. Hunt, *Explorations in Law and Society: Toward a Constitutive Theory of Law* (New York: Routledge, 1993), 25–32.

59 P. Yeager, *The Limits of Law: The Public Regulation of Private Pollution* (New York: Cambridge University Press, 1991), 25 (emphasis added).

60 Ibid., 25–6.

61 Ibid., 32.

62 See chapter 1.

63 Jenkins, *supra* note 6, 383.

64 See Chapter 1.

65 R. Unger, *Law in Modern Society* (New York: Free Press, 1976), 109.

66 F. Zakaria, 'Bigger than the Family, Smaller than the State,' *New York Times Review of Books*, 13 August 1995, 1, discussing F. Fukuyama, *Trust: The Social Virtues and the Creation of Prosperity* (New York: The Free Press, 1995).

67 M. Trebilcock, *The Limits of Freedom of Contract* (Cambridge, Mass.: Harvard University Press, 1993), 7.

68 C. Fried, *Contract as Promise: A Theory of Contractual Obligation* (Cambridge, Mass.: Harvard University Press, 1981), 132.

69 Trebilcock, *supra* note 67, 242.

70 Ibid., 9.

71 Ibid., 258.

72 C. Sunstein, *Free Markets and Social Justice* (New York: Oxford University Press, 1997), 9.

73 Ayres and Braithewaite, *supra* note 53, 7.

74 Ibid.

75 M. Valiante and W. Bogart, 'Helping "Concerned Volunteers Working out of Their Kitchens": Funding Citizen Participation in Administrative Decision Making,' *Osgoode Hall Law Journal* 31 (1993): 687.

76 Hutter, *supra* note 53, 233.

77 R. Cheit, *supra* note 53.

78 Jenkins, *supra* note 6, 231.

79 Hunt, *supra* note 58, 147.

80 M. Shultz, 'Can Dialogue Succeed Where Liberal Legalism Failed? The Reach Exceeds the Grasp,' *UCLA Law Review* 38 (1991): 1325, 1326.

81 Trubek, *supra* note 20, 45.

82 D. Engel, 'How Does Law Matter in the Constitution of Legal Consciousness?' in B. Garth and A. Sarat, *How Does Law Matter?* (Evanston, Ill.: Northwestern University Press, 1998), 109, 140–1.

83 Trubek, *supra* note 20, 46.

84 Ibid., 45.

85 Ibid., 46.

86 M. McCann, 'Law and Political Struggles for Social Change: Puzzles, Paradoxes, and Promises in Future Research,' in D. Schultz, ed., *Leveraging the Law: Using Courts to Achieve Social Change* (New York: Peter Lang Publishing, 1998), 319.

87 Ibid., 322.

88 J. Handler, *Law and the Search for Community* (Philadelphia: University of Philadelphia Press, 1990).

89 Shultz, *supra* note 80, 1327.

90 M. McCann, *Rights at Work: Pay Equity Reform and the Politics of Legal Mobilization* (Chicago: University of Chicago Press, 1994).

91 Ibid., 9.

92 M. McCann and H. Silverstein, 'Rethinking Law's "Allurements" – A Relational Analysis of Social Movement Lawyers in the United States,' in A. Sarat and S. Scheingold, eds, *Cause Lawyering: Political Commitments and Professional Responsibilities* (New York: Oxford University Press, 1998), 261.

93 See chapter 3.

94 Ibid., 'The Quandary of "Impartial" Perspective,' p. 87.

95 See G. Rosenberg, 'Positivism, Interpretivism, and the Study of Law,' *Law and Social Inquiry* 21 (1996): 435, and a reply, M. McCann, 'Causal versus Constitutive Explanations (or, On the Difficulty of Being so Positive ...)' *Law and Social Inquiry* 21 (1996): 457. I have put the description of Rosenberg as a 'positivist' in quotations because he insists his approach defies such compartmentalization and the best work should combine aspects of both approaches: 455.

96 Rosenberg, *supra* note 95, 435.

97 Ibid., 447.

98 Ibid., 447. Rosenberg suggests that the presence of union activity was the critical determinant: 449.

99 Ibid., 448.

100 McCann, *supra* note 90, 150.

101 Ibid., 4.

102 Rosenberg, *supra* note 95, 453.

103 Hunt, *supra* note 58, 166.

104 Ibid., 94.

105 See Rosenberg, *supra* note 95, 435–6: 'One school of thought argues that the law is tied to dominant interests of class, gender, race, and hierarchy and thus is incapable of helping proponents of social change.' While acknowledging the difficulties of characterization he cites the following as proponents of that position: J. Appleby, 'The American Heritage: The Heirs and the Disinherited,' *Journal of American History* 74 (1987): 798; A. Freeman, 'Racism, Rights, and the Quest for Equality of Opportunity: A Critical Legal Essay,' *Harvard Civil Rights – Civil Liberties Law Review* 23 (1988): 295; P. Gabel and D. Kennedy, 'Roll Over Beethoven,' *Stanford Law Review* 36 (1984): 1; J. Horowitz, 'Rights,' *Harvard Civil Rights – Civil Liberties Law Review* 23 (1988): 393; M. Tushnet, 'An Essay on Rights,' *Texas Law Review* 62 (1984): 1363.

106 Barnett, *supra* note 56, 162.

107 H. Arthurs, *'Without the Law': Administrative Justice and Legal Pluralism in Nineteenth-Century England* (Toronto: University of Toronto Press, 1985).

108 See Chapter 7.

109 See Chapter 8.

110 C. Smart, *Feminism and the Power of the Law* (New York: Routledge, 1989).

111 Ibid., 161.

112 Ibid., 165.

113 Ibid., 161.

114 For an illustration of this argument, based on empirical investigation of the impact of 'no fault' divorce reform on the economic conditions of

women and children, see L. Weitzman, *The Divorce Revolution: The Unexpected Social and Economic Consequences for Women and Children in America* (New York: The Free Press, 1985); but cf. H. Jacob, 'Another Look at No-Fault Divorce and the Post-Divorce Finances of Women,' *Law and Society Review* 23 (1989): 95. See the discussion of this point in chapter 3, 'Surprise – Unintended Consequences,' p. 99.

115 Smart, *supra* note 110.
116 Ibid., 51.
117 For example, see Jenkins, *supra* note 6.
118 R. Ellickson, *Order without Law: How Neighbors Settle Disputes* (Cambridge, Mass.: Harvard University Press, 1991).
119 Ibid., 4.
120 Ibid., 281.
121 Ibid., 286.
122 Some have been quick to point out that close relations can also foster some most unattractive conditions, for example, in terms of the family and domestic violence: see J. Norgren, 'Book Review: *Order without Law: How Neighbors Settle Disputes*' (1993), 16 (1993): *Legal Studies Forum* 475.
123 'Riding Herd on Coase's Cattle,' *Harvard Law Review* 105 (1992): 1141.
124 R. Ellickson, 'Controlling Chronic Misconduct in City Spaces: Of Panhandlers, Skid Rows, and Public-Space Zoning,' *Yale Law Journal* 105 (1996): 1165.
125 'Riding Herd,' *supra* note 123, 1144.
126 J. Rosen, 'The Social Police,' *The New Yorker*, 20–27 October 1997, 170.
127 E. Posner, 'The Regulation of Groups: The Influence of Legal and Nonlegal Sanctions on Collective Action,' *University of Chicago Law Review* 63 (1996): 133.
128 C. Sunstein, 'Social Norms and Social Roles,' *Columbia Law Review* 96 (1996): 903, 905.
129 T. Meares, 'It's a Question of Connections,' *Valparaiso University Law Review* 31 (1997): 579; T. Meares, 'Rewards for Good Behavior: Influencing Prosecutorial Discretion and Conduct with Financial Incentives,' *Fordham Law Review* 64 (1995): 851; T. Meares and D. Kahan, 'Law and (Norms of) Order in the Inner City,' *Law and Society Review* 32 (1998): 805.
130 D. Kahan, 'What Do Alternative Sanctions Mean?' *University of Chicago Law Review* 63 (1996): 591.
131 L. Lessig, 'The Regulation of Social Meaning,' *University of Chicago Law Review* 62 (1995): 943.
132 Ibid., 1025–34; Sunstein, *supra* note 128.
133 Rosen, *supra* note 126, 178–9.

Date	Details

Inventory Record

Details	

Product #16025

134 C. Sunstein, 'Deliberative Trouble? Why Groups Go to Extremes,' *Yale Law Journal* 110 (2000): 71.

135 Posner, *supra* note 127.

136 Rosen, *supra* note 126, 179.

137 Ibid., 175.

138 R. Kagan, 'What Makes Uncle Sammy Sue?' *Law and Society Review* 21 (1988): 717.

139 Ibid.

140 See R. Kagan, 'Adversarial Legalism and American Government,' *Journal of Policy Analysis and Management* 10 (1991): 369, 372 n. 1, for an extensive list of comparative studies involving the USA and other countries. See also R. Kagan and L. Axelrad, 'Adversarial Legalism: An International Perspective,' in P. Nivola, ed., *Comparative Disadvantages?: Social Regulations and the Global Economy* (Washington: Brookings Institution Press, 1997); some of Kagan's contentions regarding 'adversarial legalism' and his responses are contained in C. Busch et al., 'Taming Adversarial Legalism: The Port of Oakland's Dredging Saga Revisited,' R. Kagan, 'Adversarial Legalism: Tamed or Still Wild?' and C. Busch et al., 'Rights, Politics and Expertise: Righting the Balance,' *New York Journal of Legislation and Public Policy* (1999): 179, 217, and 247 respectively.

141 S. Kelman, *Regulating America, Regulating Sweden: A Comparative Study of Occupational Safety and Health Policy* (Cambridge, Mass.: MIT Press, 1981).

142 D. Vogel, *National Styles of Regulation: Environmental Policy in Great Britain and the United States* (Ithaca: Cornell University Press, 1986).

143 M. Friedland et al., *Regulating Traffic Safety* (Toronto: University of Toronto Press, 1990), 143ff.

144 J. Braithwaite, 'Negotiation versus Litigation: Industry Regulation in Great Britain and the United States,' *American Bar Foundation Research Journal* (1987): 559.

145 See *infra* notes 153–8 and 183.

146 For the use of the phrase 'American Exceptionalism' applied to the society generally, see S. Lipset, *American Exceptionalism: A Double-Edged Sword* (New York: W.W. Norton and Co., 1996). For its use applied to law, see Braithwaite, *supra* note 144, 564; and Dane Archer, quoted in *Focus on Law Studies* 12, 2 (1997): 1 with regard to the death penalty.

147 Lipset, *American Exceptionalism*, 26.

148 Ibid.

149 Ibid., 270.

150 Ibid., 26.

151 Ibid., 270.

152 Ibid.
153 For example, see V. Hamilton and J. Sanders, *Everyday Justice: Responsibility and the Individual in Japan and the United States* (New Haven: Yale University Press, 1992); J. Sanders et al., 'The Institutionalization of Sanctions for Wrongdoing Inside Organizations: Public Judgments in Japan, Russia, and the United States,' *Law and Society Review* 32 (1998): 871; S. Miyazawa, 'The Enigma of Japan as a Testing Ground for Cross-Cultural Criminological Studies' and E. Feldman, 'Patients' Rights, Citizens' Movements and Japanese Legal Culture,' in D. Nelken, ed., *Comparing Legal Cultures* (Brookfield, Conn.: Dartmouth, 1997), 195 and 215, respectively.
154 H. Jacob, 'Conclusion,' in H. Jacob et al., *Courts, Law, and Politics in Comparative Perspective* (New Haven: Yale University Press, 1996), 398; and J. Sanders, 'Courts and Law in Japan,' in ibid.
155 J. Ramseyer and M. Nakazato, *Japanese Law: An Economic Approach* (Chicago: University of Chicago Press, 1999).
156 Lipset, *supra* note 146, 227.
157 Ibid., 227, quoting Hamilton and Sanders, *supra* note 153, 158–9.
158 Ibid., 228, quoting J. Haley, *Authority without Power: Law and the Japanese Paradox* (New York: Oxford University Press, 1991), 14.
159 Vogel, *supra* note 142.
160 Ibid., 153.
161 Ibid.
162 Kagan, *supra* note 138, 723.
163 Vogel, *supra* note 142, 267.
164 Ibid.
165 Kagan, *supra* note 138, 723.
166 Kelman, *supra* note 141, 197.
167 D. Vogel, 'The "New" Social Regulation in Historical and Comparative Perspective,' in T. McCraw, ed., *Regulation in Perspective: Historical Essays* (Cambridge, Mass.: Harvard University Press, 1981), 183.
168 Ibid., 242.
169 Kagan, *supra* note 138, 727.
170 J. Prichard, 'A Systematic Approach to Comparative Law: The Effect of Cost, Fee, and Financing Rules on the Development of Substantive Law,' *Journal of Legal Studies* 17 (1988): 451.
171 Vogel, *supra* note 167, 184–5.
172 Kagan, *supra* note 138, 726.
173 Braithwaite, *supra* note 144, 574.
174 M. Glendon, *Rights Talk: The Impoverishment of Political Discourse* (New York: The Free Press, 1991), 9.

175 Kagan, 'Adversarial Legalism and American Government,' *supra* note 140, 397–8.

176 C. Epp, *The Rights Revolution: Lawyers, Activists, and Supreme Courts in Comparative Perspective* (Chicago: University of Chicago Press, 1998); N. Tate and T. Vallinder, *The Global Expansion of Judicial Power* (New York: New York University Press, 1995)

177 H. Jacob, *supra* note 154, 'Conclusion,' 394.

178 Kalman, *supra* note 48.

179 See R. Dahl, 'Decision-Making in a Democracy: The Role of the Supreme Court as a National Policy-Maker,' *Journal of Public Law* 6 (1957): 279; and A. Bickel, *The Least Dangerous Branch: The Supreme Court at the Bar of Politics* (Indianapolis: Bobbs-Merrill, 1962).

180 See J. Handler, *Social Movements and the Legal System: A Theory of Law Reform and Social Change* (New York: Academic Press, 1978).

181 G. Rosenberg, *The Hollow Hope: Can Courts Bring about Social Change?* (Chicago: University of Chicago Press, 1991); Kalman, *supra* note 48.

182 See, e.g., M. Galanter, 'Why the "Haves" Come Out Ahead: Speculations on the Limits of Legal Change,' *Law and Society Review* 9 (1974): 95; M. Galanter, *supra*, note 5; R. Mnookin and L. Kornhauser, 'Bargaining in the Shadow of the Law: The Case of Divorce,' *Yale Law Journal* 88 (1979): 950.

183 E. Feldman, 'Blood Justice: Courts, Conflict, and Compensation in Japan, France, and the United States,' *Law and Society Review* 34 (2000): 651.

184 Rosenberg, *supra* note 181, 171.

185 Ibid., 7f.

186 Ibid., 21f.

187 Ibid., 2.

188 Ibid., 27.

189 Ibid., 25.

190 Ibid., 36.

191 For example, see C. Sunstein, 'How Independent Is the Court?' *New York Review of Books*, 22 October 1992, 47; J. Simon, '"The Long Walk Home" to Politics,' *Law and Society Review* 26 (1992): 923; and see the critical reviews of M. Feeley and M. McCann and Rosenberg's response in 'Review Section Symposium – The Supreme Court and Social Change,' *Law and Social Inquiry* 17 (1993): 715; and N. Devins, 'Judicial Matters,' *California Law Review* 80 (1992): 1027.

192 Rosenberg, *supra* note 181, 338 (emphasis in original).

193 Ibid., 341.

194 M. Feeley and E. Rubin, *Judicial Policy Making and the Modern State: How the*

Courts Reformed America's Prisons (New York: Cambridge University Press, 1998).

195 D. Reed, 'Twenty-Five Years after *Rodriguez*: School Finance Litigation and the Impact of the New Judicial Federalism,' *Law and Society Review* 32 (1998): 175.

196 B. Canon and C. Johnson, *Judicial Policies: Implementation and Impact*, 2nd. ed. (Washington: Congressional Quarterly Press, 1999), 211ff.

197 P. Schuck, 'Public Law Litigation and Social Reform,' *Yale Law Journal* 102 (1993): 1763.

198 See also D. Schultz and S. Gottlieb, 'Legal Functionalism and Social Change: A Reassessment of Rosenberg's *The Hollow Hope*,' in Schultz, *supra* note 86, 169 (esp. 'Social Science and Historical Positivism'), 190–1.

199 Schuck, *supra* note 197, 1785–6.

200 Ibid., 1786.

201 See '3. Law as a Resource for (Re)Constituting Social and Political Relationships.'

202 Chapter 3, 'The Quandary of "Impartial" Perspective,' p. 84.

203 See also the criticisms of Schultz and Gottlieb, *supra* note 198, 190ff.

204 McCann, *supra* note 95, 460.

205 Further responses by Rosenberg to his critics appear in G. Rosenberg, 'Knowledge and Desire: Thinking about Courts and Social Change,' in Schultz, *supra* note 86, 251.

206 M. Glendon, 'A Beau Mentir Qui Vient de Loin: The 1988 Canadian Abortion Decision in Comparative Perspective,' *North Western University Law Review* 83 (1989): 569, 588.

207 M. Schudson, *The Good Citizen: A History of American Civic Life* (New York: The Free Press, 1998), 8.

208 Part I of the *Constitution Act, 1982*, being Schedule B to the *Canada Act* 1982 (U.K.), 1982, c. 11.

209 Ibid., s. 1.

210 Epp, *supra* note 176; the quotes are taken from the titles to chapters 9 and 10, dealing with Canada.

211 Ibid., 157–60; S. Lipset, *Continental Divide: The Values and Institutions of the United States and Canada* (New York: Routledge, 1990); W. Bogart, *Courts and Country: The Limits of Litigation and the Social and Political Life of Canada* (Toronto: Oxford University Press, 1994), chapter 1, 'Preserving Its Identity by Having Many Identities.'

212 W. Christian and C. Campbell, *Political Parties and Ideologies in Canada*, 3rd ed. (Toronto: McGraw-Hill Ryerson, 1990).

213 P. Russell, 'The Political Purposes of the Canadian Charter of Rights and Freedoms,' *Canadian Bar Review* 61 (1983): 30.

214 J. Fudge, 'The Canadian Charter of Rights: Redistribution, Recognition, and the Imperialism of Courts,' in T. Campbell et al., eds, *Entrenching Human Rights: A Skeptical Assessment* (Oxford: Oxford University Press, forthcoming 2001).

215 These points are discussed in chapter 5.

216 'Canada – The Quiet Way,' *The Economist*, 4 September 1999, 41. Saskatchewan and Manitoba did elect moderate social-democratic governments in the latter part of the 1990s.

217 P. Ryscavage, *Income Inequality in America: An Analysis of Trends* (Armonk, NY: M.E. Sharpe, 1999), chap. 7, 'International Comparisons.'

218 Lipset, *supra* note 146, 116ff.; J. Maxwell, 'Don't Be Seduced by the US Boom. Averages Lie,' *Globe and Mail*, 30 August 1999, A13.

219 Ryscavage, *supra* note 217.

220 A. Golden, 'We're Stealing from Our Kids,' *Globe and Mail*, 8 August 2000, A15.

Chapter Five: Punishment – and Capital Punishment

1 See the discussion in chapter 4, 'The Impact of Litigation Regarding Social Change – 'American Exceptionalism II,' p. 144.

2 See the discussion in chapter 3, 'Surprise – Unintended Consequences,' p. 99.

3 See the discussion in chapter 4.

4 S. Christianson, *With Liberty for Some: 500 Years of Imprisonment in America* (Boston: Northeastern University Press, 1998), x.

5 See the discussion in chapter 1, 'Why a Turning to Law?' p. 37.

6 See chapter 2.

7 Ibid., 'How Best to Deter,' p. 57.

8 Ibid.

9 F. Zimring and G. Hawkins, *Deterrence: The Legal Context in Crime Control* (Chicago: University of Chicago Press, 1973), 5.

10 Ibid.

11 A. Dershowitz, *Contrary to Popular Opinion* (New York: Pharos Books, 1992), 127–8.

12 W.A. Bogart, *Courts and Country: The Limits of Litigation and the Social and Political Life of Canada* (Toronto: Oxford University Press, 1994); see chap. 7, 'The Courts and Two Models of the Criminal Law.'

13 L. Friedman, *Crime and Punishment in American History* (New York: Basic Books, 1993), 14 (emphasis in original).

14 F. Butterfield, 'Property Crimes Steadily Decline, Led by Burglary,' *New York Times*, 12 October 1997, A1.

15 F. Butterfield, 'Homicides Plunge 11 Percent in U.S., F.B.I. Report Says,' *New York Times*, 2 June 1997, A1.

16 M. Janofsky, 'Missing Trend, Some Cities See Murders Rise,' *New York Times*, 15 January 1998, A1.

17 Butterfield, *supra* note 15, A1.

18 F. Zimring and G. Hawkins, *Crime Is Not the Problem: Lethal Violence in America* (New York: Oxford University Press, 1997), 4–6; 'Violent and Irrational – and That's Just the Policy,' *The Economist*, 8 June 1996, 23.

19 Butterfield, *supra* note 14, citing Professor F. Zimring.

20 Zimring and Hawkins, *supra* note 18, 7.

21 'Violent and Irrational,' *The Economist*, *supra* note 18.

22 W. Kaminer, 'Federal Offense,' *The Atlantic Monthly*, June 1994, 102, 105.

23 US Department of Justice, *Sourcebook of Criminal Justice Statistics* (1989), 582 as cited in Friedman, *supra* note 13, 316 f.86.

24 F. Butterfield, ' "Defying Gravity," Inmate Population Climbs,' *New York Times*, 19 January 1998, A10.

25 Zimring and Hawkins, *supra* note 18, 11.

26 L. Windlesham, *Politics, Punishment, and Populism* (New York: Oxford University Press, 1998), 224 (table 5), citing statistics from the Sentencing Project, Washington, 1997.

27 Christianson, *supra* note 4, 284.

28 Windlesham, *supra* note 26, 220.

29 J. Short, *Poverty, Ethnicity, and Violent Crime* (Boulder, Co.: Westview Press, 1997), 187.

30 Kaminer, *supra* note 22, 105.

31 T. Appleby, 'Crime Rate Falls Again, Except among Teen Girls,' *Globe and Mail*, 23 July 1998, A1, 8; W. Walker, 'Canada's Crime Rate Lowest in 20 Years,' *Toronto Star*, 22 July 1999, A1, 16.

32 F. Butterfield, 'Reason for Dramatic Drop in Crime Puzzles the Experts,' *New York Times*, 29 March 1998, A16; A. Blumstein and J. Wallman, eds, *The Crime Drop in America* (New York: Cambridge University Press, 2000).

33 'Violent and Irrational,' *The Economist*, *supra* note 18, 24; F. Butterfield, 'Drop in Homicide Rate Linked to Crack's Decline,' *New York Times*, 27 October 1997, A12.

34 'Crime in America: Defeating the Bad Guys,' *The Economist*, 3 October 1998, 35.

35 A. Lewis, 'The Noble Experiment,' *New York Times*, 5 January 1998, A19; M. Friedman, 'There's No Justice in the War on Drugs,' *New York Times*, 11 January 1998, Section 4, 19.

36 Zimring and Hawkins, *supra* note 18, 20.

37 See J. Donohue and P. Siegelman, 'Allocating Resources among Prisons and Social Programs in the Battle against Crime,' unpublished, 25 July 1996.

38 T. Meares and D. Kahan, 'Law and (Norms of) Order in the Inner City,' *Law and Society Review* 32 (1998): 805.

39 K. Ryan, 'Clinging to Failure: The Rise and Continued Life of U.S. Drug Policy,' *Law and Society Review* 32 (1998): 221.

40 M. Massing, 'The Blue Revolution,' *New York Review of Books*, 19 November 1998, 32, 36, discussing and quoting from J. Caulkins et al., *Mandatory Minimum Drug Sentences: Throwing Away the Key or the Taxpayers' Money?* (Santa Monica, Calif.: RAND Corporation, 1997).

41 'Where the Jailbirds Are,' *The Economist*, 17 July 1999, 25.

42 J. McKinley, Jr, 'Signs of a Thaw in the War on Drugs,' *New York Times*, 21 January 2001, The Metro Section, 29.

43 Ryan, *supra* note 39, 225.

44 Ibid., 233.

45 T. Egan, 'As Idaho Booms, Prisons Fill and Spending on Poor Lags,' *New York Times*, 16 April 1998, A1, 16.

46 D. Shichor and D. Sechrest, 'Three Strikes as Public Policy: Further Implications,' in D. Shichor and D. Sechrest, eds, *Three Strikes and You're Out: Vengeance as Public Policy* (Thousand Oaks, Calif.: Sage Publications, 1996), 265, 268.

47 Ibid.

48 Kaminer, *supra* note 22, 109, quoting Judge Stephen Bryer of the Federal Appeals Court (now of the US Supreme Court).

49 Lewis, *supra* note 35; and Friedman, *supra* note 35.

50 See, generally, M. Tonry, *Sentencing Matters* (New York: Oxford University Press, 1996), esp. chap. 8, 'What Is to Be Done?'

51 Short, *supra* note 29, chapter 10, 'Controlling Violent Crime.'

52 Zimring and Hawkins, *supra* note 18, chap. 11, 'Strategies of Prevention,' esp. 199ff.

53 Kaminer, *supra* note 22, 105.

54 Ibid., 109.

55 Ibid., 103.

56 S. Lipset, *American Exceptionalism: A Double Edged Sword* (New York: W.W. Norton and Co., 1996), 26.

57 Friedman, *supra* note 13, 464.

58 V. Hugo, *Écrits sur la peine de mort* (Avignon: Actes Sud, 1979), as cited in W. Schabas, *The Abolition of the Death Penalty in International Law*, 2nd ed. (Cambridge: Cambridge University Press, 1997), 295.

59 A number of jurisdictions abolished capital punishment during the nine-

teenth century. Ironically, in light of much of the United States' clinging to it, Michigan was the first jurisdiction (in 1846) to abolish capital punishment permanently: see Schabas, *supra* note 58, 5–6.

60 Ibid., 1.

61 *Protocol No. 6 to the Convention for the Protection of Human Rights and Fundamental Freedoms Concerning the Abolition of the Death Penalty*, ETS 114, *Second Optional Protocol to the International Covenant on Civil and Political Rights Aiming at the Abolition of the Death Penalty*, GA Res. 44/128, (1990) 29 ILM 1464, and *Additional Protocol to the American Convention on Human Rights to Abolish the Death Penalty*, OASTS 73, 29 ILM 1447: as cited in ibid., 2.

62 R. Hood, *The Death Penalty: A World-Wide Perspective*, 2nd ed. (Oxford: Clarendon Press, 1996), chap. 1, 'The Present Status of the Abolitionist Movement.'

63 Schabas, *supra* note 58, 295–6.

64 Ibid., 2.

65 Chapter 4, 'Law Acting in Concert with Social and Political Forces,' p. 120.

66 Schabas, *supra* note 58, 307.

67 'Comment: A Fondness for the Gallows,' *The New Yorker*, 30 November 1992, 4.

68 F. Zimring, 'On the Liberating Virtues of Irrelevance,' *Law and Society Review* 27 (1993): 9, 16.

69 F. Zimring, 'The Executioner's Dissonant Song: On Capital Punishment and American Legal Values,' in A. Sarat, ed., *The Killing State: Capital Punishment in Law, Politics, and Culture* (New York: Oxford University Press, 1999), 139.

70 W. Bowers, 'Capital Punishment and Contemporary Values: People's Misgivings and the Court's Misperceptions,' *Law and Society Review* 27 (1993): 157, 162; B. Doan, 'Death Penalty Policy, Statistics, and Public Opinion,' *Focus on Law Studies* 12 (1997): 3.

71 Bowers, 163.

72 Ibid., 162.

73 See chapter 3, 'Surprise – Unintended Consequences,' p. 99.

74 S. Holmes, 'Look Who's Questioning the Death Penalty,' *New York Times*, 16 April 2000, section 4, 1, 3.

75 Chapter 4, 'The Impact of Litigation Regarding Social Change – American Exceptionalism II,' p. 144.

76 *Furman v. Georgia* 408 U.S. 238 (1972).

77 R. Weisberg, 'Deregulating Death,' *Supreme Court Review*, [1983], 305, 315, quoted in Friedman, note *supra* note 13, 317.

78 P. Kurland, quoted in F. Zimring and G. Hawkins, *Capital Punishment and the American Agenda* (Cambridge: Cambridge University Press, 1986), x (foreword by T. Wicker).

79 Friedman, *supra* note 13, 316.

80 L. Epstein and J. Kobylka, *The Supreme Court and Legal Change: Abortion and the Death Penalty* (Chapel Hill: University of North Carolina Press, 1992), chaps. 3 and 4, and esp. pp. 82–4 and 132–4.

81 Friedman, *supra* note 13, 318.

82 J. Roberts and L. Stalans, *Public Opinion, Crime, and Criminal Justice* (Boulder, Co.: Westview Press, 1997), 229.

83 Ibid., 229–30.

84 Zimring and Hawkins, *supra* note 78, ix.

85 *Gregg v. Georgia* 428 U.S. 153 (1976).

86 Chief Justice Burger, quoted in Zimring and Hawkins, *supra* note 78, xi.

87 *McCleskey v. Kemp* 481 U.S. 279 (1987).

88 A. Sarat, 'Recapturing the Spirit of *Furman*: The American Bar Association and the New Abolitionist Politics,' *Law and Contemporary Problems* 61 (1998): 5, 5–6.

89 Epstein and Kobylka, *supra* note 80, 136.

90 Professor Carol Steiker, Harvard Law School, in an interview on the death penalty, see N. Waring, 'Capital Sentencing: Roads Taken and Not Taken,' *Harvard Law Bulletin* 49 (1998): 21, 23.

91 R. Bonner and F. Fessenden, 'States with No Death Penalty Share Lower Homicide Rates,' *New York Times*, 22 September 2000, A1, 19; B. Doan, *supra* note 70; T. Lewin, 'Who Decides Who Will Die? Even within States, It Varies,' *New York Times*, 23 February 1995, A1, B6; T. Rosenberg, 'The Deadliest D.A.,' *New York Times Magazine*, 16 July 1995, 20.

92 Friedman, *supra* note 13, 323; Rosenberg, *supra* note 91, 22; J. Brooke, 'Executions Spread from South, Becoming Part of U.S. Landscape,' *New York Times*, 14 October 1997, A1, 17.

93 '8 Oklahoma Inmates Set to Die This Month,' *New York Times*, 2 January 2001, A13.

94 Lewin, *supra* note 91.

95 S. Verhovek, 'Her Final Appeals Exhausted, Tucker is Put to Death in Texas,' *New York Times*, 4 February 1998, A1, 17.

96 Ibid.; 'Europeans Call Penalty Barbaric,' *New York Times*, 4 February 1998, A20.

97 S. Reimer, 'In the Busiest Death Chamber, Duty Carries Its Own Burdens,' *New York Times*, 17 December 2000, A1, 32.

98 T. Appleby, 'The Vengeful Society,' *Globe and Mail*, 18 November 1995, D1.

99 Ibid.

100 Ibid., quoting J. Liebman, Columbia University law professor.

101 R. Kennedy, *Race, Crime, and the Law* (New York: Pantheon Books, 1997), chap. 9, 'Race, Law, and Punishment: The Death Penalty.'

102 One of the most prominent is D. Baldus et al., 'Comparative Review of Death Sentences: An Empirical Study of the Georgia Experience,' *Journal of Criminal Law and Criminology* 74 (1983): 661. The findings of that study were rejected by the Supreme Court in *McCleskey v. Kemp, supra* note 87. See also D. Baldus et al., *Equal Justice and the Death Penalty: A Legal and Empirical Analysis* (Boston: Northeastern University Press, 1990).

103 J. McAdams, 'Racial Disparity and the Death Penalty,' *Law and Contemporary Problems* 61 (1998): 153; E. Eckholm, 'Studies Find Death Penalty Tied to Race of the Victims,' *New York Times,* 24 February 1995, B1, 4.

104 Eckholm, *supra* note 103.

105 'The Death Penalty: A Scholarly Forum,' *Focus on Law Studies* 12 (1997): 1, 7 (comments of D. Baldus).

106 Eckholm, *supra* note 103, B4; see also US General Accounting Office, *Federal Prisons: Trends in Offender Characteristics: Fact Sheet for the Chairman, Select Committee on Narcotics Abuse and Control, House of Representatives* (Washington: Office, Program Evaluation and Methodology Division, 1990) and D. Baldus et al., *Equal Justice, supra* note 102.

107 B. Herbert, 'No Room for Doubt,' *New York Times,* 21 July 1997, A17.

108 For an insistence by a proponent of capital punishment that it does deter, see McAdams, *supra* note 103, 168, citing various studies.

109 E. Van Den Haag, 'On Deterrence and the Death Penalty,' *Journal of Criminal Law, Criminology and Political Science* 60 (1969): 141, 147, quoted in Zimring and Hawkins, *supra* note 78, 183.

110 Zimring and Hawkins, *supra* note 78, 'Appendix: Deterrence and the Death Penalty,' 167.

111 Ibid., 180–1.

112 Ibid., 179–84.

113 Bonner and Fessenden, *supra* note 91.

114 P. Ellsworth and S. Gross, 'Hardening of the Attitudes: Americans' Views on the Death Penalty,' in H. Bedau, ed., *The Death Penalty in America: Current Controversies* (New York: Oxford University Press, 1997), 109 (emphasis in original).

115 A 1991 Gallup poll found that 75% of Americans approved of the death penalty, but only 13% thought that it deterred. When those who supported the death penalty were asked to choose their reason, 50% picked 'a life for a life': see 'A Fondness for the Gallows,' *supra* note 67.

116 Estimates suggest that a trial and appeals for a death sentence can cost up to three times more than the expense of imprisoning someone for life: see Rosenberg, *supra* note 91, 22; see also S. Verhovek, 'Across the U.S., Executions Are Neither Swift Nor Cheap,' *New York Times*, 22 February 1995, A1, B2.

117 Rosenberg, *supra* note 91, 22, quoting District Attorney Lynne Abraham.

118 Eckholm, *supra* note 103, B4, referring to the position of E. van den Haag.

119 Prominent columnists such as George Will and Anthony Lewis treated the televising of executions very seriously, accepting that there is a set of advantages and disadvantages to such a horror: see, e.g., A. Lewis, 'Their Brutal Mirth,' *New York Times*, 20 May 1991, A15.

120 L. Harris, 'The ABA Calls for a Moratorium on the Death Penalty: The Task Ahead – Reconciling Justice with Politics,' *Focus on Law Studies* 12 (1997): 2.

121 S. Verhovek, 'Karla Tucker Is Now Gone, But Several Debates Linger,' *New York Times*, 5 February 1998, A12.

122 M. Navarro, 'Execution without All the Attention,' *New York Times*, 10 February 1998, A10.

123 Rosenberg, *supra* note 91, 23 (emphasis in original).

124 D. Archer and R. Gartner, *Violence and Crime in Cross-National Perspective* (New Haven: Yale University Press, 1984).

125 Lipset, *supra* note 56, 145–6. Also, for Europe, see N. Nash, 'Europeans Shrug as Taxes Go Up,' *New York Times*, 16 February 1995, A10. For Canada, see S. Schlefer, 'What Price Economic Growth?' *The Atlantic Monthly*, December 1992, 113, esp. 115.

126 See the discussion in chapter 2, 'Designing Out the Problem,' p. 70.

127 Ibid., 'The Alternatives to Deterrence,' p. 63.

128 J. Donohue and P. Siegelman, *supra* note 37. See also 'Reducing Crime by Increasing Incarceration: Does This Policy Make Sense?' *Researching Law: American Bar Foundation Update* 6 (1995): 1; 'Reducing Crime by Increasing Social Spending,' ibid., 1.

129 A. Sarat, 'Capital Punishment as a Fact of Legal, Political, and Cultural Life: An Introduction,' in A. Sarat, *supra* note 69, 5, quoting J. Simon, 'Governing through Crime,' in L. Friedman and G. Fisher, eds, *The Crime Conundrum: Essays on Criminal Justice* (Boulder, Colo.: Westview Press, 1997).

130 K. Feinberg, 'How the Death Penalty Is Hurting Law Enforcement,' *Washington Post*, 4 June 1984, cited in H. Haines, *Against Capital Punishment: The Anti-Death Penalty Movement in America, 1972–1994* (New York: Oxford University Press, 1996), 178.

131 F. Butterfield, 'Death Sentences Being Overturned in 2 of 3 Appeals,' *New York Times*, 1 June 2000, A1; R. Bonner, 'Charge of Bias Challenges Death Penalty,' *New York Times*, 24 June 2000, A1, 18.

132 Zimring and Hawkins, *supra* note 78, 150; J. Wilson, 'What Death Penalty Errors?' *New York Times*, 10 July 2000, A25.

133 Windlesham, *supra* note 26, 217.

Chapter Six: Smoking

1 US Department of Health and Human Services (USDHHS), *Smoking and Health in the Americas* (Washington: Government Printing Office, 1992), 106, quoted in R. Rabin and S. Sugarman, 'Overview,' in R. Rabin and S. Sugarman, eds, *Smoking Policy: Law, Politics, and Culture* (New York: Oxford University Press, 1993), 3.

2 Ibid.

3 USDHHS, Surgeon General, *Reducing the Health Consequences of Smoking: 25 Years of Progress* (Washington: Government Printing Office, 1989), 153–61, in Rabin and Sugarman *supra* note 1.

4 USDHHS, Surgeon General 1986, chap. 2, and National Research Council 1986 in Rabin and Sugarman, *supra* note 1.

5 US Environmental Protection Agency (EPA), *Respiratory Effects of Passive Smoking: Lung Cancer and Other Disorders*, 'Environmental Tobacco Smoke' (Washington , D.C.: Government Printing Office, 1992), in Rabin and Sugarman, *supra* note 1, 4; S. Ross, 'Second-Hand Smoke: The Asbestos and Benzene of the Nineties,' *Arizona State Law Journal* 25 (1993): 713.

6 'Blowing Smoke,' *The Economist*, 20 December 1997, 59.

7 G. Collins, 'Trial Begins in Class Action Suit on Secondhand Smoke,' *New York Times*, 15 July 1997, A8.

8 R. Rabin, 'Some Thoughts on Smoking Regulation,' *Stanford Law Review* 43 (1991): 475, 485–8.

9 'Blowing Smoke,' *supra* note 6, 70.

10 USDHHS 1989, *supra* note 3, chap. 4; Rabin and Sugarman, *supra* note 1, 4.

11 'Environmental Tobacco Smoke,' *supra* note 5; Rabin and Sugarman, *supra* note 1, 4.

12 'Smoking Declines at a Faster Pace,' *New York Times*, 22 May 1992, A12, cited in Rabin and Sugarman, *supra* note 1, 4.

13 For example, a fad in the 1990s was cigars: S. Bourette, 'The Big Smoke,' *Globe and Mail*, 27 November 1995, B1.

14 M. Valpy, 'Smoke and Mirrors,' *Globe and Mail*, 20 June 1996, A2.

15 J. Gross, 'Young Blacks Link Tobacco Use to Marijuana,' *New York Times*,

22 April 1998, A1; S. Stolberg, 'Rise in Smoking by Young Blacks Erodes a Success Story,' *New York Times*, 3 April 1998, A24; cf. C. Sunstein, 'Is Tobacco a Drug? Administrative Agencies as Common Law Courts,' *Duke Law Journal* 47 (1998): 1013, 1020, citing Bureau of the Census, US Dept. of Commerce, *Statistical Abstract of the United States*, 115th ed. (Washington, 1995), 144, which documents lower rates of smoking among black teenagers.

16 A. Picard, 'Cigar Myth Clouds Deadly Truth, Journal Says,' *Globe and Mail*, 9 August 2000, A3; J. Brody, 'Increasingly, a Smokescreen of Glamour Is Hiding the Dangers of Cigars,' *New York Times*, 26 May 1996, B9. At the end of the decade there were indications that cigar smoking might be falling again: see 'Cigar Fad Goes Up in Smoke,' *Globe and Mail*, 6 October 1999, B13.

17 See 'Tobacco Habit May Cut Japan's Lead in Longevity,' *Globe and Mail*, 18 November 1995, D8; L. Snowball and J. Robertson, *Tobacco Smoking*, rev. ed. (Ottawa: Library of Parliament, Research Branch, 1996), 7.

18 B. Meier, 'Tobacco Industry, Conciliatory in US Goes on the Attack in the Third World,' *New York Times*, 18 January 1998, A14.

19 M. Levin, 'Smoke around the Rising Sun: An American Look at Tobacco Regulation in Japan,' *Stanford Law and Policy Review* 8 (1997): 99; 'Global Antismoking Efforts Face Hurdles,' *Globe and Mail*, 24 June 1997, B9.

20 J. Perlez, 'Fenced In at Home, Marlboro Man Looks Abroad,' *New York Times*, 24 June 1997, A1.

21 Rabin and Sugarman, *supra* note 1, 5.

22 See Report of the Royal College of Physicians in London (1962); Health and Welfare Canada Report (1963); and Report of the United States Surgeon General (1964) in Snowball and Robertson, *supra* note 17, 3.

23 US Department of Health, Education and Welfare (USDHEW), *Smoking and Health: Report of the Advisory Committee to the Surgeon General of the Public Health Service* (Washington: Government Printing Office, 1962) in Rabin and Sugarman, *supra* note 1, 5.

24 See, e.g., H. Sapolsky, 'The Political Obstacles to the Control of Cigarette Smoking in the United States,' *Journal of Health Politics, Policy and Law* 5 (1980): 277, 283–4.

25 For an explanation of that position, while not agreeing with it, see R. Goodin, *No Smoking: The Ethical Issues* (Chicago: University of Chicago Press, 1989), 93–5.

26 Rabin and Sugarman, *supra* note 1, 5.

27 Surgeon General, *supra* note 3.

28 J. Broder, 'Cigarette Maker Concedes Smoking Can Cause Cancer,' *New York Times*, 21 March 1997, A1; B. Meier, 'Chief of R.J. Reynolds Says

Smoking Has Role in Cancer,' *New York Times*, 23 August 1997, A7; B. Meier, 'Tobacco Executives Wax Penitent before House Panel in Hopes of Preserving Accord,' *New York Times*, 30 January 1998, A15; B. McKenna, 'Tobacco Bosses Admit Smoking Dangerous,' *Globe and Mail*, 30 January 1998, A13.

29 For a collection of essays generally critical of this shift in attitude, see R. Tollison, *Smoking and Society: Toward a More Balanced Assessment* (Lexington, Mass.: Lexington Books, 1986).

30 'Blowing Smoke,' *supra* note 6.

31 Rabin, *supra* note 8, 481.

32 'Blowing Smoke,' *supra* note 6, 59–61.

33 Ibid.

34 Rabin and Sugarman, *supra* note 1, 15.

35 For a more critical stance on this perspective, see R. Tollson and R. Wagner, *Smoking and the State: Social Costs, Rent Seeking, and Public Policy* (Lexington, Mass.: Lexington Books, 1988).

36 For Canada, the law is usefully collected and summarized in M. Grossman and P. Price, *Tobacco Smoking and the Law in Canada* (Toronto: Butterworths, 1992).

37 Sapolsky, *supra* note 24, 277.

38 R. Kagan and D. Vogel, 'The Politics of Smoking Regulation: Canada, France, the United States,' in Rabin and Sugarman, *supra* note 1, 22.

39 See chapter 3, 'Surprise – Unintended Consequences,' p. 99.

40 'Blowing Smoke,' *supra* note 6.

41 B. Meier, 'States and Cities Impose New Laws on Young Smokers,' *New York Times*, 7 December 1997, A1.

42 B. Feder, 'Youth-Smoking Study Sees Little Effect in Sting Efforts,' *New York Times*, 9 October 1997, A10.

43 Ibid.; see also J. Hersch, 'Teen Smoking Behavior and the Regulatory Environment,' *Duke Law Journal* 47 (1998): 1143; and P. Slovic, 'Do Adolescent Smokers Know the Risks?' *Duke Law Journal* 47 (1998): 1133.

44 J. Broder, 'F.T.C. Charges "Joe Camel" Ad Illegally Takes Aim at Minors,' *New York Times*, 29 May 1997, A1, B10.

45 Ibid., B10

46 B. Meier, 'Files of R.J. Reynolds Tobacco Show Effort on Youths,' *New York Times*, 15 January 1998, A10, 12.

47 S. Elliot, 'Joe Camel, a Giant in Tobacco Marketing, Is Dead at 23,' *New York Times*, 11 July 1997, C1.

48 See *infra*, 'Tort Litigation – An American Response,' p. 197.

49 W. Viscusi, *Smoking: Making the Risky Decisions* (New York: Oxford University Press, 1992), 31, table 2–4.

50 R. Sheppard, 'Profile of Teen-age Smokers,' *Globe and Mail*, 20 September 1995, A15.

51 C. Abraham, 'Grisly Warnings Take Effect,' *Globe and Mail*, 23 December 2000, A19.

52 M. Siegel and L. Biener, 'The Impact of an Antismoking Media Campaign on Progression to Established Smoking: Results of a Longitudinal Youth Study,' *American Journal of Public Health* 90 (2000): 380.

53 Kagan and Vogel, *supra* note 38, 28 and 36.

54 M. Baker, *Tobacco Smoking*, rev. ed. (Ottawa: Library of Parliament, Research Branch, 1986), 1 and 15.

55 See *Food and Drug Administration v. Brown and Williamson*, No. 98–1152, 21 March 2000, and L. Greenhouse, 'High Court Holds F.D.A. Can't Impose Rules on Tobacco,' *New York Times*, 22 March 2000, A1. See also *Brown & Williamson Tobacco Corp. v. FDA* WL 473320, 14th Cir. (1998) and Appellees' Petition for Rehearing, *Brown & Williamson* (No. 97–1604). See the debate between Merrill and Sunstein regarding these attempts to regulate on the part of the FDA: R. Merrill, 'The FDA May Not Regulate Tobacco Products as "Drugs" or as "Medical Devices,"' *Duke Law Journal* 47 (1998): 1071 and Sunstein, *supra* note 15.

56 E. Lewit et al., 'The Effects of Government Regulation on Teenage Smoking' and L. Benham, 'Comment,' *Journal of Law and Economics* (1981): 545 and 571.

57 Viscusi, *Smoking*, *supra* note 49; W. Manning et al., *The Costs of Poor Health Habits* (Cambridge, Mass.: Harvard University Press, 1991); M. Massing, 'How to Win the Tobacco War,' *New York Review of Books*, 11 July 1996, 32, 33, citing statistics in R. Kluger, *Ashes to Ashes: America's Hundred-Year Cigarette War, the Public Health, and the Unabashed Triumph of Philip Morris* (New York: Alfred A. Knopf, 1996).

58 J. Hanson and K. Logue, 'The Costs of Cigarettes: The Economic Case for Ex Post Incentive-Based Regulation,' *Yale Law Journal* 107 (1998): 1163.

59 Ibid., 1218.

60 Hersch, *supra* note 43, 1165, citing several studies including a minority that challenge the finding of price elasticity.

61 Kagan and Vogel, *supra* note 38, 28.

62 C. Bohlen, '"No Smoking," in Translation,' *New York Times*, 30 June 1996, sect. 5, 12.

63 Kagan and Vogel, *supra* note 38, 28–30 and 36.

64 R. Kagan and J. Skolnick, 'Banning Smoking: Compliance without Enforcement,' in Rabin and Sugarman, *supra* note 1, 69.

65 Grossman and Price, *supra* note 36.

66 See 'The Impact of Litigation Regarding Social Change – "American Exceptionalism II,"' p. 144.

67 C. Ross, 'Judicial and Legislative Control of the Tobacco Industry: Toward A Smoke-free Society?' *Cincinnati Law Review* 56 (1987): 317–18.

68 G. Schwartz, 'Tobacco Liability in the Courts,' in Rabin and Sugarman, *supra* note 1, 110.

69 Hanson and Logue, *supra* note 58, 1169–73; 'The Cigarette Wars,' *The Economist*, 11 May 1996, 21; and P. Carstensen et al., 'The So-Called Global Tobacco Settlement: Its Implication for Public Health and Public Policy – An Executive Summary of a Conference at the University of Wisconsin Law School,' *Southern Illinois University Law Journal* 22 (1998): 705.

70 L. Boulton, 'Tobacco Under Fire: Developments in Judicial Responses to Cigarette Smoking Injuries,' *Catholic University Law Review* 36 (1987): 643, 646–7.

71 *Cipollone v. Ligett Group, Inc.* 593 F. Supp. 1146 (D.N.J. 1984), rev'd 789 F.2d 181 3d Cir. (1986), *cert. denied* 55 U.S.L.W. 3470 (U.S. Jan. 13, 1987) (No. 86-563).

72 F. Vandall, 'Reallocating the Costs of Smoking: The Application of Absolute Liability to Cigarette Manufacturers,' *Ohio State Law Journal* 52 (1991): 405.

73 'The Cigarette Wars,' *supra* note 69.

74 'Blowing Smoke,' *The Economist*, 22 July 2000, 22; B. Meier, 'Tobacco Industry Loses First Phase of Broad Lawsuit,' *New York Times*, 8 July 1999, A1, 18.

75 Rabin and Sugarman, *supra* note 1, 9–12.

76 Ibid., 16–17.

77 M. Moorby, 'Smoking Parents, Their Children, and the Home: Do the Courts Have the Authority to Clear the Air?' *Pace Environmental Law Review* 12 (1995): 827.

78 G. Collins, 'Trial Begins in Class-Action Suit on Secondhand Smoke,' *New York Times*, 15 July 1997, A8.

79 J. Gray, 'Cigarette Makers in a $386 Billion Accord to Curb Law Suits and Curtail Marketing,' *New York Times*, 21 June 1997, A1; and J. Broder, 'Major Concessions,' *New York Times*, 21 June 1997, A1.

80 University of Wisconsin, Institute for Legal Studies, *Proceedings of the Conference on the So-Called Global Tobacco Settlement: Its Implications for Public Health and Public Policy* (Madison, Wisc.: 1998) and P. Carstensen et al., *supra* note 69.

81 K. Viscusi in an interview: see N. Waring, 'Hanson and Viscusi Dispute the True Costs of Smoking,' *Harvard Law Bulletin* 49 (1998): 24, 27; R. Epstein, 'Big Tobacco's Big Mistake,' *New York Times*, 25 June 1997, A21; 'White Smoke and Black,' *The Economist*, 28 June 1997, 16.

82 J. Hanson, in an interview: ibid., *Harvard Law Bulletin*; D. Rosenbaum,

'Health Experts Oppose Legal Protection for Tobacco Industry,' *New York Times*, 18 February 1998, A19.

83 'A Worrisome Tobacco Deal,' *New York Times*, 21 June 1997, A20; 'Holes in the Tobacco Settlement,' *New York Times*, 27 June 1997, A28.

84 B. Meier, 'In Tobacco Talks, Some Concern over the Role of Private Lawyers,' *New York Times*, 22 May 1997, A1; N. Lewis, 'House Weighs Limit on Fees in Tobacco Suits,' *New York Times*, 11 December 1997, A19.

85 'The World to Pay For,' *The Economist*, 19 April 1997, 61; J. Broder, 'Tobacco Profits May Soar under Deal,' *New York Times*, 23 September 1997, A21.

86 J. Bulow and P. Klemperer, 'The Tobacco Deal,' in M. Baily et al., eds, *Brookings Papers on Economic Activity: Microeconomics* (Washington: Brookings Institution, 1998); and 'When Lawyers Inhale,' *The Economist*, 22 May 1999, 88.

87 M. Lacey, 'Tobacco Industry Accused of Fraud in Lawsuit by US,' *New York Times*, 23 September 1999, A1.

88 J. Coutts, 'Ontario to Sue U.S. Tobacco Giants,' *Globe and Mail*, 24 April 1999, A13 (quoting Dr Jane Ashley, head of the Expert Panel on the Renewal of the Ontario Tobacco Strategy); J. Ibbitson, 'Ontario to Sue U.S. Tobacco Firms for $40 Billion,' *The National Post*, 24 April 1999, A4.

89 Stout, 'Few States Are Using Settlements in Tobacco Suit to Cut Smoking,' *New York Times*, 25 August 1999, A12.

90 L. Mather, 'Theorizing about Trial Courts: Lawyers, Policymaking, and Tobacco Litigation,' *Law and Social Inquiry* 23 (1998): 897, and G. Kelder and R. Daynard, 'The Role of Litigation in the Effective Control of the Sale and Use of Tobacco,' *Stanford Law and Policy Review* 8 (1997): 63.

91 H. Dagan and J. White, 'Governments, Citizens, and Injurious Industries,' *New York University Law Review* 75 (2000): 354.

92 D. Rosenbaum, 'Senate Is Offered Sweeping Measure to Fight Smoking,' *New York Times*, 31 March 1998, A1.

93 'National Tobacco Settlement Still Full of Surprises Two Years After It Was Signed,' *NPR: Morning Edition, National Public Radio*, 10 November 2000, transcript.

94 'When Lawyers Inhale,' *supra* note 86.

95 Coutts, *supra* note 88 and Ibbitson, *supra* note 88.

96 F. Butterfield, 'Results in Tobacco Litigation Spur Cities to File Gun Suits,' *New York Times*, 24 December 1998, A1, 13; 'Are Guns the Next Tobacco?' *Law Matters*, Summer 1999 (Chicago: American Bar Association, 1999); W. Glaberson, 'Lawyers Contend with State and Federal Efforts to Restrict Their Rising Power,' *New York Times*, 5 August 1999, A15.

97 See 'Alternatives to Deterrence,' p. 63.

98 L. Fisher, 'Alcohol, Tobacco, and Firearms: Autonomy, the Common Good, and the Courts,' *Yale Law and Policy Review* 18 (2000): 351.

99 F. Butterfield, 'Major Gun Makers Talk with Cities on Settling Suits,' *New York Times*, 2 October 1999, A1, 9; P. Barrett, 'Judge Dismisses Cincinnati's Gun-Industry Suit,' *Wall Street Journal*, 8 October 1999, B7; M. Allen, 'Cott's to Curtail Sale of Handguns,' *New York Times*, 11 October 1999, A1, 21.

100 I. Jenkins, *Social Order and the Limits of the Law* (Princeton: Princeton University Press, 1980); R.A. Samek, 'A Case for Social Law Reform,' *Canadian Bar Review* 55 (1977): 409.

101 Kagan and Skolnick, *supra* note 64, 85.

102 F. Zimring, 'Comparing Cigarette Policy and Illicit Drug and Alcohol Control,' in Rabin and Sugarman, *supra* note 1, 95.

103 Levin, *supra* note 19.

104 See *supra* 'The Perils of Nicotine – Public Attitudes and Behavior,' p. 184.

105 World Health Organization, *Tobacco or Health: A Global Status Report* (Geneva: WHO, 1997), 58–62, describing efforts in the 1990s to curtail smoking. In addition, at least up to 1993, there was significant disparity in France, in terms of smoking and gender, with 40% of males smoking but only 27% of females: see ibid., table 3.

106 Page 138.

107 The warning is 'Abus Dangereuse' – 'Overuse Is Hazardous': see Kagan and Vogel, *supra* note 38, 31.

108 Ibid.

109 Ibid.

110 Ibid.

111 See *The Economist*, 25 November–1 December 1995: 'France: A Survey,' 56.

112 L. Lessig, 'The Regulation of Social Meaning,' *University of Chicago Law Review* 62 (1995): 943.

113 'The Ineffectiveness of Law,' p. 133.

114 Kagan and Skolnick, *supra* note 64, 83.

115 Kagan and Vogel, *supra* note 38, 34.

116 R. Cohen, 'Is Paris Fuming? Yes, Despite a Legal Ban,' *New York Times*, 11 January 1997, A1, 4.

117 Kagan and Vogel, *supra* note 38, 32.

118 A. Fritschler, *Smoking and Politics: Policy Making and the Federal Bureaucracy*, 4th ed. (Englewood Cliffs, NJ: Prentice-Hall, 1989).

119 Lessig, *supra* note 112, 1025.

120 The Swiss seem to have had a similar experience: see E. Olson, 'Big Tobacco Said to Fight Swiss Smoking Laws,' *New York Times*, 15 January 2001, A8.

121 Kagan and Vogel, *supra* note 38, 28.

122 Viscusi, *supra* note 49, 35.

123 M. Schudson, 'Symbols and Smokers: Advertising, Health Messages, and Public Policy,' in Rabin and Sugarman, *supra* note 1, 210.

124 Ibid.

125 Ibid.

126 Ibid., 209; see also M. Grant, 'Controlling Alcohol Abuse,' in D. Robinson et al., *Controlling Legal Addictions* (London: MacMillan, 1989), 73–5.

127 Schudson, *supra* note 123, 217–20. Regarding such campaigns to deter consumption of alcohol and their mixed impact, see M. Grant, *supra* note 126, 73–5.

128 Schudson, ibid., 211.

129 Ibid., 212.

130 WHO, *supra* note 105, quoting from *Effect of Tobacco Advertising on Tobacco Consumption: A Discussion Document Reviewing the Evidence* (London: Economics and Operational Research Division, Department of Health, 1992).

131 See Meier, *supra* note 46 and Elliot, *supra* note 47.

132 R. Arbogast, 'A Proposal to Regulate the Manner of Tobacco Advertising,' *Journal of Health Politics, Policy and Law* 11 (1986): 393.

133 For an argument very much the other way, see H. High, *Does Advertising Increase Smoking?: Economics, Free Speech and Advertising Bans* (London: Institute of Economic Affairs, 1999).

134 Schudson, *supra* note 123, 223: 'Because cigarette advertising is a less powerful marketing tool than many people think, banning it is not likely to have a dramatic impact on the prevalence of smoking. Even so, advertising is one of the factors in the environment that encourages children and adolescents to start smoking, and there is ample justification for efforts to find public policy remedies that attack cigarette advertising.'

135 R. Moon, *The Constitutional Protection of Freedom of Expression* (Toronto: University of Toronto Press, 2000) and 'The Supreme Court of Canada on the Structure of Freedom of Expression Adjudication,' *University of Toronto Law Journal* 45 (1995): 419.

136 *RJR-Macdonald Inc. v. Canada (Attorney General)*, [1995] 3 S.C.R. 199.

137 See, e.g., S. McCarthy, 'Tobacco Advertising Ban Up in Smoke,' *Toronto Star*, 22 September 1995, A21; 'Cause for Concern in Tobacco Ruling,' *Toronto Star*, 22 September 1995, A22.

138 J. Simpson, 'The Supreme Court Should Have Butted Out of the Tobacco Issue,' *Globe and Mail*, 26 September 1995, A18.

139 See A. Coyne, 'The Supreme Court's Motto: Give Me Liberty or Give Me a Good Excuse,' *Globe and Mail*, 25 September 1995, A14; C. Hoy, 'Smoking

Is Bad, But ... Free Expression is Good,' *Law Times*, 2–8 October 1995, 7;
T. Corcoran, 'Another Defeat for Anti-smoking Zealots,' *Globe and Mail*,
22 September 1995, B2.

140 Moon, *supra* note 135.

141 See chapter 4, 'The Impact of Litigation Regarding Social Change – American Exceptionalism II,' p. 144.

142 D. Vienneau and D. Israelson, 'Ban on Cigarette Ads Rejected by Top Court – But Tobacco Firms Say They'll Consult Ottawa on Next Move,' *Toronto Star*, 22 September 1995, A1.

143 M. Strauss, 'No Deep Desire for Tobacco Ads – Agencies Fear Lucrative Accounts Gone for Good, Despite End of Ban,' *Globe and Mail*, 22 September 1995, B1. In Britain, curbs on advertising of tobacco have largely been voluntary, based on self-regulation: see P. Tether, 'Legal Controls and Voluntary Agreements,' in D. Robinson et al., *supra* note 126, 203.

144 M. Strauss, 'Tobacco Firms Set Limits for Ads,' *Globe and Mail*, 20 December 1995, B2.

145 J. Gadd, 'Tobacco Industry Alters Its Advertising Regulations,' *Globe and Mail*, 6 June 1996, A4.

146 B. McKenna, 'Cancer Society Monitors Tobacco Ads: Accuses Cigarette Firms of Disregarding Their Own Code of Conduct,' *Globe and Mail*, 26 April 1996, B4.

147 B. McKenna, 'Groups Push Ottawa for Anti-smoking Law,' *Globe and Mail*, 10 July 1996, B4.

148 W. Johnson, 'Tobacco Legislation Is Authoritarian and Opportunistic,' *Financial Post*, 4 April 1997, 13; L. Eggertson, 'Ottawa's Tobacco Bill May Face Court Challenges,' *Globe and Mail*, 2 April 1997, A4.

149 *Tobacco Act*, S.C. 1997, c. 13; S. McCarthy, 'Rock Tells Tobacco Firms to Butt Out of Legislation,' 9 December 1997, A1; J. Mahoney, 'Ottawa Remains Steadfast on Anti-smoking, PM says,' *Globe and Mail*, 8 December 1997, A1.

150 S. McCarthy, 'Rock Seeks Tobacco Reprieve,' *Globe and Mail*, 31 March 1998, A1, 10.

151 Kagan and Vogel, *supra* note 38, 30.

152 See chapter 4, '6. The Impact of Litigation regarding Social Change – American Exceptionalism II,' p. 144.

153 Kagan and Vogel, *supra* note 38, 22.

154 'Surprise – Unintended Consequences, p. 99.'

155 'Don't Ban Smokers ... Burn Them ... and Lots of Others, Too,' *The Economist*, 13 January 2001, 19.

156 See this chapter *supra*, 'The Quandaries of Advertising: The Case of Canada,' p. 206.

157 See, e.g., C. Godfrey, 'Price Regulation,' in D. Robinson et al., *supra* note 126, 110.

158 D. Johnston, 'Anti-Tobacco Groups Push for Higher Cigarette Taxes,' *New York Times*, 3 April 1997, A12; G. Collins, 'Cigarette Prices Take Big Jump: 7 Cents a Pack,' *New York Times*, 3 September 1997, A1.

159 'Taxes Prevent Lung Cancer,' *Globe and Mail*, 15 July 1993, A22.

160 R. Bonner and C. Drew, 'Cigarette Makers Are Seen as Aiding Rise in Smuggling,' *New York Times*, 25 August 1997, A1.

161 Ibid.

162 'The Smoke Surrounding Cigarette Statistics,' *Globe and Mail*, 28 April 1994, A24.

163 R. Howard, 'Tax Cut Appears to Boost Smoking – Cigarette Sales Rise 62 Percent,' *Globe and Mail*, 27 April 1994, A1; L. Eggerton, 'Price Cut Recruits Young Smokers,' *Globe and Mail*, 10 July 1997, A9.

164 'The Smoke Surrounding Cigarette Statistics,' *Globe and Mail*, 28 April 1994, A24.

165 P. Moon, 'Smugglers Go Interprovincial,' *Globe and Mail*, 28 July 1997, A1; P. Moon, 'High Taxes Make Good Smuggling,' *Globe and Mail*, 22 July 1997, A6; A. McIlroy and S. McCarthy, 'Ottawa, 5 Provinces Hit Smokers with Tax Hike,' *Globe and Mail*, 14 February 1998, A1.

166 A. Picard, 'Surgeon-General Aims to Halve US Smoking Rate,' *Globe and Mail*, 10 August 2000, A6; 'How to Get the World to Give up Smoking,' *Globe and Mail*, 9 August 2000, A12; D. Rosenbaum, 'Senators Agree on Forcing Up Cigarette Price,' *New York Times*, 28 March 1998, A1; D. Rosenbaum, 'Smoking Foes Battle the Industry's Spectra of Smuggling,' *New York Times*, 5 May 1998, A28.

167 R. DiManno, 'Second Smoking Poll Declares: Leave Well Enough Alone,' *Toronto Star*, 30 September 1996, A4.

168 I. Ross, 'Toronto Softens Smoking Law,' *Globe and Mail*, 15 April 1997, A1.

169 R. Bragg, 'Smoke Law Up from Ashes,' *Toronto Star*, 31 March 1999, A1, 21.

170 K. Honey, 'Unequal Bylaws Revive Smoking Debate,' *Globe and Mail*, 20 April 1998, A8.

171 C. Reed, 'California Smokers Fume as Law Kicks In,' *Globe and Mail*, 1 January 1998, A1, 13.

172 D. Terry, 'Barstool Rebels Defy New Ban on Smoking,' *New York Times*, 3 January 1998, A1.

173 R. Klein, 'Smoking Is Sexy Again on the Screen, and the Finger Waggers Share the Blame,' *New York Times*, 24 August 1997, sect. 2, 1.

174 Lessig, *supra* note 112, 1027; Sunstein, *supra* note 15.

175 Lessig, ibid., 1031–4.

176 C. Sunstein, 'Social Norms and Social Roles,' *Columbia Law Review* 96 (1996): 903, 905–6.
177 Gross, *supra* note 15; Stolberg, *supra* note 15.
178 Gross, ibid.
179 'The Tobacco War Goes Global,' *The Economist*, 14 October 2000, 97.
180 Kagan and Vogel, *supra* note 38, 18–19.

Chapter Seven: The Environment

1 J. Dao, 'Acid Rain Law Found to Fail in Adirondacks,' *New York Times*, 27 March 2000, A1.
2 Some would suggest that a left/right cleavage is not the best way to describe the ideological differences regarding environmentalism: R. Paehlke, *Environmentalism and the Future of Progressive Politics* (New Haven: Yale University Press, 1989), chap. 7, 'Environmentalism and the Ideological System.'
3 R. Carson, *Silent Spring* (Boston: Houghton Mifflin, 1962).
4 Quoted in D. Kevles, 'Greens in America,' *New York Review of Books*, 6 October 1994, 35, 37. See, generally, M. Kraft and N. Vig, 'Environmental Policy from the 1970s to the 1990s: An Overview,' in N. Vig and M. Kraft, *Environmental Policy in the 1990s: Reform or Reaction?*, 3rd ed. (Washington: CQ Press, 1997).
5 Kevles, ibid., 38.
6 Ibid.
7 Ibid.
8 See chapter 6.
9 *Congressional Record*, Senate, 92nd Cong., 2nd Sess., vol. 117, part 30, 38828, 2 November 1971, cited in D. Dewees et al., *Exploring the Domain of Accident Law: Taking the Facts Seriously* (New York: Oxford University Press, 1996), 323.
10 Ibid.
11 Ibid., 265.
12 Prohibitions on discharging deleterious substances have been in the *Fisheries Act* for more than 100 years, but they were set out as simple 'blanket prohibitions' that were only sporadically enforced. See the discussion in K. Webb, *Pollution Control in Canada: the Regulatory Approach in the 1980s* (Ottawa: Law Reform Commission of Canada, 1988), 11, and J. McLaren, 'The Tribulations of Antoine Ratté: A Case Study of the Environmental Regulation of the Canadian Lumbering Industry in the Nineteenth Century,' *University of New Brunswick Law Journal* 33 (1984): 203.

13 Canadian governments tolerated pollution from important industries, sometimes even protecting those industries from the full brunt of legal actions through legislation. See, e.g., discussion of the Ontario government's role in allowing the continuation of damaging air emissions from smelters in Sudbury in D. Dewees and M. Halewood, 'The Efficiency of the Common Law: Sulphur Dioxide Emissions in Sudbury,' *University of Toronto Law Journal* 42 (1992): 1. Also see D. Emond, 'Environmental Law and Policy: A Retrospective Examination of the Canadian Experience,' in I. Bernier and A. Lajoie, eds, *Consumer Protection, Environmental Law and Corporate Power* (Toronto: University of Toronto Press, 1985), 129–34.

14 D. Emond, 'The Greening of Environmental Law,' *McGill Law Journal* 36 (1991): 742. Others have traced this evolution somewhat differently: see, e.g., D. Estrin, 'Annual Survey of Canadian Law, Part 2: Environmental Law,' *Ottawa Law Review* 7 (1975): 397; J. Swaigen, 'Annual Survey of Canadian Law: Environmental Law 1975–1980,' *Ottawa Law Review* 12 (1980): 439; and Webb, *supra* note 12.

15 Emond, *supra* note 14, 747.

16 Webb, *supra* note 12.

17 There has always been a gap between environmental law as found in the statutes and regulations and as applied in practice. Because of the scientific and technical uncertainties involved, negotiation within ongoing relationships was and is the primary mode of achieving compliance. In the early years, prosecution was rarely used as a tool for bringing about compliance with environmental regulations. Thus, although statutes provided for prosecution and sanctioning, the reality was more akin to negotiation of 'regulatory agreements' between industry and governments than to 'command and control.' See M. Rankin and P. Finkle, 'The Enforcement of Environmental Law: Taking the Environment Seriously,' *University of British Columbia Law Review* 17 (1983): 35, 37–43; T. Conway, 'Taking Stock of the Traditional Regulatory Approach,' in G. Doern, ed., *Getting It Green: Case Studies in Canadian Environmental Regulation* (Toronto: C.D. Howe Institute, 1990), 25, 30–2; and Webb, *supra* note 12.

18 See Ontario's *Environmental Protection Act*, R.S.O. 1990, c. E19, s. 14.

19 Enforcement and compliance policies setting out guidance for administrators as to when to use which tools were adopted, for example, in Ontario and at the federal level. Ontario shifted to a more aggressive compliance policy in 1985, creating an Investigation and Enforcement Branch within the Ministry of the Environment, adding legal staff, and dramatically increasing the number of prosecutions.

20 For example, the 'Spills Bill,' in Ontario; directors' and officers' liability

under the *Canadian Environmental Protection Act*, 1999, S.C. 1999, c. 33, and the Ontario *Environmental Protection Act, supra* note 18.

21 'Multistakeholder consultations' were used to establish environmental initiatives under the federal process for reforming the *Environmental Contaminants Act*, R.S.C. 1985, c. E-12.

22 World Commission on Environment and Development (Brundtland Commission), *Our Common Future* (New York: Oxford University Press, 1987).

23 An ecosystem approach recognizes the link between all environmental media and the links between the living and non-living components of the earth, including humans: see T. Colborn et al., *Great Lakes, Great Legacy?* (Washington: Conservation, 1990).

24 This shift of responsibility is likely to accelerate if market-based approaches, under discussion, are established. See House of Commons, Standing Committee on Environment, *A Global Partnership: Canada and the Conventions of the United Nations Conference on Environment and Development (UNCED)* (Ottawa: House of Commons, April 1993), Recommendation 20, 46–7.

25 This is one of the major successes of the Canadian Council of Ministers of the Environment. The Council is the major intergovernmental forum in Canada for discussion and joint action on environmental issues of national, international, and global concern. It is working on the development of nationally consistent guidelines and standards in several areas, including air quality, global warming, water management, waste management, packaging, toxins, and environmental assessment: see Canadian Council of Ministers of the Environment, *1992 Strategic Overview* (Winnipeg: CCME, 1992).

26 It is also quite rare that an activity will be stopped completely or that a chemical will be banned from use.

27 R. Kaplan, 'The Coming Anarchy,' *The Atlantic Monthly*, February 1994, 44.

28 D. Vogel, *Trading Up: Consumer and Environmental Regulation in a Global Economy* (Cambridge, Mass.: Harvard University Press, 1995).

29 See *infra*, 'The Environment and International Trade,' p. 242.

30 'The Great Environment Divide,' *The Economist*, 6 April 1996, 23, describing Republican opposition to environmental laws.

31 P. Yeager, *The Limits of Law: The Public Regulation of Private Pollution* (New York: Cambridge University Press, 1991), 312–18.

32 J. Cushman, 'House Approves Major Changes in Clean Water Act from the 1970s,' *New York Times*, 17 May 1995, A1, C20; W. Stevens, 'Future of Endangered Species Act in Doubt as Law Is Debated,' *New York Times*, 16 May 1995, B7; J. Cushman, 'Clause Would End an Agency's Veto on Wetland Plans,' *New York Times*, 12 December 1995, A1, 15.

33 M. Mittelstaedt, 'Industries Urge Ontario to Ease Pollution Laws,' *Globe and Mail*, 21 May 1996, B1, 4.

34 A. McIlroy, 'Ottawa's Environmental Joy Ride,' *Globe and Mail*, 4 October 1997, D1.

35 J. Cushman, 'Business Scaling Back Plans to Defang Federal Regulations,' *New York Times*, 3 February 1996, A1, and 'Adversaries Back Pollution Rules Now on the Books,' *New York Times*, 12 February 1996, A1, C11.

36 Quoted in Kevles, *supra* note 4, 38; E. Ringquist, 'A Question of Justice: Equity in Environmental Litigation, 1974–1991,' *Journal of Politics* 60 (1998): 1148.

37 For example, see R. Bullard, ed., *Unequal Protection: Environmental Justice and Communities of Color* (San Francisco: Sierra Club Books, 1994).

38 Kevles, *supra* note 4, 39, discussing R. Gottlieb, *Forcing the Spring: The Transformation of the American Environmental Movement* (Washington: Island Press, 1993).

39 C. Hunt, 'Toward the Twenty-First Century: A Canadian Legal Perspective on Resource and Environmental Law,' *Osgoode Hall Law Journal* 31 (1993): 297, 305.

40 C. Mullan, 'Pollution Poll Trashes Tories,' *Toronto Star*, 5 January 2001, A1; M. Mittelstaedt, 'Voters, Harris Split on Green Issues,' *Globe and Mail*, 15 July 1996, A1, 4.

41 S. Terry, 'Drinking Water Comes to a Boil,' *New York Times Magazine*, 26 September 1993, 42; B. McKibben, 'An Explosion of Green,' *The Atlantic Monthly*, April 1995, 61; 'All That Remains: A Survey of Waste and the Environment,' *The Economist*, 29 May 1993; 'A New Case for Greenery,' *The Economist*, 3 June 1995, 14; T. Egan, 'Look Who's Hugging Trees Now,' *New York Times Magazine*, 7 July 1996, 28.

42 P. Knox, 'Environmental Issues Heating Up, Poll Shows,' *Globe and Mail*, 10 November 1997, A10.

43 G. Easterbrook, *A Moment on the Earth: The Coming Age of Environmental Optimism* (New York: Viking, 1995).

44 G. Easterbrook, 'Here Comes the Sun,' *The New Yorker*, 18 April 1995, 38.

45 P. Ehrlich et al., 'No Middle Way on the Environment,' *The Atlantic Monthly*, December 1997, 98.

46 Kaplan, *supra* note 27.

47 Ibid., 58. An answer to Kaplan is contained in M. Gee, 'Apocalypse Deferred,' *Globe and Mail*, 9 April 1994, D1, 3. But see T. Homer-Dixon, 'Is Anarchy Coming? A Response to the Optimists,' *Globe and Mail*, 10 May 1994, A21. See also T. Athanasiou, *Divided Planet: The Ecology of Rich and*

Poor (Boston: Little Brown & Co., 1996) and 'Green Romantics,' *The Nation,* 1 May 1995, 603.

48 R. Bailey, ed., *The True State of the Planet* (New York: The Free Press, 1995); A. Bramwell, *Ecology in the Twentieth Century: A History* (New Haven: Yale University Press, 1989) and *The Fading of the Greens: The Decline of Environmental Politics in the West* (New Haven: Yale University Press, 1994).

49 Page 133.

50 C. Giagnocavo and H. Goldstein, 'Law Reform or World Re-form: The Problem of Environmental Rights,' *McGill Law Journal* 35 (1990): 345. A more widely known 'deep ecologist' is A. Naess: see, e.g., 'The Shallow and the Deep, Long Range Ecology Movement,' *Inquiry* 16 (1973): 95. See also Yeager, *supra* note 31; and P. Elder, 'Sustainability,' *McGill Law Journal* 36 (1991): 830.

51 Giagnocavo and Goldstein, ibid., 347.

52 Ibid., 385.

53 Ibid., 350.

54 L. Cole, 'Foreword: A Jeremiad on Environmental Justice and the Law,' *Stanford Environmental Law Journal* 14 (1995): ix, xii.

55 Giagnocavo and Goldstein, *supra* note 50, 376.

56 Ibid., 347.

57 Ibid., 381.

58 Ibid.

59 Ibid.

60 See *infra*, 'The Environment and International Trade,' p. 242.

61 S. Rose-Ackerman, *Controlling Environmental Policy: The Limits of Public Law in Germany and the United States* (New Haven: Yale University Press, 1995), 35.

62 W. Bogart and M. Valiante, 'Litigation and the Environment in Canada: What We Don't Know,' unpublished, prepared for the Comparative Judicial Research Group Meeting, Florence, 1994.

63 Dewees et al., *supra* note 9, 265.

64 'Doubts on Tying Job Loss to Laws on Environment,' *New York Times,* 18 March 1996, A10.

65 S. Breyer, *Breaking the Vicious Circle: Toward Effective Risk Regulation* (Cambridge, Mass.: Harvard University Press, 1993).

66 Ibid., 11–29; G. Bryner, *Blue Skies, Green Politics: The Clean Air Act of 1970 and its Implementation* (2nd ed.) (Washington: CQ Press, 1995), 32–3, summarizing criticisms, particularly from the Office of Management and Budget.

67 Dewees et al., *supra* note 9.

68 For a fuller discussion, see ibid., 5–9.

69 See 'Instrumentalism,' p. 114.

70 Dewees et al., *supra* note 9, 265–6.

71 Ibid., 430.

72 *Comprehensive Environmental Response Compensation and Liability Act*, Pub.L. no. 96–510, 94 Stat. 2767, 42 U.S.C. 9601–75 (1982 & Supp IV, 1986)

73 Dewees et al., *supra* note 9, 419–20.

74 Ibid., 420.

75 Ibid, 420.

76 J. Tierney, 'Recycling Is Garbage,' *New York Times Magazine*, 30 June 1996, sect. 6, 24.

77 Dewees et al., *supra* note 9, 420.

78 Ibid., 423–4.

79 *Price-Anderson Act* 42 U.S.C. sec. 2210 (1946).

80 *Oil Pollution Act* 33 U.S.C. sec. 2701 (1990).

81 Dewees et al., *supra* note 9, 22.

82 Ibid., 426.

83 Ibid., 426.

84 Ibid., 431.

85 P. Passell, 'Cheapest Protection of Nature May Lie in Taxes, Not Laws,' *New York Times*, 24 November 1992, B5, 9; 'Curbing the Car,' *The Economist*, 22 June 1996, 19.

86 M. Sandel, 'It's Immoral to Buy the Right to Pollute,' *New York Times*, 15 December 1997, A19.

87 Dewees et al., *supra* note 9, 434.

88 See L. Meyer, 'Just the Facts?' *Yale Law Journal* 106 (1997): 1269; W.A. Bogart, 'The Legal Strangle,' *Literary Review of Canada*, December 1996, 11; and M. Richardson, 'Revisiting Strict Product Liability: Taking Law and Economics Further,' *Osgoode Hall Law Journal* 35 (1997): 195.

89 J. Fraiberg and M. Trebilcock, 'Risk Regulation: Technocratic and Democratic Tools for Regulatory Reform,' unpublished, Faculty of Law, University of Toronto, 1997.

90 Ibid., 73–4.

91 Ibid., 51–73.

92 N. Rescher, *Risk: A Philosophical Introduction to the Theory of Risk Evaluation and Management* (Washington: University Press of America, 1983), 114.

93 Fraiberg and Trebilcock, *supra* note 89, 60; Bryner, *supra* note 66, 3–4.

94 Fraiberg and Trebilcock, ibid., 63.

95 For another discussion of applicable criteria, see N. Gunningham et al., *Smart Regulation: Designing Environmental Policy* (Oxford: Clarendon Press, 1998), 26 and, in that same book, N. Gunningham and D. Sinclair, chap. 6, 'Designing Environmental Policy,' 375.

96 Fraiberg and Trebilcock, *supra* note 89, 47.
97 Criminal prosecutions are not discussed here. They fall under general considerations of deterrence and its alternatives: see chapter 2. One Canadian study does suggest that corporations that have received heavy fines or whose officers and directors have been prosecuted tend to spend more money on environmental protection: D. Saxe, 'The Impact of Prosecution of Corporations and Their Officers and Directors upon Regulatory Compliance by Corporations,' *Journal of Environmental Law and Practice* 1 (1991): 91.
98 For example, in Ontario the *Environmental Bill of Rights*: see P. Muldoon and R. Lindgren, *The Environmental Bill of Rights: A Practical Guide* (Toronto: Emond-Montgomery, 1995).
99 G. Rosenberg, *The Hollow Hope: Can Courts Bring About Social Change?* (Chicago: University of Chicago Press, 1991), chap. 10, 'Cleaning House? The Courts, the Environment, and Reapportionment,' 271–303.
100 *Scenic Hudson Preservation Conference v. FPC* (1965) and *Sierra Club v. Morton* (1972), cited in ibid., 273.
101 Ibid., 271–4.
102 For a study of Canada reaching broadly similar conclusions, see Hunt, *supra* note 39, 310–14.
103 See, generally, L. McSpadden, 'Environmental Policy in the Courts,' in Kraft and Vig, *supra* note 4. For a Canadian study suggesting some success (in the comparatively few cases litigated), see S. Elgie, 'Environmental Groups and the Courts: 1970–1992,' in G. Thompson et al., *Environmental Law and Business in Canada* (Toronto: Canada Law Book, 1993), 185. Another study suggests that, for a variety of reasons, it is very difficult to determine the effect of litigation in Canada with regard to protection of the environment: see Bogart and Valiante, *supra* note 62.
104 Rosenberg, *supra* note 99, 274–85. Generally, these are the conclusions reached by an earlier study: J. Handler, *Social Movements and the Legal System: A Theory of Law Reform and Social Change* (New York: Academic Press, 1978), 69: 'In environmental litigation, the courts can only be used for limited purposes. The basic problem is that courts will not substitute their judgment on the merits for that of the agency. This means that ultimately the groups will have to return to the agency and the bureaucratic contingency becomes crucial. On the other hand, courts have been used successfully for limited and extrajudicial purposes, such as gaining time and publicity, which can allow the groups to employ means other than litigation to pursue their goals.' See also R. Melnick, *Regulation and the Courts: The Case of the Clean Air Act* (Washington: Brookings Institution, 1983) and

R. O'Leary, *Environmental Change: Federal Courts and the EPA* (Philadelphia: Temple University Press, 1993).

105 W. Glaberson, 'Novel Antipollution Tool Is Being Upset by Courts,' *New York Times*, 5 June 1999, A1, 10.

106 For example, S. Rose-Ackerman, *supra* note 61, emphasizing the importance of review by courts in achieving accountability in environmental decision-making (in contrast to the German bureaucratic procedures), but without providing evidence of their effectiveness.

107 Rosenberg, *supra* note 99, 290–2.

108 Ibid., 292.

109 Chapter 4, 'The Impact of Litigation Regarding Social Change – "American Exceptionalism" II,' p. 144.

110 Rose-Ackerman, *supra* note 61.

111 D. Vogel, *National Styles of Regulation: Environmental Policy in Great Britain and the United States* (Ithaca: Cornell University Press, 1986), also discussed in chapter 4.

112 Bogart and Valiante, *supra* note 62, and Hunt, *supra* note 39.

113 Vogel, *supra* note 111, 153.

114 Rose-Ackerman, *supra* note 61.

115 For Gunningham et al. (*supra* note 95, 31) the USA's 'regulatory system is at one extreme in terms of its legalistic and adversarial nature'; see also B. Hutter, *Compliance: Regulation and Environment* (Oxford: Clarendon Press, 1997).

116 Gunningham et al., *supra* note 95, 4.

117 See, e.g., O. Young, *International Governance: Protecting the Environment in a Stateless Society* (Ithaca: Cornell University Press, 1994) and P. Haas et al., eds, *Institutions for the Earth: Sources of Effective International Environmental Protection* (Cambridge, Mass: MIT Press, 1993).

118 'No Hot Air on Global Warning,' *New York Times*, 22 June 1997, A14; 'The Rich, the Poor and Global Warming,' *Globe and Mail*, 8 December 1997, A16.

119 Vogel, *supra* note 28, 10–11; 'Dirt Poor,' *The Economist* (A Survey of Development and the Environment), 21 March 1998, 3.

120 S. Charnovitz, 'The North American Free Trade Agreement: Green Law or Green Spin?' *Law and Policy in International Business* 26 (1994): 1; B. McAndrew, 'NAFTA Criticized on Environment,' *Toronto Star*, 13 August 1997, C3.

121 Vogel, *supra* note 111, 1–3.

122 L. Caldwell, *International Environmental Policy* (Durham: Duke University Press, 1984).

123 C. Runge et al., *Freer Trade, Protected Environment: Balancing Trade Liberal-ization and Environmental Interests* (New York: Council on Foreign Relations Press, 1994); J. Cameron et al., eds, *Trade and the Environment: The Search for Balance* (London: Cameron May, 1994).

124 Vogel, *supra* note 28.

125 Ibid., 269–70.

126 Ibid., 256. Vogel also indicates that in 1993 the German government modified its recycling standards because German firms complained that some of these requirements were disadvantaging them competitively.

127 And the trading partners need not have a lesser status to be influenced. Ontario was shocked by a NAFTA report listing it as the third greatest source of pollution in North America. See S. Fine, 'Ontario Among Top Polluters,' *Globe and Mail*, 29 July 1997, A1, 4; B. McAndrew, 'Ontario Cited as 3rd Worst Polluter,' *Toronto Star*, 29 July 1997, A1, 16; S. Fine, 'Canada Put on Environmental Hot Seat,' *Globe and Mail*, 30 July 1997, A3; 'Our Pollution, Yours to Discover,' *Globe and Mail*, 30 July 1997, A12.

128 N. Kada, 'Book Review: *Trading Up,*' *Journal of Environment and Development* 5 (1996): 120.

129 R. Peduzzi, 'Book Review: *Trading Up,*' *Ecology Law Quarterly* 23 (1996): 499.

130 Ibid., 501–2.

131 J. Cushman, 'Trade Group Strikes Blow at U.S. Environmental Law,' *New York Times*, 7 April 1998, C1.

132 D. Caldwell and D. Wirth, 'Trade and the Environment: Equilibrium or Imbalance?' *Michigan Journal of International Law* 17 (1996): 563, 579–80.

133 Vogel, *supra* note 28, 269–70.

134 C. Runge, 'Book Review,' *Journal of Economic Literature* 35 (1997): 143, 144.

135 Dewees et al., *supra* note 9, 323.

136 Ibid. This is the subtitle of the book.

Chapter Eight: Pornography

1 S. Childress, 'Reel "Rape Speech": Violent Pornography and the Politics of Harm,' *Law and Society* 25 (1991): 177.

2 'Censors Through the Ages,' *The Economist*, 26 December 1993, 81.

3 See 'National Styles of Regulation – "American Exceptionalism" I,' p. 138.

4 With regard to England see, e.g., S. Easton, *The Problem of Pornography: Regulation and the Right to Free Speech* (New York: Routledge, 1994).

5 See 'Law (Re)Constituting Social and Political Relationships,' p. 126 and

'The Impact of Litigation Regarding Social Change – "American Exceptionalism" II,' p. 144.

6 See 'The Ineffectiveness of Law,' p. 133.

7 J.S. Mill, *On Liberty* (1859), chap. 1, para. 9.

8 T. Emerson, 'Toward a General Theory of the First Amendment,' *Yale Law Journal* 72 (1962–63): 877.

9 P. Devlin, *The Enforcement of Morals* (New York: Oxford University Press, 1965).

10 R. Morgan, 'Theory and Practice: Pornography and Rape,' in L. Lederer, ed., *Take Back the Night* (New York: William Morrow, 1980), 139.

11 C. MacKinnon, *Feminism Unmodified: Discourses on Life and Law* (Cambridge, Mass.: Harvard University Press, 1987), 154.

12 Easton, *supra* note 4.

13 C. MacKinnon, *Toward a Feminist Theory of the State* (Cambridge, Mass.: Harvard University Press, 1989), 204.

14 MacKinnon, *supra* note 11, 140.

15 A. Carol, *Nudes, Prudes and Attitudes: Pornography and Censorship* (Cheltenham, Eng.: New Clarion Press, 1994).

16 B. Cossman et al., *Bad Attitude/s on Trial: Pornography, Feminism, and the Butler Decision* (Toronto: University of Toronto Press, 1997), 22.

17 B. Quistgaard, 'Pornography, Harm and Censorship: A Feminist (Re)Vision of the Right to Freedom of Expression,' *University of Toronto Faculty of Law Review* 52 (1993): 132, 135.

18 Cossman et al., *supra* note 16, 25.

19 Ibid., 32.

20 Ibid., 44, 29.

21 These classifications roughly correspond to those used in R. Posner, *Sex and Reason* (Cambridge, Mass.: Harvard University Press, 1992), 366–74.

22 V. Burstyn, 'Political Precedents and Moral Crusades: Women, Sex and the State,' in V. Burstyn, ed., *Women against Censorship* (Vancouver: Douglas & McIntyre, 1985), 17.

23 D. Wildmon, *The Case against Pornography* (Wheaton, Ill.: Victor, 1986), 21, cited in Posner, *supra* note 21, 372.

24 The conservative newspaper columnist J. Kilpatrick, quoted in L. Segal, 'Does Pornography Cause Violence? The Search for Evidence,' in P. Gibson and R. Gibson, *Dirty Looks: Women, Pornography, Power* (London: British Film Institute, 1993), 10.

25 I. Kristol, 'Pornography, Obscenity and the Case for Censorship,' *New York Times Magazine*, 28 March 1971, 24, cited in Posner, *supra* note 21, 373.

26 Segal, *supra* note 24, 5, quoting various sources on the claimed impact of pornography.

27 Posner, *supra* note 21, 366.

28 L. Baron and M. Straus, *Four Theories of Rape in American Society: A State Level Analysis* (New Haven: Yale University Press, 1989), 186–7 cited in Posner, ibid., 369.

29 Childress, *supra* note 1, 183ff.

30 W. Kaminer, 'Feminists against the First Amendment,' *The Atlantic Monthly*, November 1992, 111, 115.

31 E. Donnerstein et al., *The Question of Pornography: Research Findings and Policy Implications* (New York: Free Press, 1987).

32 Childress, *supra* note 1, 184, lists the weaknesses of laboratory experiments: (a) the unreal nature of lab violence; (b) the lack of real punishment or social control; (c) subjects' inhibitions while being observed or interviewed; (d) the use of willing college students as the norm; (e) an experimenter demand effect (causing subjects to guess); (f) publication of studies mainly if they have positive results; (g) the lack of good definitions of violence and aggression; and (h) ethical inability to produce real violence.

33 Segal, *supra* note 24, 9.

34 See *infra*, 'Is Sex the Problem?' p. 261.

35 Segal, *supra* note 24, 9–10.

36 See Posner, *supra* note 21, 368 (and 33 n. 39); and Childress, *supra* note 1, 182.

37 See the discussion in Childress, *supra* note 1, 186–7; the response of B. Kutschinsky, 'The Politics of Pornography Research,' *Law and Society* 26 (1992): 447; and the reply of Childress, 'Pornography, "Serious Rape," and Statistics: A Reply to Dr. Kutchinsky,' *Law and Society Review* 26 (1992): 457.

38 Childress, *supra* note 1, 187.

39 Ibid., 187; S. Strom, 'Japan's Legislators Tighten the Ban on Under-age Sex,' *New York Times*, 19 May 1999, A6.

40 A. Dworkin, *Pornography: Men Possessing Women* (New York: Plume, 1989), 69.

41 C. MacKinnon, *supra* note 11, 269 n. 36, as cited in Posner, *supra* note 21, 365.

42 D. Dyzenhaus, *John Stuart Mill and the Harm of Pornography* (University of Toronto Law School, 1991), as cited in M. Trebilcock, *The Limits of Freedom of Contract* (Cambridge, Mass.: Harvard University Press, 1993), 72.

43 Segal, *supra* note 24, 9.

44 Posner, *supra* note 21, 372. Norway has censorship of films. This power is

aimed particularly at protecting children from depictions of violence and sexual explicitness: see W. Gibbs, 'In Norway, Movies Must Pass a Nanny Standard,' *New York Times*, 8 July 1999, B1.

45 The Scandinavian countries typically rank the highest, in terms of the position of women, in assessments by the UN Human Development Report: see J. Stackhouse, 'Women Everywhere Still Trail in Wages, Power, UN Reports,' *Globe and Mail*, 17 August 1995, A12.

46 During the 1990s the Scandinavian parliaments typically had about 40% women legislators: see 'A Parliament That Looks Like Sweden,' *New York Times*, 27 September 1994, A24.

47 L. Segal, 'Introduction,' in L. Segal and M. McIntosh, eds, *Sex Exposed: Sexuality and the Pornography Debate* (London: Virago Press, 1992), 7.

48 Ibid., 8.

49 R. Abel, *Speaking Respect: Respecting Speech* (Chicago: University of Chicago Press, 1998), chap. 6, 'The Excesses of State Regulation.'

50 C. Smart, *Feminism and the Power of Law* (New York: Routledge, 1989), 136.

51 Childress, *supra* note 1, 179.

52 Ibid., 190–2, discussing Donnerstein, *supra* note 31, 110–12.

53 Segal, *supra* note 47, 8.

54 Childress, *supra* note 1, 194, and Posner, *supra* note 21, 364 n. 32.

55 Segal, *supra* note 47, 6.

56 F. Schauer, 'Causation Theory and the Causes of Sexual Violence,' *American Bar Foundation* [1987]: 737.

57 Childress, *supra* note 1, 212.

58 *American Booksellers Ass'n v. Hudnut* (1985), 771 F.2d 323 (7th Cir.) Aff'd without opinion (1986), 106 S.Ct. 1172.

59 Abel, *supra* note 49.

60 See 'The Limits of the Law?: Pornography and the Internet,' p. 270.

61 *R. v. Butler*, [1992] 1 S.C.R. 452.

62 Section 163 of the Criminal Code, R.S.C. 1985, c. C-46, stated:

(1) Every one commits an offence who
  (a) makes, prints, publishes, distributes, circulates ... any obscene written matter, picture, model, phonograph record or other thing whatever,
  ...
(3) No person shall be convicted of an offence under this section if he establishes that the public good was served by the acts that are alleged to constitute the offence and that the acts alleged did not extend beyond what served the public good.
(4) For the purposes of this section, it is a question of law whether an act

served the public good ... but it is a question of fact whether the acts did or did not extend beyond what served the public good.

(5) For the purposes of this section, the motives of an accused are irrelevant.

(6) Where an accused is charged with an offence under subsection (1), the fact that the accused was ignorant of the nature or presence of the matter, picture, model ... is not a defence to the charge ...

...

(8) For the purposes of this Act, any publication a dominant characteristic of which is the undue exploitation of sex, or of sex and any one or more of the following subjects, namely, crime, horror, cruelty and violence, shall be deemed to be obscene.

63 The Canadian Charter of Rights and Freedoms, Part I of the *Constitution Act, 1982*, being Schedule B to the *Canada Act 1982* (U.K.), 1982, c. 11. Section 1 provides:

The Canadian Charter of Rights and Freedoms guarantees the rights and freedoms set out in it subject only to such reasonable limits prescribed by law as can be demonstrably justified in a free and democratic society.

64 *Butler, supra* note 61.
65 Ibid., 502.
66 Ibid., 479.
67 Ibid., 503.
68 Ibid., 504.
69 *R. v. Brodie*, [1962] S.C.R. 681.
70 T. Lewin, 'Canada Court Says Pornography Harms Women and Can Be Barred,' *New York Times*, 28 February 1992, B7.
71 *Butler, supra* note 61, 485.
72 R. Moon, '*R. v. Butler*: The Limits of the Supreme Court's Feminist Re-Interpretation of Section 163,' *Ottawa Law Review* 25 (1993): 361, 371, and R. Moon, 'The Supreme Court of Canada on the Structure of Freedom of Expression Adjudication,' *University of Toronto Law Journal* 45 (1995): 419.
73 R. Kramer, '*R. v. Butler*: A New Approach to Obscenity or Return to the Morality Play?' *Criminal Law Quarterly* 35 (1992): 77, 85.
74 Smart, *supra* note 50, 136.
75 Fraser Committee, *The Report of the Special Committee on Pornography and Prostitution* (Ottawa: Minister of Supply and Services, 1985). See, generally, P. Hughes, 'Tensions in Canadian Society: The Fraser Committee Report,' *Windsor Yearbook of Access to Justice* 6 (1986): 282.

76 Fraser Committee, ibid., 289.
77 Ibid.
78 B. Testa, 'The Politics of Pornography,' *Literary Review of Canada*, January 1996, 10, describing B. Arcand, *The Jaguar and the Anteater: Pornography and the Modern World* (Toronto: McClelland and Stewart, 1991) and the reaction in Quebec to English Canada's obsession with pornography.
79 Fraser Committee Report, *supra* note 75, 104.
80 D. Burton, 'Public Opinion and Pornography Policy,' in S. Gubar and J. Hoff, eds, *For Adult Users Only: The Dilemma of Violent Pornography* (Bloomington: Indiana University Press, 1989), 133, discussing various American opinion polls.
81 Testa, *supra*, note 78, 6.
82 J. Toobin, 'X-Rated,' *The New Yorker*, 3 October 1994, 70, 71.
83 Ibid.
84 Cossman et al., *supra* note 16, 10.
85 J. Fuller and S. Blackley, *Restricted Entry: Censorship on Trial* (Vancouver: Press Gang Publishers, 1995); K. Johnson, 'The Socio-Legal Governance of Obscenity in Canada, Britain and the United States,' *Canadian Journal of Law and Society* 11 (1996): 255, 266–8.
86 M. Wente, 'The Unintended Results of New Obscenity Law,' *Globe and Mail*, 15 October 1994, A2.
87 S. Lyall, 'At Canada's Border: Literature at Risk,' *New York Times*, 13 December 1993, 16.
88 *Little Sisters Book and Art Emporium v. Canada (Minister of Justice)*, 2000 S.C.C. 69; K. Makin and C. Alphonso, 'Gay Book Sellers Win the Supreme Court Case,' *Globe and Mail*, 16 December 2000, A1, 19; 'The Agents Who Seize Books at the Border,' *Globe and Mail*, 19 December 2000, A19.
89 Cossman et al., *supra*, note 16, 6–7.
90 T. McCormack, 'If Pornography Is the Theory, Is Inequality the Practice?' *Philosophy of the Social Sciences* 23 (1993): 298.
91 Testa, *supra* note 78, 7.
92 D. Lacombe, *Blue Politics: Pornography and the Law in the Age of Feminism* (Toronto: University of Toronto Press, 1994), 149.
93 G. Kolata, 'Wary Doctors Spurn New Abortion Pill,' *New York Times*, 14 November 2000, D1, 7.
94 M. Talbot, 'The Little White Bombshell,' *New York Times Magazine*, 11 July 1999, 39.
95 J. Gilmore, a founding member of the Electronic Frontier Foundation. The quote often appears on the Internet: 'The Internet Survey,' *The Economist*, 1 July 1995, 15.

96 The Internet and the Law – Stop Sign on the Web,' *The Economist*, 13 January 2001, 21; 'A Survey of Government and the Internet,' *The Economist*, 24 June 2000, insert.

97 Gambling is also on the rise on the Internet. Attempts to suppress or even regulate it may be unavailing: see 'Betting against the House,' *The Economist*, 4 September 1999, 59.

98 T. Weber, 'Porn Profits on the Internet,' *Globe and Mail*, 20 May 1997, B1; S. Schiesel, 'A Father, a Friend, a Seller of Cyberporn,' *New York Times*, 30 June 1997, C1.

99 F. Cate, 'Cybersex: Regulating Sexually Explicit Expression on the Internet,' *Behavioral Sciences and the Law* 14 (1996): 145, 147.

100 'Hands Off the Internet,' *The Economist*, 5 July 1997, 15; J. Broder, 'Let It Be – Ira Magazine Argues for Minimal Internet Regulation,' *New York Times*, 30 June 1997, C1.

101 Ibid., 'Hands Off,' *supra* note 100.

102 D. Johnson and D. Post, 'Law and Borders: The Rise of Law in Cyberspace,' *Stanford Law Review* 48 (1996): 1367, 1390.

103 'Hands Off,' *supra* note 100.

104 S. 652, 104th Cong., 2nd Sess. ss. 501ff., 1996.

105 *Reno, A.G. of The United States, et al. v. American Civil Liberties Union, et al.* (1997), 521 U.S. 844.

106 P. Mendels, 'Decision Is Expected Today on Anti-Pornography Law,' *New York Times*, 1 February 1999, C4, 'Setback for a Law Shielding Minors from Smut Web Sites,' *New York Times*, 2 February 1999, A10. These decisions struck down the *Children's Online Privacy Protection*, 15 U.S.C. sec. 6501 (1998).

107 S. Fluendy, 'Pandora's Box: Asian Regimes Struggle to Keep a Lid on the Net,' *Far Eastern Review*, 26 September 1996, 71–2.

108 'Hands Off,' *supra* note 100, 15.

109 P. Resnick and J. Miller, 'PICS: Internet Access Controls without Censorship,' *Communications of the ACM* 39 (October 1996): 87.

110 J. Rosen, 'The Social Police,' *The New Yorker*, 20 October 1997, 170, 179–80, citing the opinions of Professor L. Lessig.

111 S. Tuck, 'Internet Is Regulated Enough, CRTC Says,' *Globe and Mail*, 18 May 1999, A1, 2; T. Hamilton, 'Regulation Left to Laws, Industry and Filters,' *Globe and Mail*, 18 May 1999, A2.

112 H. Scofield, 'OECD Pledges Light Touch on the Internet,' *Globe and Mail*, 15 October 1998, D1, 5.

113 A. Harmon, 'We, the People of the Internet,' *New York Times*, 29 June 1998, C1, 10.

114 P. Mendels, 'Plan Calls for Self-Policing of the Internet,' *New York Times*, 20 September 1999, C5.

115 Fluendy, *supra* note 107, 71.

116 L. Lessig, 'The Path of Cyberlaw,' *Yale Law Journal* 104 (1995): 1743, and 'The Zones of Cyberspace,' *Stanford Law Review* 48 (1996): 1403, 1406; see also 'The Internet and the Law,' *supra* note 96.

Chapter Nine: Discrimination, the Law – and Blacks in America

1 M. Trebilcock, *The Limits of Freedom of Contract* (Cambridge, Mass.: Harvard University Press, 1993), 188.

2 'How Race Is Lived in America,' series of articles in *New York Times*, June 2000.

3 S. Lipset, *American Exceptionalism: A Double-Edged Sword* (New York: W.W. Norton and Co., 1996), chap. 4, 'Two Americas, Two Value Systems: Blacks and Whites' and esp. 'Black Progress – A Contentious Issue,' 131–8.

4 S. Holmes, 'New Reports Say Minorities Benefit in Fiscal Recovery,' *New York Times*, 30 September 1997, A1, 12.

5 Ibid.

6 As quoted in Lipset, *supra* note 3, 132–3.

7 'America's Blacks: A World Apart,' *The Economist*, 30 March 1991, 21.

8 All statistics in this paragraph, unless otherwise indicated, are taken from Trebilcock, *supra* note 1, 191.

9 F. Butterfield, 'Racial Disparities Seen as Pervasive in Juvenile Justice,' *New York Times*, 26 April 2000, A1, 19.

10 P. Applebome, 'Blacks Show Gains in Getting College Degrees,' *New York Times*, 12 June 1996, B9.

11 Ibid.; A. Hacker, *Two Nations: Black and White, Separate, Hostile, Unequal* (New York: Maxwell MacMillan, 1992); D. Strickland and C. Ascher, 'Low-Income African-American Children and Public Schooling,' in P. Jackson, ed., *Handbook of Research on Curriculum* (New York: Macmillan Publishing, 1992), 609–23.

12 A. Hacker, 'Grand Illusion,' *New York Review of Books*, 11 June 1998, 26.

13 Strickland and Ascher, *supra* note 11; S. Halpern, *On the Limits of the Law: The Ironic Legacy of Title VI of the 1964 Civil Rights Act* (Baltimore: Johns Hopkins University Press, 1995), 11–12; H. Bissinger, 'We're All Racist Now,' *New York Times Magazine*, 29 May 1994, 26.

14 S. Holmes, 'Look Who's Saying Separate Is Equal,' *New York Times*, 1 October 1995, sect. 4, 1, 5.

15 G. Fredrickson, 'America's Caste System: Will It Change?' *New York Review of Books*, 23 October 1997, 68.

16 R. Bernstein, 'Racism Is (a) Entrenched? Or (b) Fading?' *New York Times*, 8 November 1997, A11, 15.

17 The Complexities of Assessing Impact.'

18 S. Thernstrom and A. Thernstrom, *America in Black and White: One Nation, Indivisible* (New York: Simon & Schuster, 1997), 177, n. 126.

19 Ibid., 177, n. 125, citing E. Robinson, 'Black and White and Getting By,' *Washington Post*, 15 July 1996, 1.

20 I. Ayres, 'Fair Driving: Gender and Race Discrimination in Retail Car Negotiations,' *Harvard Law Review* 104 (1991): 817.

21 J. Donohue, 'Advocacy versus Analysis in Assessing Employment Discrimination Law,' *Stanford Law Review* 44 (1972): 1583, n. 122, citing L. Kahn, 'The Effects of Race on Professional Football Players' Compensation,' *Industrial and Labour Relations Review* 45 (1992): 295.

22 Ibid., 1608–9 citing 'Prime Time Live: True Colors' (ABC Television broadcast), 26 September 1991.

23 Ibid., n. 124, citing F. Crosby et al., 'Recent Unobtrusive Studies of Black and White Discrimination and Prejudice: A Literature Review,' *Psychological Bulletin* 87 (1980): 546, 555.

24 J. Kirschenman and K. Neckerman, '"We'd Love to Hire Them but ...': The Meaning of Race for Employers,' in C. Jencks and P. Peterson, eds, *The Urban Underclass* (Washington: Brookings Institution, 1991), 204.

25 F. Bloch, *Antidiscrimination Law and Minority Employment: Recruitment Practices and Regulatory Constraints* (Chicago: University of Chicago Press, 1994), 35.

26 The findings of these studies are summarized in J. Heckman and P. Siegelman, 'The Urban Institute Audit Studies: Their Methods and Findings,' in M. Fix and R. Struyk, eds, *Clear and Convincing Evidence: Measurement of Discrimination in America* (Washington: Urban Institute Press, 1993), 187.

27 M. Turner et al., *Opportunities Denied, Opportunities Diminished: Racial Discrimination in Hiring* (Washington: Urban Institute Press, 1991).

28 Thernstrom and Thernstrom, *supra* note 18, 448, and the questions they raise regarding implications of the Washington portion of the study focusing solely on private employers (and not government jobs).

29 Heckman and Siegelman, *supra* note 26, and the questions they raise regarding whether the pair were matched in every critical respect, for example, regarding the cognitive skills and other traits employers value most in hiring decisions.

30 A. Munnell et al., 'Mortgage Lending in Boston: Interpreting HMDA Data,' *American Economic Review* 86 (1996): 25.

31 P. Passell, 'Race, Mortgages and Statistics: The Unending Debate over a Study of Lending Bias,' *New York Times*, 10 May 1996, C1, 4.

32 'Race and Housing: Locked Out or Priced Out?' *The Economist*, 30 August 1997, 56.

33 K. Sack with J. Elder, 'Poll Finds Optimistic Outlook but Enduring Racial Division,' *New York Times*, 11 July 2000, A1, 23.

34 O. Patterson, 'The Paradox of Integration,' *The New Republic*, 6 November 1995, 24, 26.

35 These theories are well summarized and analysed in Trebilcock, *supra* note 1, 192–204.

36 J. Rawls, *A Theory of Justice* (Cambridge, Mass.: Harvard University Press, 1971).

37 R. Hayman, *The Smart Culture: Law, Society, and Intelligence* (New York: New York University Press, 1997).

38 R. Epstein, 'The Paradox of Civil Rights,' *Yale Law and Policy Review* 8 (1990): 299: 'There is a curious duality in the status of civil rights in the United States: massive political support for antidiscrimination legislation but little economic evidence to show how or why it does any good.'

39 Urging the repeal of anti-discrimination laws is not limited to the United States: for example, regarding Canada, see T. Flanagan, 'Human Rights and Freedom of the Press,' *Globe and Mail*, 20 May 1999, A15.

40 R. Epstein, *supra* note 38, 323, and Heckman and Verkerke, *infra* note 49.

41 J. Donohue *supra* note 21.

42 *Civil Rights Act* 42 U.S.C. 2000e (1964).

43 His main target is R. Epstein's *Forbidden Grounds: The Case against Employment Discrimination Laws* (Cambridge, Mass.: Harvard University Press, 1992).

44 Donohue, *supra* note 21, 1599–1600, estimating $1 billion in a $5.5 trillion economy.

45 Arthur Anderson and Co., *Cost of Government Regulation Study for the Business Roundtable* (1979), cited in ibid., 1600 n. 80.

46 A prominent exception is the position espoused by R. Epstein. He is generally opposed to laws protecting against discrimination, particularly regarding labour markets. However, he agrees that in the 1960s, Title VII was required to end the socially wasteful cartel – sometimes supported by state legislation – that disadvantaged blacks: see Epstein, *supra* note 43.

47 J. Smith and F. Welch, 'Black Economic Progress after Myrdal,' *Journal of Economic Literature* 27 (1989): 519, 555.

48 J. Heckman and B. Payner, 'Determining the Impact of Federal Antidiscrimination Policy on the Economic Status of Blacks: A Study of South Carolina,' *American Economic Review* 79 (1989): 138.

49 J. Heckman and J. Verkerke, 'Racial Disparity and Employment Discrimination Law: An Economic Perspective,' *Yale Law and Policy Review* 8 (1990): 276; J. Donohue and J. Heckman, 'Re-Evaluating Federal Civil Rights Policy,' *Georgetown Law Journal* 79 (1991): 1713; J. Donohue, 'The Legal Response to Discrimination: Does Law Matter?' in B. Garth and A. Sarat, eds, *How Does Law Matter?* (Evanston, Ill.: Northwestern University Press, 1998), 45; 'A Small Ripple or a Large Wave? – The Effect of Law on the Economic Progress of Minorities,' *Researching Law: An American Bar Foundation Update* 7 (1996): 1.

50 J. Donohue and J. Heckman, 'Continuous versus Episodic Change: The Impact of Civil Rights Policy on the Economic Status of Blacks,' *Journal of Economic Literature* 29 (1991): 1603.

51 'A Small Ripple or a Large Wave?' *supra* note 49, 1, 6.

52 Ibid.

53 Ibid.

54 Bloch, *supra* note 25, 1.

55 Ibid., chap. 7, 'Minority Employment Opportunities.'

56 R. Pear, 'Black and Hispanic Poverty Falls, Reducing Overall Rate for Nation,' *New York Times*, 25 September 1998, A1, 20.

57 S. Nasar and K. Mitchell, 'Booming Job Market Draws Young Black Men into the Fold,' *New York Times*, 23 May 1999, A1, 21.

58 Heckman and Verkerke, *supra* note 49, 298.

59 See this chapter, 'A Framework for Evaluating Title VII,' p. 289.

60 Donohue, *supra* note 21, 1598–9.

61 G. Rosenberg, *The Hollow Hope: Can Courts Bring About Social Change?* (Chicago: University of Chicago Press, 1991), 123–4.

62 Donohue, *supra* note 21, 1597–8, n. 64, citing J. Stimson, *Public Opinion in America: Moods, Cycles, and Swings* (Boulder, Colo.: Westview Press, 1991), 70–3, 134. Similarly, a study by the Economic Council of Canada concluded that discriminatory attitudes to immigrants of various backgrounds (racial, ethnic, etc.) appeared to decline substantially with increased contact between immigrants and residents: J. Berry, *Sociopsychological Costs and Benefits of Multiculturalism*, Working Paper no. 24 (Ottawa: Economic Council of Canada, 1991).

63 Lipset, *supra* note 3, 126.

64 S. Verhovek, 'In Poll, Americans Reject Means but Not Ends of Racial Diversity,' *New York Times*, 14 December 1997, A1, 18.

65 Sack with Elder, *supra* note 33.
66 All statistics from polls reviewed in Lipset, *supra* note 3, 115.
67 Verhovek, *supra* note 64.
68 Lipset, *supra* note 3, 125–7.
69 Verhovek, *supra* note 64.
70 Lipset, *supra* note 3, 127–8.
71 P. Sniderman and T. Piazza, *The Scar of Race* (Cambridge, Mass.: Harvard University Press, 1993), 109, as quoted in Thernstrom and Thernstrom, *supra* note 18, 501.
72 Verhovek, *supra* note 64.
73 See this chapter, 'Normative Debates Regarding Laws against Discrimination,' p. 284.
74 For a canvassing of the allegations from an anti-affirmative action perspective see Thernstrom and Thernstrom, *supra* note 18, esp. chapters 14–16.
75 N. Lemann, 'Taking Affirmative Action Apart,' *New York Times Magazine*, 11 June 1995, 36.
76 A. Wolfe, 'Affirmative Action Inc.,' *The New Yorker*, 25 November 1996, 106.
77 C. Deutsch, 'Corporate Diversity, in Practice,' *New York Times*, 20 November 1996, C1, 17.
78 R. Abelson, 'Women Minorities Not Getting to the Top,' *New York Times*, 14 July 1999, C4.
79 S. Verhovek, 'Houston Vote Underlined Complexity of Rights Issue,' *New York Times*, 6 November 1997, A1, 22.
80 Verhovek, *supra* note 64, A1.
81 W. Wilson, 'Class Consciousness' (review of R. Kahlenberg, *The Remedy: Class, Race, and Affirmative Action*), *New York Times Book Review*, 14 July 1996, 11.
82 S. Holmes, 'Quality of Life Is Up for Many Blacks, Data Say,' *New York Times*, 18 November 1996, A1, 13.
83 'A Small Ripple or a Large Wave?' *supra* note 49, 2, 3.
84 P. Burstein, 'Affirmative Action, Jobs, and American Democracy: What Has Happened to the Quest for Equal Opportunity?' *Law and Society Review* 26 (1992): 901, 910.
85 M. Selmi, 'The Facts of Affirmative Action,' *Virginia Law Review* 85 (1999): 697.
86 *Hopwood v. University of Texas Regents*, 78 F3d 932 5th Cir. (1996).
87 E. Bronner, 'U. of California Reports Big Drop in Black Admission,' *New York Times*, 1 April 1998, A1, 23.
88 W. Honan, 'Minority Applications Rise at California, Easing Fears,' *New York Times*, 29 January 1998, A14.

89 Bronner, *supra* note 87.

90 J. Rosen, 'Damage Control,' *The New Yorker*, 23 February 1998, 58.

91 S. Holmes, 'Re-Rethinking Affirmative Action,' *New York Times*, 5 April 1998, sect. 4, 5, quoting Nathan Glazer.

92 'Proposition 209 Shuts the Door,' *New York Times*, 4 April 1998, A22; F. Bruni, 'Black Students May Prefer to Say No to Berkeley,' *New York Times*, 2 May 1998, A1, 7.

93 Holmes, *supra* note 91, citing such critics of affirmative action as A. Thernstrom.

94 J. Traub, 'The Class of Prop. 209,' *New York Times Magazine*, 2 May 1999, 44.

95 W. Bowen and D. Bok, *The Shape of the River: Long-Term Consequences of Considering Race in College and University Admissions* (Princeton: Princeton University Press, 1998).

96 A. Wolfe, 'Affirmative Action: The Fact Gap,' *New York Times Book Review*, 25 October 1998, 15.

97 S. Thernstrom and A. Thernstrom, 'Reflections on the Shape of the River,' *UCLA Law Review* 46 (1999): 1583.

98 Selmi, *supra* note 85, 727.

99 Bowen and Bok, *supra* note 95, 123–5.

100 Ibid., 158–60.

101 Ibid., 167–8.

102 S. Welch and J. Gruhl, *Affirmative Action and Minority Enrollments in Medical and Law Schools* (Ann Arbor: University of Michigan Press, 1998); D. Chambers et al., 'Michigan's Minority Graduates in Practice: The River Runs through Law School,' *Law and Social Inquiry* 25 (2000): 395: Donohue, *supra* note 49, 58–61.

103 R. Dworkin, 'Is Affirmative Action Doomed?' *New York Review of Books*, 5 November 1998, 56; J. Steinberg, 'Defending Affirmative Action with Social Science,' *New York Times*, 17 December 2000, A29.

104 Wolfe, *supra* note 96, 16.

105 E. Anderson, 'From Normative to Empirical Sociology in the Affirmative Action Debate: Bowen and Bok's *The Shape of the River*,' *Journal of Legal Education* 50 (2000): 284, 285.

106 D. Clendinen, 'Helping Embattled Children in America's Cities,' *New York Times*, 31 August 1999, A22.

107 'Sorting Out School Choice,' *The Economist*, 14 September 1999, 33.

108 Ibid.

109 Lipset, *supra* note 3, 149.

110 D. Sanger, 'Bush Pushes Ambitious Education Plan,' *New York Times*, 24 January 2001, A1.

111 See 'The Impact of Litigation Regarding Social Change – "American Exceptionalism" II,' p. 144.

112 *Brown v. Board of Education* 347 US 483 (1954).

113 Rosenberg, *supra* note 61.

114 Ibid., 52.

115 For an even stronger statement regarding the ineffectiveness of *Brown* see M. Klarman, '*Brown*, Racial Change, and the Civil Rights Movement,' *Virginia Law Review* 80 (1994): 7. See also the comments critical of Klarman: M. McConnell 'The Originalist Justification for *Brown*: A Reply to Professor Klarman,' *Virginia Law Review* 81 (1995): 1937; M. Tushnet, 'The Significance of *Brown* v. *Board of Education*,' *Virginia Law Review* 80 (1994): 173; G. Rosenberg, '*Brown* is Dead! Long live Brown!: The Endless Attempt to Canonize a Case,' *Virginia Law Review* 80 (1994): 161; and D. Garrow, 'Hopelessly Hollow History: Revisionist Devaluing of *Brown* v. *Board of Education*,' *Virginia Law Review* 80 (1994): 151. But see M. Klarman, '*Brown*, Originalism, and Constitutional Theory: A Response to Professor McConnell,' *Virginia Law Review* 81 (1995): 1881.

116 Rosenberg, *supra* note 61, 111, 118, 155.

117 Ibid., 341–2.

118 C. Sunstein, 'How Independent Is the Court?' *New York Review of Books* 22 October 1992, 47.

119 R. Flemming et al., 'One Voice among Many: The Supreme Court's Influence on Attentiveness to Issues in the United States, 1947–1992'; K. McMahon and M. Paris, 'The Politics of Rights Revisited: Rosenberg, McCann, and the New Institutionalism'; D. Schultz and S. Gottlieb, 'Legal Functionalism and Social Change: A Reassessment of Rosenberg's *The Hollow Hope*,' all in D. Schultz, ed., *Leveraging the Law: Using the Courts to Achieve Social Change* (New York: Peter Lang, 1998).

120 Rosenberg, *supra* note 61, 94–106.

121 P. Burstein and M. Edwards, 'The Impact of Employment Discrimination Litigation on Racial Disparity in Earnings: Evidence and Unresolved Issues,' *Law and Society Review* 28 (1994): 79.

122 See 'Evidence Regarding Anti-discrimination Laws and Employment Opportunities for Blacks,' p. 292.

123 J. Donohue, J. Heckman, and P. Todd, 'Social Action, Private Choice, and Philanthropy: Understanding the Sources of Improvements in Black Schooling in Georgia, 1911–1960,' unpublished, presented at University of Wisconsin Poverty Research Institute, June 1997.

124 S. Wasby, *Race Relations Litigation in an Age of Complexity* (Charlottesville: University Press of Virginia, 1995), 332.

125 D. Reed, 'Twenty-Five Years after *Rodriguez*: School Finance Litigation and the Impact of the New Judicial Federalism,' *Law and Society Review* 32 (1998): 175, 181.

126 Ibid., 214–15.

127 J. Hochschild, *The New American Dilemma: Liberal Democracy and School Desegregation* (New Haven: Yale University Press, 1984).

128 D. Armor, *Forced Justice: School Desegregation and the Law* (New York: Oxford University Press, 1995), 231 (emphasis in original).

129 Ibid., 232.

130 S. Halpern, *supra* note 13, 315–16.

131 Ibid., 273ff.

132 Sunstein, *supra* note 118, 50; see also J. Simon, ' "The Long Walk Home" to Politics,' *Law and Society* 26 (1992): 923 and I. Holloway, 'Book Review: *The Hollow Hope*,' *Dalhousie Law Journal* 15 (1992): 664.

Chapter Ten: Conclusions

1 See chapter 1, 'The Growth of Law,' p. 25.

2 See chapter 4, '5. National Styles of Regulation – "American Exceptionalism" I,' p. 138.

3 See chapter 1, 'The Breakdown of Other Rules and Norms,' p. 37.

4 Ibid., 'Politics Harnesses Law,' p. 41.

5 M. Schudson, *The Good Citizen: A History of American Civic Life* (New York: The Free Press, 1998), 295.

6 See chapter 3.

7 See chapters 6, 7, and 9.

8 R. Kagan and D. Vogel, 'The Politics of Smoking Regulation: Canada, France, the United States,' in R. Rabin and S. Sugarman, eds, *Smoking Policy: Law, Politics and Culture* (New York: Oxford University Press, 1993), 85.

9 See chapter 4, 'The Ineffectiveness of Law,' p. 133.

10 See chapter 6, 'The Law, Attitudes – and Impact,' p. 203.

11 Ibid., 'Canada, Tax Increases – and Unintended Consequences,' p. 213.

12 See chapter 8.

13 Ibid., 'The Impact of Butler,' p. 266.

14 Ibid., 'The Limits of the Law: Pornography and the Internet,' p. 270.

15 See chapter 9.

16 Ibid., 'The Consensus Regarding Anti-Discrimination Laws – The War Over Affirmative Action,' p. 295.

17 W. Bowen and D. Bok, *The Shape of the River: Long-Term Consequences of*

Considering Race in College and University Admissions (Princeton: Princeton University Press, 1998).

18 See chapter 9, 'Affirmative Action as Deflection: *The Shape of the River*,' p. 301.

19 See chapter 5, 'America and Punishment,' p. 164.

20 See chapter 4, 'The Impact of Litigation Regarding Social Change – "American Exceptionalism" II,' p. 144.

21 Ibid., 'The Impact of Litigation on Popular Politics: Canada Experiments,' p. 150.

22 See chapter 6, 'Tort Litigation – An American Response,' p. 197.

23 Ibid., 'The Supreme Court of Canada, Smoking – and Free Speech,' p. 209.

24 See chapter 7, 'The Dewees Study,' p. 232; 'Environmental Litigation,' p. 238.

25 See chapter 4, '1. Instrumentalism,' p. 114.

26 See chapter 9, 'The Impact of Litigation – The Legacy of *Brown v. Board of Education*,' p. 304.

27 See chapter 8, 'The Impact of *Butler*,' p. 266.

28 See chapter 5, 'The Impact of Litigation,' p. 173.

29 See chapter 4, 'The United States as Outlier,' p. 144.

30 'POLITICS BELIEF – Is There a Crisis?' *The Economist*, 17 July 1999, 49.

31 Schudson, *supra* note 5.

32 Ibid., 273.

33 Ibid., 308.

34 P. Rycasavage, *Income Equality in America: An Analysis of Trends* (Armonk, NY: M.E. Sharpe, 1999); 'Cutting the Cookie,' *The Economist*, 11 September 1999, 26.

35 T. Skocpol, *The Missing Middle: Working Families and the Future of American Social Policy* (New York: W.W. Norton, 2000).

36 D. Kirp, 'So, Is It Back to Bowling Alone?' *The Nation*, 8 March 1999, 25, 27 (reviewing *The Good Citizen*).

37 *The Compact Edition of the Oxford English Dictionary*, vol. 2 (Oxford: Oxford University Press, 1971).

38 Learned Hand in his Spirit of Liberty speech, in G. Gunther, *Learned Hand: The Man and the Judge* (New York: Alfred A. Knopf, 1994), 549.

Index

Abrams, Floyd, 82–3
advertising. *See* smoking
affirmative action, 4, 8, 10, 289–304, 319–20; benefits of, 295–301; at Berkeley/UCLA, 300–1; College and Beyond database, 301–4; controversy over, 295–301; employment opportunities related to, 292–5; *The Shape of the River*, 301–4, 309, 320; University of Texas Law School, 299–300
alternative dispute resolution (ADR), 31
American Bar Association, 178
assessing impact of law, 91–9; comparing jurisdictions, 92–3; interrupted time series, 92; multiple time series, 94–5; plausible rival hypotheses, 93–4

behavioural decision theory, 68–9
blacks. *See* discrimination
Bloch, Farrell, 294–5
Bok, Derek, 301–4
Bowen, William, 301–4
Breyer, Stephen, 232

Canada. *See* Canadian politics, *Char-*

ter of Rights and Freedoms, environment, pornography, smoking
Canadian politics, 7, 150–3
capital punishment, 15–16, 47, 159–83, 320–1; abolition of, 169–72, 174, 179–80; and 'American Exceptionalism,' 172–3, 179; employment of, 175–7; *Furman v. Georgia*, 173–4; *Gregg v. Georgia*, 174–5; impact of litigation upon, 173–5, 324; *McCleskey v. Kemp*, 175; symbolism of, 177–80
Carlson, Rachel, 222
Centers for Disease Control, 185
Charter of Rights and Freedoms, 7, 10, 33, 151–3
China, 38
civil liability, 61–3
compliance. *See* law
context (of law), 69–70
courts, 6, 8, 14. *See also* litigation
crime, 57–9; corporate crime, 59
Cuba, 104

deregulation, 26; in Great Britain, 26–7; in United States, 26–7. *See also* privatization
Dershowitz, Alan, 163